Pervasive and Ubiquitous Technology Innovations for Ambient Intelligence Environments

Kevin Curran
University of Ulster, UK

Information Science
REFERENCE

Managing Director:	Lindsay Johnston
Senior Editorial Director:	Heather A. Probst
Book Production Manager:	Sean Woznicki
Development Manager:	Joel Gamon
Assistant Acquisitions Editor:	Kayla Wolfe
Typesetter:	Deanna Jo Zombro
Cover Design:	Nick Newcomer

Published in the United States of America by
Information Science Reference (an imprint of IGI Global)
701 E. Chocolate Avenue
Hershey PA 17033
Tel: 717-533-8845
Fax: 717-533-8661
E-mail: cust@igi-global.com
Web site: http://www.igi-global.com

Library of Congress Cataloging-in-Publication Data

Pervasive and ubiquitous technology innovations for ambient intelligence
environments / Kevin Curran, editor.
     p. cm.
  Includes bibliographical references and index.
  Summary: "This book is a collection of research on the subject matter of
human computer interaction, ubiquitous computing, embedded systems and other
areas of study which contribute to ambient intelligence"--Provided by
publisher.
  ISBN 978-1-4666-2041-4 (hardcover) -- ISBN 978-1-4666-2042-1 (ebook) -- ISBN
978-1-4666-2043-8 (print & perpetual access) 1. Ambient intelligence--
Research. I. Curran, Kevin, 1969-
  QA76.9.A48P47 2013
  004.01'9--dc23
                          2012013060

British Cataloguing in Publication Data
A Cataloguing in Publication record for this book is available from the British Library.

The views expressed in this book are those of the authors, but not necessarily of the publisher.

List of Reviewers

Adel Al-Jumaily, *University of Technology, Australia*
Noelle Carbonell, *University Henri Poincaré, France*
Joan Condell, *University of Ulster, Ireland*
Jean-Pierre George, *IRIT - Université Paul Sabatier, France*
Tom Lunney, *University of Ulster, Ireland*
Dan McCormac, *Dublin Institute of Technology, Ireland*
Maurice Mulvenna, *University of Ulster, Ireland*
Gerry Parr, *University of Ulster, Ireland*

Table of Contents

Detailed Table of Contents

Chapter 1

    Ben Graham, Letterkenny Institute of Technology, Ireland
    Christos Tachtatzis, Letterkenny Institute of Technology, Ireland
    Fabio Di Franco, Letterkenny Institute of Technology, Ireland
    Marek Bykowski, Letterkenny Institute of Technology, Ireland
    David C. Tracey, Letterkenny Institute of Technology, Ireland
    Nick F. Timmons, Letterkenny Institute of Technology, Ireland
    Jim Morrison, Letterkenny Institute of Technology, Ireland

Wireless Sensor Networks (WSNs) are gaining an increasing industry wide adoption. However, there remain major challenges such as network dimensioning and node placement especially in Built Environment Networks (BENs). Decisions on the node placement, orientation, and the number of nodes to cover the area of interest are usually ad-hoc. Ray tracing tools are traditionally employed to predict RF signal propagation; however, such tools are primarily intended for outdoor environments. RF signal propagation varies greatly indoors due to building materials and infrastructure, obstacles, node placement, antenna orientation and human presence. Because of the complexity of signal prediction, these factors are usually ignored or given little weight when such networks are analyzed. The paper's results show the effects of the building size and layout, building materials, human presence and mobility on the signal propagation of a BEN. Additionally, they show that antenna radiation pattern is a key factor in the RF propagation performance, and appropriate device orientation and placement can improve the network reliability. Further, the RSS facility in RF transceivers can be exploited to detect the presence and motion of humans in the environment.

Chapter 2

    Sean Carlin, University of Ulster, UK
    Kevin Curran, University of Ulster, UK

In this paper, the authors focus on Cloud Computing, which is a distributed architecture that centralizes server resources on quite a scalable platform so as to provide on demand' computing resources and services The authors outline what cloud computing is, the various cloud deployment models and the main security risks and issues that are currently present within the cloud computing industry.

Niall Murray, Athlone Institute of Technology, Ireland

Yuansong Qiao, Athlone Institute of Technology, Ireland

Brian Lee, Athlone Institute of Technology, Ireland

Enda Fallon, Athlone Institute of Technology, Ireland

Karunakar A K, Athlone Institute of Technology, Ireland

In future multimedia systems, seamless access to application services on different devices available to users in their vicinity, will be commonplace. The availability of these services will change as the mobile user moves. Current 3G multimedia systems do not support access to multiple applications operating on multiple different devices in context of a session or indeed seamless device session handover. Considering these requirements, the authors outline two multimedia communication platforms which potentially solve this problem. This paper describes a backward compatible architecture based on the widely adopted Session Initiation Protocol (SIP) and also outlines a clean slate approach from ITU-T SG 16 called the Advanced Multimedia System (AMS). For each of these solutions the paper describes in terms of architecture, signalling, and capability negotiation, what are viewed as the most critical functions in future multimedia systems design. The result of this comparison displays the advantages and disadvantages of each approach, and outlines solutions to satisfy challenges of current and future multimedia systems based on the service access requirement in ubiquitous environments. Furthermore, this comparison is used to suggest approaches that are best suited for future multimedia system design.

Claas Ahlrichs, Universiaet Bremen, Germany

Daniel Kohlsdorf, Universiaet Bremen, Germany

Michael Lawo, Universiaet Bremen, Germany

Gerrit Kalkbrenner, Universiaet Bremen, Germany

IT-ASSIST is a twenty months research project which has the goal to give elderly people the opportunity to profit from digital media. Suffering from age related impairments concerning vision, hearing, or dexterity and bad hand-eye coordination are challenges when designing user interfaces for elderly people. Common approaches are trying to model systems for specific impairments. In this project, the authors follow the approach to set up interfaces and systems that can be used independent from personal impairments. Customization has adapted these systems to be in accordance with personnel impairments. Common applications like photo editing, digital mailing or internet browsing in a redesigned form provide social communication accordingly. In this article, a prototype of a customized user interface, its implementation, and results of user studies are presented and discussed.

Mari Feli Gonzalez, Fundación Instituto Gerontológico Matia - INGEMA, Spain

David Facal, Fundación Instituto Gerontológico Matia - INGEMA, Spain

Ana Belen Navarro, Fundación Instituto Gerontológico Matia - INGEMA, Spain

Arjan Geven, CURE – Center for Usability Research and Engineering, Austria

Manfred Tscheligi, CURE – Center for Usability Research and Engineering, Austria

Elena Urdaneta, Fundación Instituto Gerontológico Matia - INGEMA, Spain

Javier Yanguas, Fundación Instituto Gerontológico Matia - INGEMA, Spain

The HERMES Cognitive Care and Guidance for Active Aging project proposes an integrated approach to cognitive assistance, promoting the autonomy of elderly users through pervasive technology. This work aims to describe elderly people's opinions when they are presented scenarios developed in this project. Two focus groups were organized in Austria and Spain with a view to collecting their impressions about the way in which the technological device can cover their needs; complementarily, a second session was conducted including a quantitative questionnaire. Although some participants were reluctant to use the technology, they welcomed some functionalities of the HERMES system and they considered that using them can help them to become familiar with them. Usefulness, usability, and use of real-life information for functionalities such as cognitive games are considered to be key areas of the project. This evaluation has provided the developers of the system with meaningful information to improve it and it guarantees that the system addresses elderly people's needs.

Chapter 6

In educational institutions computing technology is facilitating a dynamic and supportive learning environment for students. In recent years, much research has involved investigating the potential of technology for use in education and terms such as personalized learning, virtual learning environments, intelligent tutoring and m-learning have brought significant advances within higher education but have not propagated down to Primary Level. This paper discusses AmbiLearn, an ambient intelligent multimodal learning environment for children. The main objective of this research is to redress the limited use of virtual learning environments in primary school education. With a focus on multimodal presentation and learning environments, AmbiLearn explores the educational potential of such systems at Primary school level.

Chapter 7

The significance that Ambient Intelligence (AmI) has acquired in recent years requires the development of innovative solutions. In this sense, the development of AmI-based systems requires the creation of increasingly complex and flexible applications. The use of context-aware technologies is an essential aspect in these developments in order to perceive stimuli from the context and react upon it autonomously. This paper presents SYLPH, a novel platform that defines a method for integrating dynamic and self-adaptable heterogeneous Wireless Sensor Networks (WSN). This approach facilitates the inclusion of context-aware capabilities when developing intelligent ubiquitous systems, where functionalities can communicate in a distributed way. A WSN infrastructure has been deployed for testing and evaluating this platform. Preliminary results and conclusions are presented in this paper.

Chapter 8

An Augmented Reality (AR) is a technology which provides the user with a real time 3D enhanced perception of a physical environment with addition virtual elements—either virtual scenery, information regarding surroundings, other contextual information—and is also capable of hiding or replacing real structures. With Augmented Reality applications becoming more advanced, the ways the technology can be viably used is increasing. Augmented Reality has been used for gaming several times with varying results. AR systems are seen by some as an important part of the ambient intelligence landscape. Therefore, the authors present several types of augmentation applications of AR in the domestic, industrial, scientific, medicinal, and military sectors which may benefit future ambient intelligent systems.

Chapter 9

Michael J. Walsh, University College Cork, Ireland
John Barton, University College Cork, Ireland
Brendan O'Flynn, University College Cork, Ireland
Martin J. Hayes, University of Limerick, Ireland
Cian O'Mathuna, University College Cork, Ireland
Seyed Mohammad Mahdi Alavi, Simon Fraser University, Canada

This paper proposes a methodology for improved power controller switching in mobile Body Area Networks operating within the ambient healthcare environment. The work extends Anti-windup and Bumpless transfer results to provide a solution to the ambulatory networking problem that ensures sufficient biometric data can always be regenerated at the base station. The solution thereby guarantees satisfactory quality of service for healthcare providers. Compensation is provided for the nonlinear hardware constraints that are a typical feature of the type of network under consideration and graceful performance degradation in the face of hardware output power saturation is demonstrated, thus conserving network energy in an optimal fashion.

Chapter 10

Mark Scanlon, University College Dublin, Ireland
Alan Hannaway, University College Dublin, Ireland
Mohand-Tahar Kechadi, University College Dublin, Ireland

The popularity of Peer-to-Peer (P2P) Internet communication technologies being exploited to aid cybercrime is ever increasing. P2P systems can be used or exploited to aid in the execution of a large number of online criminal activities, e.g., copyright infringement, fraud, malware and virus distribution, botnet creation, and control. P2P technology is perhaps most famous for the unauthorised distribution of copyrighted materials since the late 1990's, with the popularity of file-sharing programs such as Napster. In 2004, P2P traffic accounted for 80% of all Internet traffic and in 2005, specifically BitTorrent traffic accounted for over 60% of the world's P2P bandwidth usage. This paper outlines a methodology for investigating a documented P2P network, BitTorrent, using a sample investigation for reference throughout. The sample investigation outlined was conducted on the top 100 most popular BitTorrent swarms over the course of a one week period.

Chapter 11

Stephen O'Shaughnessy, Institute of Technology Blanchardstown, Ireland
Geraldine Gray, Institute of Technology Blanchardstown, Ireland

A key requirement for experimental analysis in the areas of network intrusion and computer forensics is the availability of suitable datasets. However, the inherent security and privacy issues surrounding these disciplines have resulted in a lack of available "test-bed" datasets for testing and evaluation purposes. Typically, the datasets required in these cases are from system log files, containing traces of computer misuse. Therefore, there is obvious potential for the use of synthetically generated log files that can accurately reproduce these traces or patterns of misuse. This paper discusses the development, testing, and evaluation of a dataset generator tool, designed to produce such datasets, particularly those containing patterns of common computer attacks.

Chapter 12

Mikael Wiberg, Uppsala University, Sweden

Society is undergoing a major digitalization - not at least in the field of architecture. The digitalization of our built environment has also begun to reflect itself in research (see e.g., Cai & Abascal, 2006; Margolis & Robinson, 2007; Greenfield, 2006). At the cross point in-between architecture, urban development, and the digitalization of modern society, there is a major research potential – untapped and ready to be explored. This paper initiates an "architectural informatics" perspective and outlines a research agenda as to address questions of how to better integrate our built environment and digital world. This paper outlines three research themes including: 1) *Architectural composition with digital materials* (theory development), 2) *Architecture for sustainable digitization* (development of value ground), and 3) *Digitization processes & architecture as social intervention processes* (methodology development). Common to these three areas is the overall aim to *develop architectural and computational concepts and theories* as to address this common area, to *find new practice based methods* to facilitate new forms of cooperation between engineers, architects and the inhabitants of our built environment, as well as to *explore architectural informatics as a phenomenon and opportunity.*

Chapter 13

Andreas Riener, Johannes Kepler University Linz, Austria

In this paper, the author introduces a novel method for non-invasive, implicit human-computer interaction based on dynamically evaluated sitting postures. The research question addressed is whether or not the proposed system is able to allow for non-obtrusive screen content adaptation in a reading situation. To this end, the author has integrated force sensor array mats into a traditional office chair, providing sitting postures/gestures of the person seated in real time. In detail, variations in the center of pressure were used for application control, starting more generally with usability assessment of cursor control, breaking them down to simple(r) pan and zoom of screen content. Preliminary studies have indicated that such a system cannot get close to the performance/accuracy of keyboard or mouse, however its general usability, e.g., for handicapped persons or for less dynamic screen content adaptation, has been demonstrated and some future potential has been recognized.

Ambient Intelligence (AmI) is the emerging computing paradigm used to build next-generation smart environments. It provides services in a flexible, transparent, and anticipative manner, requiring minimal skills for human-computer interaction. Recently, AmI is being adapted to build smart systems to guide human activities in critical domains, such as, healthcare, ambient assisted living, and disaster recovery. However, the practical application to such domains generally calls for stringent dependability requirements, since the failure of even a single component may cause dangerous loss or hazard to people and machineries. Despite these concerns, there is still little understanding on dependability issues in Ambient Intelligent systems and on possible solutions. This paper provides an analysis of the AmI literature dealing with dependability issues and to propose an innovative architectural solution to such issues, based on the use of runtime verification techniques.

In the future, mobile and wearable devices will increasingly be used for interaction with surrounding technologies. When developing applications for those devices, one usually has to implement the same application for each individual device. Thus a unified framework could drastically reduce development efforts. This paper presents a framework that facilitates the development of context-aware user interfaces (UIs) with reusable components for those devices. It is based on an abstract description of an envisioned UI which is used to generate a context- and device-specific representation at run-time. Rendition in various modalities and adaption of the generated representation are also supported.

Chapter 16

The relationship between jurisdiction and the internet has been the subject of wide ranging discussion ever since the boom in domestic internet usage. Without clear legislation, laws have been created on an ad hoc basis, often in response to specific cases. It is difficult to predict whether any one law will ever be sufficient to cope with the great variety of alleged crimes which take place on the internet. This paper discusses the problems associated with jurisdiction on the internet, presenting sample cases which have influenced the current laws and have fuelled a long term debate that continues to get more heated especially in recent times with UK celebrities being exposed on sites such as Twitter.

Aodhan L. Coffey, National University of Ireland, Ireland
Tomas E. Ward, National University of Ireland, Ireland
Richard H. Middleton, National University of Ireland, Ireland

Designing suitable robotic controllers for automating movement-based rehabilitation therapy requires an understanding of the interaction between patient and therapist. Current approaches do not take into account the highly dynamic and interdependent nature of this relationship. A better understanding can be accomplished through framing the interaction as a problem in game theory. The main strength behind this approach is the potential to develop robotic control systems which automatically adapt to patient interaction behavior. Agents learn from experiences, and adapt their behaviors so they are better suited to their environment. As the models evolve, structures, patterns and behaviors emerge that were not explicitly programmed into the original models, but which instead surface through the agent interactions with each other and their environment. This paper advocates the use of such agent based models for analysing patient-therapist interactions with a view to designing more efficient and effective robotic controllers for automated therapeutic intervention in motor rehabilitation. The authors demonstrate in a simplified implementation the effectiveness of this approach through simulating known behavioral patterns observed in real patient-therapist interactions, such as learned dependency.

M. Amparo Navarro-Salvador, Universidad Politécnica de Valencia, Spain
Ana Belén Sánchez-Calzón, Universidad Politécnica de Valencia, Spain
Carlos Fernández-Llatas, Universidad Politécnica de Valencia, Spain
Teresa Meneu, Universidad Politécnica de Valencia, Spain

The evolution of the Internet has been spectacular in recent decades. However, the Internet is still a linear scenario, focused on showing contents and dissociated from the physical world. On the other hand, there are many social groups that don't know how to use the opportunities that ICT can offer them, such as children. In this scenario, Project Enjoy.IT! designs, develops, and validates an entertainment platform with advanced contents that will set up a practical realization of the new products and services from the Future Internet. Project Enjoy.IT! integrates the physical world as an extension of the virtual world and vice versa. Thus, the project creates an AmI system that is able to act depending on the children's knowledge and necessities. The platform is based on a Services Choreography that allows an easy, simple integration of the necessary elements to give support to interactive entertainment activities.

Irini Genitsaridi, Institute of Computer Science, FORTH, Greece
Antonis Bikakis, University College London, UK
Grigoris Antoniou, Institute of Computer Science, FORTH, Greece

Authorization is an open problem in Ambient Intelligence environments. The difficulty of implementing authorization policies lies in the open and dynamic nature of such environments. The information is distributed among various heterogeneous devices that collect, process, change, and share it. Previous work presented a fully distributed approach for reasoning with conflicts in ambient intelligence systems. This paper extends previous results to address authorization issues in distributed environments. First, the authors present the formal high-level authorization language DEAL to specify access control policies in open and dynamic distributed systems. DEAL has rich expressive power by supporting negative authorization, rule priorities, hierarchical category authorization, and nonmonotonic reasoning. The authors then define the language semantics through Defeasible Logic. Finally, they demonstrate the capabilities of DEAL in a use case Ambient Intelligence scenario regarding a hospital facility.

    J. van Hoof, Fontys University of Applied Sciences, The Netherlands
    E. J. M. Wouters, Fontys University of Applied Sciences, The Netherlands
    H. R. Marston, University of Waterloo, Canada
    B. Vanrumste, MOBILAB and Katholieke Universiteit Leuven, Belgium
    R. A. Overdiep, Fontys University of Applied Sciences, The Netherlands

Technology can assist older adults to remain living in the community. Within the realm of information and communication technologies, smart homes are drifting toward the concept of ambient assisted living (AAL). AAL-systems are more responsive to user needs and patterns of living, fostering physical activity for a healthier lifestyle, and capturing behaviours for prevention and future assistance. This study provides an overview of the design-requirements and expectations towards AAL-technologies that are formulated by the end-users, their relatives and health care workers, with a primary focus on health care in The Netherlands. The results concern the motivation for use of technology, requirements to the design, implementation, privacy and ethics. More research is required in terms of the actual needs of older users without dementia and their carers, and on AAL in general as some of the work included concerns less sophisticated smart home technology.

    Ling Feng, Tsinghua University, China
    Yuanping Li, China National Software and Service Co. Ltd., China
    Lin Qiao, Shanghai Mobile Company, China

While various ambient computing and intelligence techniques have been used to assist human beings in different aspects of their daily lives and work, this paper investigates potential ambient intelligence support in mission-critical scenarios such as firefighting. The paper reviews state-of-the-art ubiquitous techniques and tools assisting firefighting. Based upon these great research results, the authors then report the design and implementation of an ambient intelligent fire victims assistance application. By sensing the physical environment and occupants in a fire building, the system suggests the safest and fastest route along which the building occupants could evacuate; and when escaping from the building is not possible, the system tries to calm down and inform the trapped ones an action list. The channels to convey the guide assistance include traditional lights, speakers, and occupants' mobile phones (if existing). The empirical experiments show that ambient intelligence in such a fire response guide can help improve the egress time performance of building occupants. The presented ambient smart fire victims' assistance system is supposed to work at an early stage of fire in a building. As a complement of existing firefighting techniques, it still faces a number of open questions to be resolved in the future.

Search engine optimization (SEO) is the process of improving the visibility, volume and quality of traffic to website or a web page in search engines via the natural search results. SEO can also target other areas of a search, including image search and local search. SEO is one of many different strategies used for marketing a website but SEO has been proven the most effective. An Internet marketing campaign may drive organic search results to websites or web pages but can be involved with paid advertising on search engines. All search engines have a unique way of ranking the importance of a website. Some search engines focus on the content while others review Meta tags to identify who and what a web site's business is. Most engines use a combination of Meta tags, content, link popularity, click popularity and longevity to determine a sites ranking. To make it even more complicated, they change their ranking policies frequently. This paper provides an overview of search engine optimisation strategies and pitfalls.

Preface: The Rise of Mobile Computing in a Future Ambient Intelligent World

INTRODUCTION

Mobile Computing is growing at an extraordinary rate with no signs of decline in the near future (Pettey & Goasduff, 2011). This growth is tempting software developers away from traditional application development to the newer world of mobile application developing (Hakoama & Hakoyama, 2011). For instance, there has been a huge rise in the popularity of smartphones and tablets in recent years, providing health information for users to live a much healthier lives. Mobile applications exist to assist users in eating healthier foods and exercising more regularly. This should it is hoped reduce the overall number of patients admitted to hospital each year with common ailments such as heart disease, obesity and diabetes. Health organisations are beginning to realise how important and beneficial it is to be interacting with patients through mobile applications1. Due to the nature of networked mobile devices, information to and from the physician is spread rapidly. Mobile Ambient Intelligent Applications could monitor pain thresholds in out-patients so as to radically identify suffering patients (Curran, 2011).

Developers have an obligation to understand what it is that users want their mobile device to do - and do it well. In many ways, that is the ambition of ambient intelligence - providing that superior mode of achieving ideal actions on behalf of the user. One of the new aspects of modern life is the integration of social networks into everyday life. Part of the rise of social networks is the ubiquity of the mobile. Information is now everywhere at anytime. This has led to acceleration of knowledge. As the speed of mobile devices and the constant development of new technologies become available, more devices are being released with different sets of features to provide for a range of user needs. This has created a fragmented development community, as the wide range of platforms and devices available mean that development cannot be too focused on a single set-up if it is to reach a wide audience or make money. This too applies to the future of ambient intelligence. What follows next is a brief foray into the merger of mobile and ambient intelligence.

SMART PHONES AND TABLETS

One option that has to be made before the decision of whether to use a particular brand of tablet or phone is which operating system to adopt for the product. There are a number of operating systems which can be considered, but the major players for now are Microsoft with Windows Phone 7, Apple with iOS, and Google with Android.

Android was developed by a consortium of small firms known as the Open Handset Alliance which was directed by Google who then acquired the initial developer after the software's completion. Applications are developed using the Java programming language, a high level object-oriented programming language primarily through the use of the Android software development kit. The Windows Phone 7 platform provides integration with other popular services such as Windows Live, Xbox Live and Zune. Application development centres on Microsoft's Silverlight application framework and XNA development tools. Finally, iOS is the mobile platform developed by Apple. Originally known as iPhone OS, the platform has been implemented to Apple's other mobile products such as the iPad and iPod touch to help standardise their product range and to increase application compatibility between devices. The applications are developed in the Objective-C object-oriented programming language and the software development kit does not support installation on third-party hardware.

The iPad still leads the way as the gold standard of tablets but there are a number of contenders snapping at its heel. In fact, the 7" tablet market is becoming a quite competitive marketplace. With roughly half the screen area of 10-inch tablets like the iPad, 7-inch tablets offer a smaller, more convenient size. Their paperback-like dimensions also make them a natural fit for e-books. Samsung offer another Android-powered tablet, the successor of the original Galaxy Tab - the first one to run Android 4.0 Ice Cream Sandwich. The Galaxy Tab 2.0 runs Android 4.0 which is supposed to be more responsive. Amazon have released the 7" Kindle Fire that ships with a customized version of Google's Gingerbread and combined with Amazon content. In terms of exact dimensions, Both tablets have also a dual core processor with more RAM memory for the Galaxy Tab 2 with 1GB instead of 512MB for the Kindle Fire. The Samsung Galaxy Tab 2 has a lower capacity battery than Kindle Fire with a 4,000mAh in comparison with Kindle Fire 4,400. The Kindle Fire does not include a camera but the the Galaxy Tab 2 includes a rear 3 megapixel camera with a frontal VGA camera.

Figure 1. Samsung Galaxy Tab, Kindle Fire, and Acer Iconia 7"

The Acer Iconia Tab A100 comes with Android Honeycomb OS. It has both a standard micro USB connection and a micro USB port along with a micro HDMI port. This allows the tablet to be connected to an HDTV. It comes with a 1024-by-600 touch-screen LCD. Many expect Apple to compete in this space as well. There is something just 'right' about holding a 7" tablet as opposed to their much smaller or larger competitors. I for one find myself reaching for my Kindle Fire rather than my 10" iPad. I also recommend 7" for clinical trials of mobile health applications. I just feel that the patients are more inclined to interact with them if they are easier to carry and appear to be more durable than the larger tablets (where the screen seems more exposed and thus weaker).

MOBILE APPLICATION DESIGN

Human Computer Interaction (HCI) is the relationship between people and computer systems and applications (Ayob et al., 2009). Usability is a measurement of how 'easy' a product is to use. Sometimes the most important aspect underlying adoption of a product is the user interface. Apple understands this and hence their success in recent years. An interesting study (Baillie & Morton, 2009) tested two separate designs. developed. One did not adhere to HCI principles but the second was developed by following HCI standards. The findings revealed that building an application without adherence to HCI can come at a cost. This ultimate cost is that a product can perform more efficiently if it is designed to be more user-friendly. The need for good HCI is critical for future Ambient Intelligent Mobile systems development.

For each new device released on the market, many people will not have the time or patience to learn new techniques. Instead, techniques should be implemented across multiple devices to enhance the aspect of "ubi-input" (Wobbrock, 2006). Producing techniques that are consistent across numerous models can help satisfy the vast majority of users. Physical, visual, aural and cognitive disabilities all affect the user's ability to operate devices which require exact movements and co-ordinance. Despite the assistance given to disabled users of desktop applications in the form of assistive technologies such as Braille displays and alternative keyboards, making mobile devices accessible is more of a challenge. As the traditional desktop computer is controlled by the keyboard and mouse, emulating these actions with accessible hardware/software is extremely difficult on a mobile device as the majority of interaction is carried out using only the fingers.

Mobile design guidelines give developers a useful template to follow during the development of user interfaces and there exists Shneiderman's 8 Golden Rules which offer a concise summary of the key principles of interface design (Dix, 2004). These include the need to strive for consistency so that terminology, sequences and arrangements such as font size, colour and the various styles are consistent across the interface. Users should be able to perform familiar actions more efficiently by the use of certain key sequences using hotkeys as shortcuts. Feedback should be offered for any action that requires it, especially where an error has occurred and users should be informed when they have successfully completed a task or transaction perhaps through the use of prompts. There should be attempts to prevent errors by the user, but when this does occur, measures should be in place to provide recovery and it should be easy to reverse action as this encourages the user to explore the system without anxiety and with the ability to the point of entry or a previous state with which he is familiar. Finally the user should feel that he is in control of the system and that it will respond to his actions and displays and menus should be kept as simple as possible to avoid clutter and any unnecessary overload of the memory capability.

These rules do not apply to every project but they do provide a foundation which interface designers can build on. They should be implemented where possible as they will not have a detrimental effect on any system. Adherence to these guidelines will help ensure that an interface is produced which will meet its requirements in terms of necessity and usability. The above rules have been laid down for a number of years, no corresponding rules exist for mobile devices. There is a good argument for compiling similar rules to combat the weaknesses in the design of interfaces on mobile devices. A number of modifications have been suggested to the remaining guidelines to render them more suitable when applied to the design of mobile interfaces.

Consistency is particularly important in relation to mobile devices and their integration with desktop machines. A user may find it necessary to transfer documents from a home computer to a PDA and read them while travelling to work. A difference in interface design, coupled with the inevitable environmental distractions, will make the task of the user even more difficult. Certain buttons and links may not be easily identified and this can lead to further difficulties. Therefore, it makes good sense that mobile interfaces should resemble exactly that of a desktop computer. Whilst the need to prevent and correct errors on both types of interface is necessary, it is more critical on mobile devices due to the time taken by the requirement of scrolling, zooming and other functions. The physical design of the mobile device can be problematic where the device is small and buttons are placed in close proximity to each other. Care should be taken to ensure that simple operations do not initiate unplanned events which might adversely affect transactions such as online-banking. Reversal of actions allows a useful degree of flexibility for the user, and whilst it is quite difficult to install on mobile devices, it remains a necessary function. Short-term memory capacity is limited on all interfaces and this is a particular concern on mobile devices. Also, the user may be distracted by other activities and interaction with the device may not have his full attention. The use of audio input and output would go some way to solving this problem.

NEAR FIELD COMMUNICATION

Near Field Communication (NFC) is a technology that enables a device to communicate with another at a maximum distance of around 20cm or less. Currently, mobile phone manufacturers, financial organisations and mobile network providers are attempting to apply this technology to Smartphones and other handheld devices because of the opportunity to enable the consumer to use commercial services more easily. As more phone manufacturers start to include NFC chips in their mobiles, the need for applications will increase. Already marketers are looking at the possibilities of using the NFC interface alongside their traditional marketing methods such as posters. Information could also be passed to the NFC device, allowing the user to gain more information about a product or service, so this would be an efficient means of advertising. For example, it would be possible to transmit a URL to the target device so that the user would then be able to navigate to a website to get further information about a product or service in which they are interested. This is where having NFC enabled on a smartphone could prove to be very useful for consumers, enabling them to find out the best price for a product before committing to the purchase. There are many uses for NFC. They can also be used to transfer tokens at airports, which would eliminate the need for boarding cards. The passenger would check-in using their mobile and then re-confirm by swiping their phone again at the departure gate. There is also the possibility of them being able to store biometric information, which is becoming more widely developed for security.

NFC devices can be used in conjunction with image display devices like digital photo frames for displaying images very quickly. All the user needs to do is touch the photo frame with the image ready to be sent, then the connection is established and the image is sent over Bluetooth. NFC is backward compatible with RFID; therefore it is perfectly feasible to use an NFC enabled device as an RFID key. This can be used with traditional RFID access control systems as a replacement for the key fobs and cards currently used. Wireless car keys using NFC are being developed by BMW with personalised settings stored into each key. They have developed an NFC car key system which will link into the cars current navigation system which already allows for hotel reservation, and train ticket booking. Using NFC the tickets and reservations can now be stored on the NFC card which can then in turn be used to gain access to the hotel room or validate the ticket with the conductor. Applications for smartphones are starting to appear that allow the user to create their own NFC tags, an application that was developed and is being distributed for free is NXP TagWriter for the Android smartphone. The application uses the NFC enabled phone to send a signal to write contact details, URLs and SMS messages onto an NFC enabled tag which can be on items like business cards up to posters.

Microsoft's Windows 8 operating system (OS) includes built-in NFC functionality which enables Windows 8 PCs, laptops or tablets to support NFC RFID readers. To date there have only been a limited range of mobile phones that are NFC-compatible. These act as 13.56 MHz passive NFC readers and writers interrogating tags and capturing data. They then can ship this data wirelessly when within range of those tags. The use of Near Field Communication will grow as NFC support in Windows 8 should spur the new community of developers and end-product manufacturers to create new applications. NFC's use in personal devices which may now include tablets and laptops, as well as mobile phones should enable brick-and-mortar stores to link their products with the Internet.

Google Wallet (http://www.google.com/wallet) is an Android app that makes your phone your wallet. It is primarily aimed at the payments market as it stores virtual versions of your existing plastic cards on your phone. It works however by people tapping their phone to pay and redeem offers using near field communication (NFC). It is just being rolled out around the world. Google Wallet has been designed for an open commerce ecosystem. It aims to eventually hold many cards people keep in their leather wallet today. Because Google Wallet is a mobile app, it will be able to do more than a regular wallet ever could, like storing thousands of payment cards and Google Offers but without the bulk. Google hope that eventually our loyalty cards, gift cards, receipts, boarding passes, tickets, even our keys will be seamlessly synced to our Google Wallet. Every offer and loyalty point will be redeemed automatically with a single tap via NFC. The vast majority of phones however do not support NFC but Google believe that NFC will grow in popularity, and for the time being this is really a first step. Google also intend to enable older mobiles to use a more limited version of the NFC application through NFC stickers that you can place on the back of a phone.

Google are a little vague to date on this but it seems the plan is that users will be able to obtain special NFC stickers with a single credit card associated with them. Purchases made using the sticker will be relayed to the Android Wallet application on a device via the cloud. Google says it is willing to partner with everyone to help broaden support for Google Wallet and we can expect to see other operating system implementations of this technology. Google Wallet is now released on the Nexus S 4G by Google. It is possible that there may be real opportunities in the ambient intelligence arena to use the NFC on the Google phones to provide added value and services. The obvious feature is knowing the location of people.

Devices using NFC are expected to operate in environments with varying security, some with a high level of security and others that do not need any security. the technology is 'inherently secure' because of the small transmission distance however the best solution to these security issues is to have a layered security model with a minimum requirement of authentication before the start of communication. Developers can then add higher levels of security according to their application needs. This is not required by the ISO standard but will be essential for making money from the technology. So there is much room for research into these areas in secure ambient intelligent Near Field Communications.

MOBILE HEALTH

Mobile Healthcare the provision of medical applications on mobile devices to improve the health of patients. In recent years, through advances made in healthcare, people are expected to live long active lives. People are becoming more knowledgeable in how to have a better quality of life. How we get this information to help us live longer has changed. As a society in the twenty first century we are forever searching for new information. Information has become more readily available and through mobile devices, patient's views are always in close proximately to new information.

Almost everyone at some point in their life will need some type of health treatment. Whether this health treatment is from a general practitioner, surgeon or any other medical expert we want to be cared or have someone else cared for in the best possible way. Unfortunately there are current threats to the healthcare system which could reduce the quality of healthcare people will receive in the future. Since the United Kingdom fell into recession officially in January 2009, the government has been cutting funds from education, transport and various other services (Monaghan, 2009). Unfortunately the healthcare sector has also had to find ways to reduce its spending in order to save money. To save money organisations such as the NHS have been forced to cut jobs from all areas of the health sector. More than 50,000 doctors, nurses, midwives and other NHS staff are due to lose their jobs due to the most comprehensive survey of health cuts since the government came to power (Prince, 2011). With fewer nurses on wards due to these cuts, the return to long waiting lists and a rise in cancelled operations will result. Patient care will be an early casualty he warns.

Now more than ever it is important that methods can be put in place to save money for the health sector while still maintaining the highest quality of healthcare for patients. In the UK the population is predicted to increase to 70 million by the year 2027 (Travis, 2011). The number aged over 85 is expected to more than double over the next 25 years from 1.4 million in 2010 to 1.9 million by 2020 increasing to 3.5 million by 2035. The number of people aged 90 and above is set to triple, while the number of people aged 95 and above is expected to quadruple both by the year 2035. At a time where the health sector is trying to cut down on spending, there should be an emphasis on expanding the health sector for the forecasted increase in the number of older aged people and the types of healthcare treatment that they will need. Many Healthcare services are therefore faced with the problem of reducing spending while increasing resources in the next 20 years to cope with more patients. Methods must therefore be found and implemented into the health arena and mHealth applications could be beneficial to the current and future issues that affect health care

Mobile Ambient Intelligent Applications (MAIA) are extremely relevant in this world and can benefit both healthcare professionals and the public. With the current recession in the UK and across the world, the health arena has been forced to cut down spending in order to save money. MAIA can help reduce costs in the long run for any health trust. Ultimately however it is the users of MAIA who can determine whether or not the health arena can use such innovative systems to their and the physicians advantage (Curran, 2012).

CONCLUSION

Mobile devices are becoming more prevalent as our main source of information and applications are becoming the gateway to which we can access it. The mobile device industry is very much fragmented, which leaves developers making many difficult decisions in order to maximize their applications success and availability. The large corporations that control the market places do not agree on many standards and protocols, which is making the divide within the mobile device ecosystem larger.

Security is becoming the main concern for the large mobile device providers as more and more people are using mobile devices this is becoming a new market for hackers and cyber criminals. Many developers leave their applications vulnerable and many do not patch their application, which puts the users of the application at great risk of malicious intent. One of the main aspects that is cropping up amongst the mobile apps community is personalisation and user centeredness. This can be achieved by analysing the user's behaviour and preferences and identifying areas where the applications can prompt the user with a suggestion based on these, or by automatically providing information that they may want and minimizing text entry (e.g. drop down boxes). This kind of approach, as mentioned earlier, is strongly becoming characteristic of mobile applications, and this can help bypass several of the limitations of the device and its user interface if implemented correctly in the development stages. This design approach should be strongly emphasised in future application development as it will lead to more functional, user friendly applications. As apps are implicitly characteristic of compactness, ease of use, speed and functionality, it is important that the final product is able to deliver on these ideals if it is to be successful. It is important to the user that the application carries out exactly what is asked of it, with the minimum of fuss, and even just one annoying bug that impairs the app's functionality, even slightly, could turn the user off the product completely, seeking an application which does it better. This is why testing is crucial and any bugs which may visibly affect the running of the core functionality should be top-priority and stamped out immediately.

Healthcare is a multi-billion dollar industry and a vital service within society. There has been a shift in emphasis for patients, from attending hospitals and local doctor's surgeries to looking at self-monitoring and health awareness. With more health trusts attempting to embrace technology, patients are taking more control of their health. In the past the patients visited the doctor when they felt sick or unwell or had a medical problem. The doctor then provided the patient with advise, diagnosis and medication and in some cases referred them to a consultant. When the patient returned home the only person they could talk to was a relation or a neighbour. In cases where a patient had a rare condition then they would have felt extremely isolated as no one they knew would be going through the same situation.

Mobile Ambient Intelligent Applications could provide patients with support from multiple areas. This may revolutionise the healthcare sector. Control is now in the hands of the patient. This is largely down to what is known as content control. Anyone can now publish, read and review medical information due to the internet. This has shifted the medical expert from the centre of the health arena to the patient (Ayob at al., 2009).

Kevin Curran
University of Ulster, UK

REFERENCES

Ayob, N. Z. B., Hussin, R. C., Dahlan, H. M., & Malaysia, J. (2009). *Three layers design guideline for mobile application*. In 2009 International Conference on Information Management and Engineering (ICIME 2009). Kuala Lumpur, Malaysia, 3-5 April. Piscataway, NJ: IEEE.

Baillie, L., & Morton, L. (2009). Designing quick & dirty applications for mobiles: Making the case for the utility of HCI. *Proceedings of the ITI 2009 31st International Conference on Information Technology Interfaces*, June 22-25, 2009, Cavtat, Croatia, (pp. 293-298).

Curran, K. (2011). Past, current and future developments in ambient intelligence. In *Ubiquitous developments in ambient computing and intelligence: Human-centered applications*. ISBN 10: 1609605497

Curran, K. (2012). Ambient intelligence – Context aware, pervasive and making a difference in a modern world. In *Innovative applications of ambient intelligence: Advances in smart systems*. ISBN 978-1-4666-0038-6

Dix, A., Finlay, J., Abowd, G. D., & Beale, R. (2004). *Human-computer interaction* (3rd ed.). Essex, UK: Pearson.

Hakoama, M., & Hakoyama, S. (2011). The impact of cell phone use on social networking and development among college students. *The American Association of Behavioral and Social Sciences Journal, 15*(1).

Monaghan, A. (2009, 23rd January). UK recession: It's now official. *The Telegraph*. Retrieved from http://www.telegraph.co.uk/finance/recession/4321414/UK-recession-Its-now-official.html

Pettey, C., & Goasduff, L. (2011). *Gartner says sales of mobile devices in second quarter of 2011 grew 16.5 percent year-on-year; smartphone sales grew 74 percent*. Retrieved from http://www.gartner.com/it/page.jsp?id=1764714

Prince, R. (2011, 23rd February). True extent of NHS job cuts revealed. *The Telegraph*. Retrieved from http://www.telegraph.co.uk/health/healthnews/8341737/True-extent-of-NHS-job-cuts-revealed.html

Travis, A. (2011, 26th October). UK population to reach 70m by 2027. *Guardian*. http://www.guardian.co.uk/world/2011/oct/26/uk-population-70-million-2027

Wobbrock, J. (2006). *The future of mobile device research in HCI*. In CHI 2006. Quebec, Canada, 22-27 April 2006.

Wood, S. (2008, September 18th). Assessment of pain. *Nursing Times*.

ENDNOTE

[1]   http://www.nhs.uk/aboutNHSChoices/aboutnhschoices/NHSChoicesmobile/Pages/NHSChoices-mobile.aspx

Chapter 1
Analysis of the Effect of Human Presence on a Wireless Sensor Network

Ben Graham
Letterkenny Institute of Technology, Ireland

Marek Bykowski
Letterkenny Institute of Technology, Ireland

Christos Tachtatzis
Letterkenny Institute of Technology, Ireland

David C. Tracey
Letterkenny Institute of Technology, Ireland

Fabio Di Franco
Letterkenny Institute of Technology, Ireland

Nick F. Timmons
Letterkenny Institute of Technology, Ireland

Jim Morrison
Letterkenny Institute of Technology, Ireland

ABSTRACT

Wireless Sensor Networks (WSNs) are gaining an increasing industry wide adoption. However, there remain major challenges such as network dimensioning and node placement especially in Built Environment Networks (BENs). Decisions on the node placement, orientation, and the number of nodes to cover the area of interest are usually ad-hoc. Ray tracing tools are traditionally employed to predict RF signal propagation; however, such tools are primarily intended for outdoor environments. RF signal propagation varies greatly indoors due to building materials and infrastructure, obstacles, node placement, antenna orientation and human presence. Because of the complexity of signal prediction, these factors are usually ignored or given little weight when such networks are analyzed. The paper's results show the effects of the building size and layout, building materials, human presence and mobility on the signal propagation of a BEN. Additionally, they show that antenna radiation pattern is a key factor in the RF propagation performance, and appropriate device orientation and placement can improve the network reliability. Further, the RSS facility in RF transceivers can be exploited to detect the presence and motion of humans in the environment.

DOI: 10.4018/978-1-4666-2041-4.ch001

INTRODUCTION

Developments in wireless technology and sensors have resulted in a range of new applications for Wireless Sensor Networks (WSNs). One such type of WSNs is the Built Environment Networks (BENs) which can be deployed in a wide variety of applications such as environmental monitoring, surveillance and healthcare applications. WSNs are characterized by having a large number of devices (motes) with sensing capabilities, limited processing capability and wireless connectivity to other devices. The wireless capability allows the sensors to be deployed close to the phenomenon being observed while their limited memory and processing capabilities result in low cost; this allows the deployment of a large number of such devices. The motes used in WSNs usually contain a micro-controller, RF chip, sensors and often use low level operating systems such as TinyOS (Levis, Madden, Polastre, Szewczyk, Whitehouse, Woo, Gay, Hill, Welsh, Brewer, & Culler, 2005) or Contiki (Dunkels, Gr"onvall, & Voigt, 2004).

When deploying a wireless network within a building, it is vital to have an understanding of how the transmitted signals are affected through obstacles and with distance. The channel between transmitter and receiver may be a line of sight (LOS), but more likely the presence of objects such as office furniture, lab equipment and people will create obstructions and provide multiple paths (multipath) for the waves to reach the receiver. Diffraction, reflection and scattering are main causes of multipath and fading. Multipath and fading are the dominant effects on the channel as the transmitted signal propagates through the media to the receiver (Su & Alzagal, 2008). The ideal antenna radiation pattern for a mote is symmetric in all directions and would result in constant radio range and performance in a spherical radius of the mote (Su & Alzagal, 2008). In reality this uniform transmission pattern does not exist and failure to understand a mote antenna transmission pattern and how it can be affected by the environ-ment can result in network reliability issues and/or inappropriate placement of motes. There are numerous papers that investigate the relationship between signal attenuation and building materials (Jang & Healy, 2009; Wilson, 2002; Masri, Chew, Wong, & Lias, 2005) and software packages that simulate the radio frequency (RF) attenuation within buildings using ray tracing techniques (Kim & Lee, 2009). Little attention has, however, been given to the effects that antenna pattern irregularity and human presence can have on the signal strength and reliability of even a small scale network when it has been deployed.

This paper provides measurements of Received Signal Strength (RSS) from within various locations of a typical office environment during a twenty four hour period and an understanding of how signal attenuation is affected by building materials, antenna selection, orientation and both human presence and movement.

The paper is divided into sections. First we describe the experimental setup and software used. The results of the experiments are provided and discussed following this. Finally, a conclusion is given by highlighting the main outcomes of the paper.

Experimental Setup

The experiment consisted of a large number of motes deployed within an office environment for a 24 hour period. The purpose of the experiment is to measure the RSS from a large number of locations within the office. This is achieved by having multiple motes within the lab transmitting data back to a basestation. Measurements of RSS were taken using the CC2420 Received Signal Strength Indicator (RSSI) and used to build a map of the signal attenuation from the centralized basestation. The CC2420 datasheet states that the RF chip has a very linear RSSI measurement with a dynamic range of about 100 dB (Texas Instruments, n.d.). To verify this linearity stated in the datasheet a calibration test was carried out; the results confirmed the linearity was within the +/-6 dB error allowed over the majority of the dynamic range. However non-linear behaviour was highlighted at transmission powers below -85 dBm.

The use of a twenty-four hour test period means that measurements are taken when the office is occupied during the day and unoccupied at night so that the changes in RSS due to human presence can be detected. The use of a large number of motes ensures that an accurate map of RSS can be obtained.

Location and Hardware

The experiment was carried out within the WiSAR Lab which is located in the CoLab building at the Letterkenny Institute of Technology. The lab is located on the second floor and consists of four rooms with a total ground area of 95m². The four rooms consist of two general offices these being Room 204 and Room 205A, one large lab Room 205 and a machine room/store 205B. During the twenty four hour experiment all four rooms will have had people in them at some point, for the duration of the daytime working hours (09.00-17.30). More specifically room 204 has three occupants, room 205 had two and both 205A and 205B had none.

For the duration of all experiments, the basestation was located in the centre of room 205 and attached to the ceiling. This is the most central location for a basestation and has a line of sight, or a fairly unobstructed line, to most of the locations under test. The basestation was fitted with a 1/4 wave monopole vertically oriented stub antenna. Each room has a suspended ceiling at a height of 2.7 metres, with each ceiling consisting of equally sized tiles, which made an excellent grid that aided with the placement of the motes (Figure 1). All internal walls within the lab are stud partition and all external walls of the lab are concrete.

The experiment was performed at a total of seventy locations within the lab, divided into seventeen locations in Room204, thirty-three in

Room 205, eight in Room 205A, ten in Room 205B and two additional locations in the hall. Figure 2 shows a map of the mote locations within the lab, the grey circles represent the occupied workstations; the white circle represents the basestation while the orange square in the middle of room 205 represents unoccupied workstations. All walls are represented by the black line. Due to the large number of locations to be measured, the experiment was sub-divided into five separate areas of fourteen motes at any one time. With this in mind the room layout does change slightly for each experiment because of the different placement of the motes. It is not known if these small differences have an affect on the experiment results but it must be acknowledged that they exist.

The WiSAR mote (WiSAR Lab, n.d.a) was used for the transmitters in the experiments. It is based on the commonly available IEEE802.15.4 compliant Tmote Sky (Moteiv Corporation, n.d.) which uses the MSP430F1611 microcontroller and the CC2420 radio transceiver from Texas Instruments. This is a suitable test device for a BEN as it provides the data-rate and low power requirements of BEN applications. As the WiSAR mote has no USB Circuitry (Franco, Tachtatzis, Graham, Bykowski, Tracey, Timmons, & Morrision, 2010), a Tmote Sky was used as the basestation so that its USB connection could be used to connect to a database server to collect the results (Figure 3).

The Tmote sky and the WiSAR Mote incorporate an inverted-F PCB Antenna. The inverted-F PCB antenna is one of the most commonly used

Figure 1. Motes attached to ceiling

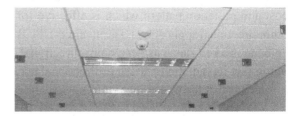

Figure 2. Layout of moto locations within the lab

1	2	3	4	5	6	7	8	9	
		Room				Room			
10	11	205A 12	13	14	15	205B 16	17	18	
19	20	21	22	23	24	25	26		
28	29	30	31 Room	32	33	34	35	36	
37	38	39	205 40	41	42	43	44		73
46	47	48	49	50	51	52	53		
55	56	57	58 Room	59	60	61	62		74
64	65	66	204 67	68	69	70	71	72	

Figure 3. WiSAR mote

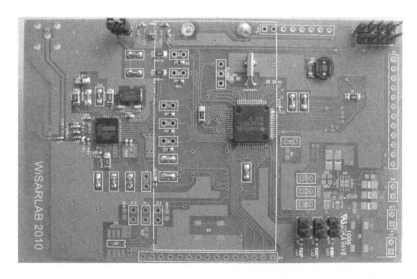

antennas at 2.4GHz mainly due to its minimal cost and radiation pattern which is effective for omnidirectional applications. The inverted-F PCB antenna is often stated as been omni-directional, but in fact its radiation pattern is directional and this means that the transmitter mote's orientation will have an affect on the RSS at the basestation. Figure 4 shows a 3D simulation of the radiation pattern for an inverted F antenna (Ember Corporation, n.d.). The strongest direction of radiation is on the X and Y axis in the direction of the antenna tip.

Figure 4. Radiation pattern of inverted F antenna (Ember Corporation, n.d.)

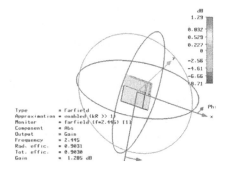

All motes were attached to the ceiling in an identical position with the antenna pointing towards the floor. This is not an ideal antenna direction, but was the most suitable in terms of mounting. With the motes positioned in this manner, the strongest RF signal will be transmitted towards the ground on the X axis and slightly towards the front of each mote. This setup was selected to highlight how incorrectly aligned antennas can affect the network were the multipath is most dominant between all locations and the basestation.

Finally, an RF sweep of the lab with a spectrum analyzer, showed that Wireless Local Area Network (WLAN) were operating on channels 1,6 and 11 at frequencies 2412MHz, 2437MHz and 2462Mhz respectively. In order to reduce the effects of interference, the experiments were performed at 2425MHz, which was found to be unoccupied by other devices.

SOFTWARE

Software was developed for both the basestation and transmitter devices for this experiment. All software was developed to run on a TinyOS platform (Levis, Madden, Polastre, Szewczyk, Whitehouse, Woo, Gay, Hill, Welsh, Brewer, & Culler, 2005). TinyOS is an open source operating system designed for wireless embedded sensor networks.

The transmitter uses a typical timer based sensor program, which wakes the microcontroller from low power mode (LPM3) every 10 seconds, performs a temperature, humidity, light and battery measurement, increments a sequence number, then transmits this along with its node id before returning to sleep (LPM3). The total transmitted packet payload length was 18 bytes.

The basestation program receives incoming packets from the radio, calculates the RSS from the incoming packet, before forwarding the received packet including the added RSS information to a database. This data is stored in a database server, connected to the basestation by USB, and all packets entered into the database are time stamped. The data in the database can then be used in two ways; it can be extracted manually for analysis, or it can be viewed as a historical plot via the WiSAR Lab webpage (WiSAR Lab, n.d.b).

RESULTS

The following results are presented in three sections; those at night when the office was empty, those during the day when people are present and an Antenna orientation section which investigates the effect of the antenna radiation pattern. The median and signal range is presented here for both the day and night set of results. The median was obtained rather than the mean as the median is unaffected by any outlying results. The fluctuation range was also obtained for both night and day to indicate the signal fluctuation at each measured location. The fluctuations were measured over 90% of the results, so to remove the effect of outlying results. The RSS medians of the night results were recorded without any human presence and show the effects of distance, mote orientation, and building materials on the signal strength. The daytime results allow the analysis of human presence on the WSN. The mote's orientation is shown at the bottom of each plot, with the X-axis perpendicular to the floor.

Night-Time (Empty Office) Results

All night time measurements were taken when the office was empty between the hours of 22.00 and 08.00. Due to the number of node locations to be measured, experiments had to be carried out over 5 consecutive nights. During this time the room layout remained constant in order to minimize any effects that may have arisen due to changes in multipath caused by changes in office layout, but as mentioned earlier small changes did occur due to the different placement of motes during the separate tests.

Figure 5 shows the median of the RSS during the night for all locations and these are the reference RSS values when the environment is constant. The RSS values range from -35 to -85 dBm, and generally nodes closest to the basesta-

tion showing the higher values and nodes further from the basestation showing lower values with the following exceptions. At this point it should be remembered that all transmitter motes are placed in a non ideal orientation.

- In Figure 5 node location 20 shows the median RSS to be -45 dBm while the nodes closer to the basestation are less. One possible explanation may be that node 20 is located directly above an equipment rack. As the node's strongest transmission path is in the direction of the floor, a reflection may be occurring from the rack to the basestation, unlike the nearby locations were the most of the RF is reaching the floor.
- In the same way location 32 has a significantly lower RSS value than location 40 which is at a similar distance from the basestation, again this may be due to the fact than location 40 is transmitting directly down to a desk area and location 32 is just on the edge of this desk area.
- As mentioned earlier the directional radiation nature of the inverted F antenna is strongest on the X axis towards the floor and slightly to the front of the mote on the Z axis. This Z axis radiation can be observed by the fact that motes located in Room205A and Room205B present a stronger RSS than the motes in Room 204,

Figure 5. Median RSSU values at night

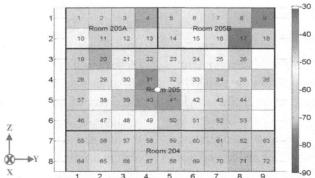

even though the motes are at a similar distance from the basestation.

Greater attenuation was observed at nodes 8, 9, 17, 18 and this can be explained by the presence of several metal enclosures in their vicinity. It should be noted that these locations were all measuring RSS values less than -85 dBm, which is outside the linear range of the CC2420's RSSI measurements.

Figure 6 shows the 90% percentile range for all locations over the night period. For example, at the location 38; 90% of the values fall within the range of -50 to -53 dBm giving a percentile range of 3 dB. The majority of the motes as expected show very little fluctuations because the surrounding environment remains constant and the multipath is unchanged. From Fig 6 the maximum percentile range observed is very small(3 dB), these small fluctuations can be justified by temperature variations and hardware tolerances.

Day Time Results

All day-time measurements were taken during working hours and as with the night measurements the experiments had to be carried out over 5 consecutive working days. During this time, the office layout was kept as constant as possible. The number of humans present and their movement

patterns during the 5 day tests would have varied slightly as can be expected in any real deployment. The lab had 5 occupied workstations for the majority of the daytime experiments located under motes 56, 65, 69 between motes 19 and 28 and between motes 37 and 46. Figure 7 shows the median of the RSS for all locations during the daytime hours.

The median RSS results from during the day are almost identical to the night time results and on first sight, suggests that human presence has no effect on RSS, but this is not the case as was seen when viewing the RSS time series. For this reason, it is necessary that the fluctuations in the measurements are considered.

Figure 8 as before shows the RSS 90% percentile range that shows the fluctuation range of RSS for all locations over the full twenty four hour period and more importantly highlights several locations that show high levels of fluctuations which were not present during the night. The black circles represent the location of occupied workstations. The highest variations were at locations 46 and 69 with RSS ranges of 13 dB and 12 dB respectively during the 24 hour period. Both of these motes were located in close proximity to an occupied workstation, showing that human presence is having a major effect on RSS. Similarly, motes 19, 56 and 60 presented larger than normal fluctuations as all of these motes were in close

Figure 6. RSS variance at night

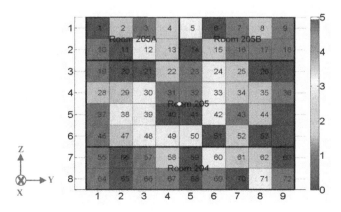

Figure 7. Median RSS values of the day

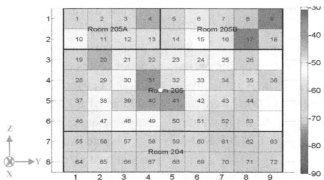

proximity to an occupied workstation. Motes 35 and 71 were located above the doorway to room 205 and 204 respectively and both showed larger than normal fluctuation, possibly due to people frequently passing under these locations as they enter and exit the lab. Mote 67 in room 204 also showed higher than normal fluctuation but in comparison to the other motes it was not in close proximity to any occupied workstations.

As an example of the RSS fluctuations experienced by a mote above an occupied workstation, Figure 9 shows the time series of the RSS for node 46 from 07.00-12.00. From 07.00-08.45 the RSS is constant at approximately -65 dBm as no humans were present in the lab. At 08.45 when someone enters room 205 and moves to workstation 1 causes the RSS to drop. At 09.00 another

person enters and sits at workstation 2 increasing the RSS. For the rest of the working day the RSS fluctuates widely while people move within the room affecting the signal strength. This plot shows the major effect on RSS of just two people in the lab and the resulting RSS fluctuations.

Figure 10 plots RSS for the same node 46 from 12.00-22.00 and it is easy to observe that the fluctuation almost disappears from 17.30, when the room becomes empty.

Antenna Orientation Results

The final test was to confirm the effect of the antenna radiation pattern, by repeating the experiment on selected locations. This time the motes were positioned in such a manner that

Figure 8. RSS variance over the 24 hour period

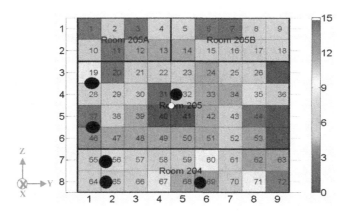

Figure 9. Node 46 RSS for 07.00-12.00 hrs

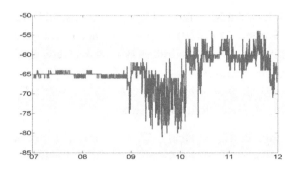

Figure 10. Node 46 RSS for 12.00-22.00 hrs

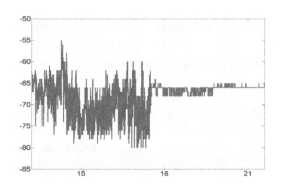

their antenna z –axes were perpendicular to the floor. With this test it was confirmed that when the antenna tip pointed towards the basestation, the RSS values were higher compared to previous setup. Additionally, the effect of human presence and movement was less, because the strongest path of radiation was in the horizontal direction unlike the previous setup that was directed downwards to the occupants.

Figure 11 shows a plot of RSS from node 46 with the new mote orientation. This location was selected because it suffered the highest fluctuation in the previous experiments. Like before, during the night and when the office was empty the RSS was constant. However, the observed median was -58 dBm instead of -65 dBm. During the day, when the office was occupied fluctuations still occurred (in the range of -53 dBm to -65 dBm) but were not as severe as in the pervious setup (-55 dBm to -80 dBm).

CONCLUSION

This paper has provided an insight into the deployment of a real WSN in a typical office environment. The results presented in this paper show the effects of the mote placement and radiation patterns. For example, a one metre move in the placement of a mote can vary the RSS by up to 20 dB. The placement of motes close to large metal objects such as filing cabinets or equipment racks can have unpredictable effects on the signal propagation. Therefore, before deploying motes within a network it is important to both understand the radiation pattern of the motes and the office layout. This information should then be used when positioning motes to ensure that their orientation effectively utilises any directional feature.

In addition, human presence within close proximity of motes greatly affects the transmission performance, both in a positive and negative manner. The results highlighted this fact by the large fluctuations of RSS over twenty four hours for motes close to occupied workstations. These fluctuations occur as the movement of a human body causes the multipath signal to change and results in unpredictable RSS, which can often result in dropped packets. The effect of human presence in the experiments carried out was heightened by the fact that the motes located above the workstations were transmitting directly down on the occupants and their movement was directly affecting the multipath. The final test confirmed

Figure 11. Node 46 RSS for 07.00-12.00 hrs

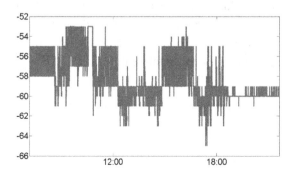

this by positioning the motes with the strongest transmission directed away from human presence, resulting in reduced fluctuations.

In summary, the findings demonstrate that the effects of both antenna orientation and human presence must be considered when designing new network protocols and deployment layouts. The results also show the potential application of using WSNs deployed in a building to detect human presence and movement. It is recommended that software simulation tools, such as those employing ray tracing techniques, should include the effect of human presence on propagation and incorporate necessary models for this when network planning. Future work is planned on implementing these results in new software models to enhance simulation tools. Longer term tests are also planned that will investigate the relationship between human presence and movement, RSS and the effects on packet error rate in this office deployment.

ACKNOWLEDGMENT

This work was carried out under the auspices of Enterprise Ireland Applied Research Enhancement (ARE).

REFERENCES

Dunkels, A., Gr¨onvall, B., & Voigt, T. (2004). *Contiki - a Lightweight and Flexible Operating System for Tiny Networked Sensors*.

Ember Corporation. (n.d.). *Designing with an inverted-F PCB antenna*. Retrieved from http://www.ember.com/pdf/120-5052-000_Designing_with_a_PCB_Antenna.pdf

Franco, F. D., Tachtatzis, C., Graham, B., Bykowski, M., Tracey, D. C., Timmons, N. F., & Morrision, J. (2010). Current Characterisation for Ultra Low Power Wireless Body Area Networks. In *Proceedings of the 8th IEEE Workshop on Intelligent Solutions in Embedded Systems (WISES 2010)*, Heraklion, Crete, Greece.

Jang, W. S., & Healy, W. M. (2009). Wireless sensor network performance metrics for building applications. *Energy and Buildings Journal*, 862-868.

Kim, H., & Lee, H. (2009). *Accelerated Three Dimensional Ray Tracing Techniques using Ray Frustums for Wireless Propagation Models*. Seoul, South Korea: Sogang Unversity.

Levis, P., Madden, S., Polastre, J., Szewczyk, R., Whitehouse, K., & Woo, A. (2005). In Weber, W., Rabaey, J. M., & Aarts, E. (Eds.), *TinyOS: An Operating System for Sensor Networks in Ambient Intelligence* (pp. 115–148). Berlin: Springer Verlag.

Masri, T., Chew, S. P., Wong, C. P., & Lias, K. (2005). *A Study of Signal Penetration into Building Materials*. Sarawak, Malaysia: University Malaysia Sarawak.

Moteiv Corporation. (n.d.). *Ultra low power IEEE 802.15.4 complaint wireless sensor module*. Retrieved from http://sentilla.com/files/pdf/eol/tmote-sky-datasheet.pdf

Su, W., & Alzagal, M. (2008). Channel propagation characteristics of wireless MICAz sensor nodes. *Ad Hoc Networks Journal*, 1183-1193.

Texas Instruments. (n.d.). *2.4GHz IEEE 802.15.4/Zigbee-ready RF Transceiver*. Retrieved from http://focus.ti.com/lit/ds/symlink/cc2420.pdf

Wilson, R. (2002). *Propagation Losses Through Common Building Materials 2.4GHz vs 5 GHz.* Los Angeles: University of Southern California.

WiSAR Lab. (n.d.a). *WiSAR Lab Development Mote.* Retrieved from http://www.wisar.org/

WiSAR Lab. (n.d.b). *WiSAR Lab Office Testbed.* Retrieved from http://monitor.wisar.ie/

This work was previously published in the International Journal of Ambient Computing and Intelligence, Volume 3, Issue 1, edited by Kevin Curran, pp. 1-13, copyright 2011 by IGI Publishing (an imprint of IGI Global).

Chapter 2
Cloud Computing Security

Sean Carlin
University of Ulster, UK

Kevin Curran
University of Ulster, UK

ABSTRACT

In this paper, the authors focus on Cloud Computing, which is a distributed architecture that centralizes server resources on quite a scalable platform so as to provide on demand' computing resources and services The authors outline what cloud computing is, the various cloud deployment models and the main security risks and issues that are currently present within the cloud computing industry.

INTRODUCTION

Cloud computing is not a new technology but rather a new delivery model for information and services using existing technologies. It uses the internet infrastructure to allow communication between client side and server side services/applications (Weiss, 2007). Cloud service providers (CSP's) offer cloud platforms for their customers to use and create their web services, much like internet service providers offer costumers high speed broadband to access the internet. CSPs and ISPs both offer services. The cloud provides a layer of abstraction between the computing resources and the low level architecture involved. The customers do not own the actual physical infrastructure but merely pay a subscription fee and the cloud service provider grants them access to the clouds resources and infrastructure. A key concept is that the customers can reduce expenditure on resources like software licenses, hardware and other services (e.g., email) as they can obtain all these things from one source, the cloud services provider. Recent studies have found that disciplined companies achieved on average an 18% reduction in their IT budget from cloud computing and a 16% reduction in data centre power costs (McFedries, 2008). This paper provides an overview of the key aspects of Cloud Computing.

DOI: 10.4018/978-1-4666-2041-4.ch002

Cloud Architecture

Cloud computing has five key attributes which grant it some advantages over similar technologies and these attributes include:

- **Multitenancy (shared resources):** Unlike previous computing models, which assumed dedicated resources dedicated to a single user or owner, cloud computing is based on a business model in which resources are shared at the network, host and application level.
- **Massive scalability:** Cloud computing *provides* the ability to scale to tens of thousands of systems, as well as the ability to massively scale bandwidth and storage space.
- **Elasticity:** Users can rapidly increase and decrease their computing resources as needed, as well as release resources for other uses when they are no longer required.
- **Pay as you go:** Users pay for only the resources they actually use and for only the time they require them.
- **Self-provisioning of resources:** Users self-provision resources, such as additional systems (processing capability, software & storage) and network resources (Mather, Kumaraswamy, & Latif, 2009).

There is a buzz around cloud computing, as users of the cloud services only have to pay for what they use and the resources that they need to cope with demanding situations can be adjusted depending on the demand. This is recognized as the cloud delivery model (SPI – see Figure 1) which consists of three services known as Software-as-a-service (SaaS), Platform-as-a-service (PaaS) and Infrastructure-as-a-service (IaaS). Software-as-a-service allows the users to utilize various applications from the cloud rather than using applications on their own computer. The cloud service provider would usually provide some sort of software development environment to allow applications to be developed for use within the cloud. The application programming interface (API) which the users use to access and interact with the software allows the user to use the software without having to worry about how or where the data is being stored or how much disk space is available as the cloud service provider will manage this for them.

Platform-as-a-service operates at a lower level than the SaaS. It is responsible for the management of the storage space, bandwidth allocation and computing resources available for the applications. It retrieves the resources needed to run the software and dynamically scales up these resources when more is needed. This service holds a key attribute of the cloud mentioned above as self-provisioning of resources. Infrastructure-as-a-service dynamically scales bandwidth allocation

Figure 1. Showing layers of the cloud delivery model

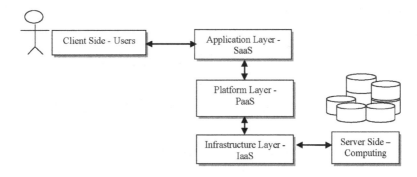

and server resources for the cloud. This service allows the cloud to operate during high traffic/demanding situations as resources are dynamically increased as they are needed. The pay as you go attribute plays a large role in this service as the user is charged for how much bandwidth or server resources are needed.

Cloud Deployment Models

There are three main types of cloud deployment models - public, private and hybrid clouds.

Public Clouds: are the most common type of cloud. This is where multiple customers can access web applications and services over the internet. Each individual customer has their own resources which are dynamically provisioned by a third party vendor. This third party vendor hosts the cloud for multiple customers from multiple data centers (see Figure 2), manages all the security and provides the hardware and infrastructure for the cloud to operate. The customer has no control or insight into how the cloud is managed or what infrastructure is available.

Private Clouds: emulate the concept of cloud computing on a private network. They allow users to have the benefits of cloud computing without some of the pitfalls. Private clouds grant complete control over how data is managed and what security measures are in place. This can lead to users having more

confidence and control. The major issue with this deployment model is that the users have large expenditures as they have to buy the infrastructure to run the cloud and also have to manage the cloud themselves.

Hybrid Clouds: incorporate both public and private clouds (see Figure 3) within the same network. It allows the organisations to benefit from both deployment models. For example, an organisation could hold sensitive information on their private cloud and use the public cloud for handling large traffic and demanding situations.

Cloud Security

Cloud computing can be considered as still in infancy however there are a number of organizations and standard bodies drafting cloud standards and APIs. There is a worry in the community about cloud computing security. One of the risks that people see is that providers have to manage potentially millions of customers and this presents a challenge (Ohlman, Eriksson, & Rembarz, 2009). What this depicts is that many people are worried that the cloud service providers will not be able to cope with the large scale of or that the infrastructure will not be able to scale properly with large amounts of usage. Privacy is important for organisations, especially when individual's personal information or sensitive information is being stored but it is not yet completely understood whether the cloud computing infrastructure will be

Figure 2. Public cloud deployment model

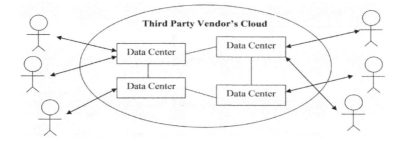

Figure 3. Showing hybrid cloud deployment model

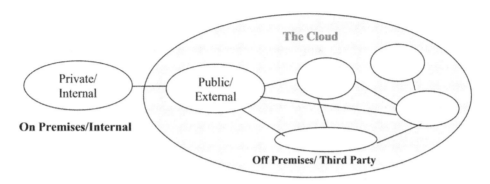

able support the storing of sensitive information without making organisations liable from breaking privacy regulations. Many believe that cloud authorisation systems are not robust enough with as little as a password and username to gain access to the system, in many private clouds, usernames can be very similar, degrading the authorisation measures further. If there was private/sensitive information being stored on a private cloud then there is a high chance that someone could view the information easier than many might believe. The customer is advised to only give their data or use the cloud providers system if they trust them.

Cloud service providers believe encryption is the key and can help with a lot of the security issues but what comes along with the benefits of encryption are the pitfalls as encryption can be processor intensive. Encrypting is not always full proof for protecting data, there can be times when little glitches occur and the data cannot be decrypted leaving the data corrupt and unusable for customers and the cloud service provider. The clouds resources can also be abused as cloud providers reassign IP addresses when a customer no longer needs the IP address. Once an IP address is no longer needed by one customer after a period of time it then becomes available for another customer to use. Cloud providers save money and do not need as many IP addresses by reusing them, so it is in the cloud provider's interest to reuse them. Too many of these idle/

used IP addresses can leave the cloud provider open to abuse of its resources. There is a period between an IP address being changed in DNS and the DNS caches holding the IP address getting cleared. If these old/used IP addresses are being held in the cache then they can be accessed which would grant a user access to the resources that are available at the IP address. Also another customer of the same cloud provider could potentially gain access to another customer's resources by navigating through the cloud provider's networks, if no/little security measures are put in place. Data and information is like a currency for cyber terrorists/crooks and clouds can hold enormous amounts of data so clouds are becoming an a attractive target for these crooks which is why cloud security must be top notch and should not be overlooked (Wayner, 2008).

Clouds API's and software-as-a-service are still evolving which means updates can be frequent but some clouds do not inform their customers that these changes have been made. Making changes to the API means changing the cloud configuration which affects all instances within the cloud (see Figure 4). The changes could affect the security of the system as one change could fix one bug but create another. The customers of the cloud provider should enquire if any updates are made and should ask about what security implementations have been put into place to secure their data and what exactly has changed with the system.

Figure 4. Showing relationships of the cloud API and other key cloud components

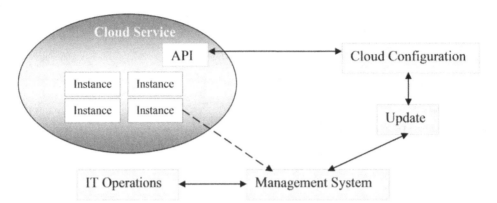

Some ways to verify if the company is right for your information is to ask is there a third party auditing their cloud or do they have any security certificates.

If a cyber criminal hacks into the cloud provider and data which belongs to the customer has been copied off the server then the customer may not know. The cloud provider will have access to the server logs and the customer will not. Multiple customers may be sharing the resources of the same servers and one customer could be using multiple hosts potentially every day. This would make tracking of the unauthorised access of the data to be nearly impossible for the cloud service provider as the data can been very widely spread throughout the cloud providers networks. Unless the cloud provider has developed some sort of monitoring software which can group/sort processes which have occurred for each user then this could be a large security risk and make attacking clouds even more attractive for cyber criminals.

Most customers will not know where their data is being stored by the cloud provider. This poses a number of issues especially if the information is important or valuable. Customers who are worried about security should ask their cloud provider where the physical servers are held, how often are they maintained and what sort of physical security measures have been taken (e.g.,

biometrics or PIN access) to restrict access to the server resources. There is a chance that the data will be held in another country which means the local law and jurisdiction would be different and could create a different security risk, as data that might be secure in one country may not be secure in another (Staten, 2009). By looking at the different views on data privacy between the US and the EU, this security risk becomes more evident as the US has a very open view on the privacy of data. The US Patriot Act grants government and other agencies with virtually limitless powers to access information including that belonging to companies whereas in the EU this type of data would be much more secure, so local laws and jurisdiction can have a large affect the security and privacy of data within a cloud (Mikkilineni & Sarathy, 2009).

CONCLUSION

One of the biggest security worries with the cloud computing model is the sharing of resources (multitenancy). Cloud service providers need to inform their existing customers on the level of security that they provide on their cloud. The cloud service providers need to educate potential customers about the cloud deployment models such as public, private and hybrids along with the pros and cons of each. They need to show their customers that they are providing appropriate security measure that will protect their customer's data and build up confidence for their service. One way they can achieve this is through the use of third party auditors (Mikkilineni & Sarathy, 2009). New security techniques need to be developed and older security techniques needed to be radically tweaked to be able to work with the clouds architecture. Plugging in existing security technology will not work because this new delivery model introduces new changes to the way in which we access and use computer resources.

REFERENCES

Mather, T., Kumaraswamy, S., & Latif, S. (2009). *Cloud Security and Privacy*. New York: O'Reilly.

McFedries, P. (2008, August). The Cloud Is The Computer. *IEEE Spectrum*.

Mikkilineni, R., & Sarathy, V. (2009). Cloud Computing and the Lessons from the Past. In *Proceedings of the 18th IEEE International Workshops on Enabling Technologies: Infrastructures for Collaborative Enterprises*, Groningen, The Netherlands.

Ohlman, B., Eriksson, A., & Rembarz, R. (2009). What Networking of Information Can Do for Cloud Computing. In *Proceedings of the 18th IEEE International Workshops on Enabling Technologies: Infrastructures for Collaborative Enterprises*, Groningen, The Netherlands.

Staten, J. (2009, March 7). Is Cloud Computing Ready for the Enterprise? *Forrester Report*.

Wayner, P. (2008, July 21). Cloud versus cloud - A guided tour of Amazon, Google, AppNexus and GoGrid. *InfoWorld*.

Weiss, A. (2007). Computing in the Clouds. *Networker*, *11*(4), 16–25. doi:10.1145/1327512.1327513

This work was previously published in the International Journal of Ambient Computing and Intelligence, Volume 3, Issue 1, edited by Kevin Curran, pp. 14-19, copyright 2011 by IGI Publishing (an imprint of IGI Global).

Chapter 3
Future Multimedia System:
SIP or the Advanced Multimedia System

Niall Murray
Athlone Institute of Technology, Ireland

Yuansong Qiao
Athlone Institute of Technology, Ireland

Brian Lee
Athlone Institute of Technology, Ireland

Enda Fallon
Athlone Institute of Technology, Ireland

Karunakar A K
Athlone Institute of Technology, Ireland

ABSTRACT

In future multimedia systems, seamless access to application services on different devices available to users in their vicinity, will be commonplace. The availability of these services will change as the mobile user moves. Current 3G multimedia systems do not support access to multiple applications operating on multiple different devices in context of a session or indeed seamless device session handover. Considering these requirements, the authors outline two multimedia communication platforms which potentially solve this problem. This paper describes a backward compatible architecture based on the widely adopted Session Initiation Protocol (SIP) and also outlines a clean slate approach from ITU-T SG 16 called the Advanced Multimedia System (AMS). For each of these solutions the paper describes in terms of architecture, signalling, and capability negotiation, what are viewed as the most critical functions in future multimedia systems design. The result of this comparison displays the advantages and disadvantages of each approach, and outlines solutions to satisfy challenges of current and future multimedia systems based on the service access requirement in ubiquitous environments. Furthermore, this comparison is used to suggest approaches that are best suited for future multimedia system design.

DOI: 10.4018/978-1-4666-2041-4.ch003

INTRODUCTION

Future multimedia networks will be a ubiquitous communication platform that allows users to enjoy continuous multimedia services in any location on any device. The user needs to be able to discover devices, discover services and capabilities, set up sessions, negotiate session characteristics, transmit data, adapt media, and modify sessions including seamless session handover, to enable best in class communication experience based on the context. A modular framework is needed to satisfy these requirements and to allow for independent evolution and development. Future multimedia communication will be based on Service Orientated Architecture (SOA) principles. Service composition will involve the collective use of multiple multimedia applications of different devices. To achieve this, it is necessary to "logically separate applications from the user's network interface device" (Jones, 2007). The separation of base session signalling from applications means application developers do not need to be concerned with session signalling. The result is an ease of development and the deployment of new applications.

The use of the Internet for voice communication has increased significantly in recent years. Using IP will allow the convergence of video, voice and many new applications in a manner not possible on traditional networks. This will enable the provision of arbitrary, new applications and services to users. As users have become accustomed to high quality of service for voice communication, the same expectations will be demanded for multimedia communication over the internet. A multimedia communication system will be required to provide the platform for these services. The question that arises is whether a backward compatible approach with extensions based on SIP is that platform or if a clean slate approach like AMS is required.

SIP has been adopted by most telecommunication standards as the de facto signalling protocol for Voice over IP. It is an IETF standard and was designed to be a generic framework to set up and tear down multimedia sessions. SIP provides a number of principal functions including; user location, user availability, endpoint capabilities and session set up and session management. RFC 4485 clearly states that SIP was not designed to emulate telephony. However, due to the universal acceptance of SIP by telephony providers, voice has become the only real application of SIP, with video being used sparingly. Through use with other existing protocols it can currently handle many other types of multimedia communication, namely; white boarding (Xiaotao & Schulzrinne, 2004), desktop sharing (Xiaotao & Schulzrinne, 2004), file transfer (Xiaotao & Schulzrinne, 2004; Zhang, 2009), but use of SIP based solutions with these applications has been minimal. Support for these has evolved through industry, academia and the many working IETF working groups like SIP, MMUSIC, SIPPING, SIMPLE. Further technological advances are required for it to become the future, all embracing platform. Based on the extensibility of SIP such an approach is possible, but the ability to control complexity in supporting current and future applications is the fundamental challenge for SIP. The Session Description Protocol (SDP) (Handley & Jacobson, 1998) has been used in conjunction with SIP to describe multimedia sessions. To extend its initial scope and address issues viewed as limiting, like the ability to advertise capabilities, SDP has undergone significant changes in recent years..

ITU-T SG 16 is in the process of defining the AMS network and terminal architectures to support future multimedia communication. In contrast to SIP, it is a "clean slate" approach. One of its primary goals is "to create a new multimedia terminal and systems architecture that supports distributed and media rich collaboration environments" (ITU-T Study Group, n.d.a). With recommendation number H.325 for the main specification, the current status described here is work in progress. As part of the design, applications will be decomposed. For devices that have multiple applications, each application's availability and capability is advertised as an independent element. Applications may be logically and physically separate from the user's control device. This is different from traditional approaches where the application intelligence and call control occurred on the same device. Through the definition of well-defined interfaces between all entities, application development is possible independent of the user control device (the container in AMS). These interfaces will enable the deployment of new applications without any infrastructure upgrades whilst also providing the facility for remote control of applications during session's, e.g., increasing the volume of a speaker from a mobile device. Such applications will include "highly converged media applications involving multiple personal and public devices" (ITU-T Study Group 16, 2008). Users will not be limited to their local device capabilities, in fact the user's device is viewed as an enabler to access and control any applications in the vicinity of the user or personal network (ITU-T Study Group 16, n.d.f). AMS proposes an XML based signalling syntax. It aims to enumerate applications, have application specific capability definition and allow asymmetric message exchange.

The remainder of this paper is organized as follows. The next section of this document discusses related work in the area and then compares AMS and SIP in terms of architecture. Next, we discuss signalling in both approaches and contrast the capability definition and negotiation mechanisms of AMS and SIP. By comparing AMS and SIP, this paper identifies which solution is better suited to become the future multimedia communications platform. Finally, we conclude this paper.

Related Work

A broad range of related work involving mobility architectures, seamless service provision and content delivery, adaptation of content based on context awareness has been completed or is ongoing. All of this work is relevant to the design of a Future Multimedia System. H.323 (H.323 v7., 2009) is a multimedia communications protocol by the ITU-T. It has rich videoconferencing capabilities and PSTN integration capabilities. It leveraged existing protocol like RTP/RTCP, adapted protocols like H.245 and Q.931 and defined new IP-centric protocols like H.225.0 for call control signalling. SIP (Handley, Schulzrinne, & Schooler, 2002) is an IETF application-layer control (signalling) protocol for creating, modifying, and terminating sessions. Extensible Messaging and Presence Protocol (XMPP) was initially designed for instant messaging but has also been extended for VoIP and other multimedia communication modes (Extensible Messaging and Presence Protocol (XMPP), n.d.). A work in progress by Sinnreich and Johnston (2010) proposes a SIP API to enable web based multimedia communications. It also suggests using metadata to describe media, displays and user controls instead of SDP.

Shacham et al., provide a solution for seamless and personalized usage of devices discovered in the vicinity of the user and provide a number of session mobility solutions (Shacham, Schulzrinne, Thakolsri, & Kellerer, 2007). Bellavista et al. (2009) incorporate the use of client and server side buffers to address seamless handover. Wu et al. (2003) provide a SIP based approach to solve ubiquitous computing. Peng et al. (2008) provide another alternative to splitting a SIP session over multiple devices based on a new SIP extension header and a split session mechanism.

Huang et al. (2010) defines XML elements according to MPEG-21 recommendations to describe heterogeneous networks and devices. The Session Description Protocol (SDP) (Handley & Jacobson, 1998) is used to describe multimedia sessions for the purposes of session announcement, session invitation, and other forms of multimedia session initiation. Service Location Protocol (Guttman, Perkins, Veizades, & Day, 1999) is discussed in this document and provides a scalable framework for discovery and selection of network services.

MULTIMEDIA COMMUNICATION ARCHITECTURES

This section describes the SIP and AMS architectures. Individual entities and their roles in supporting multimedia communication are explained.

AMS Architecture

The principle aim of the AMS architecture is to support "distributed and media rich collaboration environments" (ITU-T Study Group 16, n.d.a). It contains a number of system components; applications, the container, application servers, service nodes (SN) and Network Service Facility (NSF) nodes. Applications are elements in the AMS environment that enable communication e.g. audio, video, a flashing light. An assemblage is a group of applications used together to provide the communication experience. The container is the entity that represents the user to the network and is used to coordinate local and remote communications between applications. It has no application intelligence per se, but applications depend on the container for session establishment. It has a number of constituents; Application Registry (AR), Orchestration Manager (OM) and Transport Agent (TA) as shown in Figure 1.

The AR collates registration information from individual applications. The OM consolidates this information, interprets user preferences and coordinates events to create AMS sessions. The TA is used for signalling other containers or AMS network entities.

Standardized Interfaces will exist between all elements in AMS: application to application, applications to container and container to network. These interfaces will facilitate control signalling between applications, ensure ease in deployment of new applications and minimize the requirement for network or infrastructure upgrades. Separation of base signalling architecture (session establishment) and applications will ensure application developers do not have to be concerned with underlying signalling details (ITU-T Study Group 16, 2008). Application servers are network elements that provide services like IPTV, interactive gaming, multipoint conferencing (ITU-T Study Group 16, n.d.d). The Service Node (SN) and Network Services and Facilities (NSF) are network entities in AMS. The SN main tasks are to enable "signalling control sessions between containers and across networks" (ITU-T Study Group 16, n.d.e), perform user registration, facilitate authentication, aid NAT/FW traversal, offer QoS Control, negotiate security mechanisms and support network based services. The NSF provides services such as transcoding, session duplication and conferencing circuit.

Figure 1. Proposed AMS architecture (ITU-T study group 16, n.d.b)

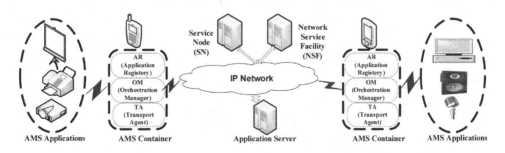

SIP Architecture

The SIP architecture comprises a number of entities as shown in Figure 2; SIP User Agent, SIP Redirect Server, SIP Proxy Server and SIP Registrar Server. Also included in Figure 2 is a Service Location Protocol (SLP) (Guttman, Perkins, Veizades, & Day, 1999) server. SLP is an IETF standardized protocol for discovering devices in a local network. Along with the SLP server, a SIP UA third party call controller (3PCC) (Rosenberg, Peterson, Schulzrinne, & Camarillo, 2004) used by Wu et al. (2003) to set up sessions involving multiple devices. The remaining entity in Figure 2 is a Multi Device System Manager (MDSM) used by Shacham et al. (2007) to enable seamless session mobility. A MDSM is a virtual SIP UA device created by joining the features of two or more existing devices and registering as one device with the multiple capabilities. SIP sets up sessions between the endpoints known as User Agents. A User Agent is as an endpoint that acts as a User Agent Client and a User Agent Server. The User Agent (UA) has two basic functions: to listen to incoming SIP messages and to send SIP messages based on user actions or incoming SIP messages. SIP servers are intermediary devices between SIP UA in a SIP enabled network. There are 3 types of server entities in SIP. The Proxy Server receives SIP messages from UA's or other proxies. It will typically have access to Location Servers which it uses to determine the next hop. Proxy servers behave like routers forwarding

SIP requests and responses. The Redirect Server responds to requests from UA's by sending its message back to the UA as opposed forwarding the message to the next hop. This information is then used by the UA agent to send the message directly to the required UA server or Proxy Server. The Registrar Server receives registration requests and updates the UA's information into a location server. Also included here a SIP enabled transcoder required to address the issue of a common codec not existing in a heterogeneous system.

Discussion: Architecture Comparison

To address access to applications residing on multiple remote devices, AMS has introduced the container as part of its architecture. With this model, the application is logically and may be physically separated from the traditional terminal. The concept of the container does not exist in SIP. All peers in SIP are SIP User agents. To address access to discovered and available applications, SIP uses third party call control to invite multiple devices to a session. In this scenario the container can be compared to the third party call controller. We have clearly defined the container constituent roles; TA, OM and AR. In SIP, the 3pcc user agent, also acting as a SLP client for application discovery, carries out the role of the container.

In a heterogeneous system, it is not very plausible that a media codec would be common to all parties. In AMS a transcoding service is part of

Figure 2. 3PCC, SLP and MDSM entities with typical SIP architecture

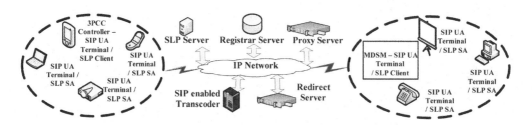

the functionality provided by the NSF. Shacham et al. (2009) overcame the problem of a common codec not existing during a SIP session through the use of "an intermediate transcoding service". To support each of the media sessions, a separate SIP dialog is required between all the nodes and the transcoder. Section 4 describes how AMS can provide more economical signalling due to its architecture when compared to SIP in this scenario.

The definition of interface between all AMS entities, allows for remote control of applications from the container or other applications. Features like this demonstrate some new approaches from AMS to satisfy the requirements of using applications from multiple devices within the context of the same session. Application specific control measures are required in SIP solutions (Xiaotao & Schulzrinne, 2004). There are similarities in the architectures, AMS service nodes can be regarded as similar to SIP proxies but as shown in this paper, the AMS architecture facilitates a more scalable signalling model.

MULTIMEDIA COMMUNICATION SIGNALLING

RFC 3726 lists the requirements for a good signalling protocol. It mentions that the "signalling protocol must be clearly separated from the control information being transported" which allows for the "independent development of both aspects and allows for control information to be carried within other protocols". In future multimedia systems, application collaboration will be commonplace and therefore the signalling protocol needs to address this requirement. The following section compares how AMS and SIP signalling are used to set up a multimedia session involving multiple applications and devices. For clarity the signalling is split up into service/application discovery and end to end signalling.

AMS Application Discovery

In order to determine what applications are available locally in the user's personal network, the container broadcasts a DiscoveryRequest message. Applications indicate their availability by replying with a RegisterRequest message. This message contains an Application Descriptor (AD), an ID and a text string for user display with other optional parameters. The container produces a consolidated message of all ADs called a Capability Descriptor (CD) which may also include user preferences. It also sends a RegisterConfirm message informing applications that they are registered. The container also updates the CD based on user preferences.

AMS End to End Signalling

Once the availability of local applications in the personal network is confirmed, the container signals the Service Node with the consolidated message via a ConnectRequest message. The Service Node determines if the calling party can be admitted based on authentication, network policy and also determines if the called party is available to accept a call. The remote container initiates a process and generates an Answer message agreeing to set up the session. The session is established at this point with the application invocation procedure. Application Capability Exchange and negotiation occurs between the applications through the containers. Call set up is now complete and media can flow directly between the applications (Figure 3).

SLP Application Discovery

Wu et al. (2003) uses the Service Location Protocol (Guttman, Perkins, Veizades, & Day, 1999) to find SIP enabled devices in local vicinity. In advance of any SIP signalling, a SLP client is used to discover local resources registered with the SLP Server. Any discovered resources will

Figure 3. Signalling to set up a session in AMS with multiple devices

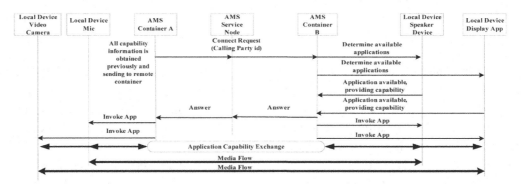

have SIP addresses at which the SIP User Agent can contact the devices.

SIP End to End Signalling

Figure 4 shows one flavour of third party call control (Rosenberg, Peterson, Schulzrinne, & Camarillo, 2004), with the user's mobile device acting as the controller, to set up a session involving a local speaker system, a local display device and a remote audio / video device. The controller device sends a separate INVITE to each of the local devices discovered using SLP. These invites have no session description. The SIP enabled speaker and display device respond with a 200 OK, which includes SDP offers. The controller uses the SDP of each of these devices, combining the media lines and sends this combined SDP within an invite message to the called corresponding node in the session which provides

both audio and video provider as shown in Figure 4. The CN responds with its own parameters for the session which are forward by the controller to the respective devices. In this way, the different media streams are associated with different hosts. There is a corresponding node (CN) to controller SIP dialog, and also controller to local devices SIP dialogs. The media sessions are between the CN and local devices.

Discussion: Signalling Comparison

The use of the third party call control model with SIP seems similar to the concept of the container in AMS. However in AMS, signalling is within the context of the same session. In SIP, there are separate dialogs between each of the entities and the controller. Parsing and manipulation of the SDP by the controller may be required in some cases, whereas the approach in AMS is to pass the capa-

Figure 4. Disaggregated media using SIP third party call control (Rosenberg, Peterson, Schulzrinne, & Camarillo, 2004)

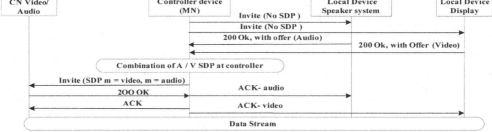

bility information to the respective applications for processing. Timeout issues and retransmission of messages have been documented using this model (Rosenberg, Peterson, Schulzrinne, & Camarillo, 2004) where automatic answering of messages (200 Ok Answer) is not possible. Literature to this point has only described basic scenarios in SIP. Further extensions are required to support sessions involving multiple controllers and other more complex applications.

To address transcoding requirements in a heterogeneous system in SIP, 3PCC is used to establish the dialogs between the transcoder and the correspondent node, and the transcoder and each of the devices used in the session. In AMS the containers contact SN on behalf of all applications involved. The SN identifies the correct NSF to use. The NSF then contacts the applications via the containers specifying session parameters required. The applications set up the data/media path with the NSF and a control path between each other. While the equivalent SIP based solution is less elegant; it is shown that through adaptation and extended signalling, SIP can be used but further work is certainly required. The use of the limiting offer/answer model of SDP hinders a more graceful SIP based solution. The current solution closely links the offer/answer to the signalling protocol.

DEVICE CAPABILITY DEFINITION AND NEGOTIATION

Capability definition of applications in future multimedia systems must be light weight, simple and extensible. Application collaboration adds further challenges to capability definition; it would be advantageous to know how individual applications can be used together, what applications reside on what devices. Media capability negotiation should be possible in a short number of messages. It may also be beneficial to specify what applications are required and optional for a session. The following sections outline a proposed

AMS approach for capability definition and session negotiation with future multimedia systems in mind. It also discusses the evolution of SDP to determine its potential to become a capability definition and negotiation mechanism for future multimedia systems.

AMS: Capability Definition and Negotiation

Some of the specifics of how AMS will provide capability definition and negotiation are still under discussion but by enumerating applications AMS will define application specific capabilities. In the proposed AMS solution, a single device can advertise itself as providing a number of different applications. When applications register with the container, they specify their capabilities. Also proposed is to introduce "preference" settings for particular applications. These capabilities shall be conveyed to the remote container as they are received from the applications, thus avoiding complex processing at the container. The remote container can pass the application capabilities to the respective applications for processing. Sample application capabilities are not included here; these will not be under the remit of AMS. These definitions will be application specific.

Figure 5 provides one way in which application capabilities for a desktop videophone, a display device and a speaker can be exchanged. The capability exchange message below describes an application list with preferences. This model of autonomous applications is easy to understand, lightweight and provides preferences and capabilities. To reduce complexity it does not specify what applications can do simultaneously, nor does it indicate what applications reside on any one device. There are many questions still outstanding about this proposed AMS solution, as it is a work in progress. It does however; provide an insight into the direction AMS are taking to satisfy capability definition.

Figure 5. Sample capability description document in AMS (ITU-T study group 16, n.d.c)

```
<!—Display Screen →
 <applicationList>
  <application preference="0" id="1" type="http://www.itu.int/xml-namespace/itu-t/h.325/display/">
   <capabilities xmlns="http://www.itu.int/xml-namespace/itu-t/h.325/display/">
   ... capabilities as specified in the associated standard ...
   </capabilities>
  </application>

 <!—Video Terminal →
  <application id="2" type="http://www.itu.int/xml-namespace/itu-t/h.325/video/">
   <capabilities xmlns="http://www.itu.int/xml-namespace/itu-t/h.325/video/">
   ... capabilities as specified in the associated standard ...
   </capabilities>
  </application>
   <application id="3" type="http://www.itu.int/xml-namespace/itu-t/h.325/audio/">
   <capabilities xmlns="http://www.itu.int/xml-namespace/itu-t/h.325/audio/">
   ... capabilities as specified in the associated standard ...
   </capabilities>
  </application>
  <application
       type="http://www.itu.int/xml-namespace/itu-t/h.325/display/">
   <capabilities xmlns="http://www.itu.int/xml-namespace/itu-t/h.325/display/">
   ... capabilities as specified in the associated standard ...
   </capabilities>
  </application>
  <application id="5" type="http://www.itu.int/xml-namespace/itu-t/h.325/camera/">
   <capabilities xmlns="http://www.itu.int/xml-namespace/itu-t/h.325/camera/">
   </application>
 <!—Speakers → <application preference="1" id="6" type="http://www.itu.int/xml-namespace/itu-t/h.325/audio/">
   <capabilities xmlns="http://www.itu.int/xml-namespace/itu-t/h.325/audio/">
   ... capabilities as specified in the associated standard ...
   </capabilities>
  </application>
 </applicationList>
```

SDP: Capability Negotiation and Negotiation Definition

SDP has evolved from a multicast of session description to a fully-fledged capability description and negotiation mechanism. The initial solution was "not intended for negotiation of media encodings" (Handley & Jacobson, 1998). It was satisfactory for broadcast applications where media stream parameters were fixed for all participants but for current and future multimedia communications this is insufficient. SDP has been extended to address these shortcomings but the complexity has also increased significantly. Here some of the significant updates to SDP are discussed and their implications.

The offer/answer model outlined in RFC 3264 (Rosenberg & Schulzrinne, 2002) was a significant addition to SDP. It allows the offering entity to create an "offer" SDP session description. Based on the contents of this offer, an answer session description is created by the receiver specifying what parameters in the offer it can use for the session. This feature added a powerful mechanism to SDP.

"Session Description Protocol (SDP) Simple Capability Declaration" (Andreasen, 2002) defined a capability declaration feature. Prior to this, SDP provided both session parameters (SDP's initial use) and session capabilities but did not explicitly distinguish between them. For example, if an audio device could support G.711 A-law and iLBC and stated so in SDP, it was agreeing to support both simultaneously, and not one or the other. Hence it had no way to indicate capability nor could not express parameter ranges or values. New attributes were added to define a capability set. Each description in the set contains information about supported media formats, but the endpoint is not committing to use any of these. It also provided an attribute to represent "ranges of numerical values".

SDPng (Kutcher, 2005) was a powerful XML based capability definition and negotiation framework and designed as a replacement for SDP. It proposed the concepts of potential and actual configurations explained below in Andreasen's solution. It was not a backward compatible solution. It did not gain any traction and work has stopped on it.

To address the ability to negotiate one or more alternative transport protocols (e.g., RTP profiles) and associated parameters (e.g., SDP attributes), Andreasen has proposed a work in progress called SDP Capability Negotiation (Andreasen, 2010). This Internet draft describes the "actual" configuration and a number of "potential" configurations in one SDP message. Actual configurations are a combination of session parameters and media stream components that can be used currently in a session with no further negotiation. The potential configurations are alternative combinations of capabilities that could be used in a session, after some negotiation. Both actual and potential configurations are sent in the SDP message. The negotiation lies in that the "answerer" can select the "actual" or one of the "potential" configurations as it desires providing the negotiated configuration for the session. This structure allows backward compatibility as the capabilities and potential configurations are in a single SDP session description (Figure 6).

Figure 6. A sample SDP message combining audio and video from two devices (Shacham, Schulzrinne, Thakolsri, & Kellerer, 2009)

```
V=0
m=audio 48400 RTP/AVP 0
c= IN IP4 audio_dev.example.com
a=rtpmap:0 PCMU/8000
m=video 58400 RTP/AVP 34
c= IN IP4 video_dev.example.com
a=rtpmap:34 H263/90000
```

Discussion: Capability Definition and Negotiation Comparison

State of the art in session description and negotiation provided by SDP has evolved to be a very powerful solution considering its initial abilities. It is backward compatible but considering future multimedia systems, it is easy to envisage high numbers of potential configurations. This leads to high processing costs and CPU usage. Use of the offer/answer mechanism also has issues. The offerer has no idea what "potential configuration" may be selected until the answer is received, but must be prepared to receive media in accordance with the offer (Andreasen, 2010). Negotiating between several transport protocols means multiple offer/answer exchanges, not satisfying the requirement of a "short number of messages", or in ideal case one round trip. Offer/Answer also only allows negotiation based on what is in the initial offer. SDP carries IP addresses and port numbers which cause NAT traversal issues. For future multimedia system, further extensions will be required and given its current complexity it does not appear as a reasonable option for future multimedia system session description and capability mechanism. We believe the AMS capability definition approach has more potential for future multimedia systems when compared to SDP. There are open questions about the AMS solution, but an alternative to SDP based approaches is required for future session description and capability negotiation (Table 1).

CONCLUSION

This paper presents a comparison between two potential solutions for future multimedia communication platforms from an architectural, signalling and capability perspective. For each solution we highlight how seamless access to services is achieved. Architecturally there are similarities but application decomposition is addressed in the AMS architecture and not in

Table 1. Comparison of AMS and SIP

	AMS	SIP
Architecture	AMS supports application decomposition by introducing the container to its architecture.	All peers in SIP are User Agents. Third Party Call Control is used to invite all peers to the session.
Signalling	Session set up involving multiple devices is within context of the same session. No parsing of capability information occurs at container.	For session set up involving multiple devices in SIP, separate SIP dialogs are required between third party call controller and each user agent. Parsing and manipulation of SDP may be required at the controller.
	AMS supports remote application control through application-to-application interfaces.	Limited support exists for remote application control in SIP. The INFO method can be used to pass application level information but no standardized mechanism exists.
	The NSF and applications setup the data/media path between each other to enable transcoding.	The third party call controller enables transcoding by creating separate SIP dialogs to between each of the devices and the transcoder.
Capability Definition	XML based mechanism, capability definition is application specific. Capability syntax is transparent to the container.	Uses SDP which has evolved to be a powerful but complex mechanism. Parsing and manipulation of SDP may be required at the controller.

SIP. Extensions to SIP address session set up for multiple devices and applications via an adjusted signalling model. SIP has evolved into a complex standard in comparison with its initial design to address new applications and requirements. Based on requirements of today, AMS provides a more scalable signalling model. Comparing the signalling required to set up sessions involving multiple devices, multiple dialogs are required with SIP, whereas in AMS all signalling is within the context of one session. Third party call control can involve SDP manipulation, whereas in AMS this processing will occur at the application with the container just acting as a conduit, passing the information to the applications. It is our belief that AMS's proposed session description model has many advantages over SDP in terms of clarity, but more importantly in terms of extensibility and complexity. As shown, SIP's is hindered by its use of SDP. A clean slate approach should produce a more elegant solution for future multimedia systems, but once point to point signalling exists, any application possible with AMS should also be possible with SIP. SIP with its adaptability and in particular its level of acceptance is likely, with extensions, to be a key part of any future multimedia communication system. Our view is that a future multimedia system, based on SIP signalling with extensions to address current issues described here and a session description approach based on what AMS are proposing will provide a solid multimedia communications platform that is extensible, backward compatible and future proof. We also conclude that it may be beneficial to introduce AMS as an overlay network. This will avoid the risk in "diluting the value of IP convergence by creating the multiple independent applications layers on top of a single IP infrastructure (NGSON Working Group of IEEE Standards Committee, 2008)" whilst also gaining from the AMS focus on services and applications. Investigation into the potential of the AMS solution as an overlay network will encompass our future work.

ACKNOWLEDGMENT

This Research Programme is supported by Enterprise Ireland through its Applied Research Enhancement fund. We also acknowledge the contribution of Paul E. Jones, Rapportuer for ITU-T Q12/16 for his assistance with AMS concepts and documentation.

REFERENCES

Andreasen, F. (2002). *Session Description Protocol (SDP)*. Simple Capability Declaration.

Andreasen, F. (2010, March 24). *SDP Capability Negotiation*.

Bellavista, P., Cinque, M., Controneo, D., & Foschini, L. (2009). Self-Adaptive Handoff Management for Mobile Streaming Continuity. *IEEE Transactions on Networks and Service Management, 6*(2).

Extensible Messaging and Presence Protocol (XMPP). (n.d.). Retrieved from http://xmpp.org/

Guttman, E., Perkins, C., Veizades, J., & Day, M. (1999). *Service Location Protocol RFC 2608*.

H.323 v7. (2009). *ITU-T Recommendation Packet Based multimedia Communication systems*.

Handley, M., & Jacobson, V. (1998). *SDP: Session Description Protocol RFC 2327*.

Handley, M., Schulzrinne, H., & Schooler, E. (2002). *SIP: Session Initiation Protocol RFC 3261*.

Haung, C.-M., Lin, C.-W., & Yang, C.-C. (2010). *Mobility Management for Video Streaming on Heterogeneous Networks*. Washington, DC: IEEE Computer Society. ITU-T Study Group 16. (n.d.a). *AMS Third generation of ITU-T Multimedia Systems and Terminals*. Retrieved from http://www.itu.int/ITU-T/studygroups/com16/ams/index.html

ITU-T Study Group 16. (2008). *Advanced Multimedia System (AMS) – AMS Project Description*. Retrieved from http://www.packetizer.com/ipmc/h325/doc_status.html

ITU-T Study Group 16. (n.d.b). *AMS Architecture*. Retrieved from http://wftp3.itu.int/av-arch/avc-site/2009-2012/AMS_emeetings/AMS-0020.zip

ITU-T Study Group 16. (n.d.c). *Advanced Multimedia System (AMS) – AMS Applications, Application Capabilities, and Capability Advertisement*. Retrieved from http://wftp3.itu.int/av-arch/avc-site/2009-2012/AMS_emeetings/AMS-0015a.zip

ITU-T Study Group 16. (n.d.d). *Advanced Multimedia System (AMS) – System Architecture*. Retrieved from http://www.packetizer.com/ipmc/h325/doc_status.html

ITU-T Study Group 16. (n.d.e). *Advanced Multimedia System (AMS) – Service Node Architecture*. Retrieved from http://www.packetizer.com/ipmc/h325/doc_status.html

ITU-T Study Group 16. (n.d.f). *Advanced Multimedia System (AMS) (2009) - H.325 Overview*. Retrieved from http://www.packetizer.com/ipmc/h325/papers

Jones, E. P. (2007). Rapporteur ITU-T Q12/16. *A Concept for the Advanced Multimedia System*. Retrieved from http://www.packetizer.com/ipmc/h325/papers/

Kutcher, O. B. (2005). *Session Description and Capability Negotiation*.

NGSON Working Group of IEEE Standards Committee. (2008). *Draft White Paper for Next Generation Service Overlay Network*.

Peng, C.-J., Chen, M.-X., & Hwang, R.-H. (2008). SSIP: Split a SIP Session over Multiple Devices. *Computer Standards & Interfaces, 29*(5).

Rosenberg, J., Peterson, J. L., Schulzrinne, H., & Camarillo, G. (2004). *Best Current Practices for Third Party Call Control (3pcc) in the Session Initiation Protocol*.

Rosenberg, J., & Schulzrinne, H. (2002). *An offer/Answer Model with the Session Description Protocol*.

Shacham, R., Schulzrinne, H., Thakolsri, S., & Kellerer, W. (2007). Ubiquitous Device Personalization and Use: The Next Generation of IP Multimedia Communications. *ACM Transactions on Multimedia Computing, Communications and Applications, 3*(2).

Shacham, R., Schulzrinne, H., Thakolsri, S., & Kellerer, W. (2009). *Session Initiation Protocol (SIP)*. Session Mobility.

Sinnreich, H., & Johnston, A. (2010). *SIP APIs for Communication on the Web*. Internet Engineering Task Force.

Wu, X., Berger, S., Sidiroglou, S., & Schulzrinne, H. (2003). *Ubiquitous Computing using SIP*. Paper presented at the International Workshop on Network and Operating System support for Digital Audio & Video.

Xiaotao, W., & Schulzrinne, H. (2004). SIPc, a Multi-function SIP User Agent. In *Proceedings of the 7th IFIP/IEEE International Conference, Management of Multimedia Networks and Services*.

Zhang, W. (2009). A Uniform Negotiation and Delivery Mechanism for SIP-based Conferencing System. In *Proceedings of the International Conference on Communication Software and Networks*.

This work was previously published in the International Journal of Ambient Computing and Intelligence, Volume 3, Issue 1, edited by Kevin Curran, pp. 20-32, copyright 2011 by IGI Publishing (an imprint of IGI Global).

Chapter 4

IT-ASSIST:
Towards Usable Applications for Elderly People

Claas Ahlrichs
Universiaet Bremen, Germany

Daniel Kohlsdorf
Universiaet Bremen, Germany

Michael Lawo
Universiaet Bremen, Germany

Gerrit Kalkbrenner
Universiaet Bremen, Germany

ABSTRACT

IT-ASSIST is a twenty months research project which has the goal to give elderly people the opportunity to profit from digital media. Suffering from age related impairments concerning vision, hearing, or dexterity and bad hand-eye coordination are challenges when designing user interfaces for elderly people. Common approaches are trying to model systems for specific impairments. In this project, the authors follow the approach to set up interfaces and systems that can be used independent from personal impairments. Customization has adapted these systems to be in accordance with personnel impairments. Common applications like photo editing, digital mailing or internet browsing in a redesigned form provide social communication accordingly. In this article, a prototype of a customized user interface, its implementation, and results of user studies are presented and discussed.

INTRODUCTION

Increased expectation of life and decreasing birthrates are leading to demographic changes (Franke, 2008). Growing parts of the population are elderly people, which suffer from personal impairments.

Due to such social changes the isolation of elderly people is increasing and commonly seen as a lack of interpersonal communication (Cacioppo, 2008). Modern technologies may help to defeat lonesomeness and regain lost social connections or even build a new social life. As we have seen from the "good old telephone" information technology

DOI: 10.4018/978-1-4666-2041-4.ch004

promotes social communication. Beside very special item based communication like interacting bowls (van der Hoog, 2004; van der Hoog, 2004b) also often used modern media like email, chat or games counteract loneliness and support interpersonal affective communication, just as well. Successful examples are Skype, WIKIPEDIA, FLICKR and YouTube, which opened new ways for social interactions.

Previous generations are familiar with the concepts of television and telephone. Unfortunately television is not known to promote social communication. This is where we want to propose an approach that aims to increase interpersonal communication of elderly people. Basis is an internet connection and a personal computer which has been modified to function like a television and video telephony device. It is based on a flat-screen and an input device that fits the needs of the user. A remote control, a joystick, a touch pad or screen or speech recognition are just a few examples for such input devices.

Unfortunately many retirement homes provide no or only very limited access to personal computers or even the Internet. Some retirement homes which provide access to this technology usually have multipurpose rooms (e.g., library or room for events) in which a few personal computers are located. Due to age related impairments (vision, hearing or dexterity) many elderly people are not able to properly interact with the installed soft- and hardware. This problem is intensified by a low acceptance rate of personal computers and the refusal to see the advantages of new technologies (Stefan, 2008; Henn, 2008). Applications like email, video telephony, browsing of pictures and Internet or reminder functionality could support and enrich the daily life in retirement homes.

How well people use, apply and understand information systems depends on the complexity the user is confronted with. It depends on the level of training and the degree of operational demands as we know that from rule or knowledge based human computer interaction models (Johannsen, 1993; Bubb, 1993).

The goal of IT-ASSIST is to bring personal computers and customized Internet services in every apartment of retirement homes, in order to help residents, caregivers and physicians to ease communication and collaboration. Therefore a system is planned with a modular hardware platform and a simplified user interface specifically designed for elderly people. The user interface should allow easy access to frequently used functions and services. Experienced and interested users could tell about the opportunities and help to motivate skeptic users.

We want to facilitate a longer, healthier life in independence and dignity within the safe environment of the own home. Goal is to decrease the isolation of elderly people and motivate social activity. Easy accesses to information and communication technologies enable social cross-linkage and therefore lead to an increased quality of life. This should be valid not only in rural or sparsely populated areas but also in cities where familial support might not be present.

This paper summarizes initial interviews of residents in local retirement homes. It describes our first exemplary user interface. The user interface and a hardware platform were implemented and are described. This platform was again evaluated and created the basis of our future work.

INITIAL INTERVIEWS

In an initial study 15 people (10 female, 5 male, between 68 and 92 years old) of three different retirement homes participated. Interviews were conducted to get an understanding of the requirements and allow a better planning of the entire system. All participants were recruited as volunteers and had minor age related impairments. The duration of the interviews ranged from 30 minutes to 2 hours depending on the needs of the interviewees.

During narrative interview sessions (Küsters, 2009) participants were asked about their needs, general mindset towards personal computers and their experiences with this technology. They were also asked to talk about applications that they felt interesting and / or had experiences with. A few applications were explained and then asked whether they could imagine benefiting from them.

The interviews were carried out by an in ethnographic studies experienced sociologist and a computer scientist. A protocol of each interview was created and subsequently discussed and evaluated by a team of pollsters, hard- and software developers, caretakers and medical instructors. Features of the first software prototype were prioritized and three user groups identified.

The following groups were identified: one small group of 3 people is already working with personal computers and has a lot experience. A large group of 8 people is interested in using personal computers and wants to learn more about it but does not know how to start or needs a lot of help. The third group of 4 people is not interested at all or does not know about the advantages.

Most participants stated to be familiar or interested in applications that involve digital music playback, video chat, browsing and editing of pictures, writing texts and emails. All of them agreed that simpler user interfaces in comparison to standard Windows PCs are important and a reminder function e.g. for birthdays, appointments or medications could proof useful.

Regarding the usability of hardware we found that the mouse seems to be very difficult to handle and residents liked the idea of using a touch screen or at least something with direct manipulation capabilities. Most of them complaint about their apartments already being crowed and did not like the idea of having another screen beside their television e.g. like another computer screen in it. However they would accept using a television for visual feedback and a remote control for interaction.

Weekly learning sessions or computer meetings were suggested where residents can exchange their experiences and help each other. These meetings could provide a public opportunity for more skeptic users to learn from their housemates. They could be motivated to use new technologies and might start to see the benefits.

The results of the interviews became the starting point for a paper prototype allowing more in depth interviews with the residents.

PAPER PROTOTYPE

A use case was created. The prototype of a user interface should meet the needs identified and defined in the prior interviews with the residents. The paper prototype was again in a similar form as described above evaluated with the residents.

Use Case

A personal computer is located in the resident's apartment and has our system installed. The computer will be turned on in the morning and turned off in the evening. This can either be done by the residents themselves or one of the caregivers. Not all residents require special attention and could do this on their own. Those residents that are not able to do this on their own can be supported by their caregiver. In the morning a caregiver comes to check on the resident and helps preparing for the day. At this point the computer could be started. Again in the evening could the resident or a caretaker turn the system off. Using a clock timer could also be an option.

The computer should be able to start and show our interface without any interaction except pressing the power button. During the day the system supports the resident with reminders, media and communication with the family, friends and assistants. Residents tend to have a lot of remote controls for their media devices like CD/DVD player, television and video recorder. We aim to integrate all of them in one solution and thereby allow a more consistent interaction across all devices.

User Interface

The first prototype had three layers: a welcome screen, a main menu and the actual programs. The welcome screen of the 1st layer provides an overview from which the main menu of the 2nd layer is accessible (see Figure 1 b). The main menu contains a list of available programs as indicated on the 3rd layer and allows the user to select and execute them.

The header of the welcome screen (see Figure 1 a) shows the resident's name, current date and time. - In public places the header could show the name of the retirement home or something similar. - A weather forecast and reminders are placed below the header. At the bottom is a button providing access to the next layer with the main menu.

The main menu consists of a list of programs. Each item in the list has an icon and name or title. By pressing one of the arrows far left or right the items in the list will be shifted in the corresponding direction. Pressing one of the directional buttons causes one item to disappear on one side and shows a new icon on the other side. In the middle of the screen the current icon is displayed larger as the others and indicates the currently selected item. Not all items in the list are displayed at once

as the screen would start to look crowded even with small lists of 10-20 programs. Therefore depending on the screen size a fixed number of items are displayed.

The items are arranged in a cycle, such a user can access all items even by pressing repeatedly one of the directional icons on the left or right hand side only. When pressing the "overview" button downright the user is returned to the welcome screen.

The programs themselves should be designed in a minimalistic way. Only necessary functionality should be available. For example a digital mailing application requires only reading, sending and replying. Font sizes and icons should be designed according to the needs of the users and allow personal adjustment.

Evaluation

The previously described prototype was already presented to the interviewees from the first iteration and other people as a computer presentation however without underlying functionality. It had interactively been adapted. The user acceptance was evaluated. New applications could be identified and implemented step by step into the prototype. In field tests in the three retirement homes the needs of the residents regarding the interaction hardware were also evaluated.

Figure 1. First two layers of the user interface. (a) welcome screen and (b) main menu

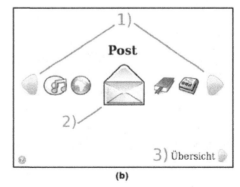

(a)　　　　　　(b)

APPLICATION PROTOTYPE

IT-ASSIST is working iteratively which means we evaluate the users' needs and wishes before any implementation. New ideas are evaluated before continuing the implementation (see Figure 2).

In this way we evaluated the profile and configuration prototype. Only after the users can imagine using the presented prototype system, we tailor the user interface to their needs and begin with the implementation. In this way we started to evaluate also the Internet prototype that is not yet sufficiently done.

During the evaluation we continuously identify services to add or to omit.

One challenging problem many elderly people are confronted with is the normal use of the Internet. Many older people are confused or frightened by the flood of information provided. Our goal is to reduce the Internet to pages tailored to the needs and interests of the interviewed. The following pages are most important for the interviewed people:

• Searching the WWW.
• Using Wikipedia.
• Searching for holiday opportunities for seniors.
• Reading the local newspaper.

Our concept is to only link to trusted websites, via a menu bar that is always present and good visible (see Figure 3). In that way loosing orientation is omitted.

The interaction and the form of presentation is mostly the same as the web browser for elderly people "Big Screen Life". Our approach is optimized for using a touch screen, but normal mouse interaction is also possible.

By clicking or touching one of the icons (Search, Wiki, Holiday, News) the user is directed to the corresponding service page. In the case that the user looses orientation, or follows a link and finds himself in an not trusted area, he can return to the safe pages by clicking again the corresponding item.

We choose Google as a representative synonym for the Internet, the World Wide Web service for searching the WWW. Googles design is simple and not overloaded with commercials.

Searching for holiday opportunities a service especially for elderly people was chosen so that the offered trips are tailored to the special needs of them.

For news reading the web service is taken from the local newspaper, most people read.

Hardware

A small (25cm * 20cm * 5cm), energy efficient computer was chosen, which is likely to fit even

Figure 2. Adapted main menu

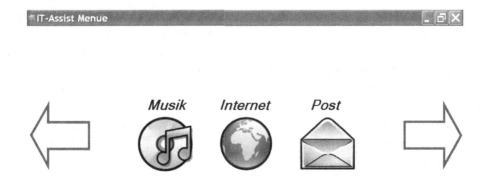

Figure 3. The IT-assist internet assistant

in small apartments. During the first iteration a television screen will be used for visual and auditory output. Most residents own a television set and do not want an extra screen in their apartments because they usually do not have the space for it. This way the apartment will not unnecessarily be crowded. A remote control and Bluetooth keyboard will be used as input devices. For people in electric wheelchairs the controller stick could be used as a mouse-type replacement. In public places, such as computer or event rooms, a touch screen will be placed which could show information about the offers of the house or newspaper articles and is hoped to motivate skeptic users to interact with the platform. However the architecture allows to interface special purpose interfaces for reduced motion control.

Software

The software was written in the programming language C# which is part of the Microsoft.NET Framework. It has a modular structure and consists of the optional welcome screen (1st layer), the application selection menu (2nd layer) and a user-dependent profile. Later is used to provide the 3rd layer. It contains a list of applications a user is interested in, information about interface specific preferences like font style and size.

Even as a first software prototype it has been developed with ease of installation in mind. It can be installed and removed just like any regular windows application which allows rapid installation and demonstration.

For most desktop interfaces the system is configured once and then shipped to all users. For people working with the computer day by day it is no problem to personalize the interface. For older people this is however not easily possible. If different people with different needs concerning the configuration of the interface use the same computer, switching profiles should be as easy as possible. The username and password concept is already too complicated.

The software prototype enables users to easily create profiles for icons, font sizes, and applications to use (see Figure 4).

For choosing the icon size a small icon with a small text is displayed. Furthermore a very big + and - button as well as a confirm button are provided. By pressing + and - the icon and the font change their size accordingly. In that way the user chooses his preferred icon and font size.

Figure 4. Configuration screen

Choosing the right applications is managed by explaining the basic functionality and the benefit from the application as well as the icon letting the user decide to accept or not.

In the end the profile is saved with the user's real name. When turning on the computer the user only searches his name in a list or starts typing it and logs in with his configuration. Thus no password is needed.

The user profile contains information about ordering, icons and titles of the applications listed in the main menu. This part is realized as a XML structure in which each entry provides information about the program (or command) to run, a path to an icon and the title itself. More general information such as font size and style are also stored in the profile. Furthermore are the size of icons, gaps and arrows adjustable.

When changing any part of the profile the effects are immediately reflected in the user interface. E.g. increasing the font size or adding a new program to the list is instantaneously noticeable. This way we do not have to start a dedicated configuration software or restart the application in order to take effect for changes, and even add previously unknown applications.

EVALUATION

For the evaluation we had a class of geriatric care takers apprentices entrusted with an entire station of a local retirement home use the system for an entire month. As part of their training they were allowed to manage a station and take care of the residents. The class had about 20 students and just about as many residents of which some were bedridden others were suffering from dementia and different impairments.

The class used two laptops, a variety of specific input devices for various impairments and our software prototype with additional applications. Two of the students volunteered to work with it and assisted the residents. Both students were given an introduction and a short training to applications installed on the laptops (most of them being third party application).

Among other applications a picture browsing and a memory training application were presented to the residents. The picture gallery was filled with pictures that had some kind of relation to the residents (e.g., relating to their family, hobbies, interests or profession). The intention was to foster the communication between the caregivers and residents. The memory training application was included as we learned from our initial interviews that many residents like to solve riddles in order to keep their memory in shape. Some residents were also introduced to Skype and shown some of the possibilities of video telephony.

We are yet to evaluate the findings of this opportunity but it seems that all three applications were accepted by the residents as we learned from our interviews with the residents and the care takers. Three residents even agreed to participate in two press meetings giving live demonstrations of the applications.

FUTURE WORK

In the future we want to implement some new features. A user profile assistant and an internet based service platform are planned. The evaluation of the work of the school class and the residents with our application will be continued.

The configuration and management of the user profiles requires further development. The interface of our current profile configuration utility is rather development oriented and not likely to be usable by the intended users or local care givers.

New users should be guided through an automatic profile generator. They should start with an empty profile and adjust their profile settings by answering questions along the way.

A platform for digital mailing, shopping, communication and further services is being planned. Residents could be supplied with a customized browser that fits their needs more properly. Like any standard browser this browser can view websites but additionally provides easy access to a selected number of (online) services (e.g., a customized mailing application or trusted online shopping portals). A similar, commercial product is called "BigScreenLive" (BigScreenLive, 2010).

A service to buy and deliver water bottles to residents' apartments could be offered just as well. Thus not all services have to be purely Internet based.

Many elderly people like social events and concerts but are somehow impaired so they cannot participate. By streaming audio and video the user can listen to those life events. But the system has to be easy to use for both sides, caregivers and residents.

The setup of the camera and the video/audio stream computer should be performed in as few and easy steps as possible. We thought about a wagon where a camera is mounted and a computer which communicates with a streaming server wirelessly. Accessing such streams as a listener should be possible using an IT-ASSIST icon.

Another application that is actually under discussion with the residents to be integrated is after the positive experiences with the video telephony to contact the general practitioner for routine health checks or for questions. What we intend to evaluate in test sessions is the user acceptance on both sides. First tests with medical specialists showed interest and surprisingly a sufficient quality of the video transmission. An open issue is the billing of such indemnification.

Furthermore the flexibility of the approach to interface different input devices to control the application will be evaluated.

CONCLUSION

In this paper we presented results after eight months of the twenty months European funded research project IT-ASSIST. The user centered design approach for giving elderly people the opportunity to profit from digital media was presented. We described the requirement phase as well as two prototyping and evaluation phases. Instead of designing systems for specific impairments interfaces that can be used independent of personal impairments were created and common applications like photo editing, digital mailing or internet browsing were accordingly redesigned.

ACKNOWLEDGEMENT

This work was partially funded by structural funds of the European Commission. The authors thank the partner Bremer Heimstiftung with its residents and care givers and the partner Igel- Rehavista for providing specific hardware components for user interaction. Only with their continuous support this work could be done.

REFERENCES

BigScreenLive. (2010). Retrieved April 8, 2010, from http://bigscreenlive.com/

Bubb, H. (1993). *Carl-Hanser Verlag*. München-Wien, Germany: Systemergonomische Gestaltung. In Ergonomie.

Cacioppo, J., & Patrick, W. (2008). *Loneliness: Human Nature and the Need for Social Connection*. New York: W. W. Norton & Co.

Franke, A. (2008). *Arbeitsmarktkompetenzen im sozialen Wandel. In Kompetenz-Bildung: Soziale, emotionale und kommunikative Kompetenzen von Kindern und Jugendlichen* (pp. 169-190). Wiesbaden, Germany: VS Verlag für Sozialwissenschaften / GWV Fachverlage GmbH.

Henn, H. (2008). Web4me – User Centric Infrastructure for Ambient Assisted Living. In *Proceedings AAL Kongress* (pp. 27-31). Berlin: VDE Verlag. ISBN 978-3-8007-3076-6

Johannsen, G. (1993). *Mensch-Maschine-Systeme*. Berlin: Springer Verlag.

Küsters, I. (2009). *Narrative Interviews. Grundlagen und Anwendungen. Wiesbaden 2009 Lehrbuch Studientexte zur Soziologie*. Germany: VS Verlag.

Stefan, F. (2008). Herausforderungen bei der Marktimplementierung von AAL-Systemen bei Anbieters von sozialen Dienstaleistungen. In *Proceedings AAL Kongress* (pp. 291-292). Berlin: VDE Verlag. ISBN 978-3-8007-3076-6

van der Hoog, W., Keller, I., & Stappers, P. J. (2004) Gustbowl: Technology Supporting Affective Communication through Routine Ritual Interactions. In *Proceedings of CHI 2004*, Vienna, Austria. New York: ACM.

van der Hoog, W., Keller, I., & Stappers, P. J. (2004 b, September/October). Connecting Mother and Sons: A Design Using Routine Affective Rituals. *Interaction*, 68–69. doi:10.1145/1015530.1015564

Chapter 5
Analysis of Older Users' Perceived Requests and Opportunities with Technologies:
A Scenario–Based Assessment

Mari Feli Gonzalez
*Fundación Instituto Gerontológico Matia -
INGEMA, Spain*

Arjan Geven
*CURE – Center for Usability Research and
Engineering, Austria*

David Facal
*Fundación Instituto Gerontológico Matia -
INGEMA, Spain*

Manfred Tscheligi
*CURE – Center for Usability Research and
Engineering, Austria*

Ana Belen Navarro
*Fundación Instituto Gerontológico Matia -
INGEMA, Spain*

Elena Urdaneta
*Fundación Instituto Gerontológico Matia -
INGEMA, Spain*

Javier Yanguas
Fundación Instituto Gerontológico Matia - INGEMA, Spain

ABSTRACT

The HERMES Cognitive Care and Guidance for Active Aging project proposes an integrated approach to cognitive assistance, promoting the autonomy of elderly users through pervasive technology. This work aims to describe elderly people's opinions when they are presented scenarios developed in this project. Two focus groups were organized in Austria and Spain with a view to collecting their impressions about the way in which the technological device can cover their needs; complementarily, a second session was conducted including a quantitative questionnaire. Although some participants were reluctant to use the technology, they welcomed some functionalities of the HERMES system and they considered that using them can help them to become familiar with them. Usefulness, usability, and use of real-life information for functionalities such as cognitive games are considered to be key areas of the project. This evaluation has provided the developers of the system with meaningful information to improve it and it guarantees that the system addresses elderly people's needs.

DOI: 10.4018/978-1-4666-2041-4.ch005

INTRODUCTION

The increase and expansion of Communication Technologies in recent years have led to the development of a series of new opportunities for leisure and social activities for older people. There are a number of studies attempting to find these applications and the relevance of these opportunities in the everyday life of elderly people (for a review, see Burdick & Kwon, 2004).

Technology can be used directly by elderly people to enhance mental well-being and expand social engagement. However, older people are often reluctant to accept any technology that aims to reduce their autonomy or minimize their cognitive or functional efforts because it would mean dependency (Buiza, Gonzalez, Etxaniz, Urdaneta, Yanguas, et al., 2008). It has been shown that the assessment of needs in elderly people can improve the functionality of technology (Walters, Iliffe, See Tai, & Orrell, 2000). In this respect, analysis and understanding of the older users' feelings when interacting with technology devices in different scenarios is a key requirement that adds value to assistive technology which could have a substantial impact on the users' daily life.

The HERMES (*Cognitive Care and Guidance for Active Aging*) project is co-funded by the European Commission within the 7th Framework Programme (http://www.fp7-hermes.eu/). Its objective is to reduce age-related cognitive decline and facilitate episodic memory, advanced activities reminding and cognitive training. It provides assistance but also promotes the autonomy of users in their daily lives, using pervasive non obtrusive technology at home and outside the home. Aging is often accompanied by different types of age-related memory changes, especially episodic memory declines (Craik, 2000). This decline implies difficulties with the memory of autobiographical events that can be explicitly stated, such as times or places. Age-related deficits are also present in attention processes, partly because of the increased difficulty of older adults to filter

out irrelevant information, to establish clear goals and to inhibit irrelevant information (Mayhorn, Rogers, & Fisk, 2004), and in executive capabilities related to abstraction capabilities, reasoning about unfamiliar problems and self-monitoring (von Hippel, 2007). To sum up, these changes result in a loss of detail of memories, a reduced ability to plan one's own life and a subsequent reduced quality of life. It is explicitly not the goal of the project to make people dependent on the HERMES system, but rather to provide support, increase the feeling of security and avoid the fear of forgetting.

The first step in this project was to carry out a requirement analysis by means of a questionnaire, focus groups, diaries, cultural probes, interviews and memory assessment (Urdaneta, Buiza, Gonzalez, Facal, Geven et al., 2009). This analysis provided us with relevant information to formulate real scenarios where the HERMES system can be used. According to Carroll (1995), scenarios contain and describe a setting, the agents or actors, their goals and purposes and the things they do. From scenarios we get a context in which the actors act with the product. The use of scenarios not only serves to aid technical development, but they are also useful in communication with the potential end-users to come up with requirements for the tools and applications that are developed within the HERMES project. The scenarios provide an instantaneous vision of a specific setting and its context and they offer a way to imagine design concepts in use (Saffer, 2007). They give us a way of describing an application and, more important, an interaction with an application in words. Because of this they can be used to communicate and transform the findings from the requirements analysis into a prototype.

Five scenarios linked to the HERMES objectives have been developed. The scenarios were composed using the results from the requirements analysis. Based on an overview of the results of the requirements analysis, five scenarios for each of the HERMES objectives have been developed:

(a) Facilitation of episodic memory, through the capture of content in audio (Petsatodis & Boukis, 2009) and video (Katsarakis & Pnevmatikakis, 2009) including when, where, who, what and why. Advanced intelligent speech and image processing techniques are being developed to index, annotate, and summarize the information captured, based on semantics extraction, events identification and inferences. The moments are intended to be easily retrievable through an accessible interface providing both browsing and searching capabilities. As the user provides some information (such as topic, location, timeframe, person involved or specific words from a conversation), the potential targets are narrowed down.

(b) Cognitive training, through games with moments that have been captured previously and that are related to contextual information. Cognitive games included in HERMES have been designed taking into account age-related changes in memory, executive processing, visual attention and visual-manual coordination, avoiding burden on these functions but stimulating them. HERMES cognitive training games will be offered through novel ergonomic interfaces, which are intended to provide aged users with comfort, flexibility and natural interaction. In particular, the HERMES end-user interface for cognitive training is implemented on multi-touch surface interface based on leading edge finger tracking technology, which enhances interaction, motivation and allows complex game features (Facal, González, Martinez, Buiza, Talantzis et al., 2009). Motivation has been taken into account, especially in order to promote users' long-term adherence to gaming experience. In this sense, computerized cognitive training has the potential of adapting stimulus automatically from users' previous performance

(successes and failures, reaction times, gaming routines).

(c) Advanced activity reminding, to assist the user's prospective memory in performing everyday tasks and to support independent living. Modelled after human associative memory, contextual cues remind the user automatically and non-disruptively, facilitating remembering in the right place, at the right time. The design of the reminders is intended to be minimally intrusive, ensuring that the system is going to be accepted by its users. Through context-awareness, HERMES will make it possible to provide the reminders when they are required, whereas intelligent processing of the captured speech and visual contents provides a way to analyze which events are going to take place, when, and where.

(d) Conversation support, on the grounds of interactive reminiscence based on the recordings of important moments in everyday life, ranging from the present back into the (shared) history of the older person and the communication partner thus facilitating sharing. The system will provide the means for older adults to share experiences and history with relatives and friends thereby making history livelier.

(e) Mobility support, to address the needs of the user outside the house with cognitive support when and where needed through a mobile device. In this respect, reminders are being designed to be location-sensitive.

The part of the work presented in this paper aims to:

(1) Check whether scenarios have been perceived as relevant and realistic.

(2) Assess the potential users' opinions about the HERMES functionalities.

Methodology

Fundación Instituto Gerontológico Matia - IN-GEMA (Spain) and CURE – Center for Usability Research and Engineering (Austria) have been involved in the evaluation of the HERMES scenarios. Both partners chose to conduct focus groups and also a questionnaire to collect some concrete, additional information. A focus group is a qualitative methodology which helps to collect the users' attitudes, preferences and initial reactions to the use of the HERMES system. Advantages of focus groups are the possibility of gathering feedback on ideas and the production of a lot of useful ideas from the users themselves. In the focus groups organized in Vienna, 6 older women attended and the one organized in San Sebastian was composed of 8 elderly people (two male and six female). The people in the evaluation of the scenarios were older adults that suffer from minor memory impairments but lead an active lifestyle.

Each focus group was split into two parts: the first part was a classical focus group and in the second part a questionnaire was used. The focus group moderator explained each of the steps and answered all questions. In the first part, the scenarios which HERMES tries to address were presented to the older participants in a PowerPoint presentation and they discussed and provided ways to solve the described issue, e.g. "You want to do some cognitive training – how do you prefer to train your cognitive abilities:

- I won't train my cognitive abilities
- I will play crosswords, puzzles, sudokus, and things like that
- I will join some memory group
- I will use a computer for my cognitive training."

The first alternative always contained the "I do not need this thing" approach. Having this statement included assured the discussion of the usefulness and relevance of each scenario for potential users. The next two alternatives were real alternatives and the last one pointed towards HERMES, e.g., the use of a machine to do the cognitive training.

In the second part of the focus group the participants were again presented with a new slide for each scenario, now describing steps needed to accomplish the desired outcome with HERMES (e.g., 1. You store appointments in HERMES; 2. HERMES asks you if you want to play a cognitive game and you can choose between different cognitive games; 3. You choose the Puzzle game; 4. The system displays puzzles of many appointments in random order; 5. You are intended to complement appointments by using these puzzles; and 6. HERMES provides feedback on the results). Also, participants had to fill out a questionnaire prepared for each scenario. This questionnaire provided the possibility of gathering feedback regarding ideas and concepts from a number of people simultaneously and in a controlled and standardized way (e.g., for the scenario "facilitation of episodic memory", the questions were: Would you use this strategy for recalling your conversation?, How would you prefer the HERMES system to start recording?, How would you prefer the HERMES system to store information?, etc.).

Results

Facilitation of Episodic Memory

Episodic memory is the memory system that captures prior experiences and uses this information to influence current behavior and plan future behavior. It is the context-bound ability to re-experience happenings from one's past, involving the ability to mentally represent a specific event and localize it in time and space (Gronlund, Carlson, & Tower, 2007). Facilitation of episodic memory was included as an objective in HERMES project because older people tend to lose track of what happened in the recent past faster than younger ones (Old & Naveh-Benjamin, 2008). From the results of the requirements analysis we know about the fact that older adults have the feeling that they forget their recent past very quickly (Buiza et al., 2008). A possibility of exploring the past is therefore very welcome for the HERMES user-group. We try to address this issue within HERMES by providing a possibility of recording important events, both at home and with the HERMES mobile device when people are out of home. Users have the possibility of recording entire conversations or just short notes to back up important events in their lives. Information stored on the mobile device will be automatically synchronized with the main system, where it will also be processed for later retrieval. By offering a central point where information is stored, we also eliminate the search through different sources of information, such as post-its, calendars and agendas.

The participants of the focus group were a little sceptical about whether they would need to record conversations at home. The scepticism was directed towards the need for detail in everyday conversations and also towards the fact that these conversations might include secrets not meant for recording. They perceived that this solution was somewhat intrusive for them and also for the people coming to their houses.

Only one participant did not see the need for recording private conversations. In general, all participants preferred the system to only record when it is programmed to do so. Some of the participants pointed out that they may use it more extensively in the future if their memory abilities become impaired. 66% of the participants would use HERMES in case they forget something important. 3 participants would use HERMES as a central data storage application for pictures, videos and the like.

With respect to how they would like to search for information, five participants would want search information using all modalities. One participant wanted to search for information by name, another wanted to search for information

by picture and another one wanted to search for information by name, time interval and place.

Cognitive Games

A common result found through the different methodologies used in the user requirements was that the most necessary requirement for independent living and for maintaining the security status in their houses was to maintain cognitive function. For example, in the questionnaire it was shown that 67.7% of the participants would appreciate a device to play some cognitive games. It is a fact that all of the elderly interviewed are aware that some cognitive training is good for them. Staying active and interested is seen as important by all the people interviewed. On the other hand, different studies have shown cognitive plasticity and learning potential in healthy elderly people (Kemperman, Gast, & Gage, 2002; Fernández-Ballesteros, Zamarrón, & Tárraga, 2005; Yanguas, Buiza, Echeverria, Galdona, González, Arriola et al., 2006). This means that for elderly people, who have been trained in a cognitive intervention, different cognitive variables can be enhanced (Buiza, Etxeberria, Galdona, González, Arriola et al., 2006).

In their daily lives, participants used crosswords, sudokus, attending memory groups (they value the opportunity to interact with other people in these groups), reading in a second language and two of them used computer games for training cognitive skills. These two people who were currently playing computerized cognitive games perceive HERMES games positively since they provided the possibility of doing cognitive training on the basis of real-life, personal information previously stored in the system (Buiza, Gonzalez, Facal, Martínez, Díaz et al., 2009).

In relation to whether participants preferred doing cognitive training on the basis of personal or fictional information, in San Sebastian five out of eight participants preferred to play with personal information while one of them preferred to play with fictitious information. Two participants in Vienna and two in San Sebastian were for a mixture of real and fictional information.

They were asked if they would like a specific cognitive game covering specific difficulties for lexical access to people names since this difficulty was ranked high on the list of problems mentioned during the requirements analysis study. Difficulties with names are one of the most salient cognitive complaints of elderly adults, especially with regard to people's names (i. e., Sunderland, Watts, Baddeley, & Harris, 1986). The reduction of processing resources related to aging increases the number of tip-of-the-tongue phenomena, which is the common and universal experience of knowing the name of something or someone that the person cannot retrieve. Juncos-Rabadán, Facal, Rodríguez, and Pereiro (2010) have recently shown that elderly adults experience more failures in word form access than young people independently of their vocabulary knowledge, but only for proper names. Accordingly to the salience of lexical access difficulties in language changes related to aging (Facal, Gonzalez, Buiza, Laskibar, Urdaneta, & Yanguas, 2009), the possibility to access a name through a guided picture search and, specifically, the possibility of strength semantic activation will be very welcome for the HERMES user-group During the focus group, participants mentioned some of the strategies that they put into practice: using alphabet searches, associating the name with something, and asking someone. These strategies are not always successful and participants indicated that they would use this HERMES game, some whenever they forget a name and others only when they were not able to remember unusual names of people.

Advanced Activity Reminding

Prospective memory is the ability to remember what you have to do in the future,, becoming aware of a previously formed plan at the right time and place. The knowledge about older adults having problems with prospective memory is well described in the literature. Laboratory studies has shown that older adults tend to have problems with this (Matthias, Jäger, & Phillips, 2008; Uttl, 2008). Martin and Schumann-Hengsteler (2001) found that the larger the resource requirements of a given prospective memory task, the more strongly older adults' performance in the task declines relative to that of younger adults, mainly since the resources available for the elderly are taken from a smaller capacity working memory. In a meta-analysis performed this same year, Uttl (2008) concluded that research shows that prospective memory declines with aging, that declines are as large or even larger than those found with classical retrospective memory tests, and that age declines in prospective memory are generally small until the 50s or 60s, and accelerate thereafter.

Three different scenarios are listed to provide an overview of this aspect: "setting a reminder at home", "setting a reminder on-location" and "setting a shopping-reminder". Answers about whether the participants would use the HERMES system to store appointments indicated that they would use it only under certain circumstances. One reason for this answer is that participants cannot decide on changing from calendar to HERMES without trying HERMES. It is hard for them to imagine how it would be to use HERMES for this task.

All participants commonly used calendars in order to remember what they have to do in the future; only one of them entered their appointments in their mobile phone. Four out of eight people answered that they always would use HERMES to store appointments. Three participants would use it in some certain circumstances and one person only sometimes. Participants were confident that the difficulty in storing an appointment in HERMES might not be too great, although they would prefer to keep using the calendar as long as possible. This feature was designed to work in a PDA with GPS and it afforded the user the possibility of being reminded of the recorded note whenever he is near the location again. In the focus groups, participants welcomed this feature. Currently, if they have to remember the address of a shop they either write it in their calendar, on a piece of paper or go into the shop and ask for a business card, or try to pay attention and make an effort in order to remember it later. Just using a PDA would be very practical in the view of participants. Most of the participants, except two, preferred to receive the reminders of their appointments both visually and by audio. Two people preferred to receive them either visually or by audio. All participants, except one, wanted to program the time of the reminder for each appointment by themselves.

When participants were asked about the difficulty level of storing an appointment in HERMES, all the participants, except one, thought that with prior training, they would be able to store the appointments and they would want reminders issued by the system. They answered that they were confident that it might not be too difficult, although they would prefer to keep using the calendar as long as possible.

HERMES also allows for setting a reminder based on location, rather than on time. Answers indicated this feature is of interest to all of the participants, in both Vienna and San Sebastian. They pointed out that it would not be hard, even though it is difficult for them to imagine how the system can do it. One participant added that it would be interesting to take photographs of the locations in order to introduce them into the system. In Spain, five out of eight always preferred reminders, two people wanted reminders only when the appointment is important, and one participant did not want reminders because he preferred to look at them but not to receive the reminders.

As it was pointed out before, "setting a shopping-reminder" is a key scenario for the advanced activity reminder function, providing the possibility to create a shopping list using the PDA. In our study, all the participants went shopping with a shopping-list. Questions for this scenario were aimed at finding out whether participants would use the HERMES portable device to make shopping lists and whether they think that it might be tedious to do this. Participants considered that they would use this function of the system, although users with less experience with technology were not sure about the tediousness of this operation.

Conversation Support

The requirement analysis revealed that a social network keeps them going when times are hard and they need to face problems. It also keeps them active and busy. The need to stay in contact with friends and family is highly important to older adults. HERMES provides possibilities to support social interaction and facilitates conversations when people are experiencing certain problems with forgetfulness by searching for contents stored in the system. In the context of active older adults, conversation support can also be understood as an electronic album or diary filled with entries of different types, e.g. video, text, pictures and audio-files. Whenever a potential end user wants to share memories with a friend, she can use HERMES to stimulate this journey to the past.

Participants agreed they would use this function of the system as support for social interaction. They considered that it could be nice to look at pictures from one's youth or to hear voices from the past, and it might also be practical: no more searching for old pictures in different places. When asked what situations participants would like to record the answers indicated that family and friends are the most interesting. In fact, they only received visits in their homes from their families and friends. Some arguments that came up during the focus group were: "It can be a nice thing to look at pictures from one's youth or to hear voices from long ago", "for nostalgic reasons", "to follow one's own development over the life span", etc.

During the requirement analysis phase many older adults mentioned the problem of meeting someone and not being able to remember the name of the person. As already described above the tip-of-the-tongue phenomena is a problem, many people and especially older adults have to deal with. Complementarily, we asked participants whether they would be interested in having the possibility to store pictures of people together with names on the HERMES PDA, sorted in categories they define themselves. Nine out of twelve participants would use the service whenever they forgot a name. In the focus group carried out in Spain, the answers indicated that all participants would use it, some whenever they forgot a name and others only when they were not able to re-member unusual names of people.

Mobility Support

Leading an active lifestyle means also being able to go out meeting family and friends. For many older adults these things are among the most important actions in their lives. According to Fernández-Ballesteros (2003), studies show that elderly people who perceive themselves as having relevant activities under control may age in a more satisfactory way (with a decrease of mortality, morbility and physical disability), than those feeling unable to control their environment.

One of the results of the requirement analysis study (Buiza et al., 2008) was the need for an active life-style for older adults in order to stay healthy. By active life style, people mean going out, meeting friends and families and the like. HERMES seeks to support older adults in doing so by providing an easy to use PDA offering the possibility to store appointments and acoustically record notes associated with these appointments. In our study, only one of the participants used his mobile phone extensively for activities such as storing addresses or appointments. Our conclu-sion from the requirement analysis is that we will develop a functionality that enables end users of HERMES to easily set reminders and to choose to add a few keywords or recorded notes to those reminders. This way, end-users have flexibility to

plan and re-plan. Additionally they can always go back to an event and refresh their memory if they feel they have forgotten the context.

Participants perceived a mobile device mainly as a telephone. They would like to record special events when they are outside the house, such as a conference, but they would not use it routinely for their daily life. It was perceived to be more productive for people with memory impairment; nevertheless, they think it would be fruitful for them as a way of acquiring further experience with communication technologies.

The answers given in the questionnaire provide us with the following: participants reported that they would use the PDA to store appointments only if these are important. Also in Spain they would record appointments if these are either too long or contain a lot of details and information. For retrieving stored appointments, participants preferred to choose between a transcribed audio file and the audio file alone. The contrary was found in Spain, most of them prefer to retrieve information, by both transcribed audio file and the audio file. However, they emphasized that when they are with someone else, they prefer to retrieve the appointments only by transcribed audio file.

CONCLUSION

The information collected through the focus groups carried out in Vienna and in Spain is simi-lar. The focus groups provided fruitful feedback about problems and needs related to older users' perceptions about how they interact with technol-ogy in home and out-of-the-home environments. Difficulties were only reported when scenarios about cognitive games or storing appointments were presented, because of difficulties with the subjective evaluation of these general concepts.

The questionnaires prepared for each scenario provided complementary information about the topics discussed in the focus groups, and also gave us the possibility to collect more concrete suggestions about some relevant topics. In this regard, in previous studies we have noticed (Subasi, Leitner, Geven, Tscheligi, & Buiza, 2009) that elderly users hardly report information on everyday problems. A more diversified approach allows us to collect different kind of information from different points of view (objective needs, subjective perceptions, affective state, shared and private potential resolutions, and so on).

Main conclusions of this study are:

1. Usefulness is the main area of interest for the older adults who participated in the study. It seems they are not interested in technological devices if these do not contribute to making their lives easier.
2. Usability is another key area for participants. Although they recognize that technology can make their lives easier, they tend to use more familiar strategies in order to cope with memory difficulties.
3. The use of real-life information is considered a key point of the HERMES system, especially regarding cognitive games. Nevertheless, privacy issues are relevant for them, not only because of privacy issues, but also because technology may interfere with social interactions if relatives and friends are not fully confident of the system.
4. Although sample size is necessarily small in this kind of research, it seems that those people with previous experience of information and communication technologies evaluate the HERMES scenarios more positively.
5. Regarding user experience, participants consider that using systems such as HERMES can help them to be familiarized with technology. In fact, although they consider HERMES more useful for people with age-related memory impairments, using it would make them more experienced and protect them against the cognitive decline in the future.

ACKNOWLEDGMENT

This work is part of the EU HERMES project (FP7-216709), partially funded by the European Commission in the scope of the 7th ICT Framework. Special thanks to all the partners of this project for the great work done in scenarios development described in this document.

REFERENCES

Buiza, C., Etxeberria, I., Galdona, N., González, M. F., Arriola, E., & López de Munain, A. (2008). A randomized, two-year study of the efficacy of cognitive intervention on elderly people: the Donostia Longitudinal Study. *International Journal of Geriatric Psychiatry*, *23*, 85–94. doi:10.1002/gps.1846

Buiza, C., Gonzalez, M. F., Etxaniz, E., Urdaneta, E., Yanguas, J., Geven, A., et al. (2008). *Technology support for cognitive decline and independent living – Presenting the HERMES project*. Paper presented at the Gerontological Society of America Conference, Washington, DC.

Buiza, C., Gonzalez, M. F., Facal, D., Martinez, V., Diaz, U., Etxaniz, A., et al. (2009). Efficacy of cognitive training experiences in the elderly: Can technology help? In *Proceedings of the 5th International Conference on Universal Access in Human Computer Interaction*.

Burdick, D., & Kwon, S. (2004). *Gerotechnology: Research and practice in technology and aging*. New York: Springer.

Carroll, J. (1995). *Scenario-based design: Envisioning work and technology in systems development*. New York: John Wiley & Sons.

Craik, F. I. M. (2000). Age-related changes in human memory. In Park, D. C., & Schwartz, N. (Eds.), *Cognitive aging* (pp. 75–92). Philadelphia: Psychology Press.

Facal, D., González, M. F., Buiza, C., Laskibar, I., Urdaneta, E., & Yanguas, J. J. (2009). Envejecimiento, deterioro cognitivo y lenguaje: Resultados del Estudio Longitudinal Donostia [Aging, cognitive impairment and language. Results from the Donostia Longitudinal Study]. *Revista de Logopedia, Foniatría y Audiología, 29*(1), 4–12.

Facal, D., González, M. F., Martínez, V., Buiza, C., Talantzis, F., Petsatodis, T., et al. (2009). *Cognitive games for healthy elderly people in a multitouch screen.* Paper presented at DRT4ALL2009 Conference, Barcelona, Spain.

Fernández-Ballesteros, R. (2003). Una perspectiva psico-social: Promoción del envejecimiento activo. [A psycho-social perspective: Promotion of active aging] In Salvador, L. A., Cabo, J. R., & Alonso, F. (Eds.), *Longevidad y vida saludable* [Longevity and healthy life]. Madrid, Spain: AECES.

Fernández-Ballesteros, R., Zamarrón, M. D., & Tárraga, L. (2005). Learning potential: a new method for assessing cognitive impairment. *International Psychogeriatrics, 17,* 119–128. doi:10.1017/S1041610205000992

Gronlund, S. D., Carlson, C. A., & Tower, D. (2007). Episodic memory. In Durso, F. (Ed.), *Handbook of applied cognition* (2nd ed.). New York: John Wiley & Sons. doi:10.1002/9780470713181.ch5

Juncos-Rabadán, O., Facal, D., Rodríguez, M. S., & Pereiro, A. X. (in press). Lexical knowledge and lexical retrieval in ageing: Insights from a tip-of-the-tongue (TOT) study. *Language and Cognitive Processes.*

Katsarakis, N., & Pnevmatikakis, A. (2009). *Face Validation Using 3D Information from Single Calibrated Camera.* Paper presented at DSP 2009, Santorini, Greece.

Kempermann, G., Gast, D., & Gage, F. H. (2002). Neuroplasticity in Old Age: Sustained Fivefold Induction of Hippocampal Neurogenesis by Long-term Environmental Enrichment. *Annals of Neurology, 52*(2), 135–143. doi:10.1002/ana.10262

Martin, M., & Schumann-Hengsteler, R. (2001). How task demands influence time-based prospective memory performance in young and older adults. *International Journal of Behavioral Development, 25*(4), 386–391. doi:10.1080/01650250042000302

Matthias, K., Jäger, T., & Philips, L. H. (2008). Adult age differences in event-based prospective memory: A meta-analysis on the role of focal versus nonfocal cues. *Psychology and Aging, 23*(1), 203–208. doi:10.1037/0882-7974.23.1.203

Mayhorn, C. B., Rogers, W. A., & Fisk, A. D. (2004). Designing technology based on cognitive aging principles. In Burdick, D. C., & Kwon, S. (Eds.), *Gerotechnology: Research and practice in technology and aging* (pp. 42–53). New York: Springer Publishing Company.

Old, S. R., & Naveh-Benjamin, M. (2008). Differential effects of age on item and associative measures of memory: a meta-analysis. *Psychology and Aging, 23*(1), 104–118. doi:10.1037/0882-7974.23.1.104

Petsatodis, Th., & Boukis, C. (2009). *Efficient Voice Activity Detection in Reverberant Enclosures using Far Field Microphones.* Paper presented at IEEE DSP2009 Conference, Santorini, Greece.

Saffer, D. (2007). *Designing for interaction: Creating smart applications and clever devices.* Berkeley, CA: New Riders.

Subasi, Ö., Leitner, M., Geven, A., Dittenberger, S., Tscheligi, M., & Buiza, C. (2009). User requirement analysis for ambient assistive living (AAL): Affective improvement of methods for technologyh acceptance evaluation. In *Evaluating new interactions in healthcare in conjunction with CHI'09*, Boston.

Sunderland, A., Watts, K., Baddeley, A. D., & Harris, J. E. (1986). Subjective memory assessment and test performance in the elderly. *Journal of Gerontology, 41*, 376–384.

Urdaneta, E., Buiza, C., Gonzalez, M. F., Facal, D., Geven, A., & Höller, N. (2009). Addressing cognition needs in three European countries with the help of technology. *The Journal of Nutrition, Health & Aging, 13*(1), 620.

Uttl, B. (2008). Transparent Meta-Analysis of Prospective Memory and Aging. *PloS One, 3*(2), e1568. doi:10.1371/journal.pone.0001568

von Hippel, W. (2007). Aging, executive functioning, and social control. *Current Directions in Psychological Science, 16*(5), 240–244. doi:10.1111/j.1467-8721.2007.00512.x

Walters, K., Iliffe, S., See Tai, S., & Orrell, M. (2000). Assessing needs from patient, carer and professional perspectives: The Camberwell Assessment of Need for Elderly people in primary care. *Age and Ageing, 29*, 505–510. doi:10.1093/ageing/29.6.505

Yanguas, J. J., Buiza, C., Echeverria, I., Galdona, N., González, M. F., & Arriola, E. (2006). *Estudio longitudinal Donostia de enfermedad de Alzheimer*. Salamanca, Spain: Tempora.

This work was previously published in the International Journal of Ambient Computing and Intelligence, Volume 3, Issue 1, edited by Kevin Curran, pp. 42-52, copyright 2011 by IGI Publishing (an imprint of IGI Global).

Chapter 6
AmbiLearn:
Multimodal Assisted Learning

Jennifer Hyndman
University of Ulster, UK

Tom Lunney
University of Ulster, UK

Paul Mc Kevitt
University of Ulster, UK

ABSTRACT

In educational institutions computing technology is facilitating a dynamic and supportive learning environment for students. In recent years, much research has involved investigating the potential of technology for use in education and terms such as personalized learning, virtual learning environments, intelligent tutoring and m-learning have brought significant advances within higher education but have not propagated down to Primary Level. This paper discusses AmbiLearn, an ambient intelligent multimodal learning environment for children. The main objective of this research is to redress the limited use of virtual learning environments in primary school education. With a focus on multimodal presentation and learning environments, AmbiLearn explores the educational potential of such systems at Primary school level.

INTRODUCTION

A learning environment is an environment where a person can learn or gain knowledge on a particular theme or topic. Traditionally, learning only took place in a classroom setting where instruction or pedagogical information was provided by a teacher/lecturer. As technology has become more

DOI: 10.4018/978-1-4666-2041-4.ch006

powerful, accessible and more pervasive, learning has migrated out of the classroom setting. In educational institutes today the use of Virtual learning environments (VLEs) has become predominant in providing an online environment for administration of course material and student assessments. However, the use of virtual learning environments in primary schools is very limited. Key findings in a study by Ofsted (2009) may suggest that this is due to the lack of the material available in relation to the range of topics covered. The presentation style of the pedagogical content also contributes to the limited use of VLEs as many of these provide information through static downloadable word documents where interactivity is limited. The focus of this research is to develop a multimodal learning environment assisting learning which is designed specifically for children. AmbiLearn combines successful techniques from virtual learning environments, serious games and multimodal interfaces. As a multimodal learning environment AmbiLearn aims to support collaborative learning with a general educational aim of encouraging children in their own learning and enabling them to take responsibly for that learning. This paper provides a review of the literature on learning environments and how they can be used effectively. Preliminary work on AmbiLearn is presented and a sample application, TreasureLearn, is described. The paper concludes by outlining future work.

VIRTUAL LEARNING ENVIRONMENTS

The term 'technology enhanced learning' is used to cover all methods of using technology as a foundation for learning such as: m-learning, e-learning and web-based learning. O'Malley et al. (2003, p.1), define m-learning as "any sort of learning that happens when the learner is not at a fixed, predetermined location, or learning that happens when the learner takes advantage of the learning opportunities offered by mobile technologies." Similar to this, e-learning can be defined as electronic learning where the learning is based upon some form of technology including, but not limited to, mobile technologies. All these concepts can encompass the use of the VLEs. In the UK most if not all of the further and higher education institutes are using a VLE such as *Blackboard* or *Moodle*. In this context the VLE is providing opportunities for distant learners, access to course content at any location, any time.

Students can catch up on missed lectures/classes, submit assignments and receive feedback at any time. This style of usage enables students to be in constant contact with the course and collaborate with other class members with for example chat boxes and open forums. JISC (2009) provide a comprehensive study of the different uses of virtual learning environments in higher education across multiple disciplines such as economics, medicine, dentistry, business, management and health science. Testimonials from both staff and students indicate high levels of satisfaction with the learning process and many suggest the results indicate a significant improvement in student learning. With each environment suited to a particular domain, it is not easy to identify which learning environment has most educational potential. A common theme amongst each is the method of providing the pedagogical content which makes it effective. An investigation of interactive multimodal learning suggests that "the most effective learning environments are those that combine verbal and non-verbal representations of the knowledge using mixed-modality presentations" (Moreno & Mayer, 2007). Since 2005 Becta has referred to the VLE as a 'learning platform' which suggests a greater emphasis on the presentation of content (Berry, 2005). The different presentation style of pedagogical content can be deemed as the critical feature needed for VLEs to be appropriate for children, supporting both auditory and visual learning styles, as demonstrated by the use of educational games.

Games as the Learning Environment

In Northern Ireland, all primary and secondary schools funded by the Department of Education and Learning (DEL) have access to the C2K network (C2K, 2010). Within this network there are resources such as educational games compatible with the aims and objectives of the Northern Ireland curriculum. In the past such edutainment software has been met with much criticism as well as some enthusiastic support. There was much hype when educational games were first released, yet educators were reluctant to adopt them. Recent studies suggest that video games promote the development of skills such as strategic thinking and creativity, offering appropriate and adaptive feedback and the embedding of cognitive strategies that can reduce task time, increase achievement and have a positive effect on student learning (Booth, 2009; Rosas et al., 2003). Mc Farlane et al. (2002) suggest that by providing a fun, playful approach games can facilitate learning in three ways: learning as a result of tasks stimulated by the content of the games, knowledge developed through the content of the game and skills arising as a result of playing the game.

Multimodal Interfaces

As an online environment, the interface to the VLE is essentially a web page. Multimodal output thus plays an important role in such systems as the style in which pedagogical content is provided affects the manner in which a student will process and learn the information. The use of audio and graphic output for portraying information enables users to visualise and further understand certain theories and facts. Using pedagogical agents in learning environments can have a positive impact on motivating students and keeping their attention (Ortiz et al., 2007). The general perception of such animated characters could be that they cause distraction and are irritating, yet certain systems have proven that an embodied agent can have a positive impact on the learning process. Lester et al. (1997, p. 359) state, "the captivating presence of the agents can motivate students to interact more frequently with agent-based educational software. This in turn has the potential to produce significant cumulative increases in the quality of a child's education over periods of months and years." Agents such as Steve (Johnson et al., 1997) and Gandalf (Thórisson, 1996) both

provide users with information effectively using verbal and nonverbal communication modalities.

As suggested, providing multimodal output for content delivery has great potential. However, multimodal input also offers many benefits for the user. Multimodal interfaces allow a more natural form of communication while certain combinations of modalities offer ease of use and fluency. Speech and pen/mouse input are arguably the most common combination of modalities as Cohen (1992) suggests and they complement each other by overcoming one's weaknesses with the other's strengths. The rise in mobile learning also strengthens this complementary input approach as device limitations can be overcome by using speech and simple pointing gestures. The use of multiple modalities is ideal within multi-user collaborative environments. A study on children's collaborative interactions suggests that sharing a physical display with multiple input devices may improve collaboration due to heightened awareness of the other user's actions and intentions (Scott et al., 2003).

AMBILEARN

The motivation for AmbiLearn has arisen from gaps in ambient multimodal learning environments in respect of children's education. In all key areas of related research, investigations have proven successful in respect of particular educational domains. Multimodal interfaces and the use of speech and pen have proven to provide complementary interfaces supporting assistance in predominately navigation and tourist systems. Studies have shown how embodied agents have had a positive effect on student learning by maintaining students' attention and hence improving motivation. Serious games have proven to be successful in motivating students and maintaining their interest in a particular educational domain and the different learning environments have facilitated a more flexible means of providing the educational content suitable to different needs of each individual. A focus of this research is to further investigate the educational potential of AmbiLearn, an ambient intelligent multimodal learning environment. AmbiLearn aims to investigate the potential of integrating multimodality and interactivity within a virtual learning environment. As a multimodal system the user can interact through speech and 2-dimensional gestures, and receive feedback through graphics, non-speech audio, speech and an animated character agent.

Architecture

AmbiLearn's architecture is shown in Figure 1, with the dialogue manager as the central component. The dialogue manager is responsible for the fusion of input data, semantic representation and decision making based upon user intentions. Here, application models are referred and multimodal presentation is generated and organized for output rendering. The pedagogical manager and domain manager relate to the pedagogical model and domain model respectively and are essentially the plug-in knowledge/content and application.

Dialogue Manager

The dialogue manager is in essence the heart of AmbiLearn. Multimodal input is fused together and represented semantically to obtain the users intentions. Based upon these intentions and the current state of application, a decision making module takes appropriate action. This action can be through the domain manager or the pedagogical manager. The domain manager initiates and terminates sessions with the application and requests and responds to information. The pedagogical manager requests, extracts and integrates relevant pedagogical information. The decision making module then sends the relevant information for multimodal presentation to be rendered for the user. In addition, personal information may be obtained by the user modeling module to amend and update a user profile.

Application Models

What differentiates AmbiLearn applications from many others is the concept of having the information available in numerous formats. One method is to use Resource Description Framework (RDF) to

Figure 1. Architecture of AmbiLearn

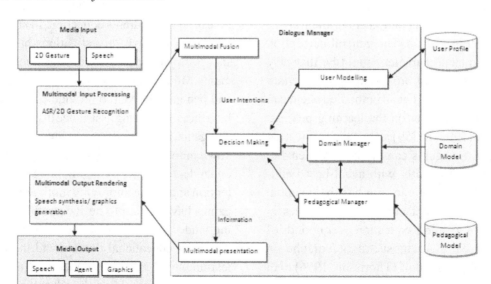

semantically represent pedagogical information on a particular theme enabling a range of applications to use it. A multimodal presentation system can thus provide content through a conversational style game, where users can interact with a character to gain further knowledge. A fact file may be used to provide a visual portrayal of the information through text, movies or images to support those pupils who prefer a visual style of learning.

TreasureLearn

The educational approach taken by AmbiLearn is demonstrated by TreasureLearn which is a treasure hunt style game. An activity diagram of TreasureLearn is shown in Figure 2 which highlights the use of multiple modalities throughout the application. General feedback will be through the medium of spoken output from a character agent. Users will interact for navigation purposes though spoken keywords or mouse/pen inputs or a combination of both. Modules within Treasure-Learn are as follows:

- **Gameplay:** In game design the game play module is concerned with the challenges a player is faced with and the actions taken to overcome the challenges. This module will essentially provide the user with the rules and game concepts. This information will be provided through the use of an embodied agent; however limited interaction occurs within this module. Depending on the user and their previous interactions, this module will provide the information regarding the level, or area of game play they are due to commence.

- **Knowledge:** A knowledge module within the game will provide the pedagogical content which will comply with the intended age group and core curriculum. This information can be provided through the embodied agent and simply provides the user with content which will need to be recalled to overcome certain challenges.

- **Challenge:** The challenge module provides the main interaction within TreasureLearn.

Figure 2. TreasureLearn activity diagram

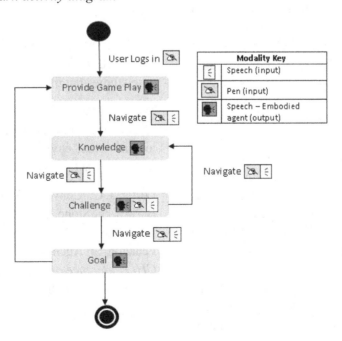

This module is responsible for accepting the knowledge the user provides and determining whether the user responded to an answer or puzzle correctly. The user input at this stage will be logged for analysis at a later stage.

- **Goal:** The goal module will provide the user with an update on their progress such as moving between levels. This module is concerned with updating the user information. At the end of each game session, i.e. each time the user plays, this module will be invoked to record and update the logged information so that an external user monitoring and assessment facility is available.

CONCLUSION AND FUTURE WORK

This paper has outlined the work to date associated with AmbiLearn, a multimodal virtual learning environment for primary school education. The multimodality of AmbiLearn will enable the user to employ a combination of speech and pen as input and offer rich feedback through the use of speech, graphics and an embodied agent. An application, TreasureLearn is being developed as a treasure hunt style game to demonstrate and test the educational potential of using multimodal presentation as a dynamic method of providing pedagogical content. AmbiLearn has a general educational aim to encourage children in their own learning and enable them to take responsibly for that learning.

AmbiLearn is being developed as an online environment using ASP.NET and Silverlight 4 as its interface technologies. Further investigation is required into the technologies of Speech recognition and the standards of Voice XML and SALT for the AmbiLearn speech capabilities. Sample pedagogical content will be tagged using the Resource Description Framework (RDF) standards to facilitate the development of a semantic search. The testing and evaluation of AmbiLearn/TreasureLearn will involve children, aged between 7 and 9 as subjects, working with the different functionalities of AmbiLearn. Pretests and Post-tests may be used to determine the learning attainment. Through questionnaires using The Fun Toolkit (Read & McFarlane, 2006) an evaluation can be carried out. Additionally using Cloud Computing as a delivery platform can open the opportunity for AmbiLearn to be accessed using mobile technologies in a ubiquitous fashion.

REFERENCES

C2K. (2010). Retrieved from http://www.c2kni.org.uk

Berry, M. (2005). *A virtual learning environment in primary education.* Retrieved from http://www.worldcitizens.net/ftp/Primary%20VLE.pdf

Booth, R. (2009, February 12). Video games are good for children – EU report. *The Guardian*, 2.

Cohen, P. (1992). The role of Natural Language in a Multimodal Interface. In *Proceedings of the 5th Annual Symposium on user interface software and technology,* Montreau, CA (pp. 143-149). New York: ACM.

JISC. (2009). *Tangible benefits of e-learning.* Retrieved from http://www.jiscinfonet.ac.uk/case-studies/tangible

Johnson, W. L., & Rickel, J. (1997). Steve: an animated pedagogical agent for procedural training in virtual environments. *SIGART Bulletin, December,* 8(1-4), 16-21.

Lester, J. C., Converse, S. A., Kahler, S. E., Todd Barlow, S., Stone, B. A., & Bhogal, R. S. (1997). The Persona Effect: Affective Impact of Animated Pedagogical Agents. In *Proceedings of the SIGCHI conference on Human factors in computing systems,* Atlanta (pp. 359-366). New York: ACM.

McFarlane, A., Sparrowhawk, A., & Heald, Y. (2002). *Report on the educational use of games: An exploration by TEEM of the contribution which games can make to the education process.* Retrieved from http://www.teem.org.uk/publications/teem_gamesined_full.pdf

Moreno, R., & Mayer, R. (2007). Interactive Multimodal Learning Environments. *Educational Psychology Review*, *19*, 309–326. doi:10.1007/s10648-007-9047-2

O'Malley, C., Vavoula, G., Glew, J., Taylor, J., Sharples, M., & Lefrere, P. (2003). *MOBILearn WP4 – guidelines for Learning/Teaching/Tutoring in a Mobile Environment.* Retrieved from http://www.mobilearn.org/download/results/guidelines.pdf

Ofsted, (2009). *Virtual learning environments: an evaluation of their development in a sample of educational settings.* Retrieved from http://www.ofsted.gov.uk/Ofsted-home/Publications-and-research

Ortiz, A., Carretero, M., Oyarzun, D., Yanguas, J., Buiza, C., Gonzalesm, M., & Etxeberria, l. (2007). Elderly Users in Ambient Intelligence: Does an avatar improve the interaction? In *Universal Access in Ambient Intelligence Environments* (LNCS 4397, pp. 99-114). Berlin: Springer.

Read, J., & McFarlane, S. (2006). Using the Fun Toolkit and Other Survey Methods to Gather Opinions in Child Computer Interaction. In *Proceedings of the 2006 conference on interaction design and children,* Tampere, Finland (pp. 81-88). New York: ACM.

Rosas, R., Nussbaum, M., Cumsille, P., Marianov, V., Correa, M., & Flores, P. (2003). Beyond Nintendo: design and assessment of educational video games for first and second grade students. *Computers & Education*, *40*(1), 71–94. doi:10.1016/S0360-1315(02)00099-4

Scott, S. D., Mandryk, R. L., & Inkpen, K. M. (2003). Understanding children's collaborative interactions in shared environments. *Journal of Computer Assisted Learning*, *19*(2), 220–228. doi:10.1046/j.0266-4909.2003.00022.x

Thórisson, K. (1996). *Communicative Humanoids: A Computational Model of Psychosocial Dialogue Skills.* Unpublished doctoral dissertation, Massachusetts Institute of Technology, Cambridge, MA.

This work was previously published in the International Journal of Ambient Computing and Intelligence, Volume 3, Issue 1, edited by Kevin Curran, pp. 53-59, copyright 2011 by IGI Publishing (an imprint of IGI Global).

Chapter 7
SYLPH:
A Platform for Integrating Heterogeneous Wireless Sensor Networks in Ambient Intelligence Systems

Ricardo S. Alonso
University of Salamanca, Spain

Dante I. Tapia
University of Salamanca, Spain

Juan M. Corchado
University of Salamanca, Spain

ABSTRACT

The significance that Ambient Intelligence (AmI) has acquired in recent years requires the development of innovative solutions. In this sense, the development of AmI-based systems requires the creation of increasingly complex and flexible applications. The use of context-aware technologies is an essential aspect in these developments in order to perceive stimuli from the context and react upon it autonomously. This paper presents SYLPH, a novel platform that defines a method for integrating dynamic and self-adaptable heterogeneous Wireless Sensor Networks (WSN). This approach facilitates the inclusion of context-aware capabilities when developing intelligent ubiquitous systems, where functionalities can communicate in a distributed way. A WSN infrastructure has been deployed for testing and evaluating this platform. Preliminary results and conclusions are presented in this paper.

INTRODUCTION

People are becoming increasingly accustomed to living with more and more technology in the hopes of increasing their quality of life and facilitating their day-to-day living. However, there are situations where technology is difficult to handle or people lack the knowledge of how to use it. Ambient Intelligence (AmI) tries to adapt technology to people's needs by incorporating omnipresent computing elements that communicate ubiquitously among themselves (Aarts & Encarnação, 2006; Lyytinen & Yoo, 2002). In

DOI: 10.4018/978-1-4666-2041-4.ch007

addition, the continuous advancement in mobile computing makes it possible to obtain information about the context and to react physically to it in more innovative ways (Jayaputera et al., 2007). Therefore, it is necessary to develop new solutions capable of providing adaptable and compatible frameworks, allowing access to functionalities regardless of time and location restrictions. Ambient Intelligence proposes three essential concepts: ubiquitous computing, ubiquitous communication and intelligent user interfaces (Aarts & Encarnação, 2006). One key aspect in any AmI-based system is the use of context-aware technologies. The context is defined as any information used to characterize the situation of an entity, which can be a person, a place or an object (Dey et al., 2001). Thus, the context includes both the users and the environmental information. This information is important for defining the interaction between users and the technology that surrounds them. The information may consist of many different parameters such as location, the building status (e.g., temperature), vital signs (e.g., heart rhythm), etc. Thus, most of the context information can be collected by distributed sensors throughout the environment and even by the users themselves.

Sensor networks are used for gathering the information needed by intelligent environments, whether in home automation, industrial applications, etc. (Sarangapani, 2007). Sensor networks need to be fast and easy to install and maintain. It is possible to distinguish between two types of sensor networks: wired and wireless. Wireless Sensor Networks (WSN) are more flexible and require less infrastructural support than wired sensor networks. Although there are plenty of technologies for implementing WSNs (e.g., Zig-Bee, Wi-Fi or Bluetooth), it is not easy to integrate devices from different technologies into a single network (Marin-Perianu et al., 2007; Cho et al., 2007). The lack of a common architecture may lead to additional costs due to the necessity of deploying non-transparent interconnection elements among different networks (Mukherjee et

al., 2006). Moreover, the developed elements are dependent on the application to which they belong, thus complicating their reutilization.

This paper describes the *Services laYers over Light PHysical devices* (SYLPH) platform. This platform is aimed at facilitating the development of AmI-based systems with context-aware capabilities by using dynamic and self-adaptable heterogeneous WSNs. These systems must be dynamic, flexible, robust, adaptable to changes in context, scalable and easy to use and maintain. Although there is currently a wide range of WSN technologies, most of them are not compatible with each other. SYLPH solves this problem by implementing a middleware that consists of additional layers added over the application layer of each WSN's stack. SYLPH implements an approach based on Service-Oriented Architectures (SOA) (Cerami, 2002). The platform provides a flexible distribution of resources and facilitates the inclusion of new functionalities in highly dynamic environments. Unlike other SOA-WSNs approaches (Marin-Perianu et al., 2007; Malatras et al., 2008), SYLPH allows both services and services directories to be embedded in devices with limited computational resources, regardless of the radio technology they use.

The next section presents the specific problem description that essentially motivated the development of a new platform. Then, it is described the main characteristics of SYLPH and briefly explained some of its components. After that, it is presented the implementation of SYLPH in a real scenario. Finally, it is presented the results and conclusions obtained.

MOTIVATION AND RELATED APPROACHES

One of the key aspects for the construction of AmI-based systems is obtaining information about the people and their environment through sensor networks. We have developed several systems based on AmI (Corchado et al., 2008). However, these developments have caused major problems when integrating sensors from different network technologies (e.g., hardware incompatibilities, reduced performance, etc.). This section presents the strengths and weaknesses of existing developments and analyzes the feasibility for implementing a new platform for integrating heterogeneous WSNs. This section also discusses some of the most important problems of existing platforms for WSNs, including their suitability for constructing intelligent context-aware systems.

The development of AmI-based systems that integrate different subsystems, especially heterogeneous WSNs, demands the creation of complex and flexible applications. As the complexity of an application increases, it needs to be divided into modules with different functionalities. Since different applications could require similar functionalities, there is a trend towards the re-utilization of resources that can be implemented as part of other systems. This trend is the best long-term solution and can be accomplished by using a common platform. However, it is difficult to carry out because the systems in which those functionalities are implemented are not always compatible with other systems. An alternative to such an approach is the reimplementation of the required functionalities. Although it implies more development time, it is generally the easiest and safest solution. Nevertheless, reimplementation can lead to duplicated functionalities and more difficult system migration.

Among the most important technologies used to implement Wireless Sensor Networks we have the ZigBee standard. The ZigBee standard allows operating in the frequency range belonging to the radio band known as ISM (Industrial, Scientific and Medical), especially in the 868MHz band in Europe, the 915MHz in the USA and the 2.4GHz in almost all over the world (Huang & Pang, 2007). The underlying IEEE 802.15.4 standard is designed to work with low-power and limited computational resources nodes (Singh et al., 2008).

ZigBee incorporates additional network, application and security layers over the 802.15.4 standard (Baronti et al., 2007). The ZigBee standard allows more than 65,000 nodes to be connected in a star, tree or mesh topology network. There are three types of ZigBee nodes: coordinator, router and end-device. The first two ones can forward data to other nodes in the network using the Ad-hoc On-demand Distance Vector (AODV) routing algorithm (Cuomo et al., 2007). End-devices can switch to a sleep mode in order to save energy achieving battery lifetimes of up to several years.

Another common standard to deploy wireless sensor networks is Bluetooth. This standard allows multiple WPAN (Wireless Personal Area Network) or WBAN (Wireless Body Area Network) applications for interconnecting mobile phones, personal computers or even biomedical sensors. Bluetooth operates also in the ISM 2.4GHz band. It allows creating star topology networks called *piconets* of up to 8 devices in which one of them acts as master and the rest as slaves. Several Bluetooth piconets can be interconnected by means of Bluetooth devices that belong simultaneously to two or more piconets, thus creating more extensive networks (known as *scatternets*) (Ilyas & Dorf, 2003).

In an AmI scenario, nodes must communicate directly with one another in a distributed way (Mukherjee et al., 2006). In a centralized architecture, most of the intelligence is located in a central node. That is, the central node is responsible for managing most of the functionalities and knowing the existence of all nodes in a specific WSN. That means that a node belonging to a certain WSN does not know about the existence of another node forming part of a different WSN, even though this WSN is also part of the system. For this reason, it is difficult for the system to dynamically adapt its behavior to changes in the infrastructure. In addition, excessive centralization negatively affects system functionalities, overcharging or limiting their capabilities. Nonetheless, this model can be improved using a common distributed architecture where all nodes in the system can know about the existence of any other node in the same system regardless of the technology or interface they use or the sub-network to which they belong. This can be achieved by adding a middleware logical layer over the existing application layers on the nodes. A distributed architecture provides more flexible ways to move functions to where actions are needed, thus obtaining better responses, autonomy, services continuity, and superior levels of flexibility and scalability than centralized architectures (Lyytinen & Yoo, 2002). In classic functional architectures the modularity and structure are oriented to the systems themselves. However, modern functional architectures such as SOA allow functionalities to be created outside the system, as external services linked to it. The term "service" can be defined as a mechanism that facilitates the access to one or more functionalities (e.g., functions, network capabilities, etc.) (Lyytinen & Yoo, 2002). Services are integrated through communication protocols that have to be used by applications to share resources in the network. Thus, distributed architectures look for the interoperability among different systems, the distribution of resources and the independence of programming languages (Lyytinen & Yoo, 2002; Cerami, 2002). Some developments try to reach integration between WSNs by implementing some kind of middleware, which can be applied as reduced versions of virtual machines, middleware or agent approaches (Marin-Perianu et al., 2007; Chen et al., 2007; Schramm et al., 2004). However, these developments require devices whose microcontrollers have large memory and high computational power, which increases costs and physical size. These drawbacks are very important when it comes to WSNs, as it is essential to deploy applications with reduced resources and low infrastructural impact, especially in AmI scenarios. A service-oriented approach is adequate for implementing in WSNs since it allows the distribution of functionalities (i.e., services) into small modules that can be executed by devices with limited computational resources, such as wireless sensor nodes.

The SYLPH platform tackles some of these issues by enabling an extensive integration of WSNs and optimizing the distribution, management and reutilization of the available resources and functionalities in such networks.

On the other hand, service-oriented architectures allow an easy integration and the reutilization of the current services, since they allow a universal communication through the use of the independent protocols of the platform, the providers and the language used. Furthermore, these architectures satisfy the requirements needed to create a wireless sensor network with authentic interoperability and scalability. By means of the hardware structure and the software architecture previously presented, the WSN nodes are provided with all the tools needed to accomplish the aims desired for a WSN, as well as to allow an easy and fast integration of the WSNs with the existing infrastructures. Next we present some related works based on service-oriented architectures to integrate wireless sensor networks.

Malatras et al. (2008) propose the exploitation of a service-oriented architecture that allows the management of services in buildings in a dynamic, coordinated and distributed way. This work presents the design of a network architecture based on the development of services and systems that specify the functional components of the architecture. The proposed architecture is compatible with general practices established in building automation environments and is centered on the business-level services. The main disadvantage of this architecture is that it is completely specific to the environment for which it is posed, so it is difficult so realize its feasibility into other scenarios.

Peng et al. (2008) present a system that defines a formal definition for a combination of services on WSNs. The main aim of this work is connect in a easy way grid computing with wireless sensor networks, The system does not only make the WSN nodes to cooperate among them in order to fulfill the application needs through a user-friendly interface, but also guarantees the quality of service integrated into the WSN. This kind of integration does not allow an autonomous operation of heterogeneous Wireless Sensor Networks, because it is necessary to deploy the grid infrastructure to manage sensor networks features.

Song and Lee (2008) present STWS (Smart Transducer Web Services), a unified Web Service for IEEE 1451 smart transducers. This research presents also a STWS prototype system that is formed by a service consumer, a service provider and a wireless sensor node. The service consumer can find the Web Services of the STWS on the service provider using SOAP/XML messages. However, this research does not integrate wireless sensor nodes from different radio technologies and does not carry the services into the nodes, but allows accessing nodes functionalities through Web Services.

Prinsloo et al. (2006) propose a service oriented architecture for the management of Wireless Sensor and Actor Networks (WSAN) that utilizes the OSGi (Open Services Gateway Initiative) framework. The service-oriented architecture proposed in this research allows for updating and modifying the application developed independently of the configuration of the nodes. Moreover, this architecture provides the user with the possibility to manage easily different types of sensors and actuators.

Avilés-López and García-Macías (2009) present TinySOA, an architecture that allows programmers to access the WSNs by means of a simple service-oriented API (Application Programming Interface). TinySOA facilitates the integration of Internet applications within WSNs and allows developers to access WSNs functionalities as services no matter the programming language they use. As other researches, this work does not embed services into sensor nodes, but uses services as interfaces to sensor functionalities.

Marin-Perianu et al. (2007) present a three-layer service-oriented architecture that adapts itself to different sensor platforms and exposes its functionalities in a uniform way. This architecture facilitates the integration of WSNs and RFID (Radio-Frequency IDentification) technologies in large-scale systems. This research uses three sensor platforms integrated by means of the UPnP (Universal Plug and Play) standard, used in business processes based on SAP software. This work also concludes that the use of a service-oriented approach is beneficial both in the design and in the implementation stages of its development.

Cañete et al. (2011) present a service-oriented middleware for Wireless Sensor and Actor Networks, called USEME middleware. USEME framework includes the USEME translator, that traduces USEME abstract language to Java or C# code. This way, USEME has been implemented in different motes using Microsoft.NET Micro Framework and Java Platform Micro Edition Virtual Machine. However, the memory and microprocessor requirements for these nodes is elevate and not adequate for low resources nodes, as they require 32-bit processors with more than 256KB of RAM.

Leguay et al. (2008) propose a novel protocol stack that brings the benefits of Service-Oriented Architectures into nodes with low resources avoiding the overhead introduced by standards based on XML. This research includes an implementation scenario using ZigBee nodes with limited memory resources. Even though the implementation of WSN-SOA is multilayered, the WSN-SOA gateways depend on OSGi and the use of Java Virtual Machines.

Nevertheless, these developments do not consider the necessity of minimizing the overload of the services on the devices. In contrast, SYLPH allows the services to be directly embedded in the WSN nodes and invoked from other nodes either in the same network or another network connected to the former. It also focuses specifically on using devices with small resources to save CPU time, memory size and energy consumption. SYLPH is presented in detail in the following section.

THE SYLPH PLATFORM

The *Services laYers over Light PHysical devices* (SYLPH) platform follows a SOA model (Lyytinen & Yoo, 2002) for integrating heterogeneous WSNs in AmI-based systems. SYLPH covers aspects relative to services such as registration, discovering and addressing. Additionally, a node can invoke functionalities offered by any other node in the system, regardless of whether they are in the same WSN or not. Some nodes in the system can integrate services directories for distributing registration and discovering services. Node registration is done in the corresponding WSN (i.e., specific network) and service registration is maintained by multiple services directories. Thus, the process of connecting new nodes to the system is performed in a dynamic way. A node can know about the existence of other nodes and the services they offer. Therefore, it can directly communicate with other nodes to perform a specific service. A SOA model was chosen because architectures based on this model are asynchronous and non-dependent on context (i.e., previous states of the system) (Lyytinen & Yoo, 2002). Thus, devices working on them do not continuously take up processing time, consume less energy, and are free

to perform other tasks. SYLPH allows services to work in a distributed way and does not depend on the lower stack layers related to the WSN formation (i.e., network layer) or the radio transmission among the nodes that form part of the network (i.e., data link and physical layers). The services can be executed from multiple wireless devices. Given that neither developers nor users have to worry about what kind of technology each node in the system uses, the experience is transparent for everybody involved. This facilitates the inclusion of context-aware capabilities into AmI-based systems because developers can dynamically integrate and remove nodes on demand.

As shown in Figure 1, SYLPH implements an organization based on a stack of layers (Sarangapani, 2007). Each layer in one node communicates with its peer in another node through an established protocol. In addition, each layer offers specific functionalities to the immediately upper layer in the stack. These functionalities are usually called *interlayer services*, which must not be confused with the services invoked from node to node. These *interlayer services* are abstract functions and independent of the implementation of the platform. The SYLPH layers are added over the existent application layer of each WSN

Figure 1. Basic schema of the SYLPH platform

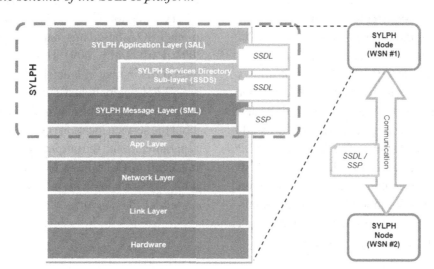

stack, allowing the platform to be reutilized over different technologies. The structure of SYLPH will now be described.

SYLPH Message Layer (SML): The SML offers the upper layers the possibility of sending asynchronous messages between two nodes through the SYLPH Services Protocol (SSP). These messages specify the origin and target nodes and the service invocation in a SYLPH Services Definition Language (SSDL) format. The SSDL describes the service itself and the parameters to be invoked. This SML not only transports the services invocations over the network, but also the services registration and search functions.

SYLPH Application Layer (SAL): The SAL allows different nodes to directly communicate with each other using SSDL requests and responses that will be delivered in encapsulated SML messages following the SSP. The SAL implements the service code (*i.e.*, firmware) from within each node, allowing each one to communicate with the SYLPH platform and invoke services located in other nodes. Moreover, there are other *interlayer services* for registering services or finding services offered by other nodes. In fact, these *interlayer services* for registering and searching services call other *interlayer services* offered by the SYLPH Services Directory Sub-layer (SDS). Therefore, the SAL can use the *interlayer services* of the SML either directly or through the SDS.

SYLPH Services Protocol (SSP): The SSP is the internetworking protocol of the SYLPH platform. SSP has functionalities similar to those of the Internet Protocol (IP). That is, it allows sending packets of data from one node to another node regardless of the WSN to which each one belongs. Every node has a unique SSP 32-bit address in the SYLPH network. Therefore, a SSP packet includes a header that describes the SSP addresses of the origin node and the destination node, as well as information for managing transmissions that involve multiple SSP packets (*i.e.*, number of SSP packet and remaining bytes).

SYLPH Services Definition Language (SSDL): The SSDL is the IDL (Interface Definition Language) used by SYLPH. Unlike other IDLs such as WSDL (Web Services Definition Language) (Cerami, 2002), SSDL does not use as many intermediate separating tags, and the order of its elements is fixed. SSDL has been specifically designed to work with limited computational resources nodes. Nodes can request the SSDS for the location of services and their specifications using SSDL.

SYLPH Services Directory Sub-layer (SSDS): The SSDS creates dynamical services tables to locate and register services in the network. A node that stores and maintains services tables is called SYLPH Directory Node (SDN). These tables are made up of a list of services entries, each of which includes the description of a service in SSDL format and the SSP address of the node that offers the service. In addition, each entry stores additional information about the service whose location and description is maintained in the network. Such information includes, for instance, a Quality of Service (QoS) rate and the last time the SDN checked if the service was available. A node in the network can make a request to the SDN to know the location (*i.e.*, network address) of a certain service. Requests are packed in SML messages and must follow the SSP. The SSDS is also used by the SAL when registering a new service.

The behavior of SYLPH is essentially similar to other SOA-based approaches (Malatras et al., 2008; Park et al., 2009). However, SYLPH has several distinctive characteristics. The first step in SYLPH begins when a node registers a new service on a SDN. The new node informs the SDN about the service location (i.e., network address), its parameters and the output values returned after its execution. Once the service has been registered in the SDN, it can be invoked by any other node in the SYLPH network.

SYLPH Basic Operation Example

The following example describes the use of SYLPH to define a new service. There is a defined service called sendRespirationData. This service collects vital signs by sensing data, which is then stored in a node that is connected to a personal computer that acts as another node in the SYLPH network. This service can be invoked by an air pressure sensor node for sending respiration data from a user to the personal computer. When a new respiration sensing node joins the SYLPH network, it looks for a SDN to find a service with the same characteristics to which it can sends the respiration data. The SSDS informs the sensor node of the network address. Hence, the sensor node periodically invokes this service, which informs the system about the respiration data. The following text represents the SSDL syntax used by developers to define this service in the node's firmware:

```
service sendRespirationData {
  input {
   string units;
   float pressure;
  };
  output {
   boolean status;
  };
};
```

After utilizing the SDDL to specify the service, developers translate definitions to specific code for the target language (e.g., C or nesC) and the microcontroller where the service will be executed. When the node registers its service in a SDN, the messages are transformed into an array of bytes which describes the service and how to invoke it from other nodes. Figure 2 shows the description of SSP (a) and SSDL (b) headers, as well as the frames involved in the sendRespirationData service definition (c), invocation (d) and response (e) when transmitted over the SSP. When a node

requests a SDN for the service definition, the SDN responds with a frame that describes the service identification, the network address of the node that stores the service, the QoS offered by the service and the definition of the input and output parameters. The frame has a SSDL header which specifies the kind of the SSDL frame (i.e., registration, definition, invocation or response), the origin and destination end-points in each node and information about the kind of QoS required by the origin node. There are *marks* to denote the input and the output parameters. Figure 2c provides an example of such kind of frame for the sendRespirationData service. Once the invoker node knows the service definition, it can make a request to the service by sending a SSP frame to the node that stores the service. This frame (Figure 2d) does not need *marks* to separate the parameters because the input parameters must follow a specific order. However, a *string end mark* must be used to know where the string-type parameter ends. Thus, the SSDL combines ease of parsing with flexibility in the type and size of the utilized parameters. The SSP header includes the target node SSP address. Finally, there is only an output parameter in the response frame (Figure 2e).

Since the aim of the platform to be as distributed as possible, it is feasible for there to be more than one SDN in the same network, so that there may be redundancy or services organized in different directories. The mechanism for discovering new services starts when a node registers itself in the SYLPH network. Then, it sends a broadcast SML message to search for existing SDNs. After receiving the broadcast message, each active SDN responds with a SML message informing the new node of its address and its directory parameters. An example of a directory parameter is whether each SDN periodically broadcasts its address and directory parameters, or if it is the rest of the nodes that must periodically poll it. After this, the new node is able to communicate with the SDNs to either obtain the list of services available in the network or register its own services. When a new

Figure 2. SSP and SSDL headers and examples of SSDL frames over SSP

1 byte	2 bytes	2 bytes	1 byte	2 bytes	1 byte	1 byte
Version	Origin Address	Destination Address	Packet ID	Fragment Control	Packet Length	Flags

a) SSP Header

1 byte	2 bytes	2 bytes	1 byte	1 byte	1 byte
Control Byte	Origin End-point	Destination End-Point	Required QoS	Sequence Number	Reserved

b) SSDL Header

10 bytes	8 bytes	2 bytes	2 bytes	1 byte	1 byte	1 byte	1 byte	1 byte
SSP Header	SSDL Header	Service ID	Node ID	*String Mark*	*Float Mark*	*Outputs Mark*	*Boolean Mark*	SSP Trailer

c) SSDL over SSP `sendRespirationData` service definition

10 bytes	8 bytes	2 bytes	4 bytes	1 byte	4 bytes	1 byte
SSP Header	SSDL Header	Service ID	*Units*	*Str. End Mark*	*Pressure*	SSP Trailer

d) SSDL over SSP `sendRespirationData` service invocation

10 bytes	8 bytes	1 byte	1 byte
SSP Header	SSDL Header	*Status*	SSP Trailer

e) SSDL over SSP `sendRespirationData` service response

SDN registers itself on the network, it sends a broadcast message to announce itself as SDN to the rest of the nodes. Then, the existing SDNs store the information on their SSDS entries lists and inform the new node its role as SDN. Any node in the network can not only offer or invoke services, but also perform as a SDN to provide services descriptions to other network nodes.

A node in a specific type of WSN (e.g., ZigBee) can directly communicate with a node in another type of WSN (e.g., Bluetooth). Therefore, several heterogeneous WSNs can be interconnected through a SYLPH Gateway. A SYLPH Gateway is a device with several hardware network interfaces (e.g., a Wi-Fi network card), each of which is connected to a distinct WSN. As an IP gateway a SYLPH Gateway does not need to implement the layers over the SML. The SYLPH Gateway stores routing tables for forwarding SSP packets among the different WSNs with which it is interconnected. The information transported in the SSP header is enough to route the packets to the corresponding WSN. If several WSNs belong to the SYLPH network, there is no difference between invoking a service stored in a node in the same WSN or in a node from a different WSN. For example, if an origin node invokes a service stored in a destination node located in a different WSN, the origin node looks for the service in a SDN present in the WSN to which it belongs. In fact, the entry stored in the services table of that SDN points to the SSP address of the SYLPH Gateway. When the origin node invokes the service in the destination node, the SYLPH Gateway forwards the call message to the destination node through its hardware interface connected to the WSN where the destination node is located.

SYLPH IMPLEMENTATION SCENARIO

In order to test the SYLPH platform and its feasibility in AmI systems, we deployed a distributed WSN infrastructure with SYLPH running over it. The infrastructure consists of two WSNs which obtain information about users and the environment automatically.

First of all a network of ZigBee nodes was deployed. These devices obtain information about the environment (e.g. smoke, temperature, etc.) and react to changes (e.g. light dimmers and fire alarms). Each ZigBee node includes an 8-bit RISC (Atmel ATmega 1281) microcontroller with 8KB of RAM, 4KB of EEPROM and 128KB of Flash memory and an IEEE 802.15.4/ZigBee 2.4GHz transceiver (Atmel AT86RF230). These devices, called n-Core Sirius-A, have both 2.4GHz and 868/915MHz versions and have several communication ports (GPIO, ADC, I2C and UART through USB or DB-9 RS-232) to connect to distinct devices, including almost every kind of sensors and actuators (Nebusens, 2011). Additionally, a network of biomedical Bluetooth sensors was deployed to monitor the users' vital signs. These sensors are placed over the users' body. Biomedical sensors allow data about the patient's vital signs to be acquired continuously. Each user carries an Electrocardiogram monitor, an air pressure sensor acting as respiration monitor, and a triaxial accelerometer for detecting falls. These Bluetooth nodes use a CSR BlueCore4 chip that includes a RISC microcontroller with 48KB of

RAM. All ZigBee and Bluetooth nodes can offer and invoke services within the network. These devices were selected because we intend to integrate them in future projects. A workstation acts as a ZigBee coordinator and is also the master node of the Bluetooth network, which is formed by the biomedical sensors as slave nodes. The Bluetooth network is, in fact, a Bluetooth scatternet (Ilyas & Dorf, 2003), as described before. This way, each slave node in the main Bluetooth piconet acts at the same time as a slave node in each Bluetooth piconet carried by each patient. Thus, each patient carries a Bluetooth piconet with a master acting as network coordinator, a slave node to interconnect with the main Bluetooth piconet and other slave nodes acting as biomedical sensors. In addition, the workstation works as a SYLPH Gateway, interconnecting both WSNs: the ZigBee automation network and the Bluetooth scatternet of biomedical sensors. The topology of this ZigBee-Bluetooth hybrid SYLPH network is depicted in Figure 3.

We have also developed an application for monitoring the state and operation of the SYLPH network. A screenshot of the monitoring application is shown in Figure 4. This application

Figure 3. Topology of the ZigBee-Bluetooth hybrid SYLPH network used in the implementation scenario

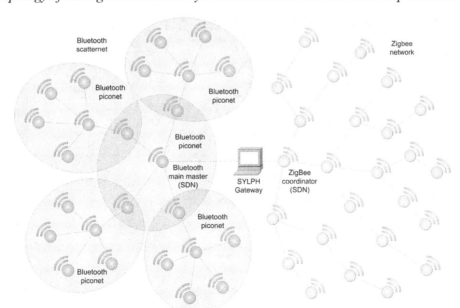

monitors all the traffic (i.e., service invocations, responses, registrations or searches) in the SYLPH network. It is necessary for the nodes to operate in *debug* mode, so that every time a node invokes a service it also invokes a monitoring service on a node connected to a computer (e.g., via a USB port). The node gathers all the invocations and forwards them to the monitoring application running on the computer. The same process is done for service responses, searches and registrations. The monitoring application makes it possible to observe when a node is searching for a certain service in the network, the services offered by the nodes, and the contents of the SSDS entries tables stored in the SDNs.

Several experiments were carried out to evaluate the performance of SYLPH, mainly to test how it handled the network formation and the services registration. The first experiment consisted of trying to form a ZigBee WSN using SYLPH. The network was made up of 50 ZigBee nodes, one acting as ZigBee coordinator and the rest as ZigBee routers. The ZigBee nodes were distributed in a mesh topology network, with less than 10 meters between adjacent routers. Each

time the ZigBee network was formed, nodes were powered on different random times, so that the logical network topology was different each time. However, there were some constraints: the maximum depth of the network (i.e., the maximum number of hops between the coordinator and any node in the network) was 5, the maximum number of neighbors of any node was 8 and the maximum number of children of any node in the network was also 8. Each time the ZigBee network was formed, the SYLPH platform was started over it with a ZigBee coordinator and a ZigBee router acting as SDNs and the other 48 ZigBee routers acting as SYLPH nodes. Each node was instructed to try to register one service on each SDN after joining the network. This experiment was run 50 times in order to measure the success ratio of the network formation and the services registration. The second experiment consisted of a dual SYLPH network made up of one 25-node ZigBee network and another 25-node Bluetooth scatternet, both of them interconnected through a SYLPH Gateway, in this case a computer. The topology of this ZigBee-Bluetooth hybrid network is the same as depicted in Figure 3 for the imple-

Figure 4. SYLPH's monitoring application GUI

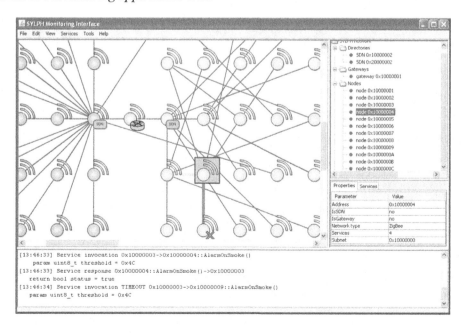

mentation scenario. The 25-node ZigBee network had similar network characteristics as in the first experiment: 10 meters as maximum between adjacent nodes (being all of them ZigBee routers except for the coordinator), 8 hops maximum depth network, 8 neighbors maximum for any node and 8 children maximum for any node. This way, the ZigBee network topology was different each time it was formed as in the first experiment. In the other hand, the Bluetooth network had a static topology formed by 5 Bluetooth piconets. Specifically, one of these piconets acted as the *main* piconet. The master of the main piconet (i.e., the main Bluetooth master) was also the node that interconnected the Bluetooth scatternet with the ZigBee network through the computer acting as SYLPH Gateway. Moreover, the 4 slaves nodes in the main piconet were also slave nodes each of them in one of the other four Bluetooth piconets. These other piconets had each of them 5 nodes: a master node, a slave node being also slave in the main piconet and 4 more slave nodes. There were also two SDNs in this experiment, one in each WSN (i.e., a SDN in the ZigBee network and another one in the Bluetooth network).

In both experiments the monitoring application was used to verify the network formation and the nodes and services registration. In the first experiment, the success ratio of network formation reached 96% while the success ratio for registration of services was 97.8%. In the

second experiment, the success ratios were 84% and 98.5% respectively. These results, shown on Figure 5, demonstrate that the inclusion of the SYLPH Gateway makes the formation of the whole SYLPH network (a difference of 12%) much harder. However, once the network is successfully formed, there is a slight difference of 0.3% in the service registration mechanism.

Two additional experiments were done using the SYLPH networks from the two first experiments. These experiments were run 50 times to calculate average measurements. In this case, the goal was to evaluate the performance of the services searches, invocations and responses in homogeneous and heterogeneous SYLPH networks. Once each network was completely formed and all the services were correctly registered, each node in the network was instructed to search all the registered services in the SDNs and then invoke each one of them once. Three factors were measured: the SDN query success ratio (i.e., the number of times the SDN answers correctly to the service searches from the nodes with respect to the total number of service searches done), the service invocation success ratio and the service response success ratio. As in the first two experiments previously described, the monitoring application was used to obtain these measurements. In the ZigBee network, the SDN query success ratio was 98.4%, the service invocation success ratio was 99.1% and the service response

Figure 5. Comparative of network formation and service registration success ratios in only-ZigBee network and ZigBee-Bluetooth hybrid network

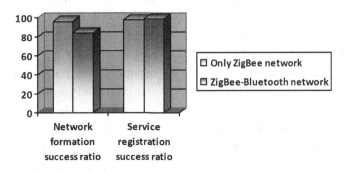

Figure 6. Comparative of SDN query, service invocation and service response success ratios in only-ZigBee network and ZigBee-Bluetooth hybrid network

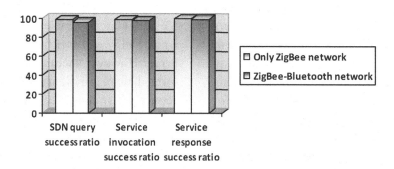

success was 99.3%. In the hybrid SYLPH network the results were 95.6%, 97.3% and 98.9%, respectively. These results are shown on Figure 6. It is possible to observe how the introduction of the SYLPH Gateway slightly affects the performance of the services searches, invocations and responses.

RESULTS AND CONCLUSION

The *Services laYers over Light PHysical devices* (SYPLH) platform presented in this paper allows wireless devices from different technologies to work together in a distributed way. These devices do not require large memory chips or fast microprocessors to exploit their functionalities. The SYLPH model was designed to be implemented on AmI-based systems. However, it can be used by any kind of complex systems as it is capable of integrating almost any functionality desired. Because the platform acts as an interpreter, the users can run services that are programmed over virtually any device, but must follow the communication protocol that all services incorporate. Services can communicate in a distributed way, even from devices with reduced computational resources. SYLPH also allows services or devices to start or stop separately, without affecting the other resources. SYLPH nodes can communicate among themselves regardless of the technology or

the programming language they use. Therefore, SYLPH-based systems are flexible and scalable and eliminate the need to use overcharged centralized nodes. In addition, sharing resources is easy and the redundancy of the services makes the systems more stable.

In conclusion we can say that although SYLPH is still under development, preliminary results demonstrate the feasibility of integrating SYLPH in AmI systems and reducing the implementation costs in terms of development and infrastructure support. The distributed approach of SYLPH makes it possible to add new components in execution time. In this respect, this model takes the design of AmI systems one step further. It is important to mention that although SYLPH was initially designed to be implemented on wireless technologies, it may be used on wired technologies as well. Even though SYLPH does not solve all the difficulties that may arise when programming firmware on embedded devices, the implementation stage is easier, especially when adding or removing nodes and functionalities dynamically.

Future work consists of improving the overall performance of the platform, especially in the network formation and the SYLPH Gateways. We also plan to add more automation and biomedical sensors and implement SYLPH in more scenarios, especially in systems already developed by the BISITE Research Group. Plans are being made to include sensors to measure ambient humidity and gas detectors. Likewise, we are expecting to add electro-dermal sensors to track the users' cognitive activity. Other planned biomedical sensors include peripheral body temperature, and surface Electromyography sensors to monitor muscle activity, while the monitor interface will be able to inject traffic in the network (e.g., invoking some service in some node from the computer) and the automatic generation of statistics (e.g., service denials).

ACKNOWLEDGMENT

This work has been supported by the Spanish Ministry of Science and Technology project TIN2006-14630-C03-03.

REFERENCES

Aarts, E. H., & Encarnação, J. L. (2006). *True visions: The emergence of ambient intelligence* (1st ed.). New York, NY: Springer.

Avilés-López, E., & García-Macías, J. (2009). TinySOA: A service-oriented architecture for wireless sensor networks. *Service Oriented Computing and Applications*, *3*(2), 99–108. doi:10.1007/s11761-009-0043-x

Baronti, P., Pillai, P., Chook, V. W. C., Chessa, S., Gotta, A., & Hu, Y. F. (2007). Wireless sensor networks: A survey on the state of the art and the 802.15.4 and ZigBee standards. *Computer Communications*, *30*(7), 1655–1695. doi:10.1016/j.comcom.2006.12.020

Cañete, E., Chen, J., Díaz, M., Llopis, L., & Rubio, B. (2011). A service-oriented approach to facilitate WSAN application development. *Ad Hoc Networks*, *9*(3), 430–452. doi:10.1016/j.adhoc.2010.08.022

Cerami, E. (2002). *Web services essentials: Distributed applications with XML-RPC, SOAP, UDDI & WSDL* (1st ed.). Sebastopol, CA: O'Reilly Media.

Chen, M., Gonzalez, S., & Leung, V. C. (2007). Applications and design issues for mobile agents in wireless sensor networks. *IEEE Wireless Communications*, *14*(6), 20–26. doi:10.1109/MWC.2007.4407223

Cho, J., Shim, Y., Kwon, T., & Choi, Y. (2007). SARIF: A novel framework for integrating wireless sensor and RFID networks. *IEEE Wireless Communications*, *14*(6), 50–56. doi:10.1109/MWC.2007.4407227

Corchado, J. M., Bajo, J., Paz, Y. D., & Tapia, D. I. (2008). Intelligent environment for monitoring Alzheimer patients, agent technology for health care. *Decision Support Systems*, *44*(2), 382–396. doi:10.1016/j.dss.2007.04.008

Cuomo, F., Luna, S. D., Monaco, U., & Melodia, T. (2007). Routing in ZigBee: Benefits from exploiting the IEEE 802.15.4 association tree. In *Proceedings of the IEEE International Conference on Communications* (pp. 3271-3276).

Dey, A. K., Abowd, G. D., & Salber, D. (2001). A conceptual framework and a toolkit for supporting the rapid prototyping of context-aware applications. *Human-Computer Interaction*, *16*(2), 97–166. doi:10.1207/S15327051HCI16234_02

Huang, Y., & Pang, A. (2007). A comprehensive study of low-power operation in IEEE 802.15.4. In *Proceedings of the 10th ACM Symposium on Modeling, analysis, and Simulation of Wireless and Mobile Systems*, Chania, Crete Island, Greece (pp. 405-408).

Ilyas, M., & Dorf, R. C. (Eds.). (2003). *The handbook of ad hoc wireless networks*. Boca Raton, FL: CRC Press.

Jayaputera, G. T., Zaslavsky, A., & Loke, S. W. (2007). Enabling run-time composition and support for heterogeneous pervasive multi-agent systems. *Journal of Systems and Software*, *80*(12), 2039–2062. doi:10.1016/j.jss.2007.03.013

Leguay, J., Lopez-Ramos, M., Jean-Marie, K., & Conan, V. (2008). An efficient service oriented architecture for heterogeneous and dynamic wireless sensor networks. In *Proceedings of the 33rd IEEE Conference on Local Computer Networks* (pp. 740-747).

Lyytinen, K., & Yoo, Y. (2002). Introduction. *Communications of the ACM*, *45*(12), 62–65. doi:10.1145/585597.585616

Malatras, A., Asgari, A., Baugé, T., & Irons, M. (2008). A service-oriented architecture for building services integration. *Journal of Facilities Management*, *6*(2), 132–151. doi:10.1108/14725960810872659

Marin-Perianu, M., Meratnia, N., Havinga, P., de Souza, L., Muller, J., & Spiess, P. (2007). Decentralized enterprise systems: A multiplatform wireless sensor network approach. *IEEE Wireless Communications*, *14*(6), 57–66. doi:10.1109/MWC.2007.4407228

Mukherjee, S., Aarts, E., Roovers, R., Widdershoven, F., & Ouwerkerk, M. (2006). *Amiware: Hardware technology drivers of ambient intelligence*. New York, NY: Springer. doi:10.1007/1-4020-4198-5

Nebusens. (2011). *n-Core: A faster and easier way to create wireless sensor networks*. Retrieved from http://www.n-core.info

Park, K.-L., Yoon, U., & Kim, S.-D. (2009). Personalized service discovery in ubiquitous computing environments. *IEEE Pervasive Computing / IEEE Computer Society [and] IEEE Communications Society*, *8*(1), 58–65. doi:10.1109/MPRV.2009.12

Peng, L., Wu, L., & Zeng, J. Z. (2008). Research on the service-oriented solution for integrating WSN with grid. *Journal of Computer Applications*, *28*, 1861–1865. doi:10.3724/SP.J.1087.2008.01861

Prinsloo, J. M., Schulz, C. L., Kourie, D. G., Theunissen, W. H. M., Strauss, T., Heever, R. V. D., et al. (2006). A service oriented architecture for wireless sensor and actor network applications. In *Proceedings of the Annual Research Conference of the South African Institute of Computer Scientists and Information Technologists on IT research in Developing Countries*, Somerset West, South Africa (pp. 145-154).

Sarangapani, J. (2007). *Wireless ad hoc and sensor networks: Protocols, performance, and control* (1st ed.). Boca Raton, FL: CRC Press.

Schramm, P., Naroska, E., Resch, P., Platte, J., Linde, H., Stromberg, G., & Sturm, T. (2004). A service gateway for networked sensor systems. *IEEE Pervasive Computing / IEEE Computer Society [and] IEEE Communications Society*, *3*(1), 66–74. doi:10.1109/MPRV.2004.1269133

Singh, C. K., Kumar, A., & Ameer, P. M. (2008). Performance evaluation of an IEEE 802.15.4 sensor network with a star topology. *Wireless Networks*, *14*(4), 543–568. doi:10.1007/s11276-007-0043-8

Song, E. Y., & Lee, K. B. (2008). STWS: A unified web service for IEEE 1451 smart transducers. *IEEE Transactions on Instrumentation and Measurement*, *57*(8), 1749–1756. doi:10.1109/TIM.2008.925732

This work was previously published in the International Journal of Ambient Computing and Intelligence, Volume 3, Issue 2, edited by Kevin Curran, pp. 1-15, copyright 2011 by IGI Publishing (an imprint of IGI Global).

Chapter 8
The Role of Augmented Reality within Ambient Intelligence

Kevin Curran
University of Ulster, UK

Denis McFadden
University of Ulster, UK

Ryan Devlin
University of Ulster, UK

ABSTRACT

An Augmented Reality (AR) is a technology which provides the user with a real time 3D enhanced perception of a physical environment with addition virtual elements—either virtual scenery, information regarding surroundings, other contextual information—and is also capable of hiding or replacing real structures. With Augmented Reality applications becoming more advanced, the ways the technology can be viably used is increasing. Augmented Reality has been used for gaming several times with varying results. AR systems are seen by some as an important part of the ambient intelligence landscape. Therefore, the authors present several types of augmentation applications of AR in the domestic, industrial, scientific, medicinal, and military sectors which may benefit future ambient intelligent systems.

1. INTRODUCTION

Ambient intelligence is a human interface metaphor referring to the environment of computing which is aware and responsive to the presence of human interaction. The aim is to place great emphasis on the aspect of being user friendly and efficient and provide support for human interaction. We are still striving for a future world where

DOI: 10.4018/978-1-4666-2041-4.ch008

we will be surrounded by intelligent interfaces that are to be placed in everyday objects. These objects will then be able to recognise but also respond invisibly to the presence of people. The interaction between the technology and the users should be natural (Aarts & Marzano, 2003; Curran, 2009). It also aims to create a system that will be able to recognise all the different scents that are in the environment.

In fact, one can argue that the holy grail of the mobile Augmented Reality (AR) industry is to find a method of delivering the right information to a user before the user needs it, and without the user having to search for it (ReadWriteWeb, 2009). The Ambient Intelligence concept builds upon ubiquitous computing and user-centric design and this paper seeks to provide a snapshot of aspects of modern Augmented Reality systems which may play important roles in the ambient computing landscapes of tomorrow. Augmented Reality systems provide contextual information to the user such as the head mounted display within a modern cockpit, by allowing the pilot firstly to see reality through the glass window then overlaying information regarding plane speed, plane trajectory and any relevant information about the current target or objectives. This process of overlaying virtual information on top of reality is the essence of AR and as technology progresses so too will the quality and functionality of these devices. It has been used more recently in the creation of car maintenance visual guides. By overlaying a virtual component and demonstrating to the user how to manipulate the counterpart physical component. The implementation of such AR applications would drastically reduce the level of knowledge required to deal with complex tasks from engineering to surgery (Zhou et al., 2008; Holden, 2011).

Augmented Reality, as a label, is credited to Tom Caudell, who coined the term when he was working at Boeing in 1992 (King, 2009). Caudell was involved in the development of one of the first AR systems; whereby users would be able to follow the installation of complex wiring looms in Boeing aircraft using a head worn device that would allow the engineers to see wiring diagrams 'projected' onto their field of vision as they worked. This significantly increased productivity and accuracy as the installations progressed without the need for engineers to constantly move back and forth between the wiring diagrams and the work location. It is thought that the first Augmented Reality (AR) system used simple wire-frame graphics, and a cumbersome head mounted display (HMD) and

was first demonstrated in 1968. The HMD was so heavy that had to be suspended from the ceiling. The system was designed by Ivan Sutherland in Harvard University (Cawood & Fiala, 1998). Augmented reality describes the way in which someone's perception of the real world, and the extraction of information from that perception by their senses, can be augmented to provide more information than can be garnered by those senses alone. All sensory input of the 'real-world' can be augmented in one way or another:

- **Sight:** Something as simple as the added graphics on a sports broadcast showing on-screen banners with scores and statistics to more sophisticated displays used in commercial and military aircraft.
- **Haptic:** Games controllers that 'rumble' when certain game-play actions take place. Mobile phones that vibrate to let you know they are ringing.
- **Hearing:** The beeping noise that is heard in an automobile when reversing, to warn the driver that they are approaching an object behind.
- **Smell:** An example being the 'Digilog' Book whose development is currently under way at Culture Technology Institute at GIST (Singer, 2010) in which the user smells scents based on the storyline.
- **Taste:** A Meta Cookie (Wilkins, 2010), has been created by researchers at the University of Tokyo, where an otherwise tasteless cookie is given 'virtual' flavour.

The possibility of group contribution areas where groups of users can interact in a shared Mixed Reality space could lead to future workspace been more useable as working environments even with participants been located remotely. When dealing with AR systems the technical requirements will be determined by the end functionality required, but most AR applications will require the tracking of real time locations and objects, 6 degrees of freedom allowing the user to move freely along 3 axis, good quality virtual elements well aligned within reality and a reliable refresh rate.

It is straightforward to define a generic Mixed Reality (MR) environment as one in which real world and virtual world objects are presented together within a single display, that is, anywhere between the extrema of the RV continuum (Milgram & Kishino, 1994). The continuum demonstrates that there are separate Real and Virtual Environments on either ends and as they blend together become a Mixed Reality (Figure 1). Augmented Reality and Augmented Virtuality are the Mixed Realities, AR primarily consists of a view of reality enhanced with virtual elements whereas AV is comprised largely of virtual elements with some features used from reality.

In this paper, we discuss the technologies used for AR, such as methods and approaches to tagging the environment. We also look at the use of the 'Magic Mirror' method of AR display, as opposed to the Magic Lens approach and advances in technology that will, for instance, mean an increased use of heads-up type displays (HUD). We discuss advances made in hardware relating to the processing power and capacity of devices used to enable AR as well as advances in sensory apparatus used to gather the additional information that is presented to the end user of any system. We keep in mind that many of the applications highlighted here could be ported to the ambient intelligence field with relative ease.

2. AUGMENTED REALITY TECHNOLOGY

The technological demands for AR are much higher than for virtual environments or VR, which is why the field of AR took longer to mature than that of VR (Van Krevelen & Poelman, 2010). The technical functions needed to provide a suitable platform for AR systems are based around a few principle capabilities. They must have the ability to read in environmental data via camera or other input while tracking the location of the user updating the virtual elements according alteration in view angle or direction. They need to provide the user with a view of the physical reality using Optical See-through, Video See-through or Projection based technology. GPS and accelerometers can be utilised in the determination of the user's location in context of the real and virtual elements around them as an aid to calculating the alignment of virtual objects to real world space. Depending on the required utility of an AR application, a specific set of different technologies will prove more compatible than others.

Figure 2 shows the release of AR applications by time and brand and measuring the search requests received for Augmented Reality through monitoring Google Trends. It shows that from before December 08 only two companies had an AR campaign, each of which only had a search volume index of 1. From December 08 there is a rise interest in Augmented Realities peaking in August as 4 new AR applications are released as part of marketing campaigns to further brand awareness. This rise in availability of AR applica-

Figure 1. Simplified representation of RV Continuum (Milgram & Kishino, 1994)

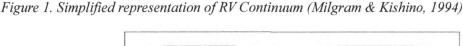
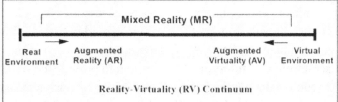

Figure 2. Brand tracking: Augmented reality (KZero Services, 2010)

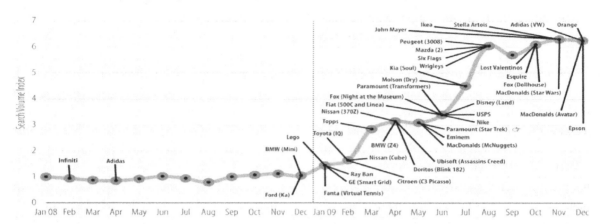

tions was facilitated in part by these companies and their use of the technology in innovative media campaigns but also due to improved computing power, the increased availability of fast wireless internet connections, the growth of social networking websites and growth in people on the web either via mobile devices or computers. AR systems can be split into two main groups depending on the type of visualisation employed for viewing reality either optical or video see-through. Optical see-through allows the user to perceive the physical world directly whereas video see-through blocks out the user's physical view of reality but then streams a video feed from a camera input to the visual output device or head mounted display.

Video See-through are the cheapest and easiest to implement. Since reality is digitised, it is easier to mediate or remove objects from reality. Also, brightness and contrast of virtual objects are matched quite easily with the real environment (Van Krevelen & Poelman, 2010). When turned off, Video See-through will not allow the user to perceive anything at all through the system or device. In contrast, Optical See-through uses optical combiners, such as mirror beam-splitters, to layer the computer generated image on top of the user's view of the environment (Höllerer & Feiner, 2004). Optical see-through is more difficult to implement as it requires the overlaying of virtual components over the users existing vi-

sion of the environment. If the system is turned off, the user will still be able to see through the device to perceive reality. Optical See-through is expected to become more viable as the technology develops. Currently, the majority of AR systems are implemented using a Video See-through display for simplistic culling and location tracking.

2.1. Magic Mirror and Magic Lens

Two common paradigms for methods to display Augmented Reality elements are known as the 'Magic Mirror' and the 'Magic Lens'. The magic mirror is a real-time display where the augmented scene being captured by a video camera is displayed, with an augmentation overlay shown on it as shown in Figure 1. As can be seen from Figure 3, the magic mirror is only suitable for static installations where the user and AR system are in a fixed location. The system above appears unwieldy when compared to modern designs of this type of system even when compared to games consoles such as the Wii and PlayStation. The cards attached to the accessories worn by the user are called the fiducial marker system, fiducial meaning trusted. These tags are used in the real-world part of the system to provide the virtual representation with the ability to render the necessary elements in three dimensions.

Figure 3. Magic mirror using fiducial marker technology

Systems, such as the Wii, with its sensor and controller provide the same sort of functionality using two infrared beams in the sensor to calculate orientation of the controller and inexpensive accelerometers, developed for NASA and the military to calculate the direction and speed of the motion of the user. This new technology is removing the need for the cumbersome marker technology shown in the picture although it is still in use for some applications. One of the newest applications for the Magic Mirror is being used in retail as a mirror! This mirror allows the user to virtually try on clothes or test make-up without actually having to change their clothes or apply and remove make-up time after time (Hickey, 2010).

Augmented Realty using the Magic Lens method is a completely different approach to accessing AR. As opposed to 'looking at' AR enhanced scenes, the magic lens method allows the user to look through an interposed medium, to a real-world image. AR elements displayed on this medium then appear to exist in the real-world image. The actual mechanism can involve a headset with the processing and computing power local to the headset and perhaps even in a mobile configuration, or sitting in front of a transparent screen positioned between user and real-world onto which the AR elements are projected in some form to overlay them onto the real-time image visible through the screen.

The HMD shown in Figure 4 can be used to provide AR elements projected into the environment such as that shown in the example in Figure 3. This example depicts the marker system where the 3Delements of the AR system are positioned using 2D 'fiducial' markers (Figure 5) in the real world. The magic lens is about to take a giant leap forward as the prominent method of access, where the general population is concerned, with the advent of technologies like Organic Light-Emitting Diode displays (OLED), that can be manufactured in thicknesses that produce a transparent and flexible display.

When these OLEDs are integrated with photodiodes on a CMOS substrate, then the possibility of producing glasses that can combine the display and camera functionality used by AR systems becomes a reality. Using glasses such as these to view the world means AR elements and

Figure 4. Schematic of HMD (Caudell & Mizell, 1992)

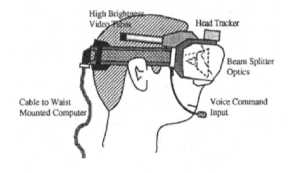

Figure 5. Fiducial markers and the magic lens

information can be shown seamlessly to the wearer based on the real-world image captured and processed in real time (Herold et al., 2008). With the addition of eye tracking technology then the display/camera becomes an interactive way to view content, or access more information through AR simply by the act of the wearer moving their eyes.

2.2. Marker versus Marker-less AR

Simultaneous Localisation and Mapping or SLAM, algorithms are at the cutting edge of development for mapping AR virtualisations onto the real-world. This approach is sounding the death knell for the fiduciary marking approach to the positioning of AR elements onto a view. SLAM, as a technology from the world of robotics, will provide a means of autonomously mapping an unknown environment or location (Bailey and Durrant-Whyte, 2006). SLAM algorithms will be used particularly in the area of mobile AR applications, where SLAM can, in conjunction with GPS and other sensory input, provide a method of discerning the location of the user in any three dimensional space and then provide AR information relevant to this space.

SLAM algorithms for AR applications have been modified as PTAM (parallel tracking and mapping) algorithms and demonstrated in prototypes on mobile handsets such as the iPhone. The phone camera uses the SLAM techniques to 'map' an area, building up an image that can be used in real-time to provide AR functionality (Klien & Murray, 2009). Steps in the PTAM process can be seen in Figure 6 where (a) a map is constructed on a book, (b) map is expanded to encompass 200 points and (c) AR elements are inserted into the scene. Figure 7 shows a purely SLAM application.

Figure 6. PTAM/SLAM iPhone application

Figure 7. Pure SLAM generated visualisation for AR

3. AUGMENTED REALITY APPLICATIONS

Because the very nature of Augmented Realities is the overlaying of additional virtual elements or information the possible uses for the technology are far reaching. There is no specific one area which can boast the most useful application of Augmented Reality since each time it is applied to a new task it will have a different mixture of benefits for the users. Augmented Realities are an ideal method for providing a large quantity of contextual information. Based on this principle the full scale to which AR will become engrained into modern society is hard to gauge, although if advances continue at the current pace AR will be used much more frequently within the next few years. Already there is a diverse selection of corporate marketing campaigns, research studies and applications out there with many more in the design stage all continuing the development and refinement of AR technology and how it is perceived by the public and private sector.

3.1. Augmented Reality in Education

The possibilities of Augmented Reality technology applications for educational purposes range from simple visualisation based learning for younger students to large complex virtual laboratories where real world hardware interacts with the virtual to recreate lab conditions. It could for instance allow the replication of experiments and reactions like that in chemistry but with no element of danger to the user. For further realism the actual simulation could be carried out in a second safe location and the results read back into the AR simulation to validate the computations. By removing the danger of associated with such tasks like operator error or mechanical error it allows a user to become familiar with the 3D visualisation of the activity without any pressure, ensuring when in the real situation they are adequately prepared. Networked laboratory hardware equipment is linkable to virtual learning environments by means of special bidirectional sensor-actuator coupling interfaces. At the moment this seems to be a quite visionary approach. Future laboratories will benefit from further developments in computer simulation technology, mobile computing and sensor/actuator devices enabling connections to be made between real-life phenomena and their virtual representation or continuation (Muller et al., 2007).

3.2. Augmented Reality for Contextual Information and Guidance

Contextual Information is extremely useful to users and as the number of AR applications rise, the industry will learn what AR is most viable for and which standards should be implemented regarding inputs, tracking and visualisation. Cur-rently existing applications on Smartphones allow the user to view tagged locations and information about them. Some are designed to provide the user with recommendations on specific shops, hotels or commercial premises and others can show the activity of nearby social networking users. Combining things such as location, the presence of other people and objects, the actions presently occurring, the user's goals and other situational components, the system discerns the user's "context" and determines how best the subject can maximize efficiency in the performance of particular tasks; in effect, the CM allows a single individual to successfully accomplish the functions of three or more individuals (Cowper & Buerger, 2003). Existing commercial uses of AR applications are mostly centred on the navigation of complex urban environments and rating local restaurants and businesses for others to view. As AR becomes more functional and viable there will be many other contextual displays such as local advertisements and environmental notifications. Through constant internet access and a wide range of virtual information, the user could be informed of changing weather conditions in the vicinity according to local forecasts.

Smartphones allow the user to interact with the Augmented Reality by either the touch screen, physically moving from one location to another can be tracked by GPS, accelerometers, a solid state compass or any additional sensors which could be attached or detached. Next generation games console manufacturers are releasing new input devices which will be AR capable. Another emerging area in AR is Haptic AR, where the user can touch a real object, a virtual object, or a real object augmented with virtual touch. AR with both sensory modalities, i.e., visuo-haptic AR, can create simulations of great realism and immersion, e.g., palpating a virtual tumour inside a real mannequin for medical training, which is not possible in a pure real or virtual environment. Haptic interfaces will allow the user to physically interact with the virtual objects within an

AR environment. This combination of several technological modules as they are developed will continue to improve the usability and functionality of current AR systems. 3D Surround Sound Effects will improve the quality of information available to the user as well as providing a choice to how each user would prefer information either visually or aurally. As experience develops within the computing industry on dealing with Augmented Reality, the first fully AR desktop will allow users to control every process of the computer through gestures and touch. With even more advanced input equipment it may be possible to use overlay virtual keyboards on flat surfaces and track the keys pressed to convert them to digital information.

3.3. Augmented Reality in Medicine

AR is beginning to be used in Medicine as a training aid for medical staff to allow them to improve their skills. In German speaking countries it was found that there was a trend away from natural delivery to caesarean sections. Even with new techniques and medicines the perinatal mortality rate had not improved since 1980. This trend, when coupled with the increased risk to the patients inherent in a caesarean delivery, led to the introduction of an AR system to facilitate the training of medical professionals in the techniques involved (Sielhorst et al., 2004). The goal of the AR system was to reduce the mortality rate by providing training for new doctors, while allowing experienced doctors to refresh their skills and knowledge. The AR simulator provides multimodal AR visualisation. Using audio, Haptic, and visual elements the proposed system consists of a body 'phantom' with a Haptic device representing the infant and software to simulate physiological and biomechanical functions. The system used a stereoscopic headset, and interaction with the phantom is facilitated by the head movements of the user. The student does not have to learn to navigate through the use of a mouse or menu, but can focus attention or bring areas of interest into the field of vision by simple movement of her/his head and looking in the direction of interest. Due to the fact that the scene is modelled internally and externally then the user can see where their instruments are inside the 'phantom' while the skin still in place. This allows them to 'view' the movements and position of the instruments without removing the skin which provides a Haptic element to the AR session.

The Haptic feedback is further enhanced by a force/torque sensor in the head of the baby which allows for interaction with the user and forceps. Software calculations based on the output of these sensors are used to simulate the level of distress and physiological responses of the patients. The software will also provide audio and visual feedback in the form of simulated instrumentation monitoring vital signs and showing various feedback with regard to foetal heart rate, blood pressure and oxygen levels. The tracking of the interaction of the user, the forceps, and the phantom and child, is facilitated by two separate systems as seen in Figure 8. External tracking is accomplished by a use of a stereo camera infra red system. Tracking of the instruments and their effects is carried out by a combination of the torque/force sensors and a called real-time augmentation in medical procedures or (RAMP), which uses retro-reflective markers and an infra-red flash and camera.

Another application for AR in the field of medicine is its use in the treatments of psychological problems such as phobias. The AR system produces an experience that gives the patient a feeling of presence. This reality judgement on the part of the patient allows their phobia to be presented to them in a manner that they perceive as real, while allowing them the tools to overcome the phobia with clinical assistance (Carmen et al., 2005). The system consists of the HMD shown in Figure 9. When worn by the patient, the image captured by a simple fire-wire or USB camera is augmented by the use of a fiducial marker based system whereby three dimensional representations of various insects are overlaid onto their field of

Figure 8. RAMP/ART AR tracking system

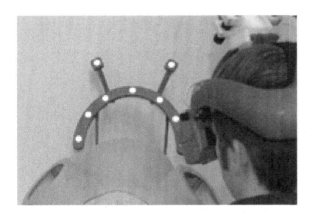

view. The images vary between dead cockroaches, through to static live or moving versions. The patients are then encouraged to either spray, swat, or actually pick up the markers and therefore the representations of the insects. This aversion therapy assists the psychologists in negating or reducing the phobic reaction to the object of the patients fear.

3.4. Augmented Reality and the Military

Augmented Reality for the battlefield soldier is a delicate balance of providing enough relevant information to the individual soldier without causing informational overload whereby the soldier is

Figure 9. HMD used in phobia research

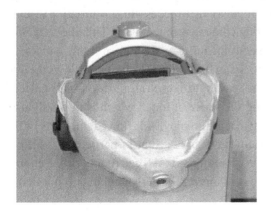

swamped with information to such a degree that he/she is rendered ineffective (Hicks et al., 2009). As part of the US Military's twenty-first Century Land Warrior program - a system called Eyekon attempts to strike this balance by minimising the amount of hardware worn and superfluous information provided. Networked communications provide strategic information that can be displayed using the eyepiece of the soldiers existing weapon in conjunction with a wearable computing system. The provision of a threat level can be represented using icons displayed in perspective, more prominent - more dangerous. The viewfinder of the weapon will, using the software developed for the system, prioritise targets, and guide the soldier between current and next best prospective target using arrows in the sight display, as well as icons and colours that will represent threat levels. The weapons sight is removable and the helmet eyepiece can be used in conjunction with this sight to 'look round corners' thus providing the same AR view to the eyepiece while using the sight as the camera element of the system.

The Eyekon AEDGE system uses three levels of human agents, these agents inputs are combined, or fused into a decision making model which provides the soldier with the best possible information as to the situation they are facing. Figure 10 and Figure 11 show this process as envisioned by a company called Tanagram Partners (Cameron, 2010), funded by the American Defence Advanced Research Projects Agency (DARPA). Outlandish as this scenario may seem, the company involved intends to have a prototype running on an iPhone by the first quarter of next year.

Drones are the future of aerial warfare and AR based control systems are the future of drone operation (Payatagool, 2008). Existing technology used to operate drones is limited and extremely difficult to learn to use, resulting in loss of life and equipment. The defence contractor Raytheon decided to employ games developers to redesign the controls and a wrap-around display of widescreen monitors to provide the operator

Figure 10. Command and control supply strategic information

Figure 11. On site spotter 'paints' a dangerous location using the AR interface

with a 120 degree field of vision. The real-time video feed from the drone is integrated with a digital overlay of buildings and terrain in the area in which the drone is operating. This interactive digital over lay is then combined with information provided about the surroundings, the drone status, and operating environment in a state of the art AR application.

American helicopter pilots are currently in trials of systems to assist them to safely maneuver their helicopters in poor visibility or bad weather. The Tactile Situation Awareness System (TSAS) uses vibrating pads integrated into flight garments to augment the information available to pilots particularly during hover operations. In conditions of poor visibility during hover the pilot can sometimes become disorientated due to the lack of visual cues from the surroundings, especially the attitude, height and relative position of the aircraft. At these times of high stress, the pilot can suffer from 'task saturation' where they simply have too much information to make best use of it all. The TSAS system allows the pilot to know where they are and how the aircraft is operating without having to access this information visually through their instrumentation. This allows them to concentrate more on the task of flying and less on processing flight data. The harness allows the pilot to process flight data on an almost subliminal level using the sense of touch which is normally used only in a minimal way during flight. Tests of this system have shown that in particularly difficult flight conditions, TSAS can reduce the likelihood of loss of aircraft or personnel due to pilot error.

3.5. Augmented Reality and the Automobile Industry

The automobile industry intends to use AR applications to display information in the driver's line-of-sight. Normally the driver would be required to look away from the road to the dashboard instrumentation to see the speed, engine temperature. Manufacturers have begun the process that will eventually lead to the inclusion of AR instrumentation and systems being included in cars that will use software, sensors and display technology that will allow this to take place (Humphries, 2010). The AR application of this information at the present time relies on cameras, various sensors and the car windscreen. General Motors are currently working on applications of this type; a prototype of the 'Enhanced Vision System' is shown in Figure 12.

Sensors include infrared, visual, potentially radar and night vision all look forward and this sensor data is then processed by the system and used to display information as AR elements on the windscreen display. Figure 12 shows a road-sign being highlighted by the system to draw the attention of the driver to perhaps the current speed limit. In-car cameras monitor the driver to see where their attention is focused, and what they are doing so that information can be targeted to the area of the view that is being looked at by the driver (Figure 13). This is also used in order that the relative position of the driver is known by the system. This better enables it to overlay the information on the real-world image in perfect registration with relation to the position of the driver. The sensor data is also used to provide road-edge projection in situations such as fog, or heavy rain, where the edge of the road is overlaid onto the windscreen providing the driver with an indication of the position of the car on the road in difficult driving conditions shown in Figure 14.

Another area that GM and other manufacturers are targeting is 'Enhanced Driver Experience'. Imagine not only a windscreen that provides you satellite navigation but that actually highlights the building that you are navigating towards as shown in Figure 15. This application of AR when combined with an OLED display sandwiched between the laminated windscreen can also be

Figure 13. Face and eye tracking

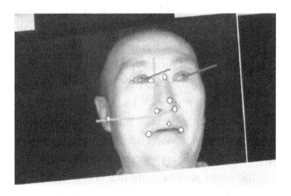

Figure 12. GM augmented reality system

Figure 14. Road edge enhancing in bad weather

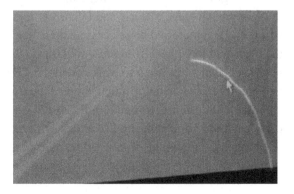

Figure 15. Satellite navigation showing destination

used, with appropriate sensors, to show pedestrians, animals and obstructions to the driver during bad driving conditions improving road safety for both the car driver and those around them.

The design process to manufacture a new car involves the use of prototypes so that designers and engineers can visualise how the new designs look and work together. The prototyping of these components can take from two to several weeks to produce. The costs involved in this process can be prohibitive. AR is being used to remove the need for the initial prototype being produced by the designers (Frund et al., 2004). The design process of most modern cars begins with a common base or chassis and standard components that are common to many manufacturers' models. This common base is placed in the AR arena, and both the arena and base are marked using the fiduciary marking system. The AR elements are created through a 3D visualisation system that `takes original 3D-CAD drawings and projects them in the AR stage to scale and in correct registration. Designers and engineers can then 'see' the parts that have been so represented, through HMD sets that allow them to walk-round the AR vehicle. This facilitates a much more detailed control of the design. Errors and conflicts between parts can lead to instant modifications without resulting in the alteration to real-world prototypes,

but by changes to the CAD drawings then being transferred to the AR element.

Only when the team is satisfied with the completed part or component does the process of building the prototype begin. The time and cost savings to the company are significant. AR is also used in the ergonomic analysis and simulation of the interior and exterior of the vehicle. The accessibility and positioning of pedals, switches and dashboard items can all be simulated. The empty space where the dashboard will be represented via AR is marked and camera systems monitor the head position or pose of the users head so that all the AR elements are produced correctly. The AR elements are again composed from 3D CAD drawings and data. Collaborative design prototypes have also been created for use primarily in the automobile industry. These systems involve multiple users using the system in an interactive way to facilitate the design process and communication between engineers and designers.

One prototype system that has moved on to real-world use involves the use of a desktop turntable that has AR markers placed on its surface. Multiple users can access the system. Local and remote users can, using HMD and networked computers with identical physical layouts on each site, view prototype components displayed in relation to the head position and orientation of individual users. His prototype is constructed from both 2D and 3D CAD drawings processed by the system to provide an AR element updated in real-time as the users change their orientation in respect to the object, and the orientation of the object in relation to the users through use of the turntable.

Users can interact with this AR rendering of the three dimensional automobile component using specially designed 'markers' to highlight areas of the model for discussion or modification (Regebrecht et al., 2006). Figure 16 shows a user point of view of the collaborative design AR system in use. The coloured markers in front of the users can be used to 'mark' the 3D AR representation of the automobile component to highlight areas of interest or debate. The AR system again provides a quicker, more economical and flexible method of prototyping components in a manner that is more integrated with the design process, feeding back directly to the CAD and engineering process. This allows for production of a physical prototype when all concerned; designers and engineers are satisfied that the component is ready.

3.6. Augmented Reality in Everyday Life

SixthSense is a wearable gestural interface that augments the physical world around us with digital information and lets us use natural hand gestures to interact with that information (Mistry & Maes, 2009). Consisting of 'off-the-shelf' components; a camera, pocket projector, mirror and mobile computing device, it is fashioned as a necklace that hangs round the users neck and connects to the computing device in the users pocket. The user can interface with the system using hand gestures that are tracked by the camera using coloured thimble-like covers for finger ends. The display for the system can be any flat surface that is available to the user and can even be used to project AR elements onto the user him/her-self. Figure 17 shows the system being used to dial the users mobile phone using a keypad projected onto their hand. Figure 18 shows the system projected a virtual wristwatch.

The AR wristwatch can be created and destroyed by simple hand-gestures of the system wearer. An example of this system worn in a head-mounted configuration is shown in Figure 19. The user is viewing and interacting with the images projected onto a suitable surface.

The system processes the video data in real time and tracks the finger-end markers or visual tracking fiducials. Several applications have been designed to show the versatility of the prototype, including book reviews being projected onto the cover of a book held by the user while browsing in a book-shop, and information relating to the ecological impact of products being projected onto the packaging of the product based on image recognition. (Mistry & Maes, 2009).

Mobile technology advances, including those demonstrated in the 'Sixth-Sense' prototypes shown in Figures 19 and 20; can be harnessed to the task of mobile gaming. Global positioning, SLAM, powerful computing, miniturised high resolution cameras, and light OLED HMDs, constitute the beginnings of the next-generation in computer gaming. The current headset and backpack wearable computer used to produce a proof-of-concept system 'AR Quake', are shown in Figure 20. AR Quake is based on the popular game by Id Software (Piekarska, 2006). The concept design used a surveying grade GPS-like system that could track user position to 50cm accuracy with 10 updates per second. Combined with magnetic and gyroscopic sensors to track

Figure 16. Collaborative design using AR

Figure 17. Mobile phone using projected keyboard

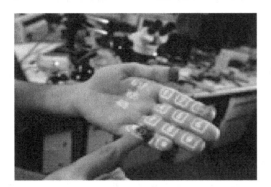

Figure 18. AR Wristwatch projected onto user

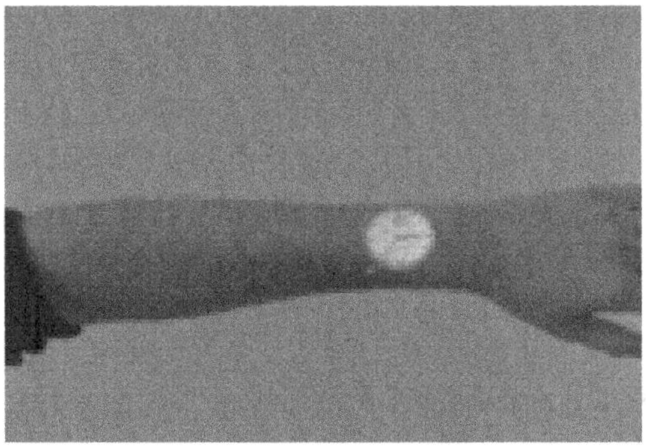

head position and orientation the system provides registration information in order that the overlaid AR elements perform as expected. Monsters and game elements appear super-imposed on the real world through the HMD and can be interacted with as in the standard version of the game; the difference being that the game arena is the real-world.

4. CONCLUSION

Domestic applications of AR in the Sports TV, gaming console, and mobile applications aside, the fact that AR is used widely in industry, medicine, and in the military means that advances in these fields will affect everyone individually and society as a whole. Computing power and display technology have advanced to the point where we

are now in the position that AR is ready to take the next step from research, small scale implementations, and high-end military applications to the mainstream. As the concept of Augmented Realities continues to rise in popularity along with the trends of internet use and multimedia entertainment, then in the future AR may be widespread and used for learning in a group and alone and perhaps for sharing collaborative workspaces.

The state of the art within the area of Augmented Realities is progressing swiftly with new creative and useful applications being developed constantly. While trends promising an increase in portable platforms which are AR enabled there are still a range of issues to deal with some of which will become apparent as the depths of AR are explored thoroughly over the coming years. New hardware technologies such as the iPhone, and Android platforms, with their powerful processors,

Figure 19. System worn in head mounted configuration

Figure 20. HMD used in AR Quake

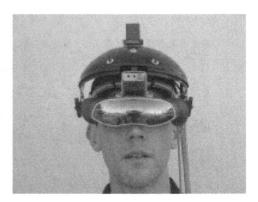

connectivity, and access to positioning systems, when coupled with software technologies such as SLAM and its variants, means that we are on the cusp of a revolution in how we interact with the world and each other.

The impact of Augmented Reality systems within the ambient intelligence field are not yet wholly visible however some aspects are such as the impact that Cloud Computing will have on the technology. Cloud computing will allow the excessive and complex computations required by an AR device to be wirelessly transmitted to a centralised machine dedicated to the task. By alleviating the majority of the computing from the user's device the necessary size will be reduced significantly. This approach could improve upon the Head Mounted Displays reducing the necessary parts to the inputs and outputs, with the calculations being done elsewhere. There are numerous ambient intelligent systems currently implemented which could benefit from such a technology.

REFERENCES

Aarts, E., & Marzano, S. (2003). *The new everyday: Visions of ambient intelligence.* Rotterdam, Netherlands: 010 Publishing.

Bailey, T., & Durrant-Whyte, H. (2006). Simultaneous localization and mapping (SLAM). *IEEE Robotics & Automation Magazine, 13*(3), 108–117. doi:10.1109/MRA.2006.1678144

Cameron, C. (2010). *Military-grade augmented reality could redefine modern warfare.* Retrieved from http://www.readwriteweb.com/archives/military_grade_augmented_reality_could_redefine_modern_warfare.php

Carmen, J. (2005). Using augmented reality to treat phobias. *IEEE Computer Graphics and Applications, 25*(6), 31–37. doi:10.1109/MCG.2005.143

Caudell, T., & Mizell, D. (1992). Augmented reality: An application of heads-up display technology to manual manufacturing processes. In *Proceedings of the IEEE Hawaii International Conference on Systems* (pp. 26-32).

Cawood, S., & Fiala, M. (1998). *Augmented reality – a practical guide.* Raleigh, NC: The Pragmatic Bookshelf.

Cowper, T., & Buerger, M. (2003). Improving our view of the world: Police and augmented reality technology. *FBI Law Enforcement Bulletin, 77*(5).

Curran, K. (2009). Ambient intelligence - the link between the sciences - paving the way where no recommender system has gone before. *International Journal of Ambient Computing and Intelligence, 1*(4), 1–2.

Frund, J., Gausemeier, J., Matysczok, C., & Radkowski, R. (2004, May 26-28). Cooperative design support within automobile advance development using augmented reality technology. In *Proceedings of the 8th International Conference on Computer Supported Cooperative Work in Design* (Vol. 2, pp. 492–497).

Herold, R., Vogel, U., Richter, B., Kreye, D., Reckziegel, S., Scholles, M., et al. (2009, June 20-22). OLED-on-CMOS integration for augmented-reality systems. In *Proceedings of the International Students and Young Scientists Workshop on Photonics and Microsystems* (pp. 19-22).

Hickey, M. (2010). *Virtual mirror – tells you how to look better.* Retrieved from http://news.cnet.com/8301-17938_105-20015260-1.html

Holden, W. (2011). *Mobile augmented reality: Forecasts, applications & opportunity appraisal.* Retrieved from http://www.juniperresearch.com/shop/viewreport.php?id=197

Höllerer, T., & Feiner, S. (2004). Mobile augmented reality. In Karimi, H. A., & Hammad, A. (Eds.), *Telegeoinformatics: Location-based computing and services.* Boca Raton, FL: Taylor & Francis.

http://io9.com/5608335/meta-cookie-can-taste-like-any-cookie-you-want-+-as-long-as-youre-willing-to-wear-the-headgear

Humphries, M. (2010). *GM experimenting with augmented reality in cars.* Retrieved from http://www.geek.com/articles/news/gm-experimenting-with-augmented-reality-in-cars-20100318/

King, R. (2009). *Augmented reality goes mobile.* Retrieved from http://www.businessweek.com/technology/content/nov2009/tc2009112_434755.htm

Klein, G., & Murray, D. (2009). Parallel tracking and mapping on a camera phone. In *Proceedings of the 8th IEEE International Symposium on Mixed and Augmented Reality* (pp. 830-86).

KZero Services. (2010). *Consulting and analytics, augmented reality brand tracking.* Retrieved from http://www.kzero.co.uk/

Milgram, P., & Kishino, K. (1994). A taxonomy of mixed reality visual displays. *Transactions on Information and Systems, 77*(12).

Mistry, P., & Maes, P. (2009). *SixthSense: A wearable gestural interface.* Cambridge, MA: MIT Media Lab.

Müller, D., Bruns, W., Erbe, H., Robben, B., & Yoo, Y. (2007). Mixed reality learning spaces for collaborative experimentation: A challenge for engineering education and training. *International Journal of Online Engineering, 3*(1), 36–42.

Payatagool, C. (2008). *War is Halo.* Retrieved from http://www.telepresenceoptions.com/2008/07/war_is_halo/

Piekarska, P. (2006). *Tinmith AR system, research into mobile outdoor augmented reality.* Retrieved from http://www.tinmith.net/

ReadWriteWeb. (2009). *Augmented reality: A human interface for ambient intelligence.* Retrieved from http://www.readwriteweb.com/archives/augmented_reality_human_interface_for_ambient_intelligence.php

Regenbrecht, H., Baratoff, G., & Wilke, W. (2005). Augmented reality projects in the automotive and aerospace industries. *IEEE Computer Graphics and Applications, 25*(6), 48–56. doi:10.1109/MCG.2005.124

Sielhorst, T., Obst, T., Burgkart, R., Riener, R., & Navab, N. (2004). An augmented reality delivery simulator for medical training. In *Proceedings of the AMI-ARCS/MICCAI Joint International Workshop on Augmented Environments for Medical Imaging* (pp. 11-20).

Singer, J. (2010). *Augmented reality e-books: Mmm, smell the Jumanji.* Retrieved from http://www.fastcompany.com/1597320/augmented-reality-e-books-bringing-jumanji-to-the-freaky-next-level

Van Krevelen, D., & Poelman, R. (2010). A survey of augmented reality technologies, applications and limitations. *International Journal of Virtual Reality, 9*(2), 1–20.

Wilkins, A. (2010). *Meta cookie – can taste like any cookie you want.* Retrieved from.

Zhou, F., Duh, H., & Billinghurst, M. (2008). Trends in augmented reality tracking, interaction and display: A review of ten years of ISMAR. In *Proceedings of the IEEE/ACM International Symposium on Mixed and Augmented Reality* (pp. 193-202).

This work was previously published in the International Journal of Ambient Computing and Intelligence, Volume 3, Issue 2, edited by Kevin Curran, pp. 16-34, copyright 2011 by IGI Publishing (an imprint of IGI Global).

Chapter 9
An Antiwindup Approach to Power Controller Switching in an Ambient Healthcare Network

Michael J. Walsh
University College Cork, Ireland

John Barton
University College Cork, Ireland

Brendan O'Flynn
University College Cork, Ireland

Martin J. Hayes
University of Limerick, Ireland

Cian O'Mathuna
University College Cork, Ireland

Seyed Mohammad Mahdi Alavi
Simon Fraser University, Canada

ABSTRACT

This paper proposes a methodology for improved power controller switching in mobile Body Area Networks operating within the ambient healthcare environment. The work extends Anti-windup and Bumpless transfer results to provide a solution to the ambulatory networking problem that ensures sufficient biometric data can always be regenerated at the base station. The solution thereby guarantees satisfactory quality of service for healthcare providers. Compensation is provided for the nonlinear hardware constraints that are a typical feature of the type of network under consideration and graceful performance degradation in the face of hardware output power saturation is demonstrated, thus conserving network energy in an optimal fashion.

1. INTRODUCTION

Ubiquitous or pervasive Body Area Networks (BANs) and their use in the healthcare application space are now beginning to reach a level of maturity wherein a number of innovative solutions are now at advanced stages of commercial development. Several projects, for instance the Complete Ambient Assisted Living Experiment (CAALYX) (Boulos et al., 2007) and Codeblue (Gao et al., 2008), are now actively promoting advances in technology and infrastructure that facilitate independent living, pre-hospital and in-hospital emergency care and disaster response. New hardware technologies, including a number of state of the art sensor node platforms, (e.g.

DOI: 10.4018/978-1-4666-2041-4.ch009

Tmote, Mica, Micaz and more recently Sentilla), are being adapted for deployment in applications where human wellness maintenance is actively addressed. A number of themes are emerging in this pre-competitive phase of development:

- The quality of the service provided to both the user and to the health care provider is crucial in terms of maximising BAN market penetration.
- Although some guaranteed level of information flow is a clear necessity for service provision factors such as energy consumption, battery life and size are proving to be just as important factors when it comes to increasing the uptake of new services and systems.
- In community health care settings support for some level of ambulatory motion must be provided without any technical concerns about information loss being a factor.
- Some hardware limitations will inevitably be a feature of the BAN devices that are worn by the user. These limitations should have no impact on the quality of service that is provided. In short BAN devices and systems should be Robust, power aware, mobile, and low cost and be readily implementable in a health care environment. This paper illustrates how these challenges can be addressed using recent developments in the area of systems science. In particular it is shown how Anti-Windup (AW) and Bumpless Transfer (BT) techniques can be applied to the design of next generation BANs that can address the aforementioned issues in an optimal fashion. Although the processing of relevant biometric information can consume valuable energy, it is clear that data transmission is the primary constraint on battery life in a BAN and can account for 70-90%

of power usage (Ares et al., 2007). The benefits of transmission power control are obvious when there exists a need for the BAN to remain operational for extended periods of time and to this end a number of wireless network power control algorithms have already been proposed (Walsh et al., 2008; Alavi et al., 2008, Walsh et al., 2009, Alavi et al., 2010, Subramanian et al., 2005, Chen et al., 2006). These schemes have exhibited some success in extending battery lifetime while concurrently providing pre-specified levels of quality of service (QoS). This equates to the provision of sufficient data to reassemble biometric waveforms, (e.g. ECK, EEG, blood oxygen levels, pulse ect.), or to reliably detecting the movement of an elderly person, in an ambient fashion, be they at home or in a care facility.

A. Remark: Practical Measurement of QoS for Dynamic Control

In this work QoS will be taken to mean an accurately tracked received signal strength (RSS) target value thereby guaranteeing a bit error rate that is below a certain predefined threshold level. There exists a body of opinion suggesting that RSS is not a suitable metric for this task, largely based on the random variability that has been observed in past mobility experiments. However this work provides practical evidence that the more stable radios that are now a feature of the 802.15.4 market can provide a basis for real time control. In this regard, the results presented here complement the claims made by a number of respected authors in defense of RSS (Ares, 2007). Moreover, no new point of principle arises in the use of any other practicable real time performance metric for BAN purposes, if and when one comes to hand.

Figure 1. The ambient healthcare environment where power control for X is initially handled by BS1. Subject X then moves in an ambulatory fashion and switching occurs between BS1 and BS2. Data is now multihopped via BS2 to BS1 and BS2 handles power control for X. Hence power controller switching has occurred between BS1 and BS2.

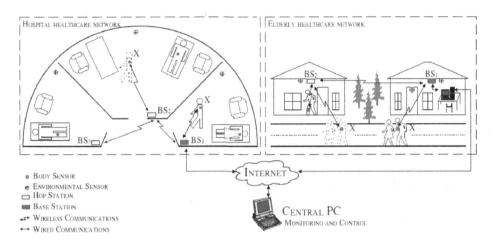

2. PERFORMANCE CONSTRAINTS IN A TYPICAL BODY AREA NETWORK

A variety of limits on performance surface sooner rather than later in a practical BAN. This section outlines the constraints that are treated by this work.

A. Hardware Limitations

When employing embedded systems in miniaturised BAN applications a number of hardware related factors are an inevitable constraint on performance. For instance the limited, necessarily quantised, and quite often saturated transceiver output power of a typical mobile node can severely degrade network performance, ultimately leading to instability if not properly addressed. In this work Anti-Windup (AW) control is shown to demonstrate graceful BAN performance degradation in the face of such constraints. AW actively seeks to minimise controller gain and also exhibits improved network energy consumption. This paper provides a novel practical example of how

to address these types of unavoidable nonlinear constraints in an optimal fashion.

B. Network Coverage

Another major challenge lies in maximizing network coverage area. Given that many of the "off-the-shelf" sensor node platforms operate using low power 802.15.4 type wireless technologies, transmission range is extremely limited, especially in the indoor environment. A multihop or mesh network topology is often proposed to extend coverage area necessitating the introduction of a switching protocol that is power aware. Figure 1 illustrates the type of scenario that is envisaged whereby subject X is being monitored and is wearing (perhaps a number of) wireless biometric devices. Initially X is in communication with base station BS_1. When X moves to an adjoining area in an ambulatory fashion, data must at some point be transmitted via BS_2 rather than BS_1 quite possibly within a mesh paradigm. It is crucial that the QoS and energy efficient properties of the BAN be retained in such a scenario. Here "bumpless transfer" (BT), (Hanus et al.,

1987), is employed to optimise this process. In the proposed BT scheme a global controller oversees multiple local loop controllers that are designed to ensure that the mesh is power aware. Depending on certain performance requirements, a sequence of switches is necessary between each controller. In essence, one controller will be operational or "on-line" while the other candidate controller(s) must be deemed "off-line" at any instant. Clearly it is necessary to be able to switch between these controllers (located at adjacent base stations) in a stable fashion. This paper presents sufficient conditions to ensure that the induced transient signals are bounded, thereby satisfying network stability requirements. To achieve this smoothly, the gap between the off and online control signals must be bounded so that the control signal driving the plant cannot induce instability.

In this work both AW and BT are applied in tandem for the first time in a practical network, thereby providing effective control of the signal entering the 'plant' (in this case the node transceiver) at any instant For the remainder of the work the term anti-windup-bumpless-transfer or AWBT is coined to denote the new technique.

This work addresses the nonlinear elements outlined above in a power control setting that is both QoS energy efficient. The necessary extensions that are required to AWBT results to account for challenges posed by wired and wireless communications are also presented. In the first instance the problem is treated for the 2 base station scenario and is subsequently extended to the general case. Traditional AWBT schemes require that the gap between the feedback measurement observed at the "off-line" controller(s), is(are) sufficiently close in magnitude to that observed at the "on-line" controller. The particular constraints imposed by the use of practical devices and in particular the use of the received signal strength (RSS) as the tracking signal observed at each successive base station is considered in detail. To this end a specific modification is proposed that delivers an AWBT scheme capable of compensate for the

differing feedback signals that naturally arise in the problem at hand.

3. FORMAL STATEMENT OF THE CONTROLLER SWITCHING PROBLEM: TWO BASE STATION SCENARIO

To determine when switching should occur the filtered downlink received signal strength indicator (RSSI) signal or the RSSI signal is considered at the mobile node. It is assumed that each base station or access point will possess the ability to transmit at a predefined maximum power level within some quantisation structure at any instant. Initially, the two node mobile ad-hoc WSN scenario depicted in Figure 2(a) is considered. When the network initializes it is assumed that the Mobile Node (MN) is unaware of its position and is transmitting data using maximum transmission power to all "listening" base stations Figure 2(a)(i).

The network connects and implements power controller switching as per Figure 2(b). The MN will subsequently receive data packets from each base station within range (in this scenario limited to BS1 and BS2). A downlink RSSI is now calculated for each received packet and this signal is subsequently filtered to remove any multipath or high frequency component, using a digital low pass filter, $F(z)$. The average speed at which the mobile node travels when considered with the environmental conditions influence the selection of the filter's parameters. Stemming from this the higher the speed and the density of sensor nodes, the lower the cut of frequency that is required. In the experiment presented in this work the filter

$$F(z) = \frac{0.25z}{z - 0.75} \quad (1)$$

was found to be satisfactory. Figure 3 illustrates how, subsequent to filtering the downlink RSSI

Figure 2. (a) Simple WSN multihop scenario. (b) The power controller switching procedure based on filtered downlink RSSI.

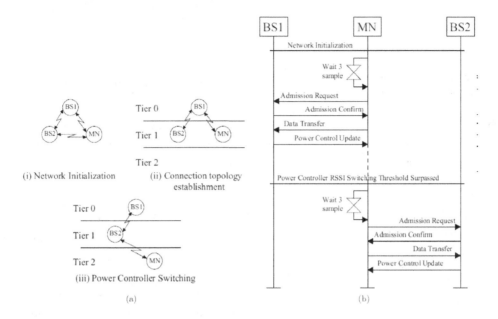

signal, the pathloss component remains. This element is shown here, and earlier by other authors (Goldsmith, 2006), to be sufficiently distance dependant to be useful for real time control. The MN now executes the algorithm presented in Table 1 comparing the resultant filtered signals, $RSSI_{Downlink\ BS\ 1}$ and $RSSI_{Downlink\ BS\ 2}$ over three

sample periods. The signals are also compared with a predefined threshold value, selected here to be -40 dBm. This threshold ensures that the base station is located in the highest possible tier of the BAN hierarchy and is also within range of the mobile node that will have routing precedence,

Figure 3. Received signal strength filtered using (1) to remove the high frequency component

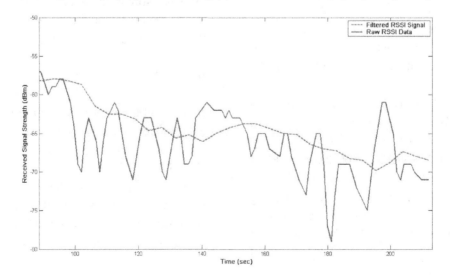

Table 1. Pseudo code for power controller switching algorithm: 2 base station example

Base Station 1 (BS1 located in tier 0)
Network Initialization
0 Downlink RSSI for BS1 recorded at MN 1 For number of sample periods = 1 to 3 2 If $RSSI_{DownlinkBS\,1} > RSSI_{DownlinkBS\,2}$
3 Or If $RSSI_{DownlinkBS\,1} > -40dBm$
4 Use power level updates from Base Station 1
Base Station 2 (BS2 located in tier 1)
Network Initialization
0 Downlink RSSI for BS2 recorded at MN 1 For number of sample periods = 1 to 3 2 If $RSSI_{DownlinkBS\,2} > RSSI_{DownlinkBS\,1}$
3 And If $RSSI_{DownlinkBS\,1} < -40dBm$
4 Use power level updates from Base Station 2

thereby satisfying a minimal latency requirement within the network.

An admission request is then sent to the base station whose downlink RSSI satisfies the switching criteria (*BS1* following network initialization). Following confirmation the mobile node implements any power level updates received from this base station. Filtering the RSSI provides the added advantage of preventing chatter, i.e., occurring too frequently, caused by any deep fades in the RSSI that may be a characteristic of the *MN* position at any instant. Furthermore the three sample period delay prior to sending an admission request ensures that jitter is not present in the system.

From Figure 2(a)(ii) and following network initialization, *MN* is now located in tier 1 of the mesh hierarchy and *BS1*, located in tier 0, dynamically manages the *MN's* power based on the uplink RSSI observed at *BS1*. At some future sampling instant, due to *MN* mobility, power controller switching is required based on the algorithm of Table 1, again by a consideration of the filtered downlink RSSI values, $RSSI_{DownlinkBS\,1}$ and $RSSI_{DownlinkBS\,2}$ and

the threshold value -40 dBm. Subsequently *MN* joins tier 2 in the hierarchy, see Figure 2(a)(iii) and power control for *MN* is now implemented through the uplink RSSI at BS2.

4. MODELLING THE NETWORK

The goal of this work is to dynamically adjust the mobile node transmitter power in a distributed manner, so that the power consumption is minimized while also maintaining sufficient transmission quality. A direct measurement of QoS is therefore an a priori requirement. In the past it has been suggested that uplink RSSI was a less than ideal metric for power control, however this claim was based on experimentation with early platforms using older radios, e.g. the Texas Instruments CC1000, where hardware miscalibration or drift was often a problem. More recently newer 802.15.4 compliant radios such as the TI CC2420, have been shown to exhibit highly stable performance and it is now commonly held that for a given link, RSSI exhibits acceptably small time-variability (Srinivasan et al., 2006). In this work the received signal strength indicator (RSSI) is therefore selected as the feedback variable to manage the control objective.

In Ares et al. (2007) a method was introduced to directly estimate the signal to noise plus interference ratio (SINR) using RSSI measurements. The SINR $\gamma\,(k)$, in terms of RSSI is given by

$$\gamma\,(k) \approx RSSI\,(k) - n(k) - C - 30 \qquad (2)$$

where the addition of the scalar term 30 accounts for the conversion from dBm to dB, $n(k)$ is thermal noise and C is the measurement offset assumed to be 45 dB.

A setpoint or reference RSSI value can therefore be selected and related directly to *PER*, as outlined in the 802.15.4 standard (International Organization for Standardization, 2007). To expand, the bit error rate (BER) for the 802.15.4 standard operating at a frequency of 2.4GHz is given by

$$BER = \frac{8}{15} \times \frac{1}{16} \times \sum_{k=2}^{16} -1^k \binom{16}{k} e^{20 \times SINR \times (\frac{1}{k}-1)}$$

(3)

and given the average packet length for this standard is 22 bytes, the PER can be obtained from

$$P\,ER = 1 - (1 - BER)^{PL}$$

(4)

where *PL* is packet length including the header and payload. *PER* is more useful here given the transceiver used to practically implement the proposed methodology, is a wideband transceiver, transmitting and receiving data in packet rather than bit format. Establishing a relationship between *RSSI, SINR, BER* and subsequently *PER* can therefore help to pre-specify levels of system performance.

A. The System Model

A systems science representation of a single base station communicating to a single mobile node is illustrated in Figure 4. The system has reference input *r(k)* (reference RSSI), the value for which is determined using (2), (3) and (4) above, guaranteeing a predefined PER. q(k) is quantization noise introduced as a result of switching between discrete power levels. The controller $K\,(z)$ has controller output *u(k)* and takes the form $K\,(z) = [K_1\,(z)\,K_2\,(z)]$ a standard two degree of freedom structure.

The plant *G(z)* is represented by $G(z) = [G_1(z)\,G_2\,(z)]$, where $G_1\,(z)$ and $G_2\,(z)$ are the disturbance feedforward and feedback parts of G(z) respectively. Given no structured disturbance model is available in the form of a transfer function, $G_1(z)$ is taken to be $G_1 = I$, where *I* is the identity matrix. $G_2(z)$ is a low pass filter with sufficient bandwidth to eliminate quantization noise. $G_2(z)$ is selected as

$$G(z) = \frac{1}{1.1z - 0.9}$$

(5)

$G_2(z)$ outputs a power level update *p(k)*, which in turn is transmitted to the mobile node. The mobile node transmitter has inherent upper and lower bounds on hardware transmission power output, represented in Figure 4 by the saturation block, the output for which is saturated output power or $p_m\,(k)$. H represents the hardware switch in the mobile node's transceiver and is taken here to be the identity matrix or $H = I.d(k)$ is a disturbance to the system and comprises of channel attenuation, interference and noise.

B. Mapping the Saturation Function

For this scenario a problem presents itself in that the saturation constraint is located at the output of the system and while there have been some advances in control design theory to deal with this type of output constraint (Turner et al., 2007), there is a vast literature covering the treatment of linear systems subject to input saturation

Figure 4. Wireless System Model with saturation block at the output

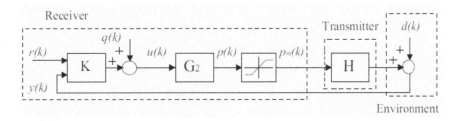

constraints (Bernstein et al., 1995) and references therein. A solution therefore lies in the mapping of the output saturation constraint to the input of the plant or the output of the controller. The saturation function is defined as

$$p_m(k) = sat(p(k)) \qquad (6)$$

where $sat(p(k)) := sign(p(k)) \times min\{|p(k)|, p_m(k)\}$ and where $p_m(k)$ is the output power saturation limit. Note the $sat(.)$ function in (6), belongs to sector $[0, 1]$ and is assumed locally Lipschitz. The following set is defined

$$P := [-p_m(k), p_m(k)] \qquad (7)$$

where $sat(p(k) = p(k), \forall p(k) \in P$. This is the set in which the saturation behaves linearly i.e. if there is no saturation present $p(k) = p_m(k)$ and the nominal closed loop system conditions are exhibited. Figure 5 portrays the system with the saturation block mapped from the output of the system to the input where $u_m(k)$ is the input to the plant. To represent the mapped saturation function we define the new set

$$U = \left[\overline{\frac{-p_m(k)}{h_{G_2}}}, \overline{\frac{p_m(k)}{h_{G_2}}} \right] \qquad (8)$$

where h_{G2} is the gain of the transfer function G_2. Recent advances in the anti-windup literature can now be applied to the problem at hand, ensuring minimal performance degradation during saturation and speedy recovery following saturation.

C. The Power Controller Switching Problem

Figure 6 illustrates the power controller switching problem for a two base station, one mobile node scenario. K_{BS1} and K_{BS2} are the same construct as $K(z)$ from the previous section. Basestation 1 is deemed "on-line" and is therefore controlling the mobile node's transmission power. The difficulty in switching between base station 1 and base station 2 is as a result of the possible difference between $p_1(k)$ and $p_2(k)$ at the time of switching. This discrepancy can exist due to incompatible initial conditions and can induce an unwanted transient and possible instability in the system. The result can be a disruption of vital health status data or indeed a loss in service altogether.

1) Conditions for stable switching:
    Assumption 1: As the work here is seeking global results, we are necessarily forced to assume that $G(z)$ is asymptotically stable. To expand given $G_2 \sim (A_p, B_p, C_p, D_p)$ in state space format and $H(z)$ is the identity matrix, if $|\lambda_{max}(A_p)| < 1$, where λ_{max} is the maximum eigenvalue, then asymptotically stable is guaranteed.
    Assumption 2: We also assume that the poles of $(1 - K_{BS1} G_2 H)(z)$ and $(1 - K_{BS2} G_2 H)(z)$ are in the open unit disc, ensuring both nominal closed loops are stable. When the above two necessary conditions are met then

Figure 5. Wireless system model with saturation block mapped from the output to the input of the system

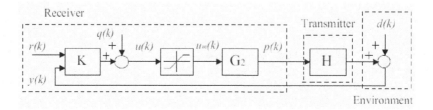

Figure 6. Wireless System Model with power controller switching

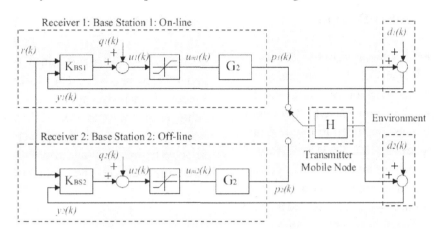

the stability of the switched system will be guaranteed if the control signals, $u_{m1}(k)$ and $u_{m2}(k)$ are sufficiently close to each other, thus an AWBT approach provides a stable solution to the power controller switching problem. $p_1(k)$ will therefore be close enough to $p_2(k)$ and should switching occur, a large unwanted transient will not be induced in the system. However an additional difficulty arises that is unique to the wireless case. As mentioned previously, in order for AWBT to be effective, the feedback measurement observed at the "off-line" controller must be sufficiently close in magnitude to the feedback measurement observed at the "on-line" controller. Clearly from Figure 6 $d_1(k) = d_2(k)$ due to differing propagation environments. This disparity can mean AWBT is unable to eliminate the difference between $u_{m1}(k)$ and $u_{m2}(k)$.

A more complex control design solution is therefore required. However prior to solving this, a linear controller must be synthesized. This controller provides pre-specified levels of stability and performance in the nominal linear closed loop i.e. when neither saturation nor switching is occurring. Following this a conservative anti-windup design is used to address the hardware saturation

constraint. Finally a modification is made to the AWBT scheme to account the differing feedback signals and to enable seamless power controller switching.

5. ANTI-WINDUP DESIGN

The technique employed here implements a two step AWBT design procedure. The first step is to design a linear power controller ignoring the inherent nonlinear constraints on the system. The control design approach adopted here is based on quantitative feedback theory (QFT) and provides both robust stability and nominal performance in the linear operational region. The second step involves using recent advances in AW theory, to minimize degradation in the face of actuator constraints. The technique employed here is the Weston-Postlethwaite AntiWindup Bumpless Transfer (WP-AWBT) synthesis technique. First presented in (Weston et al., 1998) and later in its discretized form in (Herrman et al., 2006), this approach uses an L_2 approach in conjunction with linear matrix inequality (LMI) optimization techniques to ensure that during saturation the systems performance remains as close to nominal linear operation as possible and returns to the linear operational region as quickly as possible.

A. Robust Linear Power Tracking Controller Design

Quantitative feedback theory (QFT) provides an intuitively appealing means of guaranteeing both robust stability and performance and is essentially a Two-Degree-of-Freedom (2DOF) frequency domain technique, as illustrated in Figure 6 and detailed in (Borghesani et al., 2003) and (Horowitz, 2001). The scheme achieves client-specified levels of desired performance over a region of parametric plant uncertainty, determined a priori by the engineer. The methodology requires that the desired time-domain responses are translated into frequency domain tolerances, which in turn lead to design bounds in the loop function on the Nichols chart. In a QFT design, the responsibility of the feedback compensator, $K_2(z)$, is to focus primarily on attenuating the undesirable effects of uncertainty, disturbance and noise. Having arrived at an appropriate $K_2(z)$, a pre-filter $K_1(z)$, is then designed so as to shift the closed-loop response to the desired tracking region, again specified a priori by the engineer. The approach requires that the designer select a set of desired specifications in relation to the magnitude of the frequency response of the closed-loop system, thusly achieving robust stability and performance. The design procedure in its entirety is omitted here due to space constraints, however the interested reader is directed to (Walsh et al, 2010) where a detailed description is contained. Using this techniques outlined therein $K_2(z)$ was found to be

$$K_2(z) = \frac{z - 0.6622}{0.7103z - 0.7103} \qquad (9)$$

guaranteeing a phase and gain margin equal to 50° and 1.44, respectively. The closed-loop transfer function is shaped using $K_1(z)$ ensuring the system achieves steady state around the target value of $5 \le t_{ss} \le 25(s)$ and a damping factor of $\xi = 0.5$ is selected to reduce outage probability at the outset of communication. The resultant $K_1(z)$ is

$$K_1(z) = \frac{1.4127z}{z - 0.4127} \qquad (10)$$

B. WP-AWBT Synthesis

Consider the generic AW configuration shown in Figure 7(a). As illustrated above the plant takes the form $G = [G_1 \ G_2 \ ]$, the linear controller is represented by $K = [K_1 \ K_2 \ ]$ where

$$K(z) \sim$$
$$\begin{cases} x_c (k + 1) = A_c x_c (k) + B_c y_{lin} (k) + B_{cr} r(k) \\ u_{lin} (k) = C_c x_c (k) + D_c y_{lin} (k) + D_{cr} r(k) \end{cases}$$
$$(11)$$

$\Theta = [\theta_1 \ \theta_2]$ is the AW controller becoming active only when saturation occurs. Given the difficulty in analyzing the stability and performance of this system we now adopt a framework first introduced in (Weston et al, 1998) for the problem at hand.

Figure 7. (a) A generic anti-windup scenario, (b) Weston postlethwaite anti-windup conditioning technique

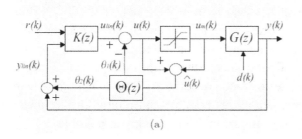

(a)

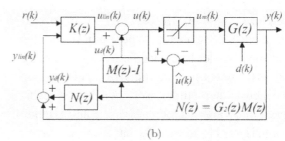

(b)

This approach reduces to a linear time invariant Anti-Windup scheme that is optimized in terms of a transfer function: $M(z)$ shown in Figure 7 (b). It was shown in (Weston et al., 1998) that the performance degradation experienced by the system during saturation is directly related to the mapping $T: u_{lin} \rightarrow y_d$. Note that from Figure 7(b) $M - I$ is considered for stability of T and G_2M determines the systems recovery after saturation, where I is the identity matrix. This decoupled representation visibly shows how this mapping can be utilized as a performance measure for the AW controller. To quantify this we say that an AW controller is selected such that the L_2-gain, $\|T\|_{i,2}$, of the operator T

$$\|T\|_{i,2} = \sup_{0 \neq u_{lin} \in L_2} \frac{\|y_d\|_2}{\|u_{lin}\|_2}$$

where the L_2 norm $\|x\|_2$ of a discrete signal $x(h)$, $(h = 0, 1, 2, 3,..)$ is

$$\|x\|_2 = \sqrt{\sum_{h=0}^{\infty} \|x(h)\|^2}$$

Static anti-windup synthesis: Static AW has an advantage in that it can be implemented at a much lower computational cost and adds no additional states to the closed loop system. Using the aforementioned conditioning technique via $M(z)$, outlined in (Turner & Postlethwaite, 2004), Θ from Figure 7(a) is given by

$$\begin{bmatrix} \theta_1 \\ \theta_2 \end{bmatrix} = \Theta \hat{u} = \begin{bmatrix} \theta_1 \\ \theta_2 \end{bmatrix} \hat{u}$$

u is derived from Figure 7(a) and Figure 7(b) respectively, as

$$u = K_1 r + K_2 y - [(I - K_2 G_2)M - I]\hat{u}$$

$$u = K_1 r + K_2 y + (K_2 \Theta_2 - \Theta_1)\hat{u}$$

Thus $M(z)$ can be written as

$$M = (I - K_2 G_2)^{-1}(-K_2 \Theta_2 + \Theta_1 + I)$$

The goal of the static AW approach is therefore to ensure that extra modes do not appear in the system. Since this will inevitably be the case it must be ensured that minimal realizations of the controller and plant are used (Herrmann et al., 2007). A state space realization can be then formed

$$\begin{bmatrix} M(z) - I \\ N(z) \end{bmatrix} \sim \begin{bmatrix} \dot{\bar{x}} \\ u_d \\ y_d \end{bmatrix} = \begin{bmatrix} \bar{A} & B_0 + \bar{B}\Theta \\ \bar{C}_1 & D_{01} + \bar{D}_1\Theta \\ \bar{C}_2 & D_{02} + \bar{D}_2\Theta \end{bmatrix} \begin{bmatrix} \bar{x} \\ \hat{u} \end{bmatrix}$$

(12)

where $\Theta = [\Theta'^1 \ \Theta'^2]'$ is a static matrix and $x, A, B_0, B, C_1, D_{01}, D_1, C_2, D_{02}$ and D_2 are minimal realizations given in the Appendix. In a similar manner to (Herrmann et al., 2007), if there exist $Q > 0$, $U = diag(v_1, \cdots, v_c) > 0$ and L such that the following LMI is satisfied, then $\|T\|$ will be less than γ.

$$\begin{bmatrix} -Q & -Q\bar{C}_1' & Q\bar{A}' & 0 & -Q\bar{C}_2' \\ - & -X & UB_0 + L'\bar{B}' & I & UD'_{02} + L'\bar{D}_2' \\ - & - & -Q & 0 & 0 \\ - & - & - & -\gamma I & 0 \\ - & - & - & - & -\gamma I \end{bmatrix} < 0$$

(13)

where

$$X = 2U + D_{01}U + \bar{D}'_1 L + UD'_{01} + L'\bar{D}'_1$$

and with

$$Q > 0, \ U = diag(v1,..vc) > 0 \ L \in \Re^{(c+n) \times n}$$

(where c = n), the minimized L_2 gain $||T||_{i,2} < \gamma$ (where γ is the L_2 gain bound on T). The '-' entries in (13) are transpose conjugate of the corresponding entries to make the LMI symmetric. In this instance Θ is given by $\Theta = LQ^{-1}$ using which the controller in (12) can be synthesized. Applying this synthesis routine to our plant given by (5) and linear controller (9), the resultant controller is $\Theta = [-0.2049\ 0.6377]'$ obtained using the LMI toolbox in Matlab.

6. MODIFIED AWBT DESIGN

A. Motivation

To motivate the need for the proposed modification to the above AWBT technique, the reader is directed to Figure 6. As mentioned previously traditional AWBT schemes require that the feedback signal entering the "off-line" controller equals or is close in magnitude to the feedback signal entering the "on-line" controller. Clearly from Figure 6 this is not the case as d_1 (k) = d_2 (k) due to differing propagation environments. As a result the AWBT controller in Figure 7(b) cannot guarantee

the controller outputs for both the "off-line" and "on-line" controllers are equal in magnitude. The result can be an unwanted transient at switching due to the incompatible controller values, possibly causing vital health status information to be lost or a total breakdown in communication.

B. Proposed Solution

The following modification compensates for the inherent discrepancy in feedback RSSI signals between the "off-line" and the "on-line" controllers. Figure 8 illustrates the modification to the system. Consider the "off-line" controller base station 2, where an additional signal $y_{diff\,2}(k)$ is included in the feedback signal. This signal comprises of

$$y_{diff\,2}\ (k) = -y_{online}\ (k)W\ (z) + y_{lin2}\ (k)W\ (z) \quad (14)$$

where $W\ (z)$ is a low pass filter removing the high frequency component present in each of the feedback RSSI signals. Note that $y_{online}(k)$ is determined by which base station is online. Therefore $y_{online}(k) = y_{lin1}$ given BS 1 is online. The signal driving the "off-line" controller then becomes

Figure 8. The proposed modified WP-AW scheme, 2 Base Station Scenario

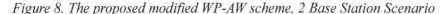

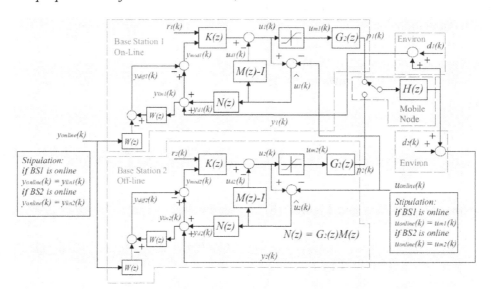

$$y_{mod2} (k) = y_{lin2} (k) - y_{diff2} (k) = y_{lin2} (k) + y_{lin1} (k)$$
$$W (z) - y_{lin2} (k)W (z)$$

$$y_{mod2} (k) = y_{lin1} (k)W (z) + y_{lin2} (k)(1 - W (z))$$
$$(15)$$

which comprises of the "dc" or low frequency component of the "on-line" feedback signal or $y_{lin1}(k)W (z)$ and the high frequency component of the "off-line" control signal $y_{lin2}(k)(1-W(z))$. Each of these signals are incorporated in the design for different reasons. Firstly driving the "off-line controller" with the "dc" component of the "on-line" control signal will ensure both controller outputs will be approximately equal or $u_1(k) \approx u_2(k)$. Retaining the high frequency component of the "off-line" feedback signal enables the "off-line" controller with the ability to compensate for deep fades in its own feedback signal. Should power controller switching then occur a large transient is avoided as the feedback conditions are compatible.

Should base station 2 become "on-line" Equation (15) becomes

$$y_{mod2} (k) = y_{lin2} (k) - y_{diff2} (k) = y_{lin2} (k) + y_{lin2} (k)$$
$$W (z) - y_{lin2} (k)W (z) = y_{lin2} (k) \qquad (16)$$

hence the modification has no effect on the system and the AWBT scheme operates as normal. This approach in essence adds a filtered additional disturbance to the system which is intuitively appealing given a perturbation of the disturbance feedforward portion of the plant G_1 will have no bearing on stability (Turner et al., 2007). Taking into account the modification (11) can be rewritten as

$$K(z) \sim$$
$$\begin{cases} x_c (k + 1) = A_c x_c (k) + B_c y_{mod} (k) + B_{cr} r(k) \\ u_{lin} (k) = C_c x_c (k) + D_c y_{mod} (k) + D_{cr} r(k) \end{cases}$$
$$(17)$$

7. EXPERIMENTATION AND DISCUSSION

This section is organized as follows: Firstly a number of system parameters and performance criteria specific to this scenario are outlined. Some results are then presented to highlight the improvements afforded by the modified AWBT scheme ignoring the inherent saturation constraints. The fully scalable experimental testbed is then introduced. Finally a series of experiments are implemented on a fully compliant 802.15.4 wireless sensor testbed. In all cases the system response is analysed first without AWBT, then with the introduction of AWBT and finally with the modified AWBT design in place.

A. System Parameters and Performance Criteria

A sampling frequency of $T_s = 1(sec)$ is used throughout and a target RSSI value of $-55dBm$ is selected for tracking, guaranteeing a PER of $< 1\%$, verified using Equations (3), (4) and (2).

The *standard deviation* of the RSSI tracking error is chosen as a performance criterion:

$$\sigma_e = \left\{ \frac{1}{S} \sum_{k=1}^{S} \left| r(k) - RSSI(k) \right|^2 \right\}^{\frac{1}{2}} \qquad (18)$$

where S is the total number of samples and k is the index of these samples. *Outage probability* is defined as

$$P_0(\%) = \frac{number of times RSSI < RSSI_{th}}{the tota \ln umber of iterations} \times 100$$
$$(19)$$

where $RSSI_{th}$ is selected to be $-57dBm$, a value below which performance is deemed unacceptable in terms of PER. This can be easily verified again using Equations (2), (3) and (4). To fully access each paradigm, some measure of power efficiency is also useful and here we define average power consumption in milliwatts as

$$P_{av} = 10^{\left|\left\{\frac{1}{S}\sum_{k=1}^{S} p_{dBm}(k)\right\}/10\right|}(mW) \qquad (20)$$

where $p_{dBm}(k)$ is the output transmission power in dBm, S is the total number of samples and k is the index of these samples.

B. Bumpless Transfer Performance

Due to the naturally occurring transceiver output power saturation nonlinearity in the system, which cannot be removed, it is difficult to ascertain the performance improvements afforded by the bumpless transfer as a standalone power controller switching scheme. Simulation can be a useful tool in this regard. Figure 9 illustrates some results were at time index 100 switching occurs between two base stations. In this instance there is a difference of 20 dBm in RSSI, between the signal received at the "on-line" base station and the RSSI signal observed at the "off-line" base station. As mentioned earlier this dissimilarity in observed RSSI is due to the propagation environment and is a realistic value based on experimental observations in an indoor environment. As a result of this feedback discrepancy the system without AWBT exhibits an extremely large transient response and indeed never achieves steady state prior to completion of the simulation. The system with AWBT in place shows improvement, however there is significant time spent below RSSI_th and as a result outage probability is still at an unacceptable level. When the modified AWBT scheme is added the outage probability is dramatically reduced highlighting the improved performance afforded by the new scheme. The results in terms of the performance criteria are summarized in Table 2.

C. Experimental Testbed Description

To illustrate the use of the proposed algorithms in practice, a scaled experiment was for-mulated bridging the gap between simulation and implementation, an important step given the unpredictable nature of the wireless channel. The Tmote Sky mote sensor node is an embedded platform using an 802.15.4 compliant transceiver and

Figure 9. Modified AWBT performance ignoring saturation constraints and where power controller switching occurs at 100 (sec)

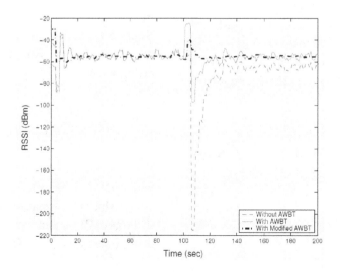

Table 2. Simulation results. Characteristics: σe - standard deviation (dbm), po - outage probability (%), pav - average power consumption (mw)

	Without AWBT	With AWBT	Modified AWBT
σe	30.59	4.445	1.603
Po	63.77	31.88	8.696
Pav	1	0.199	0.158

is selected as the primary embedded platform for this work. The Tmote platform employs the CC2420 transceiver using the Direct Sequence Spread Spectrum (DSSS) technique to code the biometric or accelerometer data. Carrier Sensing Multiple Access/Collision Avoidance (CSMA/CA) is then used to transmit the coded packets. The CC2420 transceiver on the Tmote platform provides a received signal strength indicator (RSSI) measurement in dBm by averaging the received signal power over 8 symbol periods or 128μs. Sensor data packets are framed in 802.15.4 format and transmitted using the TinyOS library function Oscope. The base station bridges packets over the USB/Serial connection to a personal computer where an interface between Matlab and TinyOS has been established using TinyOS Matlab tools written in Java.

The experimental setup shown in Figure 10(a), consists of a six Tmote nodes, two of which act as base stations or access points. A fully autono-

mous MIABOT Pro miniature mobile robot [23] is used to introduce mobility into the system, see Figure 10(b), to enable switching to occur. The first base station labeled BS_1 is connected to a PC and forwards all packets directly into the Matlab environment as discussed above. The second base station or BS_2 is a wireless device capable of gathering data from nodes within range and forwarding it in a multihop manner to BS_1 also known as the personal area network (PAN) coordinator. BS_2 is also capable of implementing power control for nodes located in lower tiers of the hierarchy as explained in the next section and illustrated by Figure 2(a). The MIABOT robot has an additional Tmote, MN, onboard and follows a trajectory along which power controller switching occurs between BS_1 and BS_2. This is equivalent to a patient or elderly person in an ambulatory environment moving outside of the range of one access point and within range of another. Smooth switching between these two access points will ensure vital health status information is not lost. The additional stationary nodes SN_1, SN_2 and SN_3, introduce interference into the system providing for a more realistic scenario. For consistency the trajectory along which the mobile robot travels remains the same. For each experiment all relevant data both visual and numerical is recorded and stored for further analysis.

Figure 10. (a) Experimental testbed scenario, (b) Miabot pro with onboard Tmote Sky node

D. Experimental Results

Figure 11(a) illustrates the experimental system response without AWBT or with the control configuration shown in Figure 6. In this scenario, switching occurs at time $t \approx 60s$ and $t \approx 120s$. Clearly without AWBT there is significant integral windup in the system, keeping both the controller at BS_1 and at BS_2 saturated for the entire duration of the experiment and making it impossible for the system to track its reference RSSI accurately. In Figure 11(b) AWBT is added to the system and some improvement is observed in tracking performance, however upon closer inspection it is apparent when power controller switching occurs

an undesirable transient is imposed on the system. The "off-line" controller output also exhibits an undesirable increase in magnitude, for instance the controller at BS_2 between 0 and 50 (sec). This is due to the discrepancy in the feedback signals or as $d_1 (k) = d_2 (k)$ (Figure 6) and results in excess power consumption in the network. The modified AWBT scheme almost eliminates this unwanted transient behaviour as shown in Figure 11(c) and this can be attributed to the modified compensators ability, when "off-line", to keep its control signal close in magnitude to the signal entering the plant despite the presence of ambiguity in the feedback signal. The results are summarized in Figure 12.

Figure 11. Experimental results where RSSI is the overall tracking signal, the dashed line is the saturated/actual controller output for base station 1 and the solid line is the saturated/actual controller output for base station 2. In this scenario, switching occurs at time $t \approx 60s$ and $t \approx 120s$. From above (a) System response without AWBT compensation, (b) System response with AWBT compensation, (c) System response with Modified AWBT compensation

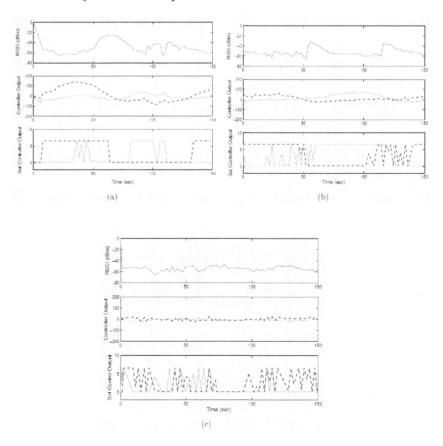

Figure 12. Results in terms of the performance criteria. Standard deviation has units dBm. Average power consumption is given in milliwatts

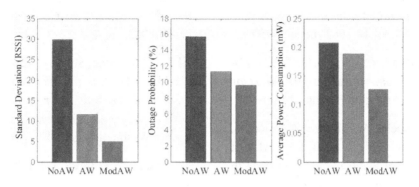

8. CONCLUSION

A novel Anti-Windup Bumpless Transfer (AWBT) scheme has been presented that enables smooth, power aware switching for networked wireless healthcare applications. The new technique facilitates the continual availability of biometric information in mesh networks that arise quite naturally in an ambulatory setting. Feedback discrepancies, hardware limitations and propagation phenomena that are posed by the use of commercially available wireless communication devices were addressed using new signal processing and robust anti-windup design tools. The approach was validated using a fully scalable 802.15.4 compliant wireless testbed. The new AWBT scheme exhibited significant performance improvements, particularly in terms of transient behaviour at power controller switching, when compared with analogous systems operating with simple dynamic control or when only Anti-Windup (AW) methods were applied in isolation. In future work the authors will apply the results presented here in a clinical study into fall detection and prevention for the elderly that will follow on from an EU Framework project in this application space.

9. ACKNOWLEDGMENT

The authors would like to acknowledge the support of Science Foundation Ireland under grant numbers 05/RFPCM/S0048 and 07/CE/I1147.

REFERENCES

Alavi, S. M. M., Walsh, M. J., & Hayes, M. J. (2009). Robust distributed active power control technique for IEEE 802.15.4 wireless sensor networks - a quantitative feedback theory approach. *Control Engineering Practice, 17*(7), 805–814. doi:10.1016/j.conengprac.2009.02.001

Alavi, S. M. M., Walsh, M. J., & Hayes, M. J. (2010). Robust power control for IEEE 802.15.4 wireless sensor networks with round-trip time-delay uncertainty. *Wireless Communications and Mobile Computing, 10*(6), 811–825.

Ares, B. Z., Fischione, C., Speranzon, A., & Johansson, K. H. (2007). On power control for wireless sensor networks: System model, middleware component and experimental evaluation. In *Proceedings of the* European Control Conference, Kos, Greece.

Bernstein, D. S., & Michel, A. N. (1995). A chronological bibliography on saturating actuators. *International Journal of Robust and Nonlinear Control, 5,* 375–380. doi:10.1002/rnc.4590050502

Borghesani, C., Chait, Y., & Yaniv, O. (2003). *The QFT frequency domain control design toolbox for use with MATLAB.* Arlington Heights, IL: Terasoft.

Boulos, M. K., Rocha, A., Martins, A., Vicente, M. E., Bolz, A., & Feld, R. (2007). CAALYX: A new generation of location-based services in healthcare. *International Journal of Health Geographics, 6*(1), 9. doi:10.1186/1476-072X-6-9

Chen, Y.-H., Lee, B.-K., & Chen, B.-S. (2006). Robust Hinf power control for CDMA cellular communication systems. *IEEE Transactions on Signal Processing, 54*(10), 3947–3956. doi:10.1109/TSP.2006.880237

Gao, T., Pesto, C., Selavo, L., Chen, Y., Ko, J.-G., Lim, J.-H., et al. (2008). Wireless medical sensor networks in emergency response: Implementation and pilot results. In Proceedings of the IEEE International Conference on Technologies for Homeland Security, Waltham, MA (pp. 187-192).

Goldsmith, A. (2006). *Wireless communications.* Cambridge, UK: Cambridge University Press.

Hanus, R., Kinnaert, M., & Henrotte, J. (1987). Conditioning technique a general anti-windup and bumpless transfer method. *Automatica, 23,* 729–739. doi:10.1016/0005-1098(87)90029-X

Herrmann, G., Turner, M., & Postlethwaite, I. (2006). Discrete-time and sampled-data anti-windup synthesis: stability and performance. *International Journal of Systems Science, 37*(2), 91–114. doi:10.1080/00207720500444074

Herrmann, G., Turner, M., Postlethwaite, I., & Guo, G. (2004). Practical implementation of a novel anti-windup scheme in a HDD-dual-stage servo-system. *IEEE/ASME Transactions on Mechatronics, 9*(3). doi:10.1109/TMECH.2004.835333

Horowitz, I. (2001). Survey of quantitative feedback theory (QFT). *International Journal of Robust Nonlinear Control, 11,* 887–921. doi:10.1002/rnc.637

IEEE. Computer Society. (2006). *IEEE Std 802.15.4: Wireless lan medium access control (mac) and physical layer (phy) specifications for low-rate wireless personal area networks (lr-wpans).* Washington, DC: IEEE Computer Society.

Srinivasan, K., & Levis, P. (2006). RSSI is under appreciated. In Proceedings of the Third Workshop on Embedded Networked Sensors EmNets.

Subramanian, A., & Sayed, A. H. (2005). Joint rate and power control algorithms for wireless networks. *IEEE Transactions on Signal Processing, 53*(11), 4204–4214. doi:10.1109/TSP.2005.857044

Turner, M., Herrmann, G., & Postlethwaite, I. (2007). Incorporating robustness requirements into anti-windup design. *IEEE Transactions on Automatic Control, 52*(10), 1842–1855. doi:10.1109/TAC.2007.906185

Turner, M., & Postlethwaite, I. (2004). A new perspective on static and low-order anti-windup synthesis. *International Journal of Control, 77,* 27–44. doi:10.1080/00207170310001640116

Walsh, M. J., Alavi, S. M. M., & Hayes, M. J. (2008, December 9-11). On the effect of communication constraints on robust performance for a practical 802.15.4 wireless sensor network benchmark problem. In *Proceedings of the 47th IEEE Conference on Decision and Control,* Cancun, Mexico (pp. 447-452).

Walsh, M. J., Alavi, S. M. M., & Hayes, M. J. (2010). Practical assessment of hardware limitations on power aware wireless sensor networks- an anti-wind up approach. *International Journal of Robust and Nonlinear Control, 20*(2), 194–208. doi:10.1002/rnc.1475

Walsh, M. J., Hayes, M. J., & Nelson, J. (2009). Robust performance for an energy sensitive wireless body area network - an anti-windup approach. *International Journal of Control*, *82*(1), 59–73. doi:10.1080/00207170801983109

Weston, P. F., & Postlewaite, I. (1998). Analysis and design of linear conditioning schemes for systems containing saturating actuators. In Proceedings of the IFAC Nonlinear Control System Design *Symposium*.

APPENDIX

Static Minimal Realizations

Given the state space realization of the plant

$$\begin{bmatrix} G_1 G_2 \end{bmatrix} \sim \begin{bmatrix} A_p & B_{pd} B_p \\ C_p & D_{pd} D_p \end{bmatrix}$$

then the minimal realization is given by

$$\bar{x} = \begin{bmatrix} x_p \\ x_c \end{bmatrix}, \bar{A} \sim \begin{bmatrix} A_p + B_p \tilde{\Delta} D_c C_p & B_p \tilde{\Delta} C_c \\ B_c \Delta C_p & A c + B_c \Delta D_p C_c \end{bmatrix}$$

$$B_0 = \begin{bmatrix} B_p \tilde{\Delta} \\ B_c \Delta D_p \end{bmatrix}, \bar{B} \sim \begin{bmatrix} B_p \tilde{\Delta} & -B_p \tilde{\Delta} D_c \\ B_c \Delta D_p & -B_c \Delta \end{bmatrix}$$

$$\bar{C}_1 = \begin{bmatrix} \tilde{\Delta} D_c C_p & \tilde{\Delta} C_c \end{bmatrix}, D_{01} = \tilde{\Delta} D_c D_p, \bar{D}_1 = \begin{bmatrix} I + \tilde{\Delta} D_c D_p & -\tilde{\Delta} D_c \end{bmatrix}$$

$$\bar{C}_2 = \begin{bmatrix} \Delta C_p & \Delta D_p C_c \end{bmatrix}, D_{02} = \Delta D_p, \bar{D}_2 = \begin{bmatrix} \Delta D_p & -\tilde{\Delta} D_p D_c \end{bmatrix}$$

This work was previously published in the International Journal of Ambient Computing and Intelligence, Volume 3, Issue 2, edited by Kevin Curran, pp. 35-55, copyright 2011 by IGI Publishing (an imprint of IGI Global).

Chapter 10
Investigating Cybercrimes that Occur on Documented P2P Networks

Mark Scanlon
University College Dublin, Ireland

Alan Hannaway
University College Dublin, Ireland

Mohand-Tahar Kechadi
University College Dublin, Ireland

ABSTRACT

The popularity of Peer-to-Peer (P2P) Internet communication technologies being exploited to aid cybercrime is ever increasing. P2P systems can be used or exploited to aid in the execution of a large number of online criminal activities, e.g., copyright infringement, fraud, malware and virus distribution, botnet creation, and control. P2P technology is perhaps most famous for the unauthorised distribution of copyrighted materials since the late 1990's, with the popularity of file-sharing programs such as Napster. In 2004, P2P traffic accounted for 80% of all Internet traffic and in 2005, specifically BitTorrent traffic accounted for over 60% of the world's P2P bandwidth usage. This paper outlines a methodology for investigating a documented P2P network, BitTorrent, using a sample investigation for reference throughout. The sample investigation outlined was conducted on the top 100 most popular BitTorrent swarms over the course of a one week period.

INTRODUCTION

The efficiency, ease of use, negligible cost (zero cost once one has a computer and an Internet connection) and the perceived anonymity of individual peers lends P2P networks well to being used for a growing number of cybercrimes, ranging from copyright infringement and virus distribution to botnet creation and control.

The content producing industry report that revenue figures are steadily declining as a result of online piracy. The IFPI's Digital Music Report (International Federation of the Phonographic

DOI: 10.4018/978-1-4666-2041-4.ch010

Industry, 2011) states that legitimate digital music distribution is up 1000% from 2004 to 2010, although total global recorded music revenues are down 31% over the same period. The report cites Internet piracy as having a significant impact on their sales. The report cites a study from 2010 entitled "Piracy, Music and Movies: A Natural Experiment" which found that physical sales would be up 72% with the abolishment of piracy in Sweden.

In 2008, P2P traffic accounted for over half of the world's Internet traffic. P2P networks especially lend themselves well to the unauthorised distribution of copyrighted material due to the abundance of material available to the downloaders. This paper presents the results of an investigation conducted on the top 100 most popular BitTorrent swarms over the course of one week. The purpose of this investigation is to quantify the scale of the unauthorised distribution of copyrighted material through the use of the BitTorrent protocol.

BITTORRENT

Based on global bandwidth usage, BitTorrent is the most popular P2P network in use today. Erman (2005) measured BitTorrent traffic was to account for over 60% of the world's bandwidth usage. The BitTorrent protocol is designed to easily facilitate the distribution of files to a potentially large number of interested parties, i.e., other peers, with minimal load on the original file source, as outlined in the BitTorrent protocol specification. This is achieved through the following steps:

1. The file is split up into a number of uniformly sized pieces or chunks – with typical chunk sizes generally ranging from 128kB to 4MB.
2. The initial source of the file creates a UTF-8 encoded ".torrent" metadata file, which includes unique SHA-1 hash values for the entire file and each of the file chunks, along with other required file information, e.g., filenames, chunk size, total file size, path information, client information, comments etc.
3. This metadata file is then shared by the creator with other users interested in acquiring the original content – either through direct distribution, e.g., email, instant messaging etc., or through the much more common method of uploading onto a torrent indexing website, such as ThePirateBay.org.
4. Users interested in downloading the available content must then download this metadata file and open it using a BitTorrent client, such as Azureus/Vuze or µTorrent.
5. The BitTorrent client is then tasked with identifying other peers who are sharing the file uniquely identified in the metadata file, i.e., other peers in the swarm. This includes identifying seeders, i.e., peers with complete copies of the content shared in the swarm, and other leechers, i.e., peers who are currently downloading the content, but are sharing the completed chunks with others. This peer discovery is achieved through a variety of methods including tracker communication, distributed hash tables and peer exchange.

The success of the BitTorrent protocol can be attributed to uploaders incurring no additional cost besides their Internet connectivity costs to share a file with many users. In practice, the original uploader need only stay connected to the swarm until a sufficient number of leechers have one full copy of the file between them. This is made possible through the leechers uploading their completed chunks of the entire file to other downloaders. Due to BitTorrent's ease of use, minimal bandwidth requirements and perceived Internet anonymity, it lends itself well as an ideal platform for the unauthorised distribution of copyrighted material, which typically has a single original source for sharing large sized files between many downloaders.

BitTorrent Peer Discovery Methods

Each leecher must be able to identify a list of active peers in the same BitTorrent swarm which has at least one chunk of the content and is willing to share it, i.e., the peer has an available open connection and has enough bandwidth to upload. The protocol is implemented in such a manner that any peer who wishes to download content from a particular swarm, must be able to communicate and share file chunks with other active peers. There are a number of methods that a peer can attempt to discover new peers who are in the swarm:

1. Tracker Communication – BitTorrent trackers maintain a list of seeders and leechers for each BitTorrent swarm they are currently tracking. Each BitTorrent client will contact the tracker intermittently throughout the download of a particular piece of content – both to report that they are still alive on the network and to download a short list of new peers on the network.
2. Peer Exchange (PEX) – Peer Exchange is a BitTorrent Enhancement Proposal (BEP) whereby when two peers are communicating, a subset of their respective peer lists, is mutually shared during the communication.
3. Distributed Hash Tables (DHT)– Within the specification of the standard BitTorrent protocol, there is no intercommunication between peers of different BitTorrent swarms. Azureus and μTorrent contain mutually exclusive implementations of distributed hash tables as part of the standard client features. These DHTs maintain a list of all recently active peers using each client and enable cross-swarm communication. Each peer in the DHT is associated with the swarm(s) in which he is currently an active participant.

It is common for BitTorrent clients to use more than one method of peer discovery to ensure the highest possible download speed, i.e., continuous access to a fresh list of peers with the desired parts of the original content.

INVESTIGATION METHODOLOGY

The initial step in investigating a cybercrime occurring on a documented P2P network involves determining the identifying factor that uniquely groups the required peers together. In a copyright infringement investigation scenario, the unique identifying factor is the content being investigated. However, in deciding to investigate a particular album or movie, etc., it must be decided how many different variations of the same content should be investigated. A predetermination should also be made on how peers are classified, who may have part of the content, e.g., one track from an album, a number of chunks of a given torrent, etc.

For the purpose of the investigation outlined as part of this paper, it was decided to investigate the most popular BitTorrent swarms, irrespective of the content being shared. The most popular BitTorrent indexing website, according to Alexa (2010), is ThePirateBay.org. In November 2010, The Pirate Bay held the Alexa global traffic rank of number 95 and is the 79th most popular website visited by Internet users in the United States. As a result, the top 100 torrents investigated were taken from those listed on The Pirate Bay overall top 100 list.

Assumptions

As with any computer forensic investigation, it is of upmost importance to identify the assumptions required to ensure accurate comprehension of any results achieved. The following list of assumptions holds true for the majority of Internet focused investigations:

1. An IP address may not uniquely identify a specific peer's computer connected to the Internet. The employment of Internet con-

nection sharing, web proxies, virtual private networks or web anonymity services such as Tor and I2P can all result in inaccuracies in the ultimate IP address identification.

2. Geo-location and ISP identification based on a given IP address is only as accurate as the databases used for lookup. For the investigation outlined in this paper, MaxMind (2010) stated that the geolocation databases used were 99.5% accurate at a country level, 83% accurate at a United States city level within a 25 mile radius and 100% accurate at the ISP level.

3. It is infeasible to detect the end-user churn rate on a given IP address due to the inconsistent dynamic IP address allocation employed by worldwide ISPs without factoring in additional available information, e.g., the end user's connection speeds, client information and more heuristic information such as an IP address downloading content from an inconsistent category.

4. Based on the size of the content being shared, it may be safe to assume that it is infeasible for users of slow Internet connections, e.g., 56kbps dial-up Internet subscribers, to partake in a swarm. This assumption can be useful for the analysis of the proportion of Internet subscribers detected throughout the investigation.

RESULTS AND ANALYSIS

For each IP address detected during the investigation, the IP geolocation databases developed and maintained by MaxMind (2010) are used to get the IP specific information such as city, country, latitude and longitude, ISP etc., being resolved. This information is then gathered and plotted as a heatmap to display the distribution of the peers involved in copyright infringement on a world map, seen in Figure 1.

Figure 1. Heatmap displaying the worldwide distribution of IP addresses discovered

Worldwide Results

The most popular content indexed by The Pirate Bay tends to be produced for the English speaking worldwide population, which is reflected in the heatmap in Figure 1, i.e., countries with a high proportion of English speaking population are highlighted in the results. As can be seen in Figure 2, the top ten countries detected account for over 53.6% of the total number of IPs found.

The assumption was made that a negligible number of dial-up users were involved in the swarms investigated due to the average required download time for the file sizes involved would have been over 69.5 hours, assuming an optimal

Figure 2. Top ten countries account for over 53.6% of the total worldwide activity

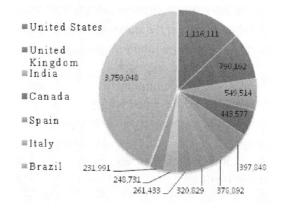

performance dial-up connection. As a result, the percentage of worldwide broadband subscribers detected during the investigation can be easily calculated based on the latest broadband subscription count from the International Telecommunication Union (2010). 2.43% of the 349,980,000 worldwide broadband subscriptions were discovered during the investigation. The percentages of broadband subscribers detected in the top 10 countries are outlined in Table 1.

United States Results

The United States was the most popular country detected with over 1.1 million unique IP addresses, which accounted for 13.15% of worldwide activity. While accounting for the largest portion of the results obtained in this investigation, this relatively low percentage suggests that BitTorrent has a much more globally dispersed users' base in comparison to other large P2P networks. For example, a 10 day investigation conducted on the Gnutella network in 2009 by Hannaway et al. (2009) it was found that "56.19% of all [worldwide] respondents to queries for content that is copyright protected came from the United States".

When the IP addresses detected during this investigation are geolocated and graphed onto a map, the large population centres can be easily identified, as can be seen in Figure 3. The state of California accounted for 13.7% of the US IPs found, with the states of Florida and New York accounting for 7.2% and 6.8% respectively. 14,202 IP addresses were identified in the most active city in the USA; Los Angeles. Chicago, New York, and Brooklyn were also identified as cities having more than then thousand unique peers identified each.

United Kingdom Results

790,162 unique IP addresses were identified in the United Kingdom. London was found to be the city with the largest number of identified IP addresses in the world and accounted for 17.2% of the total activity in the United Kingdom. Manchester, Birmingham, Brighton, Halifax, Bristol, Glasgow and Leeds were all cities with more than ten thousand IP addresses discovered. The distribution of discovered IP addresses were mainly identified in England, with significantly fewer IP addresses discovered in Wales, Scotland and Northern Ireland, as can be seen in Figure 4.

Table 1. Percentage of broadband subscribers found in each of the top ten countries

Country	Broadband Subscribers	Percentage Discovered
United States	73,123,000	1.53%
United Kingdom	17,276,000	4.57%
India	5,280,000	8.70%
Canada	9,842,000	4.51%
Spain	8,995,000	4.42%
Italy	11,283,000	3.36%
Brazil	10,098,000	3.18%
Australia	5,140,000	5.09%
Poland	4,792,000	5.19%
Greece	1,506,000	15.40%

Figure 3. IP addresses discovered during the weeklong investigation plotted onto a map of the mainland United States

Figure 4. Geographic distribution of IP addresses found in the United Kingdom

Irish Results

Of the 62,153 IP addresses identified in Ireland (Figure 5), 35,532 of those were located in Dublin. The cities of Limerick, Galway and Cork each had greater than 2000 unique IP addresses.

Figure 5. Geolocation of Irish IP addresses

CONCLUSION

The objective of this investigation is to attempt to identify the scale of the unauthorised distribution of copyrighted material worldwide. 2.43% of the world's broadband subscriber base was detected over the course of the weeklong investigation. The actual number of P2P users involved in the unauthorised distribution of copyrighted material is undoubtedly much higher than this due to the relatively small scale of this investigation. Some network factors will also have a negative effect over the results achieved, such as two or more end-users appearing as a single internet IP address though internet connection sharing, proxy services, anonymity services, etc.

ACKNOWLEDGMENT

The authors wish to acknowledge the support of Amazon.com for supporting part of this research with cloud computing time and storage through an Amazon Web Services research grant. Mark Scanlon is co-funded by the Irish Research Council for Science, Engineering and Technology and IntelIreland Ltd. through the Enterprise Partnership Scheme.

REFERENCES

Alexa. (2010). *ThePirateBay.org site info.* Retrieved from http://alexa.com/siteinfo/thepirate-bay.org

BitTorrent. (2008). *The BitTorrent Protocol specification.* Retrieved from http://bittorrent.org/beps/bep_0003.html

Erman, D. (2005). *BitTorrent traffic measurements and models.* Unpublished licentiate thesis, Blekinge Institute of Technology, Hogskola, Sweden.

Hannaway, A., & Kechadi, M.-T. (2009). An analysis of the scale and distribution of copyrighted material on the Gnutella network. In *Proceedings of the International Conference on Information Security and Privacy*, Orlando, FL.

International Federation of the Phonographic Industry. (2011). *Digital music report 2011*. Retrieved from http://www.ifpi.org/content/section_resources/dmr2011.html

International Telecommunication Union. (2010). *Report on Internet*. Retrieved from http://www.itu.int

MaxMind. (2010). *GeoLite country database*. Retrieved from http://www.maxmind.com

Scanlon, M., Hannaway, A., & Kechadi, M.-T. (2010). A week in the life of the most popular BitTorrent swarms. In *Proceedings of the 5th Annual Symposium on Information Assurance and the Academic Track of the 13th Annual New York State Cyber Security Conference*, Albany, NY (pp. 32-36).

The Pirate Bay. (n. d.). *Total top 100*. Retrieved from http://www.thepiratebay.org/top/all

This work was previously published in the International Journal of Ambient Computing and Intelligence, Volume 3, Issue 2, edited by Kevin Curran, pp. 56-63, copyright 2011 by IGI Publishing (an imprint of IGI Global).

Chapter 11

Development and Evaluation of a Dataset Generator Tool for Generating Synthetic Log Files Containing Computer Attack Signatures

Stephen O'Shaughnessy
Institute of Technology Blanchardstown, Ireland

Geraldine Gray
Institute of Technology Blanchardstown, Ireland

ABSTRACT

A key requirement for experimental analysis in the areas of network intrusion and computer forensics is the availability of suitable datasets. However, the inherent security and privacy issues surrounding these disciplines have resulted in a lack of available "test-bed" datasets for testing and evaluation purposes. Typically, the datasets required in these cases are from system log files, containing traces of computer misuse. Therefore, there is obvious potential for the use of synthetically generated log files that can accurately reproduce these traces or patterns of misuse. This paper discusses the development, testing, and evaluation of a dataset generator tool, designed to produce such datasets, particularly those containing patterns of common computer attacks.

1. INTRODUCTION

With continuing advances in the development of information technologies, the volume of data that is accrued as a result of network traffic and host machine activity is increasing at a rapid rate.

Intrusion detection and computer forensics involve sifting through such data to identify system attacks or evidence of wrong-doing. Consequently, computer forensics investigators and network administrators face the challenge of processing these ever growing volumes of data. Data mining, which can be defined as the non-trivial extraction

DOI: 10.4018/978-1-4666-2041-4.ch011

of implicit, previously unknown and potentially useful information from large amounts of data, has been well documented (Vaarandi, 2004; Abraham & de Vel, 2002; Wenke & Stolfo, 1998; Zhu & Zhang, 2001) as a successful method of identifying information of interest from data collected from network traffic or as a result of a forensics investigation.

This paper follows from (O'Shaughnessy & Gray, 2010), where the authors presented a dataset generator tool capable of generating synthetic log files containing 3 different types of computer attack pattern, the main purpose being to create test-bed datasets for the testing and evaluation of information discovery and network analysis or forensics tools.

This paper reports on the origins and usage of log file analysis, how the dataset generator tool was designed to replicate the attacks and how it was tested for accuracy using various data mining techniques. Emphasis is placed on the testing of the tool, particularly how data models, trained from the synthetically generated datasets, were applied to live data containing real computer attack instances, in order to test their accuracy in replicating both the log files and the attack signatures. Finally, the possible implications of the data models successfully identifying or misidentifying attack signatures is discussed.

2. BACKGROUND

Anyone who uses a computer will leave a trace or "fingerprint" of their activities, whether this activity is malicious or not. These usage traces are stored in the various log files generated by components on a computer or network and as such, a wealth of information on network and user activity that can be gleaned from such log files. For this reason, the authors chose to use log files to replicate the patterns of attack signatures featured in the dataset generator tool.

2.1. Types of Log File Represented by the Tool

The tool uses two different log file types to represent the attack signatures. The first type, the firewall log, records network activity to and from a host machine. The firewall log can serve as a critical component of information security, as it can be used to identify unusual or unexpected traffic patterns on a local network (Stingley, 2009). The second type, the Common Log Format log or CLF log, is the type of log file present on Web servers such as Apache or IIS and typically log a history of page requests to the server. Many differing types of computer attack signatures can be identified in this log.

Both of these log file types are ranked in the "Top 5 Essential Log Reports" by SANS (Brenton, Bird, & Ranum, 2006) and for this reason were chosen to represent the attack signatures replicated by the tool.

2.2. Categories of Attack Types

There are countless different types of attacks that are afflicted on computers and computer networks. Loosely, these attacks can be categorised as either passive or active. Passive attacks are those in which the attacker monitors transmissions and accesses data without modifying the data in any way. A passive attacker does not want the victim to know they are being attacked. Active attacks on the other hand involve the motoring and accessing of data like passive attacks, but the data is also modified in the process, to either cause malicious damage or to make some kind of gain for the attacker, whether it's financial or otherwise (Asgaut Eng., 1996).

2.3. Types of Attack Signature

The tool generates three different types of attack signatures, one passive – the Probing attack, and two active – Denial of Service and SQL Injection attacks. The challenge here was to identify how each attack signature manifests in log files and then implement the tool to successfully replicate the attack signature in the generated datasets.

2.3.1. Denial of Service (DoS)

A denial of service attack is caused by malicious attackers attempting to make computer or network resources unavailable by exhausting the resources of the host running the service, or making it unavailable by exploiting some vulnerability in the system (Houle & Weaver, 2001). The type of attack replicated by the dataset generator, known as flooding, involves saturating the target machine with communications requests, so much so that it causes the service to run very slowly or even render the service totally inaccessible.

A flooding attack will cause a significant upsurge in incoming traffic, which manifests in a log file as a large number of logon or access attempts within a short space of time. This type of attack can be identified by examining the temporal differences in the timestamp field for entries in the log file within a specified period of time.

2.3.2. Probing

A probe attack, also known as scanning, can be used by a would-be attacker as a reconnaissance tool in an attempt to reveal vulnerabilities in a system that can be exploited (Korba, 2000). The probe scans a network to search for valid IP addresses, active ports or to gather information about a computer's services, configurations and the operating system it is running on.

According to SANS 'Top 5 Essential Log Reports' (Brenton, Bird, & Ranum, 2006) a high number of error status codes (4xx) from an IP address could indicate that a probing or port scan attack is taking place on a server. The dataset generator tool replicates an access server log file in CLF to represent this type of attack, as it

contains the IP of the sender as well as the status code of the sender's request.

2.3.3. SQL Injection

SQL injection is a code injection technique that exploits a security vulnerability occurring in the database layer of an application. The malicious code is inserted into strings that are passed via HTTP to an instance of the SQL server for parsing and execution. An SQL server will execute any syntactically valid queries so any applications using SQL statements are vulnerable to this type of attack if certain precautions are not implemented.

For SQL injections to work, the attacker has to jump out of the original SQL statement. This is usually done by the single-quote ('), which is a delimiter for SQL queries, or the double-dash (--), which is a comment character in Oracle and MS SQL. Another symbol that can be used in injection attacks is the pipe (|) symbol. This symbol is used in commands to pipe the stdout of one program into stdin of another. This can be abused to execute other commands, e.g. typing |echo;id;exit|, pipes the results back to the sender (Meyer, 2008). In all, 9 distinct SQL injection signatures are replicated by the tool.

The SQL injection attack can be identified in the access request field of a HTTP request message to a server log. To represent this type of attack, the tool replicates an access server log file in CLF, containing SQL injection signatures in the access request field.

3. THE DATASET GENERATOR

The dataset generator tool is developed entirely in Java and is designed to be easily extended to cater for additional attack types. The user has the option to either customise the datasets produced by defining a number of different parameters or use the default parameters initially set in the tool. The fields representing attack signatures in the datasets are calculated randomly by the tool's custom random generator. The attack signature field values are taken from a list of possibilities contained in a series of text files, which allows ease of modification of attack signatures by editing the text files. The different dataset types available to the user are outlined below.

Clean dataset: replicates a dataset without attack signature which can be used in anomaly detection where a clean dataset is initially required to assess normal usage patterns.

Denial of Service dataset: replicates a typical flooding attack in a firewall log file. The tool produces firewall log files with sequential timestamps, such that a large number of entries, signifying a DoS attack, are identified by having shorter intervals between timestamps. The attack rows outputted are temporally sequential and correspond to the attack threshold parameter that is set by the user.

Probing dataset: replicates a log file in CLF. The attack signature here is manifested by a higher-than-normal number of 4xx status codes by a particular IP address. The number of attack rows in the dataset is randomly chosen.

SQL Injection dataset: replicates a log file in CLF. The SQL attack signatures are randomly chosen from a pool of typical attack signatures stored in an external text file. The number of attack rows in the dataset is randomly chosen.

3.1. Tool Interface

The tool's graphical user interface comprises of a series of tabbed panes which the user can choose from. Each pane in the tool represents a different dataset type and each contains default values, relevant to the particular type of dataset. Figure 1 illustrates the tool interface presented to the user upon start up, showing the clean dataset option,

set with default values. These default values can be cleared by choosing the reset option from the file drop down menu. On each pane, the user is presented with various text fields and drop-down menus and can specify parameters to be included in order to generate customised synthetic datasets containing specified computer attack signatures. There is an option to include a label field in each of the generated datasets. The label field represents the class label used in the training of the data mining models to classify each row in the dataset as either "ATTACK" or "CLEAN" data.

When the generate button is pressed, the tool generates a log file with either no attack data or one of the three pre-defined attack signatures, depending on the option chosen. The resulting dataset is written to the file and path specified by the user. The user has the option of outputting the file in comma-separated values format (.csv), text (.txt) or SQL script (.sql) formats.

Figure 2 shows an example of a generated firewall log file in CSV format. CSV format allows great portability of the generated dataset as it is supported by many spreadsheet applications and data mining tools.

Figure 3 illustrates the same output file when opened in Microsoft Excel spreadsheet application.

Figure 1. Tool interface upon start up

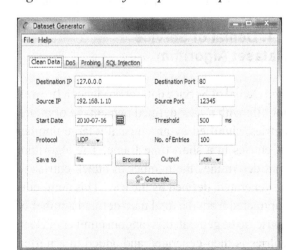

Figure 2. Generated firewall log file in CSV format

```
64.135.190.199,192.168.1.10,1296,80,UDP,2010-07-23,15:05:34.840,CLEAN
214.239.157.138,192.168.1.10,56193,80,UDP,2010-07-23,15:05:36.455,CLEAN
17.216.81.155,192.168.1.10,44133,80,UDP,2010-07-23,15:05:37.527,CLEAN
15.3.84.16,192.168.1.10,33783,80,UDP,2010-07-23,15:05:37.851,CLEAN
97.19.95.0,192.168.1.10,46551,80,UDP,2010-07-23,15:05:38.472,ATTACK
236.111.106.7,192.168.1.10,26590,80,UDP,2010-07-23,15:05:38.514,ATTACK
152.228.30.113,192.168.1.10,18424,80,UDP,2010-07-23,15:05:38.997,ATTACK
111.58.185.211,192.168.1.10,26243,80,UDP,2010-07-23,15:05:39.301,ATTACK
48.196.58.50,192.168.1.10,4349,80,UDP,2010-07-23,15:05:39.459,ATTACK
```

Figure 3. Generated firewall log file in Microsoft Excel spreadsheet format

38	64.135.190.199	192.168.1.10	1296	80	UDP	23/07/2010	15:05:35	CLEAN
39	214.239.157.138	192.168.1.10	56193	80	UDP	23/07/2010	15:05:36	CLEAN
40	17.216.81.155	192.168.1.10	44133	80	UDP	23/07/2010	15:05:38	CLEAN
41	15.3.84.16	192.168.1.10	33783	80	UDP	23/07/2010	15:05:38	CLEAN
42	97.19.95.0	192.168.1.10	46551	80	UDP	23/07/2010	15:05:38	ATTACK
43	236.111.106.7	192.168.1.10	26590	80	UDP	23/07/2010	15:05:39	ATTACK
44	152.228.30.113	192.168.1.10	18424	80	UDP	23/07/2010	15:05:39	ATTACK
45	111.58.185.211	192.168.1.10	26243	80	UDP	23/07/2010	15:05:39	ATTACK
46	48.196.58.50	192.168.1.10	4349	80	UDP	23/07/2010	15:05:39	ATTACK

4. TOOL ARCHITECTURE

The underlying architecture of the tool comprises of two main components: the data generator algorithms, which are responsible for generating datasets of a specified file format, with the desired attack signatures included, and the dataset generator engine, which facilitates the process of running the data generators to produce sufficiently accurate datasets and the output of the datasets in the correct file format to the correct location.

4.1. Denial of Service Dataset Algorithm

The Denial of Service dataset produces a firewall log file with a user defined percentage of attack entries, signified by an unusually large number of entries in a short time frame. The algorithm first determines the number of attack entries to be generated, defined by the user. This number is subtracted from the total user-defined number of entries to be generated. A random number of clean entries is then generated and added to a buffer.

The source IP and source port numbers for each entry are generated randomly. The frequency of the timestamp increment between entries is also generated randomly and is calculated between 0 and 4 times the user-defined frequency bound. This allows for a marked difference between the timestamp increments of the clean entries and the attack entries. The frequency is recalculated and added to each successive entry to produce a sequential timestamp. All other parameters in the resulting dataset are defined by the user.

Next, the user-defined percentage of attack entries is generated. As before, the source IP and source ports are generated randomly. The timestamp from the last entry in the initial generation of clean rows is used to determine the starting timestamp for the first attack entry. In this case, and of each successive entry, a random frequency is chosen between 0 and the user-defined frequency bound and added to the timestamp to give the desired increment. The attack entries are then appended to the buffer.

Finally, the remaining clean entries are calculated in the same manner as previously explained and appended to the buffer. If the noise option is chosen, then smaller timestamp increments for the clean entries are randomly calculated, giving an increment closer to that of the attack entries.

4.2. Probing and SQL Injection Dataset Algorithms

Both the Probing and SQL Injection options produce a log file in CLF so as such, the algorithms are structured the same way, the difference being the type of attack signature that is generated. The algorithms are structured into a series of loops. An outer loop controls the number of file entries generated, while three inner loops control the construction of the clean and attack entries. Two random integers are first calculated, representing the initial number of both clean and attack rows to be generated. As each clean entry is generated, a random IP address is chosen. In addition, the timestamps are incremented randomly for each entry to produce sequential entries, which are added to a buffer.

The IP address for the attack entries is user-defined. The attack entries are produced in the same manner as the clean entries, with the exception that, in the case of the Probing dataset, there are a higher number of 4xx status codes in the status field of the file and, in the case of the SQL Injection datasets, there are a higher percentage of entries containing known SQL escape character sequences in the access request field of the file. The generated attack entries are appended to the buffer.

When the third loop terminates, this process is started over again. The new value for the total number of entries is decremented by subtracting the number of entries generated in the three inner loops and the algorithm continues to loop until this value has decremented to 0, in which case all the entries have been generated. The resulting log file has sections of attack data randomly dispersed across the log file.

4.3. Dataset Generator Engine

The engine is responsible for passing the user defined parameters to the generators and gathering the resulting data from the buffers. It then writes the data to the specified file and location.

5. EVALUATION

The validity of the generator as an effective tool hinges on its performance in producing realistic log file entries containing accurate attack signature patterns. The generated datasets were individually evaluated by training a C4.5 decision tree classifier on labelled data generated from the tool. Once the model's accuracy was optimised on test data generated by the tool, the decision tree was used to classify live data, the purpose being to determine if a model trained on generated data could identify computer attacks in a real log file. RapidMiner (2010), a world-leading open-source system, was used for this evaluation.

This section details the testing and evaluation on the datasets produced by the tool, using data mining processes within the RapidMiner system. The main aim of the training process in this case is to produce a data model with a high percentage of true positives and true negatives where a high percentage of both attack rows and clean rows would be labelled correctly. This model could then be tested for accuracy against a live dataset. If the models produced from the generated datasets could accurately identify similar attack pattern signatures in live data, this would justify the accuracy of the datasets produced by the dataset generator tool.

5.1. Training the Denial of Service Dataset

The dataset generated for testing the denial of service contained 1000 rows with 5% attack data, i.e., 950 *clean* rows and 50 *attack* rows. The obvious pattern to identify in this case was the difference in the timestamp increments between each entry. As stated previously, the denial of service signature manifests as a large number of contiguous entries in the log file within a short time frame and so would have a timestamp increment that is generally smaller than that of the normal pattern of entries. In order to simulate this pattern in the data, the timestamp increment for the clean rows of data was set to 2000, which produced random timestamps between 0 and 2000 milliseconds, and the timestamp increment for the rows representing the DoS attack was set to 500 milliseconds, producing random timestamps between 0 and 500 milliseconds.

Pre-processing of this dataset primarily involved using a moving average on the timestamp increment to distinguish between attacks and sequences of valid requests that happen to come in close proximity. Moving averages are commonly used in time series data, such as this, in order to smooth out values, rather than have big differences between average values. The timestamp attribute had to be removed, as the initial decision tree identified that the attack occurred at a particular time, and so labelled all rows that occurred at that time as attack data.

In order to identify the Denial of Service attack pattern, the frequency of each entry needed to be measured and not just the particular time so the moving average was performed on the timestamp increment, which was extracted from each timestamp attribute. In addition, due to the small percentage of attack data in the dataset, boosting was used to replicate attack rows to overcome the class imbalance problem of the small proportion of attack rows in the dataset.

Cross validation was applied using 10 validations, which split the dataset into 10 models, in order to estimate the true error of the model. In each validation, 10% of rows were used for testing the model, and the remaining 90% of rows were used to train the model. The error rate was

calculated as the average error rate across the 10 models generated.

Finally, RapidMiner's implementation of the C4.5 decision tree algorithm was used to learn a decision tree from the dataset.

The decision tree for the denial of service process is shown in Figure 4. The tree shows, for the moving average of the timestamp differences, anything above 560.3 milliseconds was predicted as clean. This would be expected because the timestamp increment for the clean rows was randomly generated between 0 and 2000 milliseconds, which on average would skew the value higher than 500 milliseconds. The rows less than 560.3 were divided by the attribute "change (Time)", which represents the timestamp increment difference between each row of data. If the time difference was greater than 507 Milliseconds, then the rows were labelled as clean. Anything below 507 milliseconds was labelled as an attack row. Again this was expected because the attack row timestamp increment was randomly generated between 0 and 500 milliseconds.

The result from the RapidMiner pre-processing operations on the dataset is shown in Table 1. The data mining algorithms predicted all of the clean rows (950) i.e. 100% accuracy (true negatives). For the attack rows they predicted 296 out

Figure 4. Decision tree for the denial of service

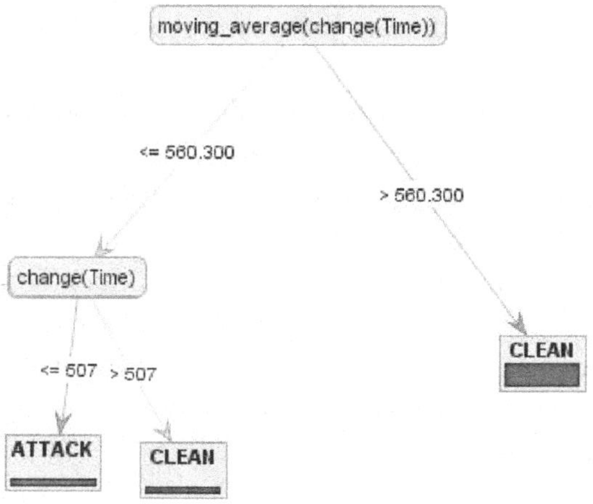

Table 1. RapidMiner pre-processing operations results

Outcome	Predicted	Total	Accuracy %
True Positive	296	300	98.7%
True Negative	950	950	100%
False Positive	0	950	0%
False Negative	4	300	1.3%

of 300 which was an accuracy of 98.7% (true positives). This means that the data mining algorithms identified less that 1.5% of attack rows incorrectly (false negatives). This high accuracy could be due to the fact that the denial of service attack has a very distinctive pattern and so was easily picked up by the data mining algorithms. Alternatively the model itself could be over-trained. Another possibility is that the timestamp increments between attack rows may be too small in comparison to the clean rows and so were easily identified, which would suggest that the generated dataset could be unrealistic. In the latter case, the dataset generator tool algorithm could be adjusted until a satisfactory output for the timestamp increments could be achieved. It should be noted that, due to time constraints, I could not locate or replicate a live dataset that contained a denial of service attack so the results here could not be tested against live data.

5.2. Training the Probing Attack Dataset

The dataset generated for the probing attack consisted of 4468 rows of data in CLF log format. Unlike the denial of service dataset, the amount of attack entries was not known since they were generated randomly by the application. The fields of interest in this type of dataset (for the purposes of predicting probing attacks) are the STATUS and IP address fields. The STATUS field is a numeric code which indicates the success or failure of a users HTTP request, i.e. their requesting of a Web

page. The error status codes, numbered 4xx, are of most interest because the probing attacker should receive a lot of these. The IP address is the ip address of the sender. In most cases, the IP address of the sender is not spoofed, as in the denial of service attack, and so is a field of interest (Meyer, 2008).

To both simplify and emphasise the difference between errors codes and other codes, the authors mapped these codes to alternative values. Any rows with containing an error code 4xx were mapped to a value of 10 and all other rows were mapped to a value of 5. The purpose of this was to introduce a value that could be used to obtain the average value for rows grouped by IP address. The reasoning here is that the rows with an error code of 10 would have a higher average than the other rows, that had a value of 5, and so could be predicted more easily by a decision tree. A moving average with a window of 5 was used to smooth this new attribute, allowing the mining algorithm to distinguish between a high concentration of errors codes, as would be typical in attack data, and a low concentration generated by error codes return to valid traffic. Cross validation was used, in a similar manner to the Denial of Service process, to estimate the error of the training model.

RapidMiner's implementation of the C4.5 decision tree algorithm was again used to mine the dataset. The results of the decision tree algorithm are shown in Figure 5.

The decision tree shows a definite prediction of probe entries for entries with a moving average of greater than 9.5. This is expected because the moving average would calculate a high percentage of attack rows as 10 or close to 10. For entries with a moving average of less than 9.5 the decision tree did miss-classify some clean entries as probe and vice versa.

This is possibly due to some clean entries having a 4xx error code and thus having a moving average of 10 or near 10. In this case, the decision tree could have labelled them erroneously as probe. Likewise, some probe entries could have contained

Figure 5. Decision tree algorithm results

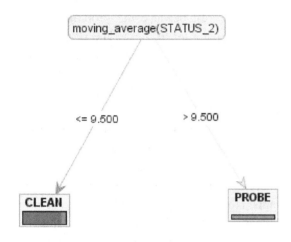

success status codes and so would have had a low moving average, miss-labelling them as clean.

5.2.1. Applying the Probe Model to Live Data

The purpose of training the dataset was to create a model that could be applied to a real dataset to determine if it could predict patterns in the live dataset that were consistent with the ones found in the model, i.e. clean or probe entries. This section details how the model was used to do this and subsequently to test the accuracy of the generated dataset in representing a probe attack. The live data sample was taken from a HoneyNet challenge (HoneyNet, 2004) and consisted of a CLF log file from an apache Web server log file that was designed specifically to be used as a honeypot. A honeypot is a computer set up to attract hackers, crackers etc. for the purposes of learning about attackers and their methods (HoneyNet, 2004). The file consists of over 202,000 entries and contains many different types of attack. As a result, the quality of the data, for the purposes of testing for attacks, was quite high. The fact that the honeypot file is machine generated, means it does not suffer from inconsistencies that befall human entered data, such as missing values and invalid data.

1400 rows from the HoneyNet log file were used as the test set. To be able to test the model, the amount of probe entries that were contained in the file had to be known so it could be determined how many entries were predicted correctly by the model. Within the 1400 rows used, 204 entries were added that were classified as probes, according to the solutions from the HoneyNet challenge (Grenier, 2004). The probe entries that were used, originated from the vulnerability scanning program Nessus (Tenable Network Security, 2010). The USER_AGENT field of the log file shows which log file entries came from the Nessus application.

The model was applied to the live data using RapidMiner's model applier operator. The results of this are illustrated in Table 2.

The figures show that the model, originally trained from the generated dataset, predicted with approximately 75% accuracy, which rows in the real dataset were probes. The number of true positives was 152 out of a possible 204 probe entries. The reason for the number of false negatives (52) could be that, similarly to the training model, certain probe entries in the live dataset contained 2xx status codes so the model classified these as clean.

5.3. Training the SQL Attack Dataset

The dataset generated for the SQLInjection example consisted of 1716 entries in CLF format. As in the case of the generated probing dataset, the number of entries that contained SQL injection sig-

Table 2. USER_AGENT field log file entry results

Outcome	Result
Number of probe entries predicted correctly (True positives)	152
Number of probe entries predicted as clean (False Negatives)	52
Total amount of true probe rows	204
Model Accuracy (% of correct predictions)	74.5%

natures was unknown because they are randomly generated. The SQL injection attack signatures used in the generated log file were taken from a solution to the HoneyNet challenge (Telmack, 2004) and also from a SANS Institute paper, which referenced this particular challenge in its explanation of SQL injection attacks (Meyer, 2008). The field that is of most importance in the CLF log file for the purposes of identifying an SQL injection attack is the access request URL. The reason for this is because the SQL injection attacker injects malicious code through HTTP requests which is essentially what the access request field shows. SQL injection attack signatures can be recognised using a regular expression search. RapidMiner is ideal for this purpose as it has facilities regular expression searching. A mapping operator was used to map all known possible combinations of regular expressions, which would identify the SQL injection entries in the access request field, to the value "SQL". All other rows were set to the default "OK". Cross validation was used to estimate the error of the training model.

The decision tree for the SQL Injection model is illustrated in Figure 6. The tree shows that for entries labelled as clean, approximately 97% of these were classified correctly (true negatives), meaning that the data mining algorithms labelled 3% of the clean rows as SQL Injection (false positive). For entries labelled as SQL Injection, approximately 75% of these were classified correctly (true positives), meaning that the data mining algorithms labelled 25% of the SQL injection rows as clean (false negatives).

5.3.1. Applying the SQL Injection Model to Live Data

Once the model was trained to a satisfactory level of accuracy, it was then applied to a live dataset. The authors used the same HoneyNet CLF log file as mentioned before, since it also contained numerous types of SQL injection attack entries. A sample of 586 entries was taken from the HoneyNet

Figure 6. Decision tree for the SQL Injection model

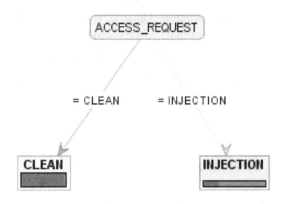

log file, which included 44 entries containing SQL injection data. These SQL entries were identified from Stelmack (2004) and Meyer (2008) as outlined previously. The results of applying the model to the live data are illustrated in Table 3.

The results show that the model identified all of the attack rows that were inserted into the live dataset. The confidence for each SQL entry was 0.74, meaning that the model was 74% confident that the identified entry was an SQL injection. This would indicate that some clean data was labelled as attack data by the model, an example of which is given below.

Examination of the dataset found a number of occurrences in the access request field that contained the following string:

GET.?D=A&M='UNION'&N=D&S=A&HT TP/1.1

Table 3. SQL Injection model results when applied to live data

Outcome	Result
Number of SQL injection entries predicted (true positives)	44
Number of Clean entries predicted (true negatives)	542
Number of SQL injection entries (known)	44
Model Accuracy (% of correct predictions)	100%

This string is a legitimate request but was picked up by the model as a SQL injection entry which illustrates that live data could contain many legitimate entries in a log file with similarities to SQL signatures and so further investigation into a more comprehensive regular expression filter is required to identify all attacks accurately.

6. CONCLUSION

This paper followed on from the authors previous work on a dataset generator for testing and evaluating knowledge discovery techniques and forensics or network security analysis tools here (O'Shaughnessy & Gray, 2010), placing greater emphasis on the testing of the tool.

Testing the tool for its ability to replicate log files with accurate attack signature patterns involved using data mining techniques to model the datasets produced by the tool and subsequently apply the models to live data, the purpose being to gauge how well the model could predict patterns of attacks in the live or unseen data. So, essentially, the success metric of the tool was measured by the effectiveness of the data mining models trained from the generated datasets at predicting the attack signature patterns in the live log files because if the models trained from the generated datasets could accurately predict similar patterns in unseen data, then it would follow that the generated datasets are accurate. Overall, the results showed that both the probing and SQL injection models were ~75% accurate in predicting the patterns of attack in the samples taken from the HoneyNet log file.

The question that arises from the results produced is: *what impact will incorrect readings have on a system?* If clean data is labelled as attack, then some legitimate traffic can be blocked. The implications here would be that important legitimate traffic would not reach its destination and in time critical systems such as ATM banking systems, this could be catastrophic. The obvious

choice here is to try and eliminate this but this is not always possible. For example, a probe attack can be quite difficult to detect as legitimate traffic can be similar to the attack data, i.e. contain 4xx error codes. On the other hand, if attack data is labelled as clean, then this traffic will get through to its intended target. The question here is, is it more important to reduce the percentage of attack data labelled as clean (false negatives) or to reduce the percentage of clean data labelled as attack (false positives)? The answer to this depends very much on the system, the type of traffic that will pass through it and the level of damage caused to the system as a result of implementing these changes.

REFERENCES

Abraham, T., & de Vel, O. (2002). Investigative profiling with computer forensic log data and association rules. In *Proceedings of the IEEE International Conference on Data Mining* (pp.11-18).

Asgaut Eng. (1996). *Passive and active attacks.* Retrieved from http://www.pvv.org/~asgaut/crypto/thesis/node10.html

Brenton, C., Bird, T., & Ranum, M. J. (2006). *Top 5 essential log reports.* Retrieved from http://www.sans.org/security-resources/top5_logreports.pdf

Grenier, C. (2004). *HoneyNet scan of the month 31: Solution.* Retrieved from http://old.honeynet.org/scans/scan31/sub/grenier/attacks.html

HoneyNet. (2004). *Scan 31.* Retrieved from http://old.honeynet.org/scans/scan31/

Houle, K. J., & Weaver, G. M. (2001). *Trends in denial of service attack technology.* Pittsburgh, PA: CERT® Coordination Centre.

Korba, J. (2000). *Windows NT attacks for the evaluation of intrusion detection systems.* Unpublished master's thesis, Massachusetts Institute of Technology, Cambridge, MA.

Meyer, R. (2008). *Detecting attacks on web applications from log files*. Bethesda, MD: SANS Institute.

O'Shaughnessy, S., & Gray, G. (2010). Development of a dataset generator for testing and evaluating knowledge discovery techniques and forensics or network security analysis tools. In *Proceedings of the 10th International Conference on Information Technology and Telecommunication*.

RapidMiner. (2010). *RapidMiner homepage*. Retrieved from http://rapid-i.com/content/view/181/190/

Stelmack, T. (2004). *HoneyNet scan of the month 31: Solution*. Retrieved from http://old.honeynet.org/scans/scan31/sub/tina_stelmack/tina_stelmack.pdf

Stingley, M. (2009). *Check point firewall log analysis in-depth*. Bethesda, MD: SANS Institute.

Tech Target. (2007). *Honeypot definition*. Retrieved from http://searchsecurity.techtarget.com/sDefinition/0,sid14_gci551721,00.html

Tenable Network Security. (2010). *Tenable nesssus*. Retrieved from http://www.nessus.org/nessus/

Vaarandi, R. (2004). A breadth-first algorithm for mining frequent patterns from event logs. In *Proceedings of the IFIP International Conference on Intelligence in Communication Systems* (pp. 293-308).

Wenke, L., & Stolfo, S. J. (1998). Data mining approaches for intrusion detection. In *Proceedings of the 7th Conference on USENIX Security* (Vol. 7).

Zhu, P., & Zhang, C. (2001). Data mining for network intrusion detection: A comparison of alternative methods. *Decision Series*, *32*(4), 635–660. doi:10.1111/j.1540-5915.2001.tb00975.x

This work was previously published in the International Journal of Ambient Computing and Intelligence, Volume 3, Issue 2, edited by Kevin Curran, pp. 64-76, copyright 2011 by IGI Publishing (an imprint of IGI Global).

Chapter 12
Making the Case for "Architectural Informatics":
A New Research Horizon for Ambient Computing?

Mikael Wiberg
Uppsala University, Sweden

ABSTRACT

Society is undergoing a major digitalization - not at least in the field of architecture. The digitalization of our built environment has also begun to reflect itself in research (see e.g., Cai & Abascal, 2006; Margolis & Robinson, 2007; Greenfield, 2006). At the cross point in-between architecture, urban development, and the digitalization of modern society, there is a major research potential – untapped and ready to be explored. This paper initiates an "architectural informatics" perspective and outlines a research agenda as to address questions of how to better integrate our built environment and digital world. This paper outlines three research themes including: 1) Architectural composition with digital materials (theory development), 2) Architecture for sustainable digitization (development of value ground), and 3) Digitization processes & architecture as social intervention processes (methodology development). Common to these three areas is the overall aim to develop architectural and computational concepts and theories as to address this common area, to find new practice based methods to facilitate new forms of cooperation between engineers, architects and the inhabitants of our built environment, as well as to explore architectural informatics as a phenomenon and opportunity.

DOI: 10.4018/978-1-4666-2041-4.ch012

1. INTRODUCTION: TOUCHING THE "MATERIAL GROUND" FOR ARCHITECTURAL INFORMATICS

Our society is undergoing a major digitalization - not at least in the field of architecture. The digitalization of our built environment has also begun to reflect itself in research (see e.g., Cai & Abascal, 2006; Margolis & Robinson, 2007; Greenfield, 2006). At the same time, the digital is increasingly becoming a natural architectural element (Greenberg, 2006; Wiberg, 2011). As the digital gets integrated in our built environment, typically addressed as ambient computing, it creates and enables new functionality for buildings, new opportunities for building construction, and new architectural expressions. With this development follows that the digital is neither possible nor meaningful to separate from the social, the physical, and the material world. Rather, we find meaning inn texturized and working *compositions* made up of physical, digital and social elements (for a further discussion see e.g., Robles & Wiberg, 2010; Wiberg & Robles, 2010; Wiberg, 2011).

For the research program "architectural informatics" as presented in this paper this is a guiding vision in which no categorical distinction is made between the physical and the digital in the first place. On the contrary, the physical, the digital and the social is now to a large extent integrated in our everyday lives. The history of informatics research shows that with full clarity. People shape digital technology and the digital technology is shaping us. Several concepts have over the years succeeded each other in informatics research to make this point. 'Socio-technical systems' (Hirschheim & Klein, 1989) was one of the first concepts formulated to point to the fact that technical and social systems are fundamentally inseparable and as such constituting a socio-technical materiality. The concept of a "duality of technology" (Orlikowski, 1992) was further developed as a concept aimed at describing the relationship between the social and the technical world. When the complete fu-sion of the physical and digital occur, there is no point in further distinguish these elements. This knowledge led to the development of the present concept of 'sociomateriality' (Orlikowski, 2007; Orlikowski & Scott, 2008) or simply 'materiality' (Leonardi & Barley, 2008) aimed at highlighting how social practices relate to the material in our increasingly digitalized society.

In the modern society our built environment and our digital reality are increasingly defining our social, cultural and professional everyday lives. With this as a point of departure a number of researchers in recent years have stressed the importance of closer interdisciplinary collaboration between the fields of architecture and IT research (see e.g., Streitz et al., 2002, p. 555; Jones et al., 2005; Sengers et al., 2004). Despite this obvious fact, very little has been done in order to build strong research on an integrative approach of the two areas (Mitchell, 2000; McCullough, 2004; Wiberg, 2005). The research agenda as presented in this paper is an attempt to contribute to this need.

At the core of this research program is an opportunity to reach new knowledge in the joint, interdisciplinary area that we think of as *"architectural informatics"* (for a further motivation see Robles & Wiberg, 2011). We view *architectural informatics* as the study of the entangled design and practice of digital material use at the scale of architecture. Such entanglements manifested through architectural composition of known architectural materials and new digital materials requires the development of architectural theory, including concept development capable of framing and describing new spatial and temporal dimensions of new architectural forms. As will be further elaborated through the three research themes presented in this paper the research program on architectural informatics takes this material understanding of our reality as an important point of departure.

The rest of this paper is structured as follows. First we present a number of research questions that serves the purpose of illustrating the current research challenges facing this area. Moving on from these challenges identified this paper then present three research themes designed to address these challenges. With a point of departure in these three areas we then reflect on different methodological approaches needed to explore this area followed by a discussion on potential results from this exploration. The paper ends with the sketching out of a research agenda that might leverage current research on ambient computing into the area of architectural informatics.

Research Questions and Interdisciplinary Research Challenges

The overall research questions guiding our research program on *'Architectural Informatics'* are all of a strong interdisciplinary kind and as such they also serve as a common starting point for the involved parties in our research environment. The questions are also deliberately formulated as to work across the three thematic areas of the research program as will be described later on in this paper. The main research questions include e.g.: - *How can architectural theory be developed with regards to architectural informatics?, - How can new architectural compositions that include digital materials be described, conceptualized and historically anchored in architecture?, - How is architectural thinking effected by the possibilities of digital technologies as new architectural elements? - Will the current developments lead to new forms of cooperation between engineers, architects and their clients? If so, how can these forms of cooperation be further described and methodologically supported?*

These are examples of research questions that will be further explored through the research program's three overarching research themes.

The Research Program's Three Overarching Research Themes

The research program *Architectural Informatics* consists of three major research themes motivated by the inquiries in this application. These include: 1) *Architectural composition with digital materials* (pragmatic advancement and theory development), 2) *Architecture for sustainable digitalization* (the development of values), and 3) *Digitalization processes & architecture as social intervention processes* (methodology development). These three will be simultaneously explored and below these three are further described in detail.

1. *Architectural composition with digital materials* (pragmatic advancement and theoretical developments)

    Within this research theme we will undertake specific research efforts aimed at increasing the documentation of good pragmatic examples and illustrative expressions of how the digital manifest itself in architectural compositions. This empirical material will then be used to inform theory development in this important area. A starting point will be in the history of architecture with regard to compositional thinking. Another starting point will be in modern texturation theory (Wiberg, 2011), which has to a large extent targeted architectural compositions with digital materials. With our partners who are working with digital architecture for the modern indoor environment we also aim at furthering the integration of video/audio in the architecture of the modern home as well as look into digitalization and development of mobile solutions in support of a building's heating system, ventilation system, solar panels, etc.

2. *Architecture for sustainable digitization* (development of value ground for architectural informatics)

This research theme is intended to move from broad issues of architecture and so called "green technologies"/Green IT to issues of sustainability (broadly speaking at the range from material development and material choices to the creation of sustainable life worlds for the people inhabiting our built environment) as to expand our value ground for good architecture. The theme is based upon the idea of *sustainable digitalization* of our built environment including digitalization of architectural design processes, architecture, infrastructure and the life cycles of various infrastructures – reaching from traditional architecture to the ultra-modern digital infrastructures.

As emphasized by Rodden and Benford (2003) architecture and infrastructure changes works along on a much longer time span than gadgets and services (Table 1). A better understanding of sustainability in terms of integration of architecture and digital technologies is therefore important to reach, both from an economic and environmentally sound perspective as in the creation of good, and long-term sustainable environments. Fundamentally, this is a question of development of architectural values in relation to the digitaliza-

tion of our society and in particular in relation to the digitalization of our built environment.

Looking into related work in this area we notice that Rodden and Benford (2003) further expands this perspective in their research with an illustration of the methodological approaches taken to this date in IT research in relation to different scales of the physical, (ranging from small stuff (stuff) to large construction sites (sites) Figure 1). From this graph it is evident the initiatives taken and the technologies developed in proportion to *scale*, and what kind of studies that mainly has so forth been undertaken in this area. At the same time this graph also shows with clarity a large, empty and largely unexplored area of the chart (see gray area in Figure 1) in terms of opportunities for method development, technology development, and understanding of digitalization, where the scale reaches architectural scale (the range of "services" to "site" in the graph). This in itself is a clear call for *architectural informatics.*

In relation to the graph (Figure 1) our research program on architectural informatics will work with empirical cases that in different ways explore

Table 1. Time spans for architectural informatics in relation to scale (Rodden & Benford, 2003)

Brands Level	Dominant Skills	Inhabitants Role	Representations	Time to Make Change
Site	Civil Engineers Architects Regulatory Bodies Builders	Coordination with external expert Involvement in planning	Maps, Site Engineers Plans and Planning Bodies Notations	Months to Years
Structure	Regulatory Bodies Builders Painters	Coordination with experts Some advanced DIY expertise	Engineering plans Architectural Draws	Weeks to Months
Skin	Regulatory Bodies	Coordination with expert Some advanced DIY expertise	Architectural views and diagrams	Weeks to Months
Services	Service Providers	Coordination with service providers DIY enthusiast	Specialized diagrams, notations and models associate with each service.	Days
Space Plan	Designers Painters Inhabitants	Coordination with experts Inhabitant based decoration DIY enthusiast	Simple Layouts Feng Shui	Hours to Days
Stuff	Inhabitants	Introduction and movements of Stuff	Design Magazines	Minutes to Hours

Figure 1. Current research activities undertaken in relation to architectural scale and positioning of the architectural informatics research program (Rodden & Benford, 2003)

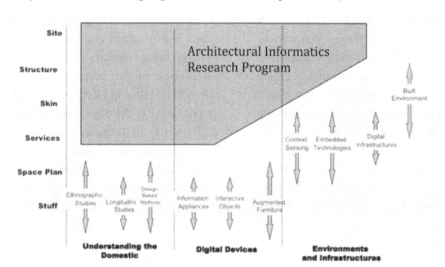

these empty spaces of the graph with a particular focus on the scale between "services" and "site". This will be done by following and participating in ongoing cases and projects together with companies and architects affiliated with this research program.

3. *Digitization processes & architecture as social intervention processes* (methodology).

Planning and change in our built environment is also to a great extent a matter of *social intervention processes* where the final building and the planning of its context and its immediate environment is a manifestation of the process that in turn led to the decisions on which the new architecture is based. This concern, that context is also an important element of a design, and not just something that influences the design process, has most recently been noted in IT research (see e.g., Wiberg, 2011). In this interweaving of architecture and its context, and across architecture and social processes, it is also important to find new ways of supporting *temporal thinking* on the integration of architecture and digital technologies. As for today, and to a large extent, various

supporting tools have been developed to support *spatial thinking* in the field of architecture - from simple support for sketching, via blueprint drawing to the most advanced 3D and CAD software in support of advanced design and visualization of complex architecture. With a focus on processes there's a need for new knowledge that can inform the development of alternative methods of high relevance to the architecture profession's modern challenges of thinking about architecture in terms of temporal flows of people, activities and objects.

2. A METHODOLOGICAL CHALLENGE: THE RESEARCH PROGRAM'S OVERALL APPROACH

There are a number of methodological challenges associated with a research program on architectural informatics. As to tackle these challenges a number of sub-projects will be put together and conducted as to achieve more in-depth knowledge of relevance to the development of architectural theory and practice, and to build the field of *architectural informatics* as an interdisciplinary and internationally well-established field of knowledge. To achieve these ambitious goals the research program will: 1) prioritize and research sub-projects with high potential for exploring links between architecture, historical/cultural perspectives in combination with architectural prototyping with modern digital technologies and materials, 2) prioritize sub-projects with clear links to international research collaborations, and finally 3) prioritize sub-projects which highlights international perspectives on the modern society's challenges related to architectural and technological sustainability.

The methodological approach will further build on the ideas of leading practice and action research in order to cooperate with, follow and document the leading practice in the field. Further on, it will actively seek to transform and influence architectural practice. This, through the application of new knowledge produced within the research program directly into the specific sub-projects that the research program's industry partners are working with.

3. WHERE WE MIGHT BE HEADING: THE RESEARCH PROGRAM'S OVERALL RESULTS

The research program as outlined in this paper can have a major impact on a number of different levels. For architectural practice we see this as a unique opportunity to create a stable platform for the exchange of ideas, critical reflection and method development. By encouraging meetings between architects, IT designers, engineers and their clients the practice of architectural informatics is also directly affected throughout this research program. The research program will also open up for new opportunities to experiment with digital technologies (including so called "new materials", see e.g., Margolis & Robinson, 2007; Brownell, 2008; Wiberg, 2011) in architecture which in turn open of opportunities to achieve new knowledge about e.g. digitalized ventilation systems, smart

home solutions, alarm systems, flexible room solutions, digital/interactive art, home media centers, mobile systems of indoor climate control, lighting systems, heating consumption control systems, etc.

For architectural theory and for method and methodology development there are also great achievements to be reached within this research program. Through a number of sub-projects undertaken in which digital technologies are being explored in its implementation in the public space and integrated in modern indoor and outdoor architecture there are great opportunities for methodological lessons to be learnt from these real life processes. As such, the research program's results will therefore contribute to both the development of methods and theory development, as well as to the practical development of the area constituted by an integration of architecture and digital technology – results valuable both for practice and academia.

Through the activities and sub-projects undertaken within this research program will contain it is our intention that will lead to a number of practical results of importance for the further development. These results include the development of knowledge to further the development of: 1) digital infrastructures for future cities and sustainable living, 2) better standards for digitalizing buildings and cities, including results valuable for smart grid solutions, 3) communication solutions (and protocols) to allow for easy integration of various building technologies, and 4) visualizations and interfaces (adjusted to a wide range of media - from embedded wall displays to mobile devices, pads and ordinary computers). By reaching results on several different levels it is our intention that the research program should be relevant both for the development of computational and architectural theory as well as for the profession of modern architecture.

4. CONCLUSION

In this paper we have presented our research program on architectural informatics. The research program has been motivated by the current development towards new materialities in which the digital becomes an integrated material in a number of areas including full-scale architecture. As presented in this paper a focus on integration across digital technologies and architecture opens up new research opportunities for e.g. the development of energy-efficient buildings, smart homes, and new innovative solutions for future housing. Given this current development we might ask the question of how this might present a new horizon for research on ambient computing, i.e. the research area closest related to the integration of digital technologies with our built environment. From our perspective we find that likely, and in closing and to be more specific we think that this new horizon will include a number of research challenges for ambient computing. First of all, a focus on architectural informatics will imply a focus on *digital installations at architectural scale*. Further on, in order to conduct this research on architectural scale there is a need to also *move from lab prototyping to real world cases*. As a third implication following from this the real world cases also implies a *movement from the research lab to the public setting*. Methodologically, it follows from this movement a need to develop methods capable of *shifting perspective from the fictional to the real* (e.g. to move forward from e.g. "scenario based design" methods). Finally, when working with these real world cases it will not only concern *what can be built (i.e. design) but also our already built environment* and its current use. This will call for theoretical development in terms of sustainable ambient computing. From our perspective we see these challenges as landmarks – marking out an interesting new horizon for future research on ambient computing.

REFERENCES

Brownell, B. (2008). *Transmaterial 2: A catalog of materials that redefine our physical environment*. Princeton, NJ: Princeton Architectural Press.

Cai, Y., & Abascal, J. (2006). *Ambient intelligence in everyday life*. Berlin, Germany: Springer-Verlag.

Greenfield, A. (2006). *Everyware – the dawning age of ubiquitous computing*. Indianapolis, IN: New Riders.

Hirschheim, R., & Klein, H. (1989). Four paradigms of information systems development. *Communications of the ACM, 32*(10), 1199–1216. doi:10.1145/67933.67937

Jones, Q., Grandhi, S., Terveen, L., & Whittaker, S. (2005). People-to-people-to-geographical places: The P3 framework for location-based community systems. *Computer Supported Cooperative Work, 13*, 249–282. doi:10.1007/s10606-004-2803-7

Leonardi, P. M., & Barley, S. R. (2008). Materiality and change: Challenges to building better theory about technology and organizing. *Information and Organization, 18*, 159–176. doi:10.1016/j.infoandorg.2008.03.001

Margolis, L., & Robinson, A. (2007). *Living systems – Innovative materials for architecture and design*. Boston, MA: Birkhäuser.

McCullough, M. (2004). *Digital ground: Architecture, pervasive computing, and environmental knowing, cloth*. Cambridge, MA: MIT Press.

Mitchell, W. (2000). *City of bits – Space, place and the Infobahn*. Cambridge, MA: MIT Press.

Orlikowski, W. J. (2007). Sociomaterial practices: Exploring technology at work. *Organization Studies, 28*(9), 1435–1448. doi:10.1177/0170840607081138

Orlikowski, W. J., & Scott, S. V. (2008). Sociomateriality: Challenging the separation of technology, work and organization. *Academy of Management Annals*, *2*(1), 433–474. doi:10.1080/19416520802211644

Robles, E., & Wiberg, M. (2011). From materials to materiality. *Interactions (New York, N.Y.)*, *18*(1). doi:10.1145/1897239.1897248

Rodden, T., & Benford, S. (2003, April 5-10). The evolution of buildings and implications for the design of ubiquitous domestic environments. In *Proceedings of the CHI Conference on Human Factors in Computing.*

Sengers, P., Kaye, J., Boehner, K., Fairbank, J., Gay, G., Medynskiy, Y., & Wyche, S. (2004). Culturally embedded computing. *Pervasive Computing, 3*(1).

Streitz, N. A., Tandler, P., & Müller-Tomfelde, C. (2002). Roomware: Toward the next generation of human-computer interaction based on an integrated design of real and virtual worlds. In Carroll, J. (Ed.), *Human computer interaction in the next millennium.* Reading, MA: Addison-Wesley.

Wiberg, M. (2005). *An architecturally situated approach to place-based mobile interaction design.* Paper presented at the Location Awareness & Community Workshop at the 9th European Conference on Computer-Supported Cooperative Work.

Wiberg, M. (2011). *Interactive textures for architecture and landscaping – digital elements and technologies.* Hershey, PA: IGI Global.

Wiberg, M., & Robles, E. (2010). Computational compositions: Aesthetics, materials, and interaction design. *International Journal of Design*, *4*(2), 65–76.

This work was previously published in the International Journal of Ambient Computing and Intelligence, Volume 3, Issue 3, edited by Kevin Curran, pp. 1-7, copyright 2011 by IGI Publishing (an imprint of IGI Global).

Chapter 13
Display Content Adaptation Using a Force Sensitive Office Chair

Andreas Riener
Johannes Kepler University Linz, Austria

ABSTRACT

In this paper, the author introduces a novel method for non-invasive, implicit human-computer interaction based on dynamically evaluated sitting postures. The research question addressed is whether or not the proposed system is able to allow for non-obtrusive screen content adaptation in a reading situation. To this end, the author has integrated force sensor array mats into a traditional office chair, providing sitting postures/gestures of the person seated in real time. In detail, variations in the center of pressure were used for application control, starting more generally with usability assessment of cursor control, breaking them down to simple(r) pan and zoom of screen content. Preliminary studies have indicated that such a system cannot get close to the performance/accuracy of keyboard or mouse, however its general usability, e.g., for handicapped persons or for less dynamic screen content adaptation, has been demonstrated and some future potential has been recognized.

1. AmI TECHNOLOGY IN AN OFFICE ENVIRONMENT

Traditionally, office work is concerned with (1) using the keyboard for input operations and (2) precise point, click, and drag&drop operations using the computer mouse. However, as more and more people spending their working day in front of the screen, beside the "processing-centered tasks" a new class of interaction gains more and more importance: The computer (screen) as "reading device" for scientific papers, e-books, newspapers, and other information-rich information. While conventional computer work requires frequent user inputs, the usage as an electronic reading device often comes along with a "relaxed", reclined sitting posture, with hands – most the

DOI: 10.4018/978-1-4666-2041-4.ch013

time – away from both keyboard and mouse. In this "mode of operation", however, scarce interaction with the computer, e.g., for moving invisible screen areas into focus, for turning pages, for magnifying interesting data, and so on, has to be necessarily enabled.

To address this problem, i.e., leaving the reader in a comfortable sitting posture but at the same time allowing him/her for convenient (limited) application control, the utilization of ambient intelligence (AmI) technology is expected to serve as a feasible solution. According to (Crutzen, 2006), one of the characteristics of AmI technology is that smart objects will make our whole lives relaxed and enjoyable – AmI will be capable of (1) meeting needs, (2) anticipating and responding intelligently to spoken or gestured wishes, and (3) desires without conscious mediation. To pick up on this vision, we propose a non-invasive, natural behaving sitting posture controlled input/feedback system integrated into a common office chair, and providing the computer user with implicit functionalities for controlling the screen content on display. The operating principle is thereby based upon the proven fact that people naturally lean towards items and adjusts their position in order to better inspect them (Harrison & Dey, 2008).

The research question addressed in this work is

RQ: whether or not it is possible to (conveniently) use a non-invasive, implicit sitting posture acquisition system integrated into a common office seat for unobtrusive, non-disruptive screen content adaptation (e.g., zoom, pan) in a relaxed, probably reclined, reading situation.

1.1. Related Approaches

Since Doug Engelbart's, "Mother of All Demos" (Engelbart, 1968), where he demonstrated the computer mouse (Engelbart, 1970) to the public for the first time, many research groups all over the world have investigated alternative approaches

for interacting with the computer employing different levels of accuracy and workload. Harrison and Dey (2008) were, to our best knowledge, the first who recognized the need for inconspicuous, implicit assistance in the considered tasks. Their system "Lean and Zoom" follows a camera-based approach for magnifying screen content based on the measured face-screen distance. Even though this system shows good performance and demonstrates ease of use, the usability is to some extent restrictive as the user has – on desired magnification – to move the whole body towards the screen and furthermore, the utilization of cameras is in general somehow problematic. For example, cameras have to be calibrated before usage in order to estimate correct camera parameters like metric information (Sauer et al., 2006), both angle and distance to the camera are limited (Sippl et al., 2010) (this is particularly true for Webcams integrated into computer screens), they are susceptible to varying lighting conditions, reliable distance/position detection is often compromised already by small motions of the head (Sippl et al., 2010), computer vision algorithms to be applied are, in relation to the finally used control commands, too complex, etc.

Other feasible approaches for unobtrusive detection of body movement, gestures/postures, or any other expressive body language to be used for implicit interaction with the computer are, admittedly all with their specific drawbacks, eye movement (Jacob, 1990) or gaze gestures (Drewes et al., 2007; Drewes & Schmidt, 2007; Sippl et al., 2010; Luca et al., 2007). Common to all technologies using movements of the eye are a number of limitations, such as contact lenses or spectacles, lighting conditions (brightness, shadows), or posture and movement of the head. The "Midas-touch problem" (Jacob, 1990) indicates that reducing the dwell time when inspecting the displays leads to unstable system behavior, however, increasing the dwell time too much prevents undisturbing, „relaxed" usage. In addition, the eye is normally used for triggering output – using it as „input sensor" is unnatural and may result in further conflicts or even user distraction.

Recently, increasing effort has been put into research focused on electrooculography (EOG) (Bulling et al., 2008, 2011), and electroencephalography (EEG) (Choi & Lee2006; Knezik & Drahansky2007; Felzer & Nordmann, 2008). The approach is to use the changing electrical potential of brain waves generated by the eye movements or detected during EEG measurements. However, also here are a number of limitations preventing the universal application of these techniques such as that the eye can rapidly get tired incapacitating further usage, blinking/winking of the eyes has to be incorporated, a (test) person's head has to be equipped with physical electrodes, sweating on the scalp may gives rise to low amplitude tracings (short circuit caused by saline), and others. A complete different approach in form of a balance disk (type "IKEA Virrig") with a set of embedded sensors (e.g., ball switches for tilt sensing or a compass for measuring rotational movements) was used by Holleis et al. (2006) and Schmidt et al. (2004) for hands-free control of the mouse cursor. Application in edutainment/gaming indicated some problems and restrictions caused by missing precision and latency – which, in the end, disallows also this system to be used for solving the here addressed problem.

Summary

All of the related technologies/systems for implicit and „relaxed" screen content adaptation discussed previously have shown some drawbacks or limitations, prohibiting its universal, particularly non-distractive, application, and calling for a new, less susceptible solution. In the following, we present with the "force sensitive office chair" one potential solutions considering the aforementioned issues.

Outline

The rest of the paper is structured as follows. The next Section 2 presents a general system overview to allow for non-invasive, posture controlled, screen content adaptation, Section 3 presents two case studies conducted to assess the quality and usability of such a device. The final Section 4 concludes the paper, draws some conclusions for practical application, and discusses potentials for future improvements.

2. A FORCE SENSITIVE SITTING POSTURE RECOGNITION SYSTEM

In this work we present our initial findings on a non-invasive, implicit, sitting posture based screen content adaptation system. The underlying functional principle are force sensitive array (FSA) mats, integrated into both seating and backrest of a standard office chair (Figure 1). The arrays allows for dynamic tracking of sitting posture variation, i.e., person movements in the seat.

In more detail, the underlying technological assembly and principle of sitting posture sensing/processing is as follows. For real time recognition of postures, XSensor pressure sensor technology (http://www.xsensor.com/pressure-imaging/), built up from pressure sensing matrices with specialized electronics connected to a computer, was employed. Each "sensor mat" consists of a matrix of capacitive sensors (in our case, using two mats of type "PX100:48.48.02", 48 by 48 sensors each, covering a sensing area of about $61 \times 61 cm^2$) formed into a continuous film. This film is connected to an electronics module that translates the physical compression of each cell of the matrix into a capacitance value that is correlated to pressure. After preprocessing, 16 bit pressure values are forwarded to the application (Java) via USB-Interface, dynamic link library (DLL), and JNI-Wrapper at a maximum of $100 Hz$. With such a system even slight variations in the

Figure 1. Technically, the underlying functional principle of the sitting posture-aware seat prototype is based on force sensitive mats integrated into seating and backrest, and allowing for dynamic tracking of sitting postures

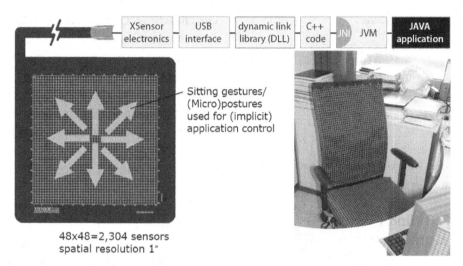

pressure distribution between the two surfaces can be detected.

For processing of sensor data a 3-staged approach is followed in the software application.

1. **Sitting posture acquisition:** As soon as a person is seated (determinable by a weight threshold exceeded on the seat map), the 48 by 48 array of force sensitive sensors (sensor size/spatial resolution 1 by 1) for both seating and backrest is read out once and buffered for later reuse (zero pressure filtering).

2. **Zero pressure filter:** After the "single image snapshot", data from the two pressure sensitive mats is continuously recorded at an update rate of about $10Hz$. In order to keep data quantity to be processed as low as possible, with – at the same time – not loosing information accuracy, the initial gathered pressure image was deducted from all further images. The result is a zero matrix with sparse entries indicating changed sensor values only (for clarification see Figure 5). Dynamic center of pressure values are then derived from these sparse matrices.

3. **Center of pressure (COP):** The center of pressure (COP) (Ferencz et al., 1993) is calculated for each frame and for both seating and backrest. COP is used as it can be calculated much more efficient than processing the whole matrix several times a second, with same quality of results when used for cursor control or content adaptation (zoom/pan). Separately for the two force sensor array mats, deviations in (x,y) from the initial position of COP (x_0, y_0) are determined in real time, and used for application control. In the given cases (see Section 3), the sensor sheet attached to the seating alone is used for cursor control (in the form indicated in Listing 1), seat mat and y-coordinate (for controlling the zoom level; $y < y_0$ zoom out, $y > y_0$ zoom in) of the backrest mat are used for screen content adaptation.

3. PRELIMINARY STUDIES

In order to assess the quality and usability of this, generally spoken, "sitting posture based input de-

Listing 1. Mapping between center of pressure (seat) and screen cursor position

```
// seat map
// x,y represents COP coordinates
if (xi > xj)
xcursor += (xi-xj)*corrfactX;
if (yi > yj)
ycursor += (yi-yj)*corrfactY;
..
xj = xi;
yj = yi;
```

vice", user studies were conducted whose findings will be presented in the following.

3.1. Case 1: Sitting Postures for Mouse Cursor Control

For the reasons substantiated in the introduction, but also to discover the general capabilities of such a system, the initial (and, of course, ultimate) goal – supported by the high update rate of the force sensitive arrays – was to implement a input device for controlling the cursor on the screen in real time and with similar behavior as the computer mouse. If this goal can be achieved, any other control task (such as the suggested screen content adaptation) can be easily implemented as a specialization from the underlying general system.

3.1.1. Cursor Movement

While the direction of movement of the cursor on the screen was related to the (x, y)-position of the center of pressure, the distance to the origin (derived from first pressure image) was used to control the moving speed of the cursor towards the indicated direction. The performed experiment was a classical movement task described first by Fitts' in the corresponding law.

Fitts' index of performance (IP) (Fitts, 1954; Fitts & Peterson, 1964) was found to be a valuable predictor of the movement time in any cursor positioning task and has become the standard method to identify performance differences between input devices like mouse, keyboard, joystick, etc. (Slocum, 2005) and thus, should also be applied as metric for assessing the usability of the current setting. Chin and Barreto (2006a, 2006b) found that the bigger part of interaction between a human and a computer is covered by "point and click" actions. Nevertheless, in the first study we evaluated point actions only – once the cursor hits the destination/circle (by moving over), the next target is generated and displayed. MacKenzie et al. (2001) evaluated the accuracy of different types of computer pointing devices and found that the mouse was the fastest device and the joystick the slowest; the mouse also had the flattest learning curve. Another important result of the study was that the accuracy measures with an independent contribution to pointing device throughput were able to discriminate among devices. This work (MacKenzie et al., 2001) can be extended by adding, for the first time, a measure for a sitting posture based input device.

3.1.2. Evaluation

During software implementation and first user tests we experienced that mouse input (point/ movement only, click omitted) would be always immeasurable faster compared to the pressure sensitive seat interface, at least for untrained users and most likely due to the fact of slow movement contingency in the seat. (Higher responsiveness of posture changes would allow for increased cursor movement speed, but, at the same time, would make it even more difficult to accurately point to a small target). To qualitatively assess the usability of a sitting posture controlled cursor control system, a Fitts' law test was implemented and conducted, comparing a point operation using a keyboard's numeric keys 1 to 9 (except 5) as "keyboard mouse" and the seat posture interface (Figure 2). The times for reaching the circular objects with either the keyboard or the "seat-steered" cursor were recorded into files for later evaluations. One test series encompassed 30 mea-

Figure 2. User view (without labeling) for the Fitt's law test comparing keyboard and posture interface

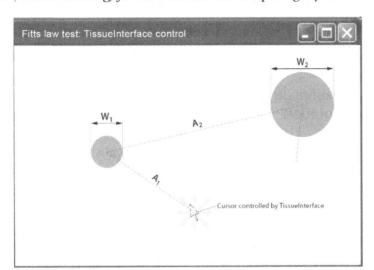

suring points with each input technology. Also, in this – compared to mouse input considerably slower – case, the keyboard input is much faster compared to the posture control (Figure 3). As already the movement time alone (for 10 test runs) clearly shows a high deviation between the two interface types (more than double the time, much higher variance: $\overline{x}_{keyboard} = 4.57 \pm 2.66 sec.$, $\overline{x}_{seat} = 11.47 \pm 5.65 sec.$), the "index of performance" (IP) was no more calculated.

In this preliminary test study it became evident that the utilization of a force sensitive seat inter-

face cannot replace the classical mouse input, at least not for high dynamic, precise mouse cursor control as generally required by (healthy) computer users. It has to be noted, however, that this input device still can get a chance to be used by handicapped people as its general usability has been proven. It is a matter of fact, for example, those physical disabilities, like spinal cord injuries or spinal dysfunctions, incapacitates a population of people to use classical input devices like mouse, keyboard or joystick (Chin & Barreto, 2006a). Given the increasing penetration with, and usage of computers in working life, for daily activities,

Figure 3. Case study employing "Fitts' law" for testing the usability of the pressure sensitive seat interface in relation to keyboard control (using "arrow keys")

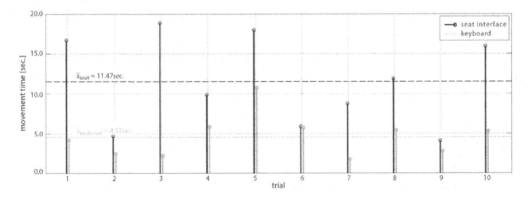

and in social communication over the Internet it is of essential importance to make computers and the Internet also available to these individuals with disabilities.

3.2. Case 2: Non-Invasive, Implicit Screen Content Adaptation

From the results of the first study we were brought back down to earth, investigating in a second study the potential of such an interface for limited control tasks, such as dynamic screen content adaptation as claimed in the research question (Figure 4). Such a application is not aimed to replace traditional controls like keyboard or mouse, but to provide the computer user with limited possibility for implicitly control applications in "relaxed" situations as when reading electronic news, ebooks, or even scientific papers. Much potential is seen in such tasks, where optimization with respect to interaction performance (movement time) and positioning accuracy is not the central matter. Quite the contrary -- the focus is not on qualitative measures, but on usability assessment for implicit, convenient, non-distracting, potentially emotionally influenced application control.

Basically, the same setting as in the previous study was used for the tests, however, only relative movements were evaluated and no precise positioning on pixel granularity was requested.

First tests with applied zero pressure filter and more complex COP calculation algorithms, as described by Siebenthal (1998) (Sections 3.6.3 through 3.6.6) (neighboring method, i.e., sum of squared distances), showed good user experience and control behavior (Figure 5). Nevertheless, detailed user studies and qualitative assessment of the interface characteristics, are ongoing and will be published elsewhere.

The parametrization of this interface would be, by all means, application specific, allowing, for instance, when reading newspapers, to bring the previous/next page on display when exceeding a certain threshold in left/right movement, or to define the manner of how to browse through an archive of images, control a media player, or studying extensive data tables – with specific functions each.

4. CONCLUSION

In this work we have shown that a non-invasive, dynamic sitting posture acquisition system integrated into a common office chair can be used for implicitly and intuitively control standard computer applications, however, with both limited point/movement performance and accuracy. Nevertheless, such a input system can gain excess value for a special group of handicapped people,

Figure 4. The mat attached to the backrest (y-axis only) is used for controlling the "zoom level" of the screen content. When sitting upright (left-hand side), the content is shown in original size (100%), the more leaning forward (right-hand side), the higher the magnification of the screen content

Figure 5. In case of magnification (by leaning forward), weight stabilizing on the seating can be used to scroll (pan) continuously through the screen content by dynamically evaluating changes in the center of pressure. The right image shows typical pressure images (with applied zero pressure filter) together with the corresponding COP points

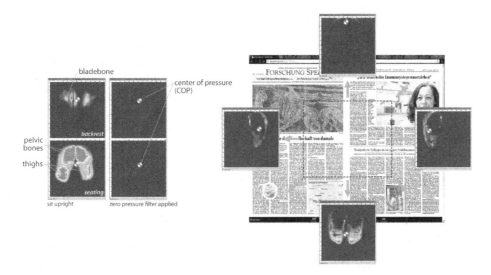

such as those with spinal cord injuries. A second, even more promising field of application, is its use as assistive technology, e.g., to employ computers as reading devices for newspaper or scientific papers. Future experiments have to be conducted to improve on the behavior of the interface (linkage sitting posture – application control) and to verify the supposed lower cognitive workload (or distraction) when using this interface instead of keyboard or mouse.

REFERENCES

Bulling, A., Roggen, D., & Tröster, G. (2008). It's in your eyes: Towards context-awareness and mobile hci using wearable eog goggles. In *Proceedings of the 10th International Conference on Ubiquitous Computing* (pp. 84-93). New York, NY: ACM Press.

Bulling, A., Ward, J. A., Gellersen, H., & Tröster, G. (2011). Eye movement analysis for activity recognition using electrooculography. *IEEE Transactions on Pattern Analysis and Machine Intelligence*, *33*(4), 741–753. doi:10.1109/TPAMI.2010.86

Chin, C., & Barreto, A. (2006a). Electromyograms as physiological inputs that provide efficient computer cursor control. In *Proceedings of the WSEAS International Conference on Mathematical Biology and Ecology*, Miami, FL.

Chin, C., & Barreto, A. (2006b). Performance comparison of electromyogram-based computer cursor control systems. *WSEAS Transactions on Biology and Biomedicine*, *3*, 118.

Choi, S. H., & Lee, M. (2006). Brain computer interface using EEG sensors based on an fMRI experiment. In *Proceedings of the International Joint Conference on Neural Networks* (pp. 4656-4663).

Crutzen, C. K. M. (2006). Invisibility and the meaning of ambient intelligence. *International Review of Information Ethics, 6*(12), 52–62.

Drewes, H., Atterer, R., & Schmidt, A. (2007). Detailed monitoring of user's gaze and interaction to improve future e-learning. In *Proceedings of the 4th International Conference on Universal Access in Human-Computer Interaction: Ambient Interaction* (pp. 802-811).

Drewes, H., & Schmidt, A. (2007). Interacting with the computer using gaze gestures. In C. Baranauskas, P. Palanque, J. Abascal, & S. DinizJunqueira Barbosa (Eds.), *Proceedings of the 11th IFIP TC13 International Conference on Human-Computer Interaction*, Rio de Janeiro, Brazil (LNCS 4663, pp. 475-488).

Engelbart, D. C. (1968). *The demo.* Retrieved from http://sloan.stanford.edu/MouseSite/1968Demo.html

Engelbart, D. C. (1970). *U. S. Patent 3541541: X-Y position indicator for a display system.* Washington, DC: U. S. Patent and Trademark Office.

Felzer, T., & Nordmann, R. (2008). Evaluating the hands-free mouse control system: An initial case study. In K. Miesenberger, J. Klaus, W. Zagler, & A. Karshmer (Eds.), *Proceedings of 11th International Conference of Computers Helping People with Special Needs*, Linz, Austria (LNCS 5105 pp. 1188-1195).

Ferencz, D. C., Zhenxing, J., & Chizeck, H. J. (1993). Estimation of center-of-pressure during gait using an instrumented ankle-foot orthosis. In *Proceedings of the 15th Annual International Conference on Engineering in Medicine and Biology Society* (pp. 981-982).

Fitts, P. M. (1954). The information capacity of the human motor system in controlling the amplitude of movement. *Journal of Experimental Psychology, 47*(6), 381–391. doi:10.1037/h0055392

Fitts, P. M. (1992). The information capacity of the human motor system in controlling the amplitude of movement. *Journal of Experimental Psychology. General, 121*(3), 262–269. doi:10.1037/0096-3445.121.3.262

Fitts, P. M., & Peterson, J. R. (1964). Information capacity of discrete motor responses. *Journal of Experimental Psychology, 67*(2), 102–113. doi:10.1037/h0045689

Harrison, C., & Dey, A. K. (2008). Lean and zoom: proximity-aware user interface and content magnification. In *Proceeding of the Twenty-Sixth Annual SIGCHI Conference on Human Factors in Computing Systems* (pp. 507-510). New York, NY: ACM Press.

Holleis, P., Kranz, M., Winter, A., & Schmidt, A. (2006). Playing with the real world. *Journal of Virtual Reality and Broadcasting, 3*(1).

Jacob, R. (1990). What you look at is what you get: Eye movement-based interaction techniques. In *Proceedings of the SIGCHI Conference on Human Factors in Computing Systems* (pp. 11-18). New York, NY: ACM Press.

Knezik, J., & Drahansky, M. (2007). Simple EEG driven mouse cursor movement. *Advances in Soft Computing, 45*, 526–531. doi:10.1007/978-3-540-75175-5_66

Luca, A. D., Weiss, R., & Drewes, H. (2007). Evaluation of eye-gaze interaction methods for security enhanced PIN-entry. In *Proceedings of the Australian Computer-Human Interaction Conference*, Adelaide, Australia (pp. 199-202). New York, NY: ACM Press.

MacKenzie, S., Kauppinen, T., & Silfverberg, M. (2001). Accuracy measures for evaluating computer pointing devices. In *Proceedings of the CHI Conference on Human Factors in Computing Systems* (pp. 9-16). New York, NY: ACM Press.

Sauer, K. L., Yfantis, E. A., Teruel, M. B., & Elkhater, R. W. (2006). A novel approach to camera calibration as part of an hci system. *Journal of Systemics. Cybernetics and Informatics, 4*(1), 8–13.

Schmidt, A., Holleis, P., & Kranz, M. (2004). Sensor Virrig – A balance cushion as controller. In *Proceedings of the Workshop on Playing with Sensors in Conjunction UbiComp.*

Siebenthal, T. (1998). Online-erfassung von handschrift mit einer videokamera (Doctoral dissertation, Universität Bern). *Neubrückstrasse, 10,* 3012.

Sippl, A., Holzmann, C., Zachhuber, D., & Ferscha, A. (2010). Real-time gaze tracking for public displays. In B. de Ruyter, R. Wichert, D. V. Keyson, P. Markopoulos, N. Streitz et al. (Eds.), *Proceedings of the First International Joint Conference on Ambient Intelligence* (LNCS 6439, pp. 167-176).

Slocum, J. (2005). A breakdown of the psychomotor components of input device usage. Usability News, 71.

This work was previously published in the International Journal of Ambient Computing and Intelligence, Volume 3, Issue 3, edited by Kevin Curran, pp. 8-17, copyright 2011 by IGI Publishing (an imprint of IGI Global).

Chapter 14
On Dependability Issues in Ambient Intelligence Systems

Marcello Cinque
Università di Napoli Federico II, Italy

Antonio Coronato
Institute of High Performance Computing and Networking (ICAR), Italy

Alessandro Testa
Università di Napoli Federico II and Institute of High Performance Computing and Networking (ICAR), Italy

ABSTRACT

Ambient Intelligence (AmI) is the emerging computing paradigm used to build next-generation smart environments. It provides services in a flexible, transparent, and anticipative manner, requiring minimal skills for human-computer interaction. Recently, AmI is being adapted to build smart systems to guide human activities in critical domains, such as, healthcare, ambient assisted living, and disaster recovery. However, the practical application to such domains generally calls for stringent dependability requirements, since the failure of even a single component may cause dangerous loss or hazard to people and machineries. Despite these concerns, there is still little understanding on dependability issues in Ambient Intelligent systems and on possible solutions. This paper provides an analysis of the AmI literature dealing with dependability issues and to propose an innovative architectural solution to such issues, based on the use of runtime verification techniques.

1. INTRODUCTION

Future computing platforms will surround human activities during their everyday life. Adaptive hardware/software architectures, characterized by context-aware services and immediate responsiveness to human needs and habits, will replace today's static platforms, towards the goal of Ambient Intelligence (AmI) environments and systems (Cook et al., 2009). Such systems will be based on a large number of heterogeneous devices, from handheld and wearable devices operated by users to smart sensing and actuating devices embedded in the surrounding environment, able to interact with each other spontaneously by exploiting different communication links. In this context,

DOI: 10.4018/978-1-4666-2041-4.ch014

applications will have to make effective use of the resources available on-the-fly, and adapt to different hardware and software, and even firmware configurations.

Recently, we are witnessing the application of the AmI concept even to critical application scenarios, such as smart hospitals (Coronato et al., 2008), ambient assistance to elder people (Nehmer et al., 2006), and disaster recovery (Chang et al., 2009). It becomes thus crucial to devise AmI systems capable to fulfill stringent dependability requirements, in order to avoid catastrophic consequences, such as the loss of human life in the case of healthcare applications. Building AmI systems with verifiable dependability properties is paramount also for increasing their level of acceptance. Non-technical and not experienced users will need to trust AmI systems in order to delegate to them critical decisions about their lives (i.e., whether or not to administer a given drug during a therapy, when alarms are raised by the AmI system which monitors the patient).

At the same time, the dependability level of AmI systems is challenged by severe impairments, due to their open and evolving nature. An AmI system operates proactively, does its job automatically with minimal human intervention, it interacts with humans by speech, gestures, and other forms of natural communication and it should provide its service in astable, robust and reliable way, even in the presence of component malfunctions, power/battery break down, or other exceptional conditions. Generally, faults in a system are unavoidable and they make a system less available, reliable, safe, and secure. This combination of heterogeneity, mobility, dynamism, sheer number of devices, accidental failures, and the presence of unavoidable software and hardware defects makes increasingly difficult to build AmI systems with verifiable dependability properties.

Despite these compelling issues, there is still little understanding in the literature on the dependability delivered by current research proposal for AmI environments and on the methods

and techniques needed to build more dependable AmI systems in the next future. The attention to dependability issues in AmI systems is also witnesses by recent European Union initiatives, such as the SERENITY (System Engineering for Security and Dependability) Project (Mana, 2007) that aims to provide security and dependability in Ambient Intelligence systems (AmI).

This paper aims to provide a contribution towards a better understanding of the dependability concept when applied to such novel computing systems. In particular, in Section 2 we review the recent related research focused on dependability issues in AmI systems, with the goal of putting in the foreground the issues that still remain unresolved. We group such issues in fundamental, technological, and architectural issues, depending on their peculiarity. Then, in Section 3 we discuss about a potential solution to the pinpointed issues, based on the application of runtime verification techniques (Leucker et al., 2007) to AmI systems, in order to have a continuous feedback on their operation and to design adaptable restoration actions to unpredictable failures. Finally, Section 4 ends the paper with conclusions and ongoing challenges.

2. RELATED RESEARCH ON DEPENDABILITY ISSUES IN AmI SYSTEMS

Currently, the provision of appropriate means to enforce and/or to assess the dependability of AmI Systems remains an unsolved issue. The recent research on related areas is however progressively recognizing the need of fundamental research, methods, and techniques to build dependable and secure AmI systems, or to implement AmI systems with verifiable dependability properties. The issues emerged in the literature in order to reach these ambitious goals are discussed in the following, according to three main categories:

fundamental issues, technological issues, and architectural issues.

2.1. Fundamental Issues

The definitions of dependability, its attributes, threats and means, considered until today, have to be reviewed in the new context of Ambient Intelligence. While AmI systems share several characteristics of traditional computing systems, they also introduce novel dependability threats, due to their highly evolvable and dynamic nature. Such new threats call for new means to be adopted to reach an adequate dependability and/ or security level.

In Simoncini (2003), the author presented a new "global" view of the concept of "dependability", which has to start from the basic intrinsic characteristics of the AmI components (of a computer, of a network, of an infrastructure, of a set of services, of the interested managing and user bodies, of the society) to grow up and reach reliance in "ambient dependability". The realization of such view requires the analysis of new threats and fault types as well as the definition of extended dependability attributes, like "acceptable availability under attack", "data delivery resilience under accidental failures", and other.

Simoncini introduced several drivers for research over the next few years and he suggested some considerations for future work, with respect to the four main typologies of dependability means, i.e., *fault prevention, fault tolerance, fault removal*, and *fault forecasting* (Avizienis et al., 2004).

Fault prevention means are used to prevent the occurrence or introduction of faults. In the context of AmI, this calls for a formal definition of novel accidental and malicious faults which may be introduced in an AmI system. With reference to security threats, the definition of policies is needed in order to prevent the introduction of vulnerabilities due to human factors in critical "socio-technical" systems.

Fault removal techniques are instead used to reduce the number and severity of faults. To this aim, novel statistical testing and robustness testing techniques should be defined for such evolvable systems.

Fault tolerance means are adopted to avoid failures in the presence of residual faults, which escape the prevention and removal means. In the case of AmI systems, it is important to consider that the majority of faults are transient in nature, even if they may lead to catastrophic consequences. In order to define proper countermeasures, such faults should be carefully classified and characterized, based on their causes, triggers, and manifestation. A preliminary analysis on such threats is performed in Section 2.2.

Fault forecasting embraces the set of techniques to estimate the present number, the future incidence, and the likely consequences of faults. In the context of AmI, it could be useful to define specific fault-injection techniques to build dependability benchmarks to compare competing systems and architectures on an equitable basis. In addition, specific tools for the on-line monitoring of an AmI system need to be defined, in order to statistically characterize the system based on realistic data gathered from the field of operation. The collected data can then be used to improve successive generations of systems and to define proper fault tolerance strategies at runtime, as better detailed in Section 3.

In Lindwer et al. (2003) the *energy*, the *fault-tolerance* and the *mobility* represent the fundamental issues to be faced for developing the next-generation of smart environments. In particular, authors highlight the problem of the high spatial correlation among the nodes and link failures in these systems, due topological constraints and the common dependency from external events.

Finally, it is widely recognized that the lack of a clear definition of dependability needs represents an issue for AmI Systems, as well as for safety critical systems, and for eHealth monitoring applications, as documented in Bohn et al. (2003), in Di Giacomo et al. (2008) and in Serpanos et al. (2008).

2.2. Technological Issues

The recently proposed prototypes of AmI Systems present severe technological limitations, which introduce several threats to the dependability of the overall system. Being the system usually composed by low-cost, battery-powered and wireless-enabled devices, their correct functioning is affected by the capacity of batteries, the unreliability and variability of wireless communications, the mobility of users, the risk of physical damage, etc. In addition, the presence of hardware faults, due to defects and interference, and the presence of residual software bugs further complicate the picture.

These threats are in part discussed in Killijian et al. (2004), where authors discuss about the limited device lifetime and communication due to low electrical energy and the poor physical protection of mobile devices which can make them prone to physical damage, if deployed in a harsh environment. Therefore authors raise the issue of realizing a fault- and intrusion-tolerant collaborative data backup for AmI systems. They consider a scenario where it is needed to protect the backed-up data against denial-of-service attacks and availability problems due to failures. The need for such fault-tolerant service is justified by the increasing dependency of users on the availability, integrity and confidentiality of data transmitted by mobile devices and by the risks related to their use in a hostile, public environment.

In Alemdar et al. (2010) technologies based on Wireless Sensor Networks (WSN) are considered as one of the key research areas to favor the development of future healthcare industries. The authors illustrate the state of the art on WSN-based AmI Systems for healthcare with related benefits, issues and challenges. It is interesting to note that several challenges and open research problems for AmI Systems are indicated, in particular for

dependability problems. In this work it is reported an analysis of open issues divided by layers. The majority of dependability issues result to be concentrated in the physical layer, where the scarce transmission power and the small size of antennas particularly compromise the resilience of the communication. In particular, the reduced Signal-to-Noise Ratio (SNR) causes high bit error rates and reduces the capacity of the network to reliably cover the area of interest. Similar dependability issues are discussed for the transport layer. The scarce computation power of sensor devices does not allow implementing complex, reliable transport protocols, with control flow and retransmission. On the other hand, the loss of even a single packet may result in a significant hazard. This is a major impairment to medical monitoring systems, dealing with life-critical data. In such systems, the resilient delivery of medical data could result vital for monitored patients.

A survey of the technologies of ambient intelligence systems (Cook et al., 2009) shows several challenges and opportunities that AmI researchers will face in the coming years. The authors organize the contributing technologies into five areas: *Sense, Reason, Act, Human-Computer Interface* and *Secure*. In the last area, *Secure*, they highlight some dependability issues; for example, at the sensor level, the sensor reliability, the error handling process, and the errors due to misconfiguration can create security vulnerabilities. To ensure security in sensor networks, the designer must consider these factors together with sensor communication channel reliability/availability and sensor data integrity and confidentiality. An ongoing challenge for AmI researchers is mentioned about the design of self-testing and self-repairing AmI software that can offer quantitative quality-of-service guarantees and a high degree of dependability.

2.3. Architectural Issues

In the literature, there is still a lack of a commonly accepted architecture to build the AmI systems of the future, with predictable dependability properties. This issue is considered in Simoncini (2003), where the author pointed out the concepts of "architecture" and "system" need to be redefined in the context of AmI systems, in order to properly define "ambient dependability" attributes, threats and means.

In Bohn et al. (2005), authors define a dynamic system able to adapt itself to the current situation. They claim that, in order to guarantee dependability requirements, the system architecture has to be manageable, controllable and it has to provide means for the prediction of the system correctness at runtime. In Nehmer et al. (2006), authors proposed an integrated system approach for living assistance systems based on ambient intelligence technology. They claim that the construction of trustworthy, robust, and dependable living assistance systems is a challenging task which requires novel software engineering methods and tools, and novel approaches for dependable self-adapting software architectures, able to react to changes due to frequent failures and reconfiguration events, which become the norm, rather than the exception. In addition, self-adapting multi-modal human-computer interfaces must be devised, since even the wrong interaction with humans may represent an obstacle for the dependable operation of the system.

Georgalis et al. (2009) argue that the most important architectural property in an AmI architecture is the fault-tolerance. The fault tolerance, in the context of an AmI architecture, has to be able to isolate failures, to eliminate single points of failure, to restart failing services before that are used by the clients, and finally to provide mechanisms for notifying the fault level about the irreparable failure of a specific service.

Coronato and De Pietro (2010) pointed out that the design of AmI applications in critical systems requires rigorous software-engineering-oriented approaches. The authors proposed a set of formal tools and a specification process for AmI, which have been devised to lead the developer in designing activities and realizing software artefacts.

Zamora-Izquierdo et al. (2010) propose a platform that provides a home automation architecture, called DOMESTIC, able to satisfy current and future needs in indoor environments. Although the architecture is claimed to be robust and dependable, there is neither evidence nor experimental study assessing the dependability level.

In Duman et al. (2010) it is defined an Ambient Intelligent Environment (AIE) as a multitude of interconnected systems composed by *embedded agent* with computational and networking capabilities which form a ubiquitous, unobtrusive, and seamless infrastructure that surrounds the user. These intelligent agents are integrated into AIEs to form an intelligent "presence" to identify the users and be sensitive and attentive to their particular needs, based on a publish-subscribe communication infrastructure. The intelligent agents are dynamic and capable to keep a high level of dependability of a network structure preserving the resilience and the fault tolerance. They suggest, as future work, to investigate the proposed AmI system in a truly distributed and real AIE with a richer set of sensors and actuators.

The adoption of the Service Oriented Architecture (SOA) is gaining popularity in the AmI literature, due to its flexibility, composability, and interoperability properties, and to the large availability of commercial and open source implementations. For instance, in Perez et al. (2009) authors present a SOA-based approach to implement reliable platforms for the integration of heterogeneous devices in AmI scenarios. The approach defines a Device Profile for Web Service (DPWS) to access tiny mobile devices via high-end applications based on the OSGi platform (Hall & Cervantes, 2004) and running on mobile phones, automobiles, industrial automation equipment, etc.

Some solutions focus on the dependable delivery of data. In Chakraborly (2007) authors propose a trust-based routing protocol able to ensure the delivery of event data from sensors to actuators in an Ambient Intelligence environment even in the presence of faults; the dependability is measured in terms of a trust value for the node. It is also performed a security analysis of the effects of malicious nodes.

Although the introduced architectures in this section, propose solutions and different techniques to create AmI systems, currently, there is not a single reference architecture for AmI systems. On the other hand, we believe it is unlikely that a reference architecture will be assumed as a standard de-facto in AmI systems, as SOA, publish-subscribe, and agent-based architectures are all promising solutions for smart environments. What we note, however, is the scarce attention of current architectural proposal to dependability issues. Even when a solution is claimed to offer dependability guarantees, these claims are not supported by experimental evidence. This is partially due to the lack of a state-of-practice on the dependability evaluation of such complex and dynamic systems, which prevent to build AmI systems with predictable and verifiable dependability properties.

3. ARCHITECTING DEPENDABLE AmI SYSTEMS

Recent contributions on AmI systems are starting to focus on architectural issues, as discussed in the previous section. Despite these efforts, which represent fundamental contributions to resolve specific problems under given assumptions, the problem of architecting AmI systems with predictable and verifiable dependability properties still represents a critical open issue. The problem lies in the highly evolvable and dynamic nature of such systems, which, coupled with the unpredictability of hardware and software faults,

exacerbates the definition of fault tolerance means, and compromises the application of fault forecasting techniques, due to the non-reproducibility of their behavior. In other terms, AmI systems do not allow the application of techniques based on the a-priori knowledge of the system itself, even because, being AmI systems relatively young, there are no field failure data or experience reports available on their failure behavior. Given the high dynamicity and heterogeneity of these systems (which behavior is strongly influenced by the mission they need to accomplish), and given the absence of a reference architecture, we believe that the knowledge on the system behavior needs to be acquired during the actual execution of the system, and to be adapted continuously to current system dynamics. This allows to tailor the intervention of fault tolerance means based on the current situation (what we call *situation-aware fault tolerance*).

Based on these considerations, our proposal towards the definition of dependable AmI architectures is to adopt *Runtime Verification* techniques (Rosu & Havelund, 2005) to acquire continuous knowledge on the execution state of the system and to assess, verify, and enforce its dependability level.

Runtime verification is the discipline of computer science that deals with the study, development, and application of verification techniques that allow checking whether a run of a system under scrutiny satisfies or violates a given correctness property (Leucker, 2009). The goal of runtime verification (Barringer, 2004) is to determine, at every time step, if the system is currently meeting its correctness requirement (in our case, dependability attributes); a description of system correctness is a set of formally specified, high-level and time-evolved behaviors that have been determined to be necessary for correct system operation. It can be used to automatically evaluate test runs, either on-line, or off-line analyzing stored execution traces; or it can be employed on-line, during the operation of the system, potentially steering the application back to a safety region if a property is violated.

In detail, runtime verification enables the checking of correctness properties with respect to system implementations. It concerns the application of a lightweight formal verification (model-checking) during the execution of the system by checking traces of events generated from the system run against the correctness properties. When a property is violated, a recovery strategy is triggered. The technique scales well since just one model of computation is considered, rather than the entire state space like in model-checking (Clarke et al., 1999). Such a technique can be used both for testing prototypes before deployment and for monitoring the final system after deployment.

We expect runtime verification to become a major verification technique especially for systems in which the behavior depends heavily on the environment and operational conditions. In other words, the behavior of highly dynamic systems such as adaptive, self-organizing, self-healing, or pervasive systems depends heavily on the environment and changes over time, which makes their behavior hard to predict and analyze prior the execution. To ensure certain correctness properties, the runtime verification can become part of the architecture of such dynamic systems, independently from the specific architectural model adopted. Definitively, it is worth noting that static verification techniques, when they do not lead to problems like decidability or state space explosion, can prove completely the correctness of specifications. For this reason they are considered to be stronger than runtime verification techniques. However, the correctness of specifications does not imply the correctness of implementation. This is particularly true for pervasive applications whose behavior can strongly depend on operating conditions. As an example, an RFID reader can fail to detect a tagged user depending on 1) the orientation of the antenna, 2) the power of the antenna itself, 3) the position of the tag on body, 4) the existence of an object between the

tag and the reader at the time of reading, etc. All these conditions are difficult to verify with static techniques. In contrast, runtime verification of the prototype system in the real domain of application can make possible the collection of traces that can be used to tune the system, or to recognize faulty components.

Therefore, a runtime checker helps both to react to failures at runtime, that is, by detecting the problem and by triggering the most proper recovery actions, based on the current situation gathered from the system (situation-aware fault-tolerance), and to identify and correct permanent bugs to improve future versions of the system.

Figure 1 shows an example of use of a runtime checker: while the system is running, the *Runtime Checker* checks if the system is currently meeting its correctness properties (the specification).

For instance, we can consider an application of long-term vital signs monitoring (Figure 2). It relies on a wireless body sensor network used to monitor physiological parameters. The body sensor network includes specific biomedical sensors (e.g., oximeter, ECG, pulsimeter, etc.); these sensors communicate with a sink node (i.e., a PDA) that sends the data to a workstation over an IP network.

Such an application is characterized by 1) high user mobility; 2) limited resources (e.g. devices battery); 3) unreliable connections; etc. All these considerations make the application quite critical especially considering that some of those vital signs can be monitored in order to control a medical device (e.g., a pump that release glucose to the patient) or to launch alarms (e.g., in case of heart attack).

Several kinds of failures can occur; but, runtime verification mechanisms may help in monitoring the correct execution of the entire system. As an example, a runtime checker can be adopted to monitor a correctness property on the level of power of any mobile and wireless device and to launch recovery strategies, which imply the use of spare components, in order to avoid service

Figure 1. Running system with support of the runtime checker

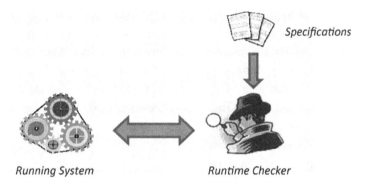

interruption. Or, the checker can raise alarms when vital signs data are no longer acquired by the sink according to established correctness properties, e.g., on the inter-arrival frequency, on the percentage of data loss, and so on, in order to discard poor data streams (due to temporary communication failures) which could affect negatively the decisions taken by the system.

This approach helps to afford the complexity and variability of AmI systems, since it does not require to know in advance all the failures that may affect the system, but it only requires to define the

correctness properties to be verified continuously. The violation of such known correctness properties helps to trigger recovery actions, independently from the particular failure or misuse conditions which caused it.

CONCLUSION AND ONGOING CHALLENGES

In this paper, we have reported the recent open issues on the dependability of Ambient Intelligence

Figure 2. A vital signs monitoring application

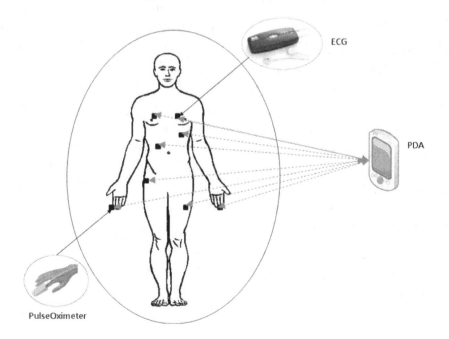

Systems, classified in fundamental, technological and architectural issues. What appears clear is that the path towards the production of dependable AmI system is still long, and more research effort is needed to reach this compelling goal. Our contribution to this goal is the idea of applying Runtime Verification techniques. Given the absence of a reference architecture, the lack of past experiences and field data, and the high dynamicity and heterogeneity of such systems, the idea of acquiring continuous knowledge on the system behavior, to enforce the fulfillment of correctness properties, seems a promising one to achieve more stable and dependable AmI systems in the future.

REFERENCES

Alemdar, H., & Ersoy, C. (2010). Wireless sensor networks for healthcare: A survey. *Computer Networks*, *54*(15), 2688–2710. doi:10.1016/j.comnet.2010.05.003

Avizienis, A., Laprie, J., Randell, B., & Landwehr, C. (2004). Basic concepts and taxonomy of dependable and secure computing. *IEEE Transactions on Dependable and Secure Computing*, *1*(1), 11–33. doi:10.1109/TDSC.2004.2

Barringer, H., Goldberg, A., Havelund, K., & Sen, K. (2004). Rule-based runtime verification. In *Proceedings of the 5th International Conference on Verification* (pp. 44-57).

Bohn, J., Coroama, V., Langheinrich, M., Mattern, F., & Rohs, M. (2005). Social, economic, and ethical implications of ambient intelligence and ubiquitous computing. In Weber, W., Rabaey, J., & Aarts, E. (Eds.), *Ambient intelligence*. New York, NY: Springer. doi:10.1007/3-540-27139-2_2

Bohn, J., Gärtner, F. C., & Vogt, H. (2003). Dependability issues of pervasive computing in a healthcare environment. In *Proceedings of the Statistical Process Control Conference* (pp. 53-70).

Chakraborty, S., Poolsappasit, N., & Ray, I. (2007, July 8-11). Reliable delivery of event data from sensors to actuators in pervasive computing environments. In S. Barker & G. JoonAhn (Eds.), *Proceedings of the 21st Annual IFIP WG 11.3 Working Conference on Data and Applications Security*, Redondo Beach, CA (LNCS 4602, pp. 77-92).

Chang, Z., & Hao, Y. (2009).The research of disaster recovery about the network storage system base on "safety zone". In *Proceedings of the Conference on Apperceiving Computing and Intelligence Analysis* (pp. 290-293).

Clarke, E. M., Grumberg, O., & Peled, D. A. (1999). *Model checking*. Cambridge, MA: MIT Press.

Cook, D., Augusto, J., & Jakkula, V. (2009). Ambient intelligence: Technologies, applications, and opportunities. *Pervasive and Mobile Computing*, *5*(4), 277–298. doi:10.1016/j.pmcj.2009.04.001

Coronato, A., & De Pietro, G. (2010). Formal design of ambient intelligence applications. *IEEE Computer*, *43*, 60–68.

Coronato, A., & Esposito, M. (2008). Towards an implementation of smart hospital: A localization system for mobile users and devices. In *Proceedings of the Sixth Annual International Conference on Pervasive Computing and Communications* (pp. 715-719).

Di Giacomo, V., Felici, M., Meduri, V., Presenza, D., Riccucci, C., & Tedeschi, A. (2008). Using security and dependability patterns for reaction processes. In *Proceedings of the 19th International Conference on Database and Expert Systems Application* (pp. 315-319).

Duman, H., Hagras, H., & Callaghan, V. (2010). A multi-society-based intelligent association discovery and selection for ambient intelligence environment. *ACM Transactions on Autonomous and Adaptive Systems, 5*(2).

Georgalis, Y., Grammenos, D., & Stephanidis, C. (2009). Middleware for ambient intelligence environments: Reviewing requirements and communication technologies. In C. Stephanidis (Ed.), *Proceedings of the 5th International on Conference on Universal Access in Human-Computer Interaction. Part II: Intelligent and Ubiquitous Interaction Environments* (LNCS 5615, pp. 168-177).

Hall, R., & Cervantes, H. (2004). An osgi implementation and experience report. In *Proceedings of the Consumer Communications and Networking Conference* (pp.394-399).

Killijian, M., Powell, D., Banâtre, M., Couderc, P., & Roudier, Y. (2004). Collaborative backup for dependable mobile applications. In *Proceedings of the 2nd Workshop on Middleware for Pervasive and Ad-Hoc Computing.*

Leucker, M., & Schallhart, C. (2009). A brief account of runtime verification. *Journal of Logic and Algebraic Programming*, *78*(5), 293–303. doi:10.1016/j.jlap.2008.08.004

Lindwer, M., Marculescu, D., Basten, T., Zimmennann, R., Marculescu, R., Jung, S., & Cantatore, E. (2003). Ambient intelligence visions and achievements: Linking abstract ideas to real-world concepts. In *Proceedings of the Design, Automation and Test in Europe Conference and Exhibition* (pp. 10-15).

Mana, A., Rudolph, C., Spanoudakis, G., Lotz, V., Massacci, F., Malideo, M., & Lopez-Cobo, J. S. (2007). Security engineering for ambient intelligence: A manifesto. In Mouratidis, H., & Giorgini, P. (Eds.), *Integrating security and software engineering: Advances and future visions* (pp. 244–270). Hershey, PA: IGI Global.

Nehmer, J., Karshmer, A., Lamm, R., & Becker, M. (2006). Living assistance systems: An ambient intelligence approach. In *Proceedings of the 28th International Conference on Software Engineering* (pp. 43-50).

Peréz, J., Álvarez, J., Fernández-Montes, A., & Ortega, J. (2009). Service-oriented device integration for ubiquitous ambient assisted living environments. In J. A. Pérez, J. A. Álvarez, A. Fernández-Montes, & J. A. Ortega (Eds.), *Proceedings of the 10th International Work-Conference on Artificial Neural Networks: Part II: Distributed Computing, Artificial Intelligence, Bioinformatics, Soft Computing, and Ambient Assisted Living* (LNCS 5518, pp. 843-850).

Rosu, G., & Havelund, K. (2005). Rewriting-based techniques for runtime verification. *Automated Software Engineering*, *12*, 151–197. doi:10.1007/s10515-005-6205-y

Serpanos, D., & Henkel, J. (2008). Dependability and security will change embedded computing. *IEEE Computer*, *41*(1), 103–105.

Simoncini, L. (2003). Architectural challenges for "ambient dependability". In *Proceedings of the 9th IEEE International Workshop on Object-Oriented Real-Time Dependable Systems* (p. 245).

Zamora-Izquierdo, M., A., Santa, J., & Gomez-Skarmeta, A., F. (2010). An integral and networked home automation solution for indoor ambient intelligence. *IEEE Pervasive Computing / IEEE Computer Society [and] IEEE Communications Society*, *9*(4), 66–77. doi:10.1109/MPRV.2010.20

This work was previously published in the International Journal of Ambient Computing and Intelligence, Volume 3, Issue 3, edited by Kevin Curran, pp. 18-27, copyright 2011 by IGI Publishing (an imprint of IGI Global).

Chapter 15

An Abstract User Interface Framework for Mobile and Wearable Devices

Claas Ahlrichs
Universitaet Bremen, Germany

Michael Lawo
Universitaet Bremen, Germany

Hendrik Iben
Universitaet Bremen, Germany

ABSTRACT

In the future, mobile and wearable devices will increasingly be used for interaction with surrounding technologies. When developing applications for those devices, one usually has to implement the same application for each individual device. Thus a unified framework could drastically reduce development efforts. This paper presents a framework that facilitates the development of context-aware user interfaces (UIs) with reusable components for those devices. It is based on an abstract description of an envisioned UI which is used to generate a context- and device-specific representation at run-time. Rendition in various modalities and adaption of the generated representation are also supported.

INTRODUCTION

Desktop computers present no longer the only affordable technology with reasonable computing power. Over the last decades a new trend in computing has emerged: mobile computing. In recent years, mobile computing platforms have become available to the broad masses. Their price

has decreased and today almost everybody can profit from devices, like smartphones or personal digital assistants (PDAs).

Nowadays many people use mobile phones, MP3 players or digital cameras in their daily lives. All of these devices provide functionality which can be accessed via a UI. They are typically graphically represented and must ensure an appropriate level of usability and information presentation in order to let users control the provided

DOI: 10.4018/978-1-4666-2041-4.ch015

functionality. However, usability and information presentation are rather often neglected. E.g. using applications of mobile phones may be a burden as their UIs are still frequently based on desktop applications. Instead of creating an application that is specialized to solve a (single) problem, desktop applications are usually rather general purpose and feature-rich. While this may be a useful approach for desktop computers, it is not for mobile and wearable devices as they significantly differ from stationary systems (e.g., in terms of size, usage, computing power, etc.). Unnecessary features tend to hinder usability than being a useful extension when being in a mobile setting.

Not having expert knowledge on creating UIs for wearable and mobile scenarios makes it hard to develop applications for such devices. The heterogeneous nature of the hardware of these devices intensifies this problem as existing UIs are unlikely to be reused. A unified framework, that offers reusable components and facilitates UI development, could reduce development efforts and decrease programming errors.

UIs could be described in an abstract manner, so called abstract user interfaces (AUIs). AUIs can be used to transport information just like regular UIs. They are used to specify what is presented rather than how information is presented. Thus no concrete representation or visualization is defined instead a single AUI description can be represented in multiple ways. Furthermore an AUI can easily be adapted according to user preferences, device constraints or contextual information.

RELATED WORK

Several frameworks for automatic UI generation already exist. Three of them are listed and summarized as follows. Most frameworks can also be used to create wearable and mobile computing applications.

- **WUI Toolkit**: Witt et al. (2005) introduced ``a toolkit for context-aware UI development for wearable computers'' called wearable user interface (WUI) toolkit. It was designed and developed to meet requirements of wearable computers and aimed to ease development of WUIs. The toolkit first utilized reusable UI components and was based around a model-driven approach. It support self-adapting UIs without being limited to specific interaction devices or graphical UIs (Witt, 2005; Witt, Nicolai, & Kenn, 2007).

- **Huddle**: Huddle is a system that uses an abstract description language for automatic generation of task-based UIs for appliances in a multi-device environment (e.g. a home theater or presentation room). It makes use of an XML-based language for describing functionalities of appliances in those environments (e.g., televisions, DVD players, printers or microwave ovens). Huddle has been used to generate graphical and speech interfaces for over thirty appliances on mobile phones, handhelds and desktop computers (Nichols & Myers, 2007; Nichols, Myers, Litwack, Higgins, Hughes, & Harris, 2004; Nichols, Rothrock, Chau, & Myers, 2006).

- **SUPPLE**: SUPPLE is an alternative to creating UIs in a hand-crafted fashion. Instead UIs are automatically generated with respect to a person's device, abilities and preferences. It is based around an abstract UI describing its functionality rather than its representation. The actual generation of UIs with SUPPLE is interpreted as an optimization problem (Gajos & Weld, 2004; Gajos, Weld, & Wobbrock, 2010).

AbstractUI

The AbstractUI framework eases development of applications using AUIs. It has been specifically designed to meet requirements of mobile and wearable devices. Furthermore development efforts are reduced as the same application can be used on multiple devices. A context-aware representation of an AUI can be generated at run-time.

Application developers describe what is to be displayed rather than how an envisioned UI is displayed. While doing so developers make use of several UI components and can interact with them just like they would with standard UI components of other toolkits and frameworks. Once an application is completed, it is passed to a renderer which in turn takes care of the concrete representation.

The requirements and limitations of the AbstractUI framework are listed in the following. Furthermore a general overview of the framework is given.

Requirements

The AbstractUI framework has been designed and implemented in consideration of several requirements.

- **Device independent UI description**: The UI is to be described in a way that allows the rendering on a wide range of devices and usage of UI toolkits or frameworks. It should be specified on an abstract level that is independent of a particular rendering software (e.g., AWT, SWT, GTK+, etc.) or device (e.g., PDA, head-mounted display (HMD), etc.).

- **Reusability of components**: Reusability of UI components allows a more productive and effective development of wearable and mobile applications. Instead of creating an application from scratch with a specialized interface, a list of default UI components (that are likely to be reused) should be identified and provided for reusage. The identified components are not expected to be exhaustive, meaning that

they can be used to create a wide range of applications but certainly not all possible ones.

- **Support for integration of context**: Gathered contextual information (by sensors, user, wearable) can help to optimize the rendering of a UI. The usage should not be restricted to internal software components but also permitted to be directly used within applications developed with the AbstractUI framework. A global storage place for context information would allow the propagation of newly gained or changed contextual information.

- **Extensibility**: New ways of displaying information emerge from time to time and create the necessity to adapt the rendering process. Existing UI components may be required to be rendered in a different way or new UI components may need to be integrated into the toolkit. The identified list of UI components is not exhaustive and therefore the AbstractUI framework must permit the addition of new UI components.

- **Support for distribution of toolkit components**: Wearable and mobile systems are typically very limited in terms of available computing power and energy consumption. Therefore the possibility to distribute an application across multiple systems in a network should be considered e.g., a wearable system could act as a display of a wearable application and communicate with a second system (with more computing power) on which the actual wearable application is executed.

- **Support for multi-modal information presentation**: UIs of wearable and mobile devices are not restricted to graphical representations. In fact there are cases in which a graphical representation is not the preferred way to display information e.g. when walking, crossing the street or in general when a user's visual attention is occupied by a real world task. Some information can equally well be displayed using tactile or auditory interfaces. The UI components should be designed in a way that allows the possibility to render them in a non-visual modality.

General Overview

The implementation of the AbstractUI framework makes frequent use of design patterns found in Gamma, Helm, Johnson, and Vlissides (1994) e.g., the Abstract Factory (Gamma, Helm, Johnson, & Vlissides, 1994, p. 87) and the Observer (Gamma, Helm, Johnson, & Vlissides, 1994, p. 293) design pattern have been applied several times.

A set of five UI components is provided by the AbstractUI framework, which was chosen as their concrete representations cover a broad range of commonly used UI components. Even though this set is not exhaustive, it enables application developers to create a fairly large amount of applications. The UI components of the AbstractUI framework are summarized as follows.

- **Text**: Is used to display text-related information. Depending on the context, it could be represented as a label, text box or text area. Thus also allowing user inputs.
- **Trigger**: Enables users to execute actions (e.g., send form or save file). It will typically be represented as a labeled button, but could also be displayed as part of a menu.
- **Choice**: Is responsible for displaying selection-related information (e.g., month, weekday, etc.). The most obvious representation is probably the combo box. However depending on the context it is being used in, a check box, radio buttons or a list might also be suitable.
- **Container**: Is a component that allows the addition of child components. It will usu-

ally be represented as some sort of panel or dialog box.
- **Screen**: Is a top level container and will typically represent as a window.

The Composite design pattern (Gamma, Helm, Johnson, & Vlissides, 1994, p. 163) has been applied to all of the above components and allows treating of individual components and compositions in a uniform way. Compositions and individual components do not need to be distinguished, thus reducing development efforts.

Each UI component represents a certain kind of data (e.g., a text, an action or a choice) and thereby has an individual data model. The data models were designed in a way that allows easy interchangeability e.g. the same data model can be implemented to store its information in the device it is being used on or retrieve its data from a remote computing machine.

Contextual information (e.g., environmental information, user's mental state, etc.) can be represented in the AbstractUI framework. It provides a globally accessible storage point for such information. The context information is represented as a simple key-value pair (e.g., 'illumination' → 'bright'). Furthermore, all UI components are equipped with a way to represents the context they are being used in.

Having used above components to create an AUI, one can pass it to a renderer and have a concrete representation build for it.

Limitations

The design of the framework is not limited to a specific programming language nor does it suggest one in particular. Nonetheless, the implementation of the AbstractUI framework has been done in Java and therefore can only be used on Java-enabled devices. Future versions will target additional programming languages and may include support for the .Net programming environment or the iPhone/iPad; thus extending the range of supported devices. Projects like XMLVM (2011) could be utilized for such a purpose.

Although UIs for wearable and mobile devices are not limited to graphical representations, the primary focus of the proposed framework will be on graphical output. The existence of other output modalities (e.g., auditory and tactile) was kept in mind during the development and renderers using them can be created.

AbstractUI provides five basic UI components (*Text, Trigger, Choice, Container, Screen*) that can be used to create applications. Even though many applications can be created with them, there are still a lot that cannot be represented with those five components. However, missing UI components can be added to the AbstractUI framework.

Even though the AbstractUI framework supports distribution of framework components across multiple machines no actual implementation exists that does so. The default data models and event providers do not utilize network capabilities. However, further families of data models and event providers can be created to do so.

Evaluation

Description of User Study

The idea of the user study was to compare Witt's WUI toolkit (Witt, Nicolai, & Kenn, 2007) to the AbstractUI framework from the viewpoint of an application developer. Consequently, a part of the conducted user study was to use both toolkits and create applications with them.

A total number of 12 subjects took part in the user study. Most of them were students at University Bremen (10 subjects) while the remaining ones were local staff members (2 subjects). 10 of them were male and 2 female. All subjects were between 23 and 31 years old (average age was 25).

At the beginning of the user study, each subject was asked to fill out a simple questionnaire. They reported their age, gender and whether or not they had used the toolkits beforehand. Furthermore

subjects rated their Java-skills on a scale from 1 to 10 (1 meaning very poor to 10 meaning very good) as well as their English-skills also on a scale ranging from 1 to 10.

Subjects were given several minimalistic examples demonstrating the use of key components for both toolkits (e.g., *Trigger* in AbstractUI framework and *ExplicitTrigger* in WUI toolkit). The examples for the AbstractUI framework and WUI toolkit contained the same functionality. One example for each key component and toolkit was presented to the subjects (4 exercises * 2 toolkits = 8 examples). Furthermore an overview of the four key components and where to find them in the corresponding toolkit was given to the subjects.

Subjects could then look through the resources and ask questions at their own ledger. They were told that that all resources were allowed to be used throughout the entire user study. Once they felt comfortable with them they started with the programming exercises.

A total number of four exercises (one for each key component), which had to be completed with both toolkits, were part of the user study. Subjects were told to have about 5 to 8 minutes to solve a given problem in a particular toolkit. Once the exercise was completed in one toolkit, they were asked to fill out a NASA-Task Load Index (TLX) form. The same exercise was then completed using the remaining toolkit and the subjects were asked to fill out another NASA TLX form. Having completed the exercise with both toolkits, subjects were asked to rate how well they could solve the exercise in each toolkit on a scale from 1 to 10. This was repeated for all exercises.

The programming was done using Eclipse IDE (Eclipse Foundation, 2011) with preconfigured Java-projects. The projects contained two sets of empty Java-classes, one set for each toolkit.

The order of all exercises was changed with each subject as well as the order of the toolkits for each exercise. The sequence of both was balanced across all subjects.

Having completed all exercises the subjects were asked whether or not they felt to have mixed up the toolkits. They were also asked to rate their overall experience with both toolkits on a scale from 1 to 10. The user study was then finished with an informal interview in which all subjects were given a chance to comment on everything they felt noteworthy.

Results

The subjects' NASA TLX and usability ratings were analyzed using a paired t-test (two-tailed). The findings will be depicted in the following.

The NASA TLX rating of the AbstractUI framework and the WUI toolkit was statistically significant ($p < 0.01$). The average NASA TLX rating for both toolkits can found in Figures 1 and 2. The latter illustrates the average NASA TLX rating for each subject, whereas the first shows the overall NASA TLX rating of both toolkits. The average NASA TLX rating for the AbstractUI framework was 26.80 and 43.43 for the WUI toolkit (0 meaning a very low task load index and 100 meaning a very high task load index).

The usability rating of both toolkits was also statistically significant ($p < 0.01$). The average usability rating for each subject is illustrated in Figure 4. Figure 3 shows the average usability rating for both toolkits. Subjects' usability ratings averaged for the AbstractUI framework at 9.28 and the WUI toolkit at 4.92 (1 meaning very poor to 10 meaning very good).

Discussion

All 12 subjects completed the entire user study without complications. Most of them rated their

Figure 1. Average NASA TLX rating of all subjects (0 meaning a very low task load index and 100 meaning a very high task load index)

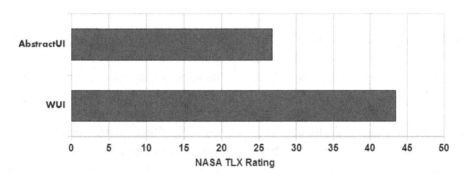

Figure 2. Average NASA TLX rating of each subject

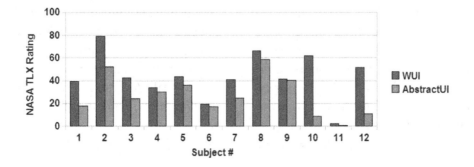

Figure 3. Average usability rating of all subjects (1 meaning very poor to 10 meaning very good)

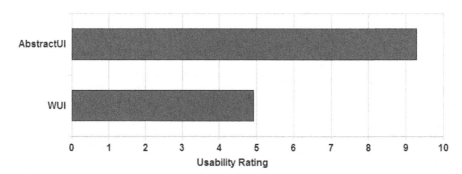

Figure 4. Average usability rating of each subject

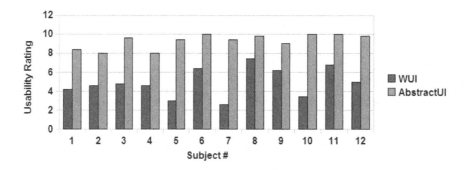

own Java- and English-skills to be good (rating ≥ 7). The average subject required about an hour in order to complete the user study. The fastest subject required about 40 minutes while the slowest subject needed almost 90 minutes.

Some subjects commented on the toolkits during the informal interview session. Several of them were complaining about the inconsistent interfaces and weird naming conventions of the WUI toolkit. All of them commented on how easy and straight forward the AbstractUI framework was when comparing to the WUI toolkit. One subject was so pleased that he was already looking forward to programming with the AbstractUI framework when having to complete an exercise using the WUI toolkit. Other subjects felt that they spent 80% of their time understanding and programming with the WUI toolkit while the remaining 20% were used for the AbstractUI framework and

paperwork. Furthermore, several subjects told the interviewer that they were fans of the slim source code they produced while completing the exercises with the AbstractUI framework.

From observation of the subjects, it became quite clear that the AbstractUI framework is simpler and more intuitive to use. The results support this. The NASA TLX ratings of all subjects for both toolkits were statistically significant and show that the AbstractUI framework requires less workload than the WUI toolkit. Statistically significant was also the usability rating of both toolkits and indicate that the AbstractUI framework is more usable than the WUI toolkit.

The results of the experimental evaluation indicate that the AbstractUI framework outperforms the WUI toolkit in terms of usability.

CONCLUSION AND FUTURE WORK

A framework for developing context-aware UIs on mobile and wearable devices has been introduced. Reusable UI components and an abstract description are used in order to generate concrete representations. Furthermore, a user study has been conducted which compared the WUI toolkit to the AbstractUI framework from the viewpoint of an application developer. The results indicate that the AbstractUI framework outperforms the WUI toolkit in terms of usability.

In the course of working on the AbstractUI framework, several ideas were generated e.g. porting the AbstractUI framework to different programming languages (e.g., dotNet, Objective-C, JavaScript, Ruby, etc.) or comparing the AbstractUI framework with further frameworks in the 'Related Work' section. The first would allow the use of the AbstractUI framework on various devices (e.g., iPhone, Windows Phone, etc.). Furthermore, the implementation of UI generation as an optimization problem is a very interesting approach (Gajos & Weld, 2004) and will certainly be looked into.

REFERENCES

Eclipse Foundation. (2011). *Explore the Eclipse universe.* Retrieved from http://www.eclipse.org/

Gajos, K. Z., & Weld, D. S. (2004). Supple: Automatically generating user interfaces. In *Proceedings of the 9th International Conference on Intelligent User Interfaces* (pp. 93-100). New York, NY: ACM Press.

Gajos, K. Z., Weld, D. S., & Wobbrock, J. O. (2010). Automatically generating personalized user interfaces with supple. *Artificial Intelligence, 174*(12-13), 910–950. doi:10.1016/j.artint.2010.05.005

Gamma, E., Helm, R., Johnson, R., & Vlissides, J. M. (1994). *Design patterns: Elements of reusable object-oriented software.* Reading, MA: Addison-Wesley.

Nichols, J., & Myers, B. A. (2009). Creating a lightweight user interface description language: An overview and analysis of the personal universal controller project. *ACM Transactions on Computer-Human Interaction, 16*(4), 1–37. doi:10.1145/1614390.1614392

Nichols, J., Myers, B. A., Litwack, K., Higgins, M., Hughes, J., & Harris, T. K. (2004). Describing appliance user interfaces abstractly with xml. In *Proceedings of the Workshop on Developing User Interfaces with XML: Advances on User Interface Description Languages.*

Nichols, J., Rothrock, B., Chau, D. H., & Myers, B. A. (2006). Huddle: Automatically generating interfaces for systems of multiple connected appliances. In *Proceedings of the 19th Annual ACM Symposium on User Interface Software and Technology* (pp. 279-288). New York, NY: ACM Press.

Witt, H. (2005). A toolkit for context-aware user interface development for wearable computers. In *Proceedings of the Doctoral Colloquium at the 9th International Symposium on Wearable Computers.*

Witt, H., Nicolai, T., & Kenn, H. (2007). The WUI-toolkit: A model-driven UI development framework for wearable user interfaces. In *Proceedings of the 27th International Conference on Distributed Computing Systems Workshop* (pp. 43). New York, NY: ACM Press.

XML VM. (2011). *Overview.* Retrieved from http://xmlvm.org/

This work was previously published in the International Journal of Ambient Computing and Intelligence, Volume 3, Issue 3, edited by Kevin Curran, pp. 28-35, copyright 2011 by IGI Publishing (an imprint of IGI Global).

Chapter 16
The Problems of Jurisdiction on the Internet

Róisín Lautman
University of Ulster, UK

Kevin Curran
University of Ulster, UK

ABSTRACT

The relationship between jurisdiction and the internet has been the subject of wide ranging discussion ever since the boom in domestic internet usage. Without clear legislation, laws have been created on an ad hoc basis, often in response to specific cases. It is difficult to predict whether any one law will ever be sufficient to cope with the great variety of alleged crimes which take place on the internet. This paper discusses the problems associated with jurisdiction on the internet, presenting sample cases which have influenced the current laws and have fuelled a long term debate that continues to get more heated especially in recent times with UK celebrities being exposed on sites such as Twitter.

1. INTRODUCTION

What if information on the website of a company in country A, is considered defamatory, an infringement of copyright, or an interference with a business relationship, by a company in country B? What if the allegedly wronged party sues for one of the foregoing causes of action in country A? Would the company in country B have to undergo the trauma, expense, and inconvenience

DOI: 10.4018/978-1-4666-2041-4.ch016

of defending itself in country A? Cases such as this highlight the importance of jurisdiction, the authority of the defendant over the subject matter that has led to the prosecution, the authority of the prosecuting court over the defendant, despite their geographical location and the locations in which the crimes were committed. Jurisdiction generally describes any authority over a certain area or certain persons. In the law, jurisdiction sometimes refers to a particular geographic area containing a defined legal authority. Determining jurisdiction in a case of internet crime has proved to be near impossible in many cases and in some cases it has appeared that the determining of jurisdiction has relied on opinion rather than fact (Whitehead & Spikes, 2006).

With the recent passing of the Digital Economy Act (passed in UK parliament on 7th of April 2010) the debate over internet jurisdiction has become highly public, with many people, including those the act claims to benefit, fiercely opposing its law, protesting that it is too severe and close minded. It has also in recent times exploded as a topic of conversation where a married footballer was named on Twitter as having an injunction over an alleged affair with a reality TV star. This particular footballer was eventually identified in Parliament as Ryan Giggs by Liberal Democrat MP John Hemming during a Commons question on privacy orders. The MP using parliamentary privilege to break the court order, said it would not be practical to imprison the 75,000 Twitter users who had named the player (Letts, 2011). This again was a problem of jurisdiction in that UK authorities simply knew that they could not ultimately defend against the 'chatter' on the Internet. This paper discusses the problems associated with jurisdiction on the internet, presenting well known cases which have influenced the current laws and have fuelled a long term debate that continues to get more heated.

2. COUNTRY SPECIFIC LAWS GOVERNING INTERNET JURISDICTION

Since the boom of domestic internet usage in the mid to late 1990's, new laws have been created to help dictate what should be considered as correct and legal use of the internet. This section of the paper will document and explain some of the most significant laws to have been passed in an attempt to govern the internet. The first real act governing the use of data in the UK in response to the introduction of computerised systems and networks in an industrial capacity was the Data Protection Act (DPA), first introduced in 1983 and amended in both 1987 and 1998. The DPA does not have much jurisdiction over internet usage as it mainly governs the holding of data on computerised systems and can only be applied if data has been transferred over the internet in a way that does not comply with the DPA, for example if it has been sent from a company's system that has the right to hold the data to a company's system that has no right to hold the data. The majority of laws that have come into force governing the use of the internet have been aimed at child protection, a major issue on the internet. In the UK it is illegal both online and offline to:

- Entice or coerce a child under 16 to engage in sexually explicit conduct
- Import or transport obscenity using telecommunications public networks
- Knowingly receive child pornography or advertise child pornography
- Depict minors (or appear to be minor) engaged in sexually explicit conduct (even in pseudo-form)
- Advertise sexually explicit conduct by giving the impression that minors are engaged in sexually explicit conduct

However the law does not govern explicit material that is transported into the UK, a problem of geographical jurisdiction. In cases like this, courts will rely on the country which has jurisdiction over the material to prosecute using their laws. In a child protection case this is rarely a major problem as, although there are not many laws governing the internet, many countries have laws governing child protection on the internet as this is publicly acknowledged to be one of the largest risks posed by the internet.

The US Congress has passed 3 major laws to govern child protection online. The Communications Decency Act, or CDA (1996), was Congress's first law to govern child protection. It made it illegal to place content that could be classified as 'indecent' on the internet where a child could access it. However, in 1997 it was ruled that the law was unconstitutional (did not comply with the US constitution) in that it suppressed the right to free speech by adults. In 1998 a more exclusive version of the CDA was passed, the Child Online Protection Act dictated that commercial websites most request users to verify their age before allowing them access to sexually explicit material. However the law again came up against the constitution, in 1999 a permanent injunction was ordered against its enforcement and in 2003 it was declared unconstitutional. Another law to be passed by the US Congress governing child protection was the Child's Internet Protection Act in 2000 which dictated that all schools and libraries that received federal government funding must install pornography blocking software on all their computers. This law encountered a constitutional argument from the Eastern District of Pennsylvania which ruled that the library portion of the law was unconstitutional; however after an appeal from the US government the Supreme Court overturned the Eastern District of Pennsylvania's ruling. As well as these child protection laws, the USA also has a number of laws in place to govern copyright, which can be argued has become a victim of the digital revolution (Sander, 1999).

The Digital Millennium Copyright Act (DMCA), which was made law in the USA in October 1998, made it illegal to facilitate unauthorized access to copyrighted works. Unlike the UKs Digital Economy Act, it did not hold Internet Service Providers responsible for users accessing file sharing sites but rather targeted those who created and maintained the sites (Lee, 2006). The DMCA only governs works that are complete and therefore are fully copyrighted and so in 2005, in response to the rise of the early release of products such as films and software before the company who is responsible for the product has made it publicly available and filming in movie theatres, the Family Entertainment

and Copyright Act was introduced (Dean, 2004). In 2000, Ireland introduced the Copyright and Related Rights Act in an attempt to give artists and copyright holders the right to claim ownership over intellectual property such as sound recordings and writing, and the right to prosecute if the copyright has been deemed to have been broken (ISB, 2000). The most recent (and perhaps most controversial) legislation that has been passed in the UK regarding internet jurisdiction is the UK's Digital Economy Act (DEA). The act claims to protect the economy of the music and film industry by dissuading users by forcing Internet Service Providers to contact suspected offending users and restrict the broadband connection to an address if it has been proven that file sharing has taken place at that address and also block sites that are suspected of facilitating file sharing. Due to mass opposition to this penalty, it has been decided that fines shall be tested for one year and then it shall be decided by government whether or not to introduce restrictions to broadband service. The act comes after a massive rise in file sharing which many record companies and film studios have argued have broken copyright.

3. INTERNET JURISDICTION STANDARDISATION

The laws discussed in the previous section are all subject to geographical jurisdiction, meaning they are only enforceable if the person who is held responsible for the crime committed the crime within the borders of the country. There have been a number of attempts by international organizations to standardize copyright laws in order to remove the problem of geographical jurisdiction in copyright cases. In 2004 the European Union introduced the Intellectual Property Rights Enforcement Directive, which covers all civil courts in the member states of the EU. The directive addresses the intentional infringement of copyright on a commercial scale and aiding infringement of copyright (Nilsson, 2009).

The most recent international move to standardize laws governing the internet, and therefore removing a majority of jurisdiction problems, is the controversial Anti-Counterfeiting Trade Agreement (ACTA). The agreement is the result of negotiations between the USA, the EU and countries such as Japan, South Korea, Mexico and Australia on the international practice of file sharing. ACTA, which has not yet been introduced, dictates that ISPs all over the world would be held responsible for instances of file sharing if they did not impose a penalty on customers suspected of file sharing, such as restricting or removing their broadband connection. The area which many countries readily agree on in regard to the internet is the area of child protection and its jurisdictions. In order to combat international child abuse rings, the international authority Interpol works with 188 countries to help catch and prosecute child offenders. The introduction of the DEA comes after many campaigns by large record companies and film studios that have sought to force ISPs to monitor their users to prevent file sharing. A landmark case in this long running campaign was the case of the Irish subsidiaries of EMI, Sony BMG, Universal and Warner against Eircom, Irelands largest ISP which began in March 2007. The record companies argued that Eircom was aware that the file sharing was taking place on their servers and yet had failed to implement measures to prevent this, such as software that filters internet traffic and can block specified recordings. In October of 2007, Eircom stated that it would not be feasible for them to run the specialised software on their servers and that they were not legally obliged to monitor the traffic on their servers (RTE, 2008).

Another case which has publicised file sharing and has fuelled the arguments of record companies and film studios is the case of the well known torrent search site piratebay.org. Torrents are quite simply the most common file type used for downloading. The pirate bay is based in Sweden and was initially launched in 2003 by the Swedish anti copyright organization *The Piracy Bureau*. In 2008 a criminal and civil prosecution case was brought against them and a Swedish businessman called Carl Lundström, who was accused of selling services to the site, by the Swedish Court supported by the International Federation of the Photographic Industry. The prosecutors claimed that in maintaining and hosting the site they had facilitated users in breaking copyright law. The defendants were found guilty on 17th April 2009 and sentenced to one year imprisonment and a fine of 2.7 million euro. This case was a landmark in the battle between file sharers and the companies that to claim to be adversely affected by this practice. In this case, personal jurisdiction was placed upon these website operators, despite that fact that none of the operators had directly contacted any users of the site and encouraged them to break copyright (Murphy, 2009).

In the case of copyright infringement on the internet, many people argue that it is hard to find the victim in many of the cases; however there are darker sides to internet crime which have very clear victims. With the rise of 'home-shopping', more and more people are transferring debit and credit card details over the internet which, on an unsecured network, can be extremely risky. Skilled hackers have been known to hack into many types of networks, such as online shopping and banking networks and view customers entire bank account details. Some criminal organizations have made an international business out of trading thousands of these stolen account details. In 2006, six men were convicted in Moscow of manufacturing 5000 false credit cards using stolen account details and selling them both in Russia and abroad (Rianovosti, 2006). The men were sentenced by Russian courts however it can be argued that as they sold the false credit cards to other countries apart from Russia, they facilitated credit card fraud in other countries and so they could also be liable to face trial in those countries. The most heavily legislated area of the internet is the area of child protection. Although internet crimes involving children can take place across a global network, many countries have been quick to act in these cases, despite geographical jurisdiction, for example in 2006 the U.S and international authorities charged 27 people in nine U.S states and three countries in connection to an international child pornography ring. However, in less developed countries which do not have a strong legal and justice system, cases of child pornography are rarely discovered and prosecuted and therefore result in child pornography from theses less developed countries being distributed internationally.

4. OPPOSITION TO INTERNET JURISDICTION

The majority of protests against acts such as the Digital Economy Act and the proposed Anti-Counterfeiting Trade Agreement have been based on issues regarding human rights. Groups such as the UK's House of Lord's Joint Committee on Human Rights has stated that "at the moment the Bill defines a process of appeals with no presumption of innocence" and that "[this] process will be applied irrespective of the sanction or evidence" (Arthur, 2010). The DEA has been described as indiscriminate as, in an age where most UK households have internet access on multiple machines such as laptops and PCs and an increasing amount of cafes and hotels offering internet access to their customers, it could affect members of the public who have not violated the act.

Another argument on the topic of human rights is the right to privacy. To prosecute in a copyright infringement case, a user's internet activity must be tracked and logged and then this information must be passed from the ISP to the company lodging the infringement complaint. Human rights groups argue that this is too intrusive by removing users' right to privacy while they are browsing. The DEA has also received criticism from key ISPs. UK ISP

TalkTalk is the first UK ISP to take a stand against the measures proposed by the DEA. They have stated that they will refuse to hand over customer details to any rights holder unless a court order can be obtained ordering them to do so and neither will they comply with the technical measures imposed by the bill, such as disconnecting or restricting a customer's broadband connection (Arthur, 2010). It has been debated that the current laws for imposing jurisdiction in internet cases, particularly in copyright cases, that the laws will not apply jurisdiction fairly, especially personal jurisdiction. It has been said that under the new DEA, personal jurisdiction will be exercised over innocent parties as the act targets the owner of the connection, not particular users.

The major argument in internet jurisdiction has been how to determine who should jurisdiction be applied to? And once that has been decided, how can they be held accountable? All connections to the internet have an Internet Protocol address (or IP address) and it is this address that prosecutors use to locate file sharing offenders. However, due to the rise in copyright infringement prosecution, experienced internet users have developed methods which can prevent companies from connecting an offending IP address to a user. The most common and long established method is the proxy server. A proxy server will navigate the internet on your computers behalf, acting as a relay between the internet and your machine, therefore any activity that could be punishable is tracked back to a server and not a user. This causes problems in determining jurisdiction, meaning that a rights holder who wishes to prosecute for an infringement of copyright must find a way to prove the service provider responsible, something which this paper has shown has been very difficult to do in past cases. Businesses have also risen out of the need to 'cover your browsing tracks' by hiding an IP address for a subscription fee. This is effect makes it impossible for a copyright holder to locate copyright infringements and therefore impossible to apply personal jurisdiction to a specific user.

The only chance a copyright holder will have for prosecution is if they can prove that the subscription site is operating primarily for the use of illegal file sharing and therefore personal jurisdiction can be applied to the site. However this is very difficult to prove as a majority of these sites are advertised as merely aiding internet privacy and therefore can be argued as protecting user's human rights to privacy. The rise in wireless technology has also posed a problem in determining jurisdiction over file sharing cases. Any computer with the facility to connect to a wireless network can use a household's wireless connection without being inside the house, if the signal is strong enough to reach outside. It can be very easy to hack a household wireless connection, with step by step guides being made available online. This can result in wrongful accusations as it is the household router's IP address that is tracked, not an individual machine, therefore the household can be prosecuted for breaching copyright by illegal file sharing. It has been argued, even by intellectual property solicitors, that IP addresses alone are not enough to establish a firm case of file sharing. In 2008 Michael Coyle, an intellectual property solicitor with the firm Lawdit, stated that "The IP address alone doesn't tell you anything. Piracy is only established beyond doubt if the hard-drive is examined." It was revealed in 2008 that the file sharing site PirateBay had been inserting random IP addresses; even of people who may not even know what file sharing is, into their list of downloaders, to mislead investigators (BBC, 2008).

5. CONCLUSION

The problems of internet jurisdiction are constantly evolving, as each new law is passed it creates loopholes, which in turn fuels the technology designed to take advantage of these loopholes. The main problem which seems to affect every law that is made is what exactly qualifies as a crime? Not all cases of internet jurisdiction are black and white and therefore it is impossible to create a blanket law that can be applied to all cases. It can only be said that when it comes to jurisdiction and the internet, it is an ongoing fight with no clear winners or losers on either side.

REFERENCES

Arthur, C. (2010, February). *Opposition to digital economy bill grows.* Retrieved from http://www.guardian.co.uk/technology/2010/feb/05/digital-economy-bill

BBC. (2008, February). *Games firms 'catching' non-gamers.* Retrieved from http://news.bbc.co.uk/1/hi/technology/7697898.stm

Dean, K. (2004, November). *A kinder, gentler copyright bill?* Retrieved from http://www.wired.com/politics/law/news/2004/11/65796

ISB. (2000). *Copyright and related rights act.* Retrieved from http://www.irishstatutebook.ie/2000/en/act/pub/0028/index.html

Lee, T. (2006). *Circumventing competition: The perverse consequences of the digital millennium copyright act: Policy analysis, no. 564.* Washington, DC: Cato Institute.

Letts, Q. (2011, May 24). *Good man John Hemming brought an end to the farce.* Retrieved from http://www.dailymail.co.uk/debate/article-1390215/Ryan-Giggs-super-injunction-John-Hemming-brought-end-farce.html#ixzz1O24eCqmw

Murphy, D. (2009, April 17). *The Pirate Bay founders sentenced to prison, website soldiers on.* Retrieved from http://www.engadget.com/2009/04/17/the-pirate-bay-founders-head-to-prison-website-soldiers-on/

Nilsson, H. (2009, October). *Sweden implements IP rights enforcement directive for copyright.* Retrieved from http://www.twobirds.com/English/News/Articles/Pages/Sweden_implements_IP_Rights_Enforcement_Directive_for_Copyright.Aspx

Rianovosti. (2006, June 16). *Moscow court gives lengthy jail terms to credit card fraud gang.* Retrieved from http://rianovosti.com/russia/20060616/49635773.html

RTE. (2008, April 21). *Eircom rejects record firms' claims.* Retrieved from http://www.rte.ie/business/2008/0421/eircom.html

Sanders, J. (1999). The regulation of indecent material accessible to children on the Internet. *Catholic Law*, 125-129.

Whitehead, R., & Spikes, P. (2003, July). *Determining Internet jurisdiction.* Retrieved from http://www.nysscpa.org/cpajournal/2003/0703/features/f072403.htm

This work was previously published in the International Journal of Ambient Computing and Intelligence, Volume 3, Issue 3, edited by Kevin Curran, pp. 36-42, copyright 2011 by IGI Publishing (an imprint of IGI Global).

Chapter 17
Game Theory:
A Potential Tool for the Design and Analysis of Patient-Robot Interaction Strategies

Aodhan L. Coffey
National University of Ireland, Ireland

Tomas E. Ward
National University of Ireland, Ireland

Richard H. Middleton
National University of Ireland, Ireland

ABSTRACT

Designing suitable robotic controllers for automating movement-based rehabilitation therapy requires an understanding of the interaction between patient and therapist. Current approaches do not take into account the highly dynamic and interdependent nature of this relationship. A better understanding can be accomplished through framing the interaction as a problem in game theory. The main strength behind this approach is the potential to develop robotic control systems which automatically adapt to patient interaction behavior. Agents learn from experiences, and adapt their behaviors so they are better suited to their environment. As the models evolve, structures, patterns and behaviors emerge that were not explicitly programmed into the original models, but which instead surface through the agent interactions with each other and their environment. This paper advocates the use of such agent based models for analysing patient-therapist interactions with a view to designing more efficient and effective robotic controllers for automated therapeutic intervention in motor rehabilitation. The authors demonstrate in a simplified implementation the effectiveness of this approach through simulating known behavioral patterns observed in real patient-therapist interactions, such as learned dependency.

DOI: 10.4018/978-1-4666-2041-4.ch017

1. INTRODUCTION

There are numerous movement-based motor rehabilitation devices commercially available which have proven to successfully aid the recovery of patients suffering hemiparesis after stoke (Bouzit, Popescu, Burdea, & Boian, 2002; Gomez, 1997; Muto, Herzberger, Hermsdörfer, Miyake, & Pöppel, 2007). Robotic movement-based rehabilitation therapy has many advantages over conventional manual rehabilitation, such as; reducing the burden on the healthcare system, the ability to deliver low cost well controlled repetitive training sessions, and quantitative assessment of motor recovery (Banala, Kulpe, & Agrawa, 2007). However, the major drawback over manual rehabilitation is the loss of human insight and intuition which is used by the therapist to regulate how and when assistance is offered to a patient. Current control system approaches do not take into account the highly dynamic and interdependent nature of the relationship which exists between a patient and their therapist. For example, an experienced therapist will very quickly notice when a patient is making less effort to engage during periods of assistance. In such cases the therapist may reduce the amount of assistance they offer in order to coax more effort from the patient. This is an example of a strategy adoption by the therapist based on their experience of the patient's behavior. In the same situation, a robotic controller lacking the therapist's experience might increase the level of assistance to such a patient in a naïve attempt to provide assistance. This action is counterproductive since the robot is taking more of the rehabilitation burden from the patient who can complete their task with less effort than they have the ability to offer. In such cases the patient is no longer contributing maximum effort and the resulting therapy will not be as efficacious.

A. Introduction to Common Rehabilitation Robotics Control Strategies

One of the most common controller strategies used in robotic rehabilitation therapy systems is the fixed kinematic control approach. Research suggests that the fixed kinematic control strategy is suboptimal because it abolishes variability, an intrinsic property of neuromuscular control (Jezernik, Scharer, Colombo, & Morari, 2003). A significant concern is that this strategy may force the central nervous system into a state of "learned helplessness" (Grau, Barstow, & Joynes, 1998; Wool, Siegel, & Fine, 1980) since the neural systems are not being challenged to explore alternative motor patterns on their own accord.

A more intuitive controller based on the "assist-as-needed" (AAN) paradigm is also widely used by movement-based rehabilitation robots. A comparison study of the efficacy of fixed trajectory algorithms against AAN algorithms on recovery of locomotion ability in completely spinalized adult mice was undertaken by Cai et al. (2006). The results of this study show that mice undergoing AAN robotic training exhibited faster and more pronounced recovery than mice given fixed robotic training. However, the paper concludes that an exact optimal AAN algorithm still needs to be developed. We believe that approaches such as AAN can be improved further through a better understanding of the complex dynamic interactions that exist between patient and therapist during periods of assistance. Current approaches ignore the complexity which drives a patient's actions, motivation and behavior in response to their therapist's assistance and therefore is not sufficient for administering optimized therapy. We feel that understanding these dynamics is crucial to developing rehabilitation systems that can offer quality recovery matching that of a competent therapist. Here we advocate the use of agent-based modeling for analysing patient-therapist interactions with a view to designing more efficient and effective robotic controllers for automated therapeutic intervention in motor rehabilitation.

B. Introduction to Agent-Based Modeling and Game Theoretic Principles

Agent-based modeling and simulation (ABMS) is a relatively new approach used to model complex systems composed of interacting 'agents' (human or otherwise). These agents are often described by simple rules and behavior for interacting with other agents and completing tasks. The main strength behind this approach is the principle of self-organization. Agents learn from their experiences, and adapt their behaviors so that they are better suited to their environment. As the models evolve, structures, patterns and behaviors can emerge that were not explicitly programmed into the original models, but instead surfaced through the agent interactions with each other and their environment (Macal & North, 2010).

A typical agent-based model is made up of three components:

1. A set of *agents,* their attributes and behaviours.
2. A set of agent *relationships* and methods for how to interact.
3. An environment '*a game*'.

In order to develop an agent based model these three elements must be identified, defined and programmed.

Agent-based modeling has been applied exhaustively in both the social sciences (economics, management, political and social psychology) and the formal sciences (computer science, biology, physics and statistics). This approach of modeling has proven to be useful for modeling phenomena which are not easily modeled by other approaches (Macy & Willer, 2002). The applications of agent based modeling are plentiful, range from modeling the stock market (Arthur, Durlauf, & Lane, 1997) to networking engineering (P2P file share) and predicting the spread of epidemics (Zhang, 2007).

The interaction between a therapist and patient is clearly then a problem for which an agent based approach is well suited as the individual interacting elements are clearly nonlinear decision making entities whose behavior arises out of a complex series of interactions. These interactions are driven by a range of motivations, desires, beliefs and intentions which are difficult to quantify and simulate through any other means. Consequently we feel the approach will be of utility here and merits investigation as so far as the authors are aware the methods of agent based modeling has not been previously applied to the design of automated controller systems for neurorehabilitation.

C. Introduction to the Principles of Game Theory

The agent based modeling of the behaviors of the patient and the therapist (and subsequently its automated counterpart) is an essential element for the investigation being undertaken here. However, the development of the interactivity between these agents through modification of behavior based on experience and observation of each other's action is key to producing the types of behavior observed in real life patient-therapist interaction. To provide the required dynamics in this instance we harness ideas from the mathematics of Game Theory. Game Theory is a branch of mathematical analysis developed to study social decision making in situations of competition and conflict. Typically these games consist of two or more competitive participants (agents) where the outcome of a participant's choice of action depends critically on the actions of others. When played iteratively, participants can through the adoption of strategies derived from the participant's model of their opponent achieve improved payoff over time (Chiba & Hiraishi, 1998).

The interaction between a patient and their rehabilitation therapist can be considered as an instance of such a competitive game in which the patient is seeking maximum success at the rehabilitation task but with minimal energy expenditure. The therapist on the other hand wishes to seek the patient deploy maximum effort or expenditure of energy during the rehabilitation tasks. However it is not obvious from the therapist's viewpoint how much effort the patient possesses and how much of it they are expending on a trial by trial basis. Consequently the therapist must balance giving assistance to complete the task and therefore maintain motivation with the need to engage the patient as fully as possible with the task.

Game theory is then clearly applicable in this scenario. In the next section we will develop these ideas further and show through example how it can be applied to investigate patient-therapist interactions.

2. METHODS

We apply the ideas of the previous section through very simple models of patient motivation and behavior. Simple as the formulations are they will demonstrate significant exploratory and explanatory power through the production of plausible patterns of behavior in patient-therapist (therapist/ agent/controller) interaction. We start by defining each player's desires, objectives and outcomes according to a basic mathematical formulation.

A. The Patient Model

The patient's primary input to the game is the effort they exhibit during a therapy session. We called this parameter E_p (Patient Effort). Patient effort could be measured through energy exerted, force applied, measures of central nervous system activity etc – the details of the physical measurement is not important at this stage as only an abstraction of the interaction is examined in this

work. We also assume that the patient desires to recover the use of their effected limb; hence their objective is to successfully complete each motor task they are assigned, to the best of their ability. We can model this objective mathematically by stating that,

The patient desires to maximize G where,

$$G = \sum_{i=1}^{N} T_i \qquad (1)$$

where,

T_s = Task Completion status: $T_i \in [0,1]$
N = Number of trials in therapy session.

In this case $T_i \in [0,1]$ where 0 represents the task has not progressed at all and 1 represents the task is complete. For example, perhaps the task is to move a weight from one position to another. In such a case, patient effort might be measured in cm of movement that the patient generates (similarly for robotic effort) and therefore T can represent how far the patient movement task has progressed. In such a case T=1 would correspond to the weight being successfully moved to the target position.

One could consider this desire to maximize Gas reflecting the patient's motivation through gratification. Clearly this is something which could be experimented with in exploratory scenarios.

We also need some measurement of the patient's recovery. A reasonable assumption would be that we can gauge the recovery of the patient based on the amount of effort they offered during the complete set of rehabilitation therapy sessions. We can therefore say that a measure of the patient recovery is given by,

$$R = \sum_{i=1}^{N} E_{p(i)} \qquad (2)$$

B. The Therapist (Robotic Assistance) Model

The therapist's primary input to the game is the effort they offer to the patient in order to complete a task. We called this parameter E_r (Robot Effort). In a motor rehabilitation task this robotic effort could as in the therapist example be a physical measurement such as force applied, however as previously stated the details are not important in this example. The simplified formulation of the therapist's motivation is to assist the patient in completing a motor task. In the ideal situation,

The therapist desires to offer,

$$E_r = [E_n - E_p] \qquad (3)$$

where,

E_n = Effort needed to complete task

Now that we have defined the preliminary models for our patient and therapist we can focus on designing a model of the interaction. The structure of this 'game' will determine how the agents interact with each other and will affect the behavioral patterns that emerge. In the following section we develop three different behavioral models for our robot therapist and describe the 'game' dynamics of each simulation which will control the agent's interactions.

3. SIMULATIONS

Our preliminary model defined above, which is admittedly very basic, can be used to demonstrate plausible patterns observed in real patient-therapist interactions. In this section we illustrate this by simulating interesting interactions between patient and therapist. We start by simulating a scenario in which learned dependency occurs; this simulation is of significant interest as its occurrence is quite common in rehabilitation therapy. However, we then proceed to show how through experimenting with alternative robotic agent (the model therapist) behavior we can predict and limit its occurrence, thus optimizing the resulting recovery rate.

A. Simulating Learned Dependency

In this instance we model the patient as being 'lazy', desiring to offer the minimal effort possible to complete a task. To simulate this effect we program the patients to offer less and less motor effort each turn so long as the task is cooperatively completed.

$$E_{p(i)} = E_{p(i-1)} + \Delta E \qquad (4)$$

where,

if $(T(i) = 0)$, $\Delta E = 0.1$
if $(T(i) = 1)$, $\Delta E = -0.1$
Note: The values chosen for ΔE are arbitrary and only serve to reflect some change in the patient's effort.

We model the therapist in this instance (a naïve robotic actuator) as a player who will always provide the additional assistance required to complete the task.

$$E_r = [E_n - E_p]$$

We then model the interaction through a round based game with $N=100$.

Results

Given the rules as designed, it is clear that after several iterations the patient will offer almost no effort and yet still 'successfully' complete the rehabilitation task thanks to the additional effort

Figure 1. Learned dependency

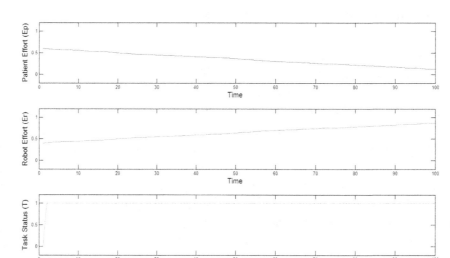

offered by the 'over helpful' therapist. This can be observed in Figure 1.

It is interesting to note that, whereas the patient received constant gratification of 'successfully' completing each motor task, their recovery R as defined as the sum of the patient efforts (area under the curve) is low. This result is as we would expect in the case of learned dependency.

Now that we have observed a plausible behavior we can experiment with developing alternative robot behavior so as to reduce the likelihood of this occurrence through basing the robot's behavior on its experiences of previous patient effort.

B. Developing Alternative Robotic Behavior to Counter Learned Dependency

The following simulations purpose is to explore how the patient will react to random bursts of no assistance while they are falling into the pattern of learned dependency.

Instead of always assisting the patient to complete a task regardless of their input effort, we instead modify the robot to naïvely assist the patient only for the first half of our session. Then for the second half of the session we get the robot

to randomly stop offering assistance to the patient for short periods of time. For this example, the moment of no assist will be chosen by generating a number between (1-6).

Such that,

if (n < 6), $E_r = [E_n - E_p]$
if (n =6), $E_r = 0$ (5)

Results

The results of this simulation are interesting as they still show the effect of learned dependency; however its occurrence is less severe and takes longer to manifest. This can be observed in Figure 2, since the gradient of the curve Ep is less linear than in Figure 1.

We can clearly see the patient effort level E_p declining up until the halfway point (while the robot is still mindlessly assisting the patient). Then, as the robot behavior switches to randomly offer no assistance we see a drop in the task completion status. Consequently, as the patient loses the gratification of completing their task they react by starting to increase their effort levels again. Whereas this is a very simple simu-

Figure 2. Countering learned dependency

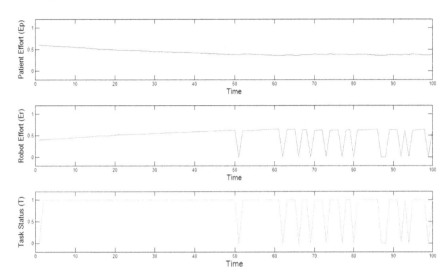

lation, it accurately replicates a real patient reaction. We can see that the recovery rate R of the patient under this robotic therapist model is higher than that in the previous model, since the patient was encouraged to offer more effort.

In simulation 3 we take this model and try to advance it to show how we can effectively reduce learned dependency even further and regain positive efforts from our patient.

C. Simulation 3: Replicating Therapist Coaxing Effect

In this simulation we show how it is possible to replicate a desired behavior which an experienced therapist might employ during periods of assistance when they realize a patient is no longer contributing sufficient effort to complete a task. We call this strategy 'effort coaxing'.

To achieve this we take a similar approach as in simulation 2. However, this time instead of randomly reducing the robot's assistance to zero for short periods of time, we instead reduce the amount of assistance it offers by some small amount. We then hold this value constant for a random period of time, for example 10 trials.

if $(n < 6)$, $E_r = [E_n - E_p]$

if $(n = 6)$, $E_r = [E_n - E_p] - \Delta E$ (6)

Results

Figure 3 clearly shows the patient effort levels responding to the periods of lack of assistance. At these moment the patient loses gratification i.e., $T(i) = 0$, and therefore starts to increase their effort until they rebalance the completion status $T(i) = 0$. Since the assistance level is being held constant this coaxes the patient to keep increasing their effort until they match the effort need to complete the task. This effect can be observed as the slight rises in the plot of patient's effort. We can also observe a rise in the patient's recovery R, as would be expected in a real therapy session.

Comparison of the Recovery Outcome of Each Simulation

To compare the three therapist behavioral models developed, we simulated 10 therapy sessions consisting of 100 iterations for each of the con-

Figure 3. Replicating therapist coaxing effect

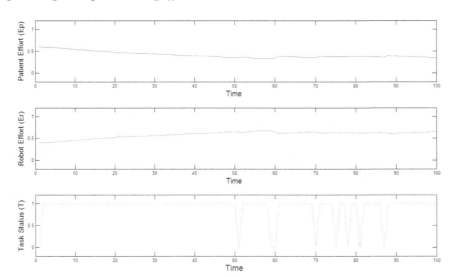

Table 1. Recovery results of simulations

	Simulation #1	Simulation #2	Simulation #3
Recovery (R)	33.8181	35.8954	38.6840
(R / Max patient Effort)	56.36%	59.82%	64.46%

trol strategies. We then computed the average recovery rate R as per Equations 2, for each of the models. The results of this experiment are described in Table 1.

It should be noted that we are using the same patient model for each of the simulations and that only the therapist model has been modified between simulations. Therefore, we can simply examine the magnitude of the recovery R of the patient to determine how biasing the robots behavior affected the patient's recovery.

At first glance the difference between the patient's recovery rate R of the models might seem non-substantial. To better appreciate these results we need to examine the percentage difference of patient effort between the simulations. For example, there is approximately an 8 percentage point increase in patient effort between simulation 1 and simulation 3.

4. DISCUSSION AND CONCLUSION

A key objective of this paper is to investigate if agent-based models are a suitable approach for developing conceptual models of the interactions between a patient and their therapist with a view to improving the design of robotic assistance devices for automated therapy. As an illustration of this approach we have developed a simple model which demonstrates behavior which could be described as 'learned dependency' – a phenomenon observed in real patient-therapist interaction. We have shown that it is possible to capture interesting patient-therapist dynamics with respect to patient effort through such simulations. We further show how through minor adaptation of the therapist agent we can alter the interaction elicited from the patient agent in a way that is commensurate with observed real patient responses. The results of this simulation show how appropriate interaction strategies for the therapist can reduce the manifestation of suboptimal interactions such as learned dependency and as a result increase the efficiency of the resulting therapy session (in this abstraction). Finally we demonstrate how such simple models can be further adapted to replicate a desired behavior used by an experienced therapist to coax more effort out of their patient. Our results clearly indicate an increase in patient effort during this simulation. Whereas these simulations are admittedly simplistic, they serve to prove the potential of using an agent based modeling approach in replicating some of the phenomena observed in real patient-therapist dynamics.

This work is only a simple illustration of an approach that we feel may be useful in the design of automated assistance systems for motor rehabilitation. The models used while simple already demonstrate a powerful ability to replicate and explore the dynamics between a patient and therapist. This modeling power should be of great utility in the design and deployment of neurorehabilitation control systems.

REFERENCES

Arthur, W. B., Durlauf, S. N., & Lane, D. A. (1997). *The economy as an evolving complex system II. SFI studies in the sciences of complexity*. Reading, MA: Addison-Wesley.

Banala, S. K., Kulpe, A., & Agrawa, S. K. (2007, April 10-14). A powered leg orthosisfor gait rehabilitation of motor-impaired patients. In *Proceedings of the IEEE International Conference on Robotics and Automation,* Rome, Italy (pp. 401-407).

Bouzit, M., Popescu, G., Burdea, G., & Boian, R. (2002). The Rutgers Master II-ND force feedback glove. In *Proceedings of the 10th Symposium on Haptic Interfaces for Virtual Environment and Teleoperator Systems*, Orlando, FL (p. 145).

Cai, L. L., Fong, A. J., Liang, Y., Burdick, J., Otoshi, C. K., & Edgerton, V. R. (2006). Effects of assist-as-needed robotic training paradigms on the locomotor recovery of adult spinal mice. In *Proceedings of the IEEE/RAS-EMBS International Conference on Biomedical Robotics and Biomechatronics* (pp. 62-67).

Chiba, K., & Hiraishi, K. (1998). Iterated continuous prisoner's dilemma game and its usefulness in analyzing multi-agent systems. In *Proceedings of the IEEE International Conference on System, Man and Cybernetics* (pp. 644-649).

Gomez, D. (1997). *A dexterous hand master with force feedback for virtual reality.* Unpublished doctoral dissertation, Rutgers University, Rutgers, NJ.

Grau, J. W., Barstow, D. G., & Joynes, R. L. (1998). Instrumental learning within the spinal cord: I. Behavioral properties. *Behavioral Neuroscience, 112*, 1366–1386. doi:10.1037/0735-7044.112.6.1366

Jezernik, S., Scharer, R., Colombo, G., & Morari, M. (2003). Adaptive robotic rehabilitation of locomotion: A clinical study in spinally injured individuals. *Spinal Cord, 41*, 657–666. doi:10.1038/sj.sc.3101518

Macal, C. M., & North, M. J. (2010). Tutorial on agent-based modelling and simulation. *Journal of Simulation, 4*, 151–162. doi:10.1057/jos.2010.3

Macy, M. W., & Willer, R. (2002). From factors to actors: Computational sociology and agent-based modeling. *Annual Review of Sociology, 28*, 143–166. doi:10.1146/annurev.soc.28.110601.141117

Muto, T., Herzberger, B., Hermsdörfer, J., Miyake, Y., & Pöppel, E. (2007, October 29-November 2). Interactive gait training device 'walk-mate' for hemiparetic stroke rehabilitation. In *Proceedings of the IEEE/RSJ International Conference on Intelligent Robots and Systems*, San Diego, CA (pp. 2268-2274).

Wool, R. N., Siegel, D., & Fine, P. R. (1980). Task performance in spinal cord injury: Effect of helplessness training. *Archives of Physical Medicine and Rehabilitation, 61*, 321–325.

Zhang, J. (2007). An evolutionary game model of resources-sharing mechanism in P2P networks. In *Proceedings of the Workshop on Intelligent Information Technology Application* (pp. 282-285).

This work was previously published in the International Journal of Ambient Computing and Intelligence, Volume 3, Issue 3, edited by Kevin Curran, pp. 43-51, copyright 2011 by IGI Publishing (an imprint of IGI Global).

Chapter 18
Enjoy.IT!:
A Platform to Integrate Entertainment Services

M. Amparo Navarro-Salvador
Universidad Politécnica de Valencia, Spain

Ana Belén Sánchez-Calzón
Universidad Politécnica de Valencia, Spain

Carlos Fernández-Llatas
Universidad Politécnica de Valencia, Spain

Teresa Meneu
Universidad Politécnica de Valencia, Spain

ABSTRACT

The evolution of the Internet has been spectacular in recent decades. However, the Internet is still a linear scenario, focused on showing contents and dissociated from the physical world. On the other hand, there are many social groups that don't know how to use the opportunities that ICT can offer them, such as children. In this scenario, Project Enjoy.IT! designs, develops, and validates an entertainment platform with advanced contents that will set up a practical realization of the new products and services from the Future Internet. Project Enjoy.IT! integrates the physical world as an extension of the virtual world and vice versa. Thus, the project creates an AmI system that is able to act depending on the children's knowledge and necessities. The platform is based on a Services Choreography that allows an easy, simple integration of the necessary elements to give support to interactive entertainment activities.

INTRODUCTION

The Internet evolution has been spectacular in the last decades. The Internet has grown from a simple message exchange tool to become a macro showcase for the knowledge of the world. The Internet is also everywhere and when you want: you can access via computer, mobile, laptop even television. It is worth to remake that nowadays the Internet is driven by Social Networks and new ways of uploading content and communication range. Despite all these advances the Internet world is still a linear preestablished scenario, fo-

DOI: 10.4018/978-1-4666-2041-4.ch018

cused on showing contents and dissociated from physical world.

On the other hand, there are many groups who, despite being very proactive in their real activities, they don't see the need or don't know how to use the opportunities that ICT can offer them. ICT can provide them with new and more powerful services and they can also directly benefit from the interaction potential that the Internet offers society.

Focusing more on the field of entertainment, it is worth to highlight several aspects. Currently, ICT is focused on entertainment for the youth are totally networked: online videogames and entertainment connecting players together have online communities associated. The online ways allow people to connect each other, to share all kind of information and, ultimately, to have the possibility to access to places, context and individuals hardly reachable by other ways. The new entertainment ICT are networked but not fully integrated into the environment; there is a number of individual and collective constraints that hinder the full development and implementation of new technological applications in the main aspects of people's day-by-day. We are thinking about a world where ICT is fully integrated into basic psychosocial processes, into the political, economical and cultural structure.

Finally, it is worth noting the current status of socio-cultural field, which is the recipient of this project. The current provision of the socio-cultural sphere needs a qualitative transformation that allows the full integration of ICT into the environment of the person, in an internal (psychological) and external (social) level. The point is that the different technological tools and devices can be connected and share information to each other about the individual's conditions, capabilities, emotions, reasoning, needs, choices, etc. The entertainment ICT have to be totally and properly integrated into the environment within the person that is paying attention on it. The point is that a person can freely interact without being aware of the presence of ICT.

In this context Project Enjoy.IT! (http://www.proyectoenjoyit.es) is born, whose main objective is to design, develop and validate an entertainment platform with advanced contents which will set up a practical realization of the new products and services from the Future Internet. The project may cause a significant and differentiating impact in this related scenario, enabling help to blur the lines that are still separating the ICT of the real world. The project may also enhance the evolution of the Internet towards a more dynamic and complex world. A world where the relationship with the physical world is closet, and in which all users are, in an easy way and at the same time, creators and effective receivers of the knowledge. By creating this platform we pretend to promote the use of ICT by users which are not familiarized with this kind of technologies, such as children.

The following paper explains, in the first instance, the objectives that the project aims to obtain with their execution. In the second instance, the materials and methods which will be employed to the project development are explained. In this section, a state of the art of actual videogames and entertainment is described. In the third instance, we present the results Project Enjoy.IT! Project aims for and which technology is going to be used. Finally, a discussion about how the Project will affect to children is explained, enclosed by future researches.

OBJECTIVES

Project Enjoy.IT! is a pre-industrial prototype which will set up a technological platform of personalized, ubiquitous and collaborative services. These services will be oriented to management, coordination and support of intensive applications of knowledge and dynamic, multimedia and multimodal contents. All these services will be applied in the field of entertainment, recreational and educational activities and animation in selected environments, always being based on high content of ICT capabilities.

By this reason, the first objective o the Project is to design, develop and validate an entertainment platform and advanced contents which is going to be a practical realization of new products and services of the Future Internet.

In addition, the implementation of this project, aims to promote the use of ICT by users which are not familiarized with this kind of technologies. In this case they will be children.

In third place, the project expects to develop innovative research lines such as the integration of the user in the chain of provision of services, who will be the potential beneficiary of the results and who is participating in its conception and design from the first moment.

Moreover, this Project aspires to remarkably contribute to the investigation and development of innovative technology in three of the five pillars of the Future Internet. Focusing of this objective, the first one is the Internet of Things (ITU, 2005; Sundmaeker, Guillemin, Friess, & Woelfflé, 2010). Project Enjoy.IT! wants to integrate the physical world as an extension of the virtual world and vice versa. Thus, the system intelligence and the users' interaction can overcome the digital barriers. Project Enjoy.IT! is going to create an AmI (Riva, Vatalaro, Davide, & Alcañiz, 2005) system which will be able to act depending on the user's necessities. But this AmI network will not only be able to realize received requests but also be aware of the user's identity and his context, customs and circumstances.

The second mainstay of the Future Internet is the Internet of Knowledge and contents. In this research line, Project Enjoy.IT! will create and automatically associate content and knowledge elements linked to the Internet of Things which will be instantly extended to the Internet of People and will also create tools for generating and using content in an easy and powerful fashion, taking advantage of these new capabilities in a way that they are reflected on entertainment applications developed in the virtual world.

Finally, the third mainstay of the Future Internet to be developed is the Internet of People. This will be especially due to the entertainment and educative goal effort being the scope of this project, specific to promote the integration of all people in the use and enjoyment of applications, customizing roles and interaction to suit the differentiating characteristics of all people including those with special needs or disabled ones. Of course, this research area will devote special attention to ensure that these new capabilities don't jeopardize the privacy of users and securing inherent knowledge generated in the process and communications security.

MATERIALS AND METHODS

Performing a global vision of the video games existing nowadays, it is worth noting two types of video games for Project Enjoy.IT!. On the one hand there are online videogames. Online videogames are those played via the Internet regardless of the platform. They can either be multiplayer games played with other people, or single player games which played by solo users. Focusing on multiplayer games, they are games which involve a mode for various players. They are often played via the Internet or other network with other people connected to it. The theme of these videogames can be collaborative or competitive. The first group of them, the collaborative ones, are interesting videogames for Enjoy.IT!. A cooperative game is a game in which two or more players do not compete, but rather strive to achieve the same objective and therefore earn or lose as a group. Role-playing games are the most common form of a cooperative game, in spite of not being always like that. In such games, players (acting of characters) are generally seeking similar objectives.

On the other hand, there are serious games. A serious game is a game designed for a different purpose other than pure entertainment. Serious games are learning tools which have pedagogical and educational objectives that enable players to obtain a set of predominantly practical knowledge and skills. The game by itself is a motivating factor for students, it gets meaningful and leisure learning, it promotes teamwork and it has great flexibility in its use. For this reason, what we aim to achieve with Project Enjoy.IT! video gaming platform is that children learn while they are playing. At the same time, they will be developing in both the psychomotor activity and the psychosocial levels (Sánchez, 2007; Ritterfeld, Cody, & Vorderer, 2009).

The interaction form of these games should be different from the usual: we want children to perform a series of activities linked by a common story. In this story they will have to move and interact with the environment, either through sensors responding to his actions, or using the new available game controllers that make users stand up from the chair and use their body to move the remote control and the character at the same time, such as Wiimote or PlayStation Move. Even using Microsoft Kinect, where gestures and spoken commands are used to control the game. Moreover, in order to create a transparent environment, sensors and remote controllers used will be hidden.

Otherwise, we aim to integrate all this technologies into the world of the socio-cultural animation, which focuses on the development of recreational activities for children of all ages. This animation currently does not include ICT for the realization of the games and that is where Project Enjoy.IT! is going to give a change with this type of combined experience. Thus, the Project desires to go beyond what exists today in the world of video games: it wants to enhance the interactive possibilities not just with the remote control but also with the environment, within a broad space where entertainment activities can be executed in a way that include both video games and physi-

cal activity, without the user being aware of the technology that is behind all the environment.

In order to create this platform, an architecture based on Services Choreography is going to be used. This fact will facilitate the installation and fault tolerance in the environment which will be surrounded by sensors. The sensors will collect the data independently from the central system (Fernández, Mocholí, Moyano, & Meneu, 2010).

EXPECTED RESULTS

Project Enjoy.IT! aims to create a digital and interactive entertainment platform for children. A complete role-playing adventure of interconnected games is being built. Ten groups of twenty children (9-10 years old) from the Polytechnic University of Valencia's Summer School will participate on it. Each group will be a village from a region and shall solve the same problem. Natural resources are near extinction and children have to begin a journey around an imaginary world in order to find several pieces from a magical object which will solve the problem. Using the recovered pieces the magical object will be assembled, always bearing in mind the collaborative spirit to promote positive values among children. The adventure will be composed by around twenty different games. A different technology will be used in each game. Each game will be multiplayer, collaborative (among children and different groups) and interconnected to the whole adventure, using a Social Network. All the advances of each group could be consulted by every player and by children's parents.

This adventure will be expressed in a modular and scalable platform that allows an easy and simple integration of the necessary elements to give support to interactive entertainment activities. To achieve all the above, the architecture in Figure 1 is proposed, which is based on a Services Choreography.

Services Choreography specification is targeted for composing interoperable, peer-to-peer

Figure 1. Proposed platform architecture

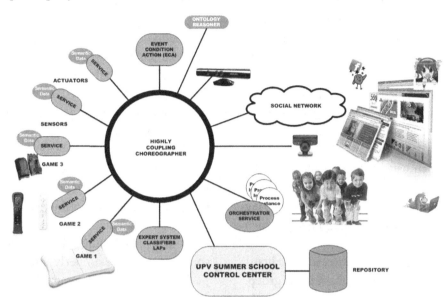

collaborations between any type of participant regardless of the supporting platform or programming model used by the implementation of the hosting environment. Choreography has no centralised control, which is instead shared between domains, where each is able to carry out its own activities according to its role in a peer-to-peer model, applying a global behavioural contract. The perspective is neutral to any of the participants in any interactions, and execution and/or central control are the responsibilities of the participants themselves. Using the choreographer, services and devices are able to exchange information in a distributed way because choreographed processes are independent and can communicate with each other to define its workflow execution. This model makes easy to turn the connection and disconnection of services dynamically and it's capable of using different types of sensors and configurations (Fernández, Lázaro, & Benedí, 2009).

Use of choreography for interconnecting services requires the use of a common exchange language that allows services to be understood. This is achieved with an architecture that includes a semantic layer in the choreographer to improve communication among sensors, actuators, and services in the system. The use of Ontology Services and Machine Reasoning for the description of data from sensors allows to make a more accurate interpretation of information obtained from them, and allows the system to automatically detect sensors and services available in each moment (Fernández et al., 2009).

Service choreography involves the Orchestration of both manual and automated processes. Orchestration addresses application execution in a host-bound fashion. There is a centralised control mechanism which directs activities, each of which is an interaction between services (generally constrained to Web services). These apply a behavioural contract between partners in a binary model. This enables one to define an executable, and to a lesser sense, an abstract model of stateful interactions, but only from the perspective of the controller. Orchestration defines executable behaviour and how it is to be achieved, and events are centrally controlled. By these reasons, it is also included in the architecture an Orchestrator of Services connected to the choreographer who supports the use of workflows to describe processes graphically. Workflows are a formal specification of the implementation of processes that can be dynamically executed by a computer-based system. Using these tools a non-expert can create complex processes, enabling them to be managed automatically by a system, without the need of writing any line of source code.

It is noteworthy that it will exist a control centre where the evolution of the context could be observed in a centrally way. This will be made interviewing each part of the system. Thus, the summer school monitors will control the evolution of each group, how many groups are playing at the same time, where they are playing, which children are playing, etc.

There is also a repository where all data items will be stored as well as the progress of each group.

The games will be interconnected to the whole adventure, using a private Social Network. All the advances of each group in the adventure will be consulted by every players, monitors and children's parents. Players will be able to view and modify their profile, consult milestones achieved by any group, see the groups' positions on the map as well as upload and view photos, contribute to various forums related to the places they visit. Contents will be generated by the users and by the system, from the information captured by the sensors and the intelligence of the platform.

Another thing to note it is that used sensors must be wireless as far as possible in order to create a transparent environment for the user. Next, there are several examples of sensors and their possible use: movement sensors, to know when children enter to a room; position sensors, to know their position in the campus; barrier sensors, to know when they cross a door; light actuators, to control the environmental lights depending on the story, microphones and speech processing, to interact to the system; IP cameras, to create augmented reality.

DISCUSSION

The technological platform proposed is projected to make technology accessible to children and to provide personal and social benefits arising from the use of ICT. It will also contribute to the development of a significant set of values, beliefs, thoughts and attitudes as well as to the development of several physical and cognitive skills. The integration of ICT in the individual's environment will allow to change the contexts of interaction, to reach the inner child, defining and mediating her personal experience. The purpose is to bring the ways in which children define their own world so that ICT can be properly integrated.

The aim is to adapt personal and social experiences of children in order to provide benefits to them. It is sure that the new entertainment ICT and the platform in which we are working, besides being a primary cognitive tool in the sense that the players enhance mental skills, and allow the development of new ways of thinking, will also contribute to promote social relationships, cooperative learning, the development of capacities for creativity, communication and reasoning, the storage and processing of large amount of information, the automation of tasks, and other essential components of the interaction and the physical and psychosocial growth.

With this new entertainment platform, Project Enjoy.IT! will set up a practical realization of the new products and services from the Future Internet. It will be promoted the use of ICT by users which are not familiarized with this kind of technologies, such as children. The AmI system will immerse the users (children) in a world that will interact to them without being aware of what technology are they using.

The first step will be a pilot on 2011, where new videogames using AmI will be tested by several groups of 20 children ten years old. The second step will be the test of the whole platform on July 2012 by 200 children. Future researches will include different ages of children by including new games as well as the ability to set the difficulty of the games according to age.

REFERENCES

Fernández, C., Lázaro, J. P., & Benedí, J. M. (2009). Workflow Mining Application to Ambient Intelligence Behavior Modeling. In *Proceedings of Universal Access in HCI, Part II (HCII 2009)* (LNCS 5615, pp. 160-167).

Fernández, C., Mocholí, J. B., Moyano, A., & Meneu, T. (2010). *Semantic Process Choreography for Distributed Sensor Management.* Paper presented at the International Workshop on Semantic Sensor Web (SSW 2010).

International Telecommunication Union (ITU). (2005). *ITU Internet Reports 2005: The Internet of Things*. Geneva, Switzerland: Author.

Ritterfeld, U., Cody, M. J., & Vorderer, P. (2009). *Serious Games. Mechanisms and effects*. London, UK: Routledge.

Riva, G., Vatalaro, F., Davide, F., & Alcañiz, M. (2005). *Ambient Intelligence*. Amsterdam, The Netherlands: IOS Press.

Sánchez, M. (2007, September 19-21). *Buenas Prácticas en la Creación de Serious Games (Objetos de Aprendizaje Reutilizables)*. Paper presented at the IV Simposio Pluridisciplinar sobre Diseño, Evaluación y Desarrollo de Contenidos Educativos Reutilizables (SPDECE 2007).

Sundmaeker, H., Guillemin, P., Friess, P., & Woelfflé, S. (2010). *Vision and challenges for realising the Internet of Things*. Brussels, Belgium: European Commission.

Chapter 19

DEAL:
A Distributed Authorization Language for Ambient Intelligence

Irini Genitsaridi
Institute of Computer Science, FORTH, Greece

Antonis Bikakis
University College London, UK

Grigoris Antoniou
Institute of Computer Science, FORTH, Greece

ABSTRACT

Authorization is an open problem in Ambient Intelligence environments. The difficulty of implementing authorization policies lies in the open and dynamic nature of such environments. The information is distributed among various heterogeneous devices that collect, process, change, and share it. Previous work presented a fully distributed approach for reasoning with conflicts in ambient intelligence systems. This paper extends previous results to address authorization issues in distributed environments. First, the authors present the formal high-level authorization language DEAL to specify access control policies in open and dynamic distributed systems. DEAL has rich expressive power by supporting negative authorization, rule priorities, hierarchical category authorization, and nonmonotonic reasoning. The authors then define the language semantics through Defeasible Logic. Finally, they demonstrate the capabilities of DEAL in a use case Ambient Intelligence scenario regarding a hospital facility.

INTRODUCTION

Ambient intelligence (AmI) is a new wave of information technology that integrates microprocessors into everyday objects in order to improve the quality of everyday life. AmI environments

DOI: 10.4018/978-1-4666-2041-4.ch019

include heterogeneous intelligent devices that communicate by means of ad-hoc wireless networks. Each intelligent device acts as an autonomous entity that controls resources, handles requests and shares information and services with other entities. The core difference between AmI and traditional systems is the formers' user centric approach. AmI systems adapt and respond to people by acknowledging their presence and gestures instead of the other way around.

Ambient Intelligence is a multidisciplinary approach as presented in Aarts (2004) and Remagnino and Foresti (2005), since it requires the convergence of many areas of Computer Science in order to fulfill its purpose. Therefore, it has introduced new research challenges in many areas, including the field of access control. The implementation of access control is vital in order to develop a secure AmI system. Each intelligent device should be able to specify access policies to the resources that it controls. However, the special characteristics of AmI environments make the specification and implementation of access control problematic.

Ambient Intelligence environments are characterized by the imperfect nature of context information. Aboud, Dey, Brown, Davies, Smith, and Steggles (1999) defined context as "any information that can be used to characterize the situation of an entity. An entity is a person, place or object that is considered relevant to the interaction between a user and application, including the user and applications themselves". Henricksen and Indulska (2004) characterize four types of imperfect context information: unknown, ambiguous, imprecise, and erroneous. Sensor or connectivity failures (which are inevitable in wireless connections) result in situations, that not all context data is available at any time. When data about a context property comes from multiple sources, then context may become ambiguous. Imprecision is common in sensor-derived information, while erroneous context arises as a result of human or hardware errors.

Moreover, AmI environments are characterized by their open and dynamic nature. In an open and dynamic environment participating entities enter or leave the environment at random times and without prior notice. Such entities are expected to have different goals, experiences and perceptive capabilities. They may use distinct vocabularies to describe their contexts, and may even have different levels of sociality. Due the unreliable and restricted (by the range of the transmitters) wireless communications, direct communication with all entities may not always be feasible.

In this paper we study the problem of authorization, as a basic part of access control in Ambient Intelligence environments, and provide a fully distributed approach to address it. Authorization is the process of specifying an access control policy that is used to determine whether a requester, with a given valid identity, is permitted to consume a particular requested service.

We propose a formal high-level logic-based language for addressing authorization issues in AmI environments. Our work builds on our previous work on a distributed model for contextual reasoning, called *Contextual Defeasible Logic* (*CDL*) (Bikakis & Antoniou, 2010, 2011; Bikakis, Antoniou, & Hassapis, 2011). CDL is based on Defeasible Logic (Antoniou, Billington, Governatori, & Maher, 2001; Nute, 1994), which is skeptical, rule-based, and uses priorities to resolve conflicts among rules. CDL also adopts ideas from *Multi-Context Systems* (*MCS*) (Giunchiglia & Serafini, 1994). A MCS consists of a set of logical theories called *contexts*, and a set of inference rules (i.e., *mapping rules*) that enable information flow between different contexts. In CDL, the Multi-Context Systems model is enriched through defeasible rules, and priority relations that provide a preference ordering on system contexts to represent their comparative reliability. Although CDL provides a flexible approach for reasoning about context in distributed environments, it does not address authorization issues. In this work we implement an authorization language as an extension of the language of CDL in order to address the access control requirements of Ambient Intelligence systems. We emphasize on the expressive power of the language in specifying authorization policies of distributed systems.

The rest of this paper is structured as follows. In the next section, we describe an Ambient Intelligence motivating scenario regarding a hospital facility emphasizing on its authorization requirements. Then we provide a thorough description of the authorization problem by presenting its basic concepts and the desirable characteristics of an authorization language. In the Background section, we describe the main features of Defeasible Logic and Contextual Defeasible Logic. Then we introduce an authorization language, called DEAL; we present its syntax (alphabet and rules), main characteristics and semantics. In the last two sections we present a comparison with related approaches, summarize and discuss future research directions.

MOTIVATING SCENARIO

In this section we describe a motivating scenario from the ambient intelligence domain that refers to a hospital facility. We aim to automate hospital processes while preserving the safety of medical data.

Description

The hospital of the scenario consists of three autonomous departments: The Cardiology department for diagnostic heart or circulation services, the X-ray department for diagnostic imaging services, such as MRI (Magnetic resonance imaging), and the Gastroenterology department for diagnostic gastrointestinal services. Each department is equipped with a computer hosting a database server. The database stores information about equipment, medical examinations and personnel of the department.

The secretariat of the hospital hosts another database that stores administrative data about doctors, patients and more general information about diseases and the hospital departments.

All hospital computers are connected through a local wired network. Each computer is also equipped with Bluetooth, so that doctors can access their local data through their Bluetooth-enabled smartphones. Upon receiving a request for accessing their local data, department computers determine to accept / reject access based on the following access-control policy:

1. Doctors are authorized to access their patients' examinations.
2. Trainees are authorized to access patient examinations if the patients' doctors permit it.
3. Retired doctors are not authorized to access patients' examinations.
4. Statement 3 is preferred to statement 1.

If the local information is not sufficient to determine whether the access request should be served, the computer collects relevant context information from other information sources, e.g., the secretariat database.

Consider the case that Alice, a pathologist working for the hospital, enters the cardiology department. Her smartphone establishes a connection with the Bluetooth computer and identifies the department. Then, as it has been set up by Alice, it reminds her about pending events that are relevant to the department, e.g., a reminder to ask for Bob's (one of her patients) cardiology exams. Alice issues a request to access the exams through her smartphone. The department computer receives the request along with information about the device that issued the request (e.g., the name of its owner). It, then, issues a query to the secretariat computer asking for information about Alice's status. When it gets the information that Alice is a doctor working for the hospital, it determines that access should be authorized to Alice and provides the results of Bob's exams to her smartphone.

Charles is a trainee of Alice. In the same time that Alice is in the cardiology department, Charles visits the X-ray department. Following a similar procedure with Alice, Charles uses his smartphone to issue a request to access Bob's X-rays exams. To determine about the acceptance of the request, the department computer sends a query to the secretariat computer asking for information about Charles. After receiving the information that Charles is a trainee of Alice, the department computer then attempts to contact Alice to get her permission to provide the results of Bob's exams to Charles. Since Alice's smartphone was located some minutes ago at the cardiology department, the permission request is delivered to Alice's smartphone through the computer of the department. Alice sends her permission through her smartphone and the local hospital network, and the X-ray department computer determines to provide Charles with access to Bob's X-rays.

Dan is also a doctor who used to work for the same hospital but has recently retired. Before retiring, he was responsible for Alice's patient, Bob. Dan can still use his smartphone to interact with the hospital computers. Through his smartphone he issues a request to the Gastroenterology department to access Bob's gastroenterological examinations. The computer of the department gets information from the secretariat computer that Dan has just retired; therefore it rejects his request.

The context information flow of the scenario is depicted in Figure 1. Double arrows represent the users' initial requests to access services, while single arrows represent requests to collect relevant information in the process of answering the service requests.

Figure 1. Context information flow

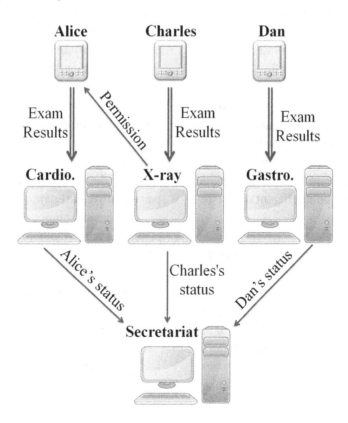

Assumptions and Challenges

The implementation of the scenario described above requires the combination of technologies from various fields including Human-Computer Interaction, Wireless Networks and Knowledge Representation and Reasoning (KRR). Our focus is on issues related to KRR. We implicitly make the follow simplifying assumptions for issues that are out of the scope of this paper.

- There is an available infrastructure for communication between the computers of the hospital and the doctors' smartphones. The hospital computers communicate through the hospital local wired network, while communication between the computers and the doctors' smartphones is enabled by Bluetooth.
- Each device is aware of parts of the knowledge that the other devices possess. For instance, each computer department is aware of the type of knowledge stored in the secretariat's database.
- Each device has some minimum computing capabilities that are sufficient to conduct some simple reasoning tasks.
- Since our focus is on the authorization problem, we make identification and authentication assumptions. Specifically, we assume that the requesters are correctly identified and their identities are verified successfully when an intelligent device receives a request.

The specific problem that we focus on in this paper is:

"How to address distributed authorization in an environment characterized by distribution of the available relevant knowledge to several heterogeneous entities, taking into account the openness and dynamicity of the environment, the restrictions posed by wireless communications, and potential cases of missing or ambiguous information."

THE AUTHORIZATION PROBLEM

In this section we describe the authorization problem in the domain of Ambient Intelligence. First, we analyze the basic concepts and notations of authorization. Then, we define the desirable characteristics of an authorization language for Ambient Intelligence environments.

Basic Concepts and Notations

In this subsection we define the concepts of *request pair*, *authorization statement*, *authorization conflict* and *authorization policy*.

Devices in Ambient Intelligence environments act as autonomous entities by sending and receiving requests from other entities. Using such requests, devices aim at consuming services that other entities provide. The pair that consists of the requesting entity and the requested service is called *request pair*.

In an Ambient Intelligence environment, authorization issues arise when an entity receives a request that is either sent from a device or is perceived through human interaction. An *authorization statement* (also known as *authorization*) expresses either permission - *positive authorization* - or denial - *negative authorization* - for a particular request pair.

The basic components of an authorization statement are listed below.

- **Service:** In an authorization statement the service has the form of a query (e.g., "*open(File)?*"). It is usually decomposed into two additional elements, an *action* and an *object*, that represent the right to perform an action on a resource object, and the resource itself, respectively.

- **Grantor:** The entity that provides the authorization for a specific request pair. In case the grantor is omitted from the authorization statement, it is assumed to be the local system.
- **Grantee:** The entity that receives the authorization for consuming a specific service. The grantee component may also refer to a group of entities indicating that every entity of the group receives the same authorization.

Another basic concept is the *authorization conflict*. An authorization conflict describes the problematic state where a positive and a negative authorization may be applied for the same grantor, grantee and service components. The resolution of an authorization conflict requires the specification of a preference among the contradictory authorizations. The following conflict resolution options could be used:

- **Denial-preference:** The negative authorization is preferred over the positive one. In this case, the grantor finally denies providing the service to the grantee.
- **Permission-preference:** The positive authorization is preferred over the negative one. In such case, the grantor permits the grantee to consume the service.
- **No-Preference:** Neither of the two authorizations is preferred thus the grantor neither permits nor denies the grantee to consume the service. The system may handle this case according to the specific application needs (e.g., as system error).

Given a particular request pair, the decision of whether the requester should be provided or denied the requested service is based on the *authorization policy* of the system. An authorization policy consists of a set of authorizations and conditions under which they are determined.

Logic-based approaches for the specification of authorization policies have been proven very successful since they offer significant advantages, e.g., simplicity, flexibility, formality, expressivity and modularity. In logic-based approaches, an authorization policy is defined as a set of logical rules. A logical rule that is contained in an authorization policy is called *authorization rule*. An authorization rule can either be a *final rule*, which concludes to an authorization decision; or an *intermediate rule*, which specifies an intermediate conclusion. Two authorization rules are called *conflicting* (or *contradictory*) if their conditions can be simultaneously satisfied and their conclusions result in an authorization conflict.

Desirable Characteristics

In this subsection we describe in detail the desirable capabilities of an authorization language for distributed environments.

The expressive characteristics that should be provided by an authorization language are listed below.

- Negative authorization
- Rule priorities
- Hierarchical category authorization
- Nonmonotonic reasoning
- Distributed authorization

A *negative authorization* expresses the denial of a grantor to provide a service to a grantee. The specification of negative authorizations is required in order to block specific request pairs. In the hospital scenario, negative authorization can be used to implement the third statement, which denies access to medical files to doctors who have retired. An authorization language should be able to support negative authorizations in order to easily specify such simple authorization statements.

Rule priorities is a feature that enables the specification of a priority relation over a set of rules. The priority relation can be used to denote a preference on a pair of conflicting rules. This feature is useful in many common scenarios that involve multiple authorization rules, which may potentially lead to inconsistencies (authorization conflicts). In the hospital scenario, statements 1 and 3 could lead to a contradiction (authorization conflict). Statement 4, however, can be encoded as a rule priority that gives preference to statement 3; therefore in case both statements (rules) may be applied for a given scenario, the system accepts only the conclusion of statement 3 as a valid conclusion. An authorization language should be able to support rule priorities in order to easily specify consistent policies with multiple authorization rules.

Hierarchical category authorization is a feature that enables the inheritance of authorizations, which are specified on hierarchical categories. Hierarchical categories express structured elements, which may refer to any relevant entities, such as users, devices, services, actions or objects. In our scenario, we can define the general class of doctors, as well as trainee doctors as a specific subclass of doctors. All authorizations that refer to a class of objects (e.g., permission to doctors for accessing medical data), are also applied to all its subclasses (e.g., permission to trainee doctors for accessing medical data). The components of an authorization that can be associated with hierarchical categories are: (a) the grantee; (b) the service; (c) the action; and (d) the object.

Nonmonotonic reasoning is a form of reasoning in which the acquisition of new knowledge can cause earlier conclusions to be withdrawn. It was developed to model commonsense reasoning used by humans. Such form of reasoning is supported by nonmonotonic logics, such as Defeasible Logic, where defeasible rules supporting contradictory conclusions may block each other's conclusions, and rule priorities can be used to resolve such conflicts. *Negation as failure* is another type of nonmonotonic reasoning, where conclusions can be derived based on the absence of certain information. In our scenario, if there is no informa-

tion about the retirement of Dan, the system will determine to provide him with the authorization to access Bob's exams. When such information is entered into the system, such authorization will become invalid.

Distributed authorization is a form of authorization that may be based on both local knowledge and external information. Distributed authorizations are required in many cases in order to decrease authorization work load in an entity or in order to confirm an authorization decision by another trusted entity. In our motivating scenario, authorization to Charles is based on information residing in three different devices: (a) the X-rays department computer, which stores the local privacy policy; (b) the secretariat computer that stores information about doctors and their trainees; and (c) Alice's smarthone, which provides the final permission. In open and dynamic distributed environments, we distinguish two different approaches for the exchange of knowledge with external entities. An authorization framework can adopt either of them in order to support distributed authorizations.

- **Connection-based approach:** This approach is based on runtime communications and information gathering from third-party entities. The authorizer must establish connections with the external entities that he wishes to communicate with, in order to receive relevant information.
- **Credential-based approach:** This approach is based on credentials. Credentials represent knowledge in specific file forms that are issued from entities in the environment. Credentials may contain simple facts such as "Alice is a doctor" or more complicated policy statements. The credentials are usually provided to the authorizer by the requester, either together with the request, or at runtime according to the communication protocol.

The connection-based approach is a more direct approach, since the authorizer must establish a direct connection with the third-party entity that maintains the required information. Moreover, this approach is more dynamic and flexible, since it provides runtime third-party information flow that can be specified in the authorization policy. Its main disadvantage is that it is more time demanding, because the exchange of knowledge with external entities requires additional time for the third-party communications.

On the other hand, the credential-based approach requires only the process of extracting the credential information into the local authorizer knowledge. This approach is indirect since the authorizer receives the required information (in the form of credentials) usually from the requesting entity, which may not be related with the third-party entity that issued the credentials. It is also more static in the sense that it does not provide "fresh" information that is gathered during the process of the request, since credentials may have been issued any time earlier. The indirect and static nature of this approach results in more risks on the secure information flow.

Concluding this brief comparison, we argue that choosing the right approach depends on the specific requirements of the application. An interesting potential future direction would be to study a hybrid solution, which will combine the advantages of both approaches.

BACKGROUND

The authorization language that we propose in this paper has been developed on top of *Defeasible Logic* (Antoniou, Billington, et al., 2001; Nute, 1994), and its distributed variant called *Contextual Defeasible Logic* (*CDL*) (Bikakis & Antoniou, 2010, 2011; Bikakis et al., 2011). Before presenting the language in detail, below we give some background information on the two formalisms.

Defeasible Logic

Defeasible logic is a simple and efficient rule based non-monotonic formalism that was originally created by Donald Nute (1994). A thorough research on the formalism is also provided in Antoniou, Billington, et al. (2001). The logic has been extended over the years and several variants have been proposed. The main focus of the logic is to be able to derive conclusions from incomplete and sometimes conflicting information. Thus, the logic was developed to support "tentative" conclusions (defeasible conclusions) and conflict resolution. In case of conflicting information, the logic provides a conflict resolution approach based on a priority relation over the set of rules. In case of incomplete information, the logic is able to express defeasible conclusions; such conclusions can be withdrawn in the presence of new information.

A defeasible theory consists of three main elements: a set of *facts*, a set of *rules* and a *superiority relation* on the set of rules. Facts represent indisputable statements. Rules are classified into two categories: *strict rules* and *defeasible rules* (fuller versions of defeasible logics include also defeaters). Strict rules are "classical" rules in the sense that whenever their premises are indisputable (e.g., facts) then so are their conclusions. On the other, defeasible rules can be defeated (their conclusions are invalidated) by stronger contrary evidence. The superiority relation is a binary relation defined over the set of rules. The superiority relation determines which rule is stronger in case of a conflict between two competing rules.

Reasoning in Defeasible Logic is "skeptical". This derives from the fact that when there is some support (a combination of facts and rules) for concluding A, but there is also support for concluding the negation of A ($\neg A$), neither of the conclusions is derived, and the logic consults the priority relation to resolve the conflict. If the support for A (or $\neg A$) has priority over the support for $\neg A$ (resp. A), then A (resp. $\neg A$) is concluded.

Governatori, Maher, Billington, and Antoniou (2004) describe Defeasible Logic and its variants in argumentation theoretic terms. A model theoretic semantics is discussed in Maher (2002).

Contextual Defeasible Logic

Contextual Defeasible Logic implements a distributed nonmonotonic reasoning approach by combining ideas from Defeasible Logic and Multi-Context Systems. Multi-Context Systems (Giunchiglia & Serafini, 1994) can be abstractedly defined as a set of contexts, which can be thought of as logic theories, and a set of inference rules (known as mapping or bridge rules) that enable information flow between different contexts.

In CDL, a MCS C is defined as a collection of contexts. A context, C_i, is defined as a tuple (V_i, R_i, T_i), where V_i is the vocabulary used by C_i (a set of positive and negative literals), R_i is a set of rules, and T_i is a partial preference ordering on C. R_i consists of a set of local rules and a set of mapping rules. The body of a local rule is a conjunction of local literals (literals that are contained in V_i), while its head is labelled by a local literal. Local rules are classified into strict rules, and defeasible rules. Mapping rules associate local literals with literals from the vocabularies of other contexts (foreign literals). To deal with ambiguities caused by the interaction of mutually inconsistent contexts, mapping rules are also modelled as defeasible rules, while preference information from T_i is used to resolve any potential conflicts.

DEAL LANGUAGE

In this section we present the formal high-level logic-based language *DEAL (DistributEd Authorization Language)* for expressing authorization policies in distributed environments. First, we describe its syntax. Then, we illustrate its expressive characteristics through examples from the hospital scenario. Finally, we provide the language semantics in detail.

DEAL Alphabet

The alphabet of DEAL consists of five sets of symbols: the *constants* (C), the *variables* (V), the *predicate symbols* (P), the *logical symbols* (L) and the *rule labels* (R).

Constants and variables are used in the classical sense. A constant has a specific non-changing value referring to an environment entity while a variable has a changing value that ranges over the set of constants C. Constant symbols start with a lowercase letter while variable symbols start with an uppercase letter.

Predicate symbols are used to denote relations or properties of relevant entities. DEAL uses the following predicate symbols:

- **belongs(X, Y):** Represents that an element X belongs to a category of elements Y. Moreover, it may represent that a category of elements X is a subcategory of category Y. X and Y may take values either from C (sets of constants) or V (set of variables).
- **right(X, Y):** Represents the privilege to perform an action X to a resource Y. Arguments X, Y may also represent a category of actions and a category of resources, respectively. Both arguments may take values either from C or V.
- **grant(X, Y, Z):** Represents a positive authorization (permission) that is given by a grantor X to a grantee Y for a service Z. Arguments Y, Z may also represent categories of entities and services respectively. All arguments may take values either from C or V. Moreover, the service specified in Z may be represented by a *right* predicate.
- **granted(Y, Z):** Represents a positive authorization in the exact same sense as it is specified for predicate *grant*. The only dif-

ference is that the grantor is omitted as it is assumed to be the local system.

- **superior(*X, Y*):** Represents that given a pair of conflicting rules (*X, Y*), the rule with label *X* is preferred to the rule with label *Y*. Both *X* and *Y* take their values from the set of rule labels R.
- **User defined predicates:** A user is able to define any predicate of *n*-arity in order to represent knowledge for a particular application domain. For example, if an application of a particular company requires the specification of the property "*manager*" in order to represent persons that are project managers, the user is able to define the application dependent predicate *isManager(X)*.

A predicate symbol or its negation is defined as a *literal* in DEAL. The specification of a predicate negation and its semantics are explained below in the description of DEAL logical symbols.

DEAL language supports the following logical symbols:

- **Strong Negation:** DEAL supports strong negation (i.e., classical negation) with the use of "¬" symbol. Strong negation can be used in front of any predicate to denote contradictory knowledge from what the predicate expresses. In other words, given a data element *p,* which is a grounded predicate, then ¬ *p* represents the contradictory data element. Strong negation in front of *grant* or *granted* predicates expresses negative authorization.
- **Weak Negation:** DEAL supports weak negation (i.e., negation as failure) with the use of *not* keyword. Weak negation can be used in front of any predicate to denote the absence of the predicate from the knowledge base. In other words, given a data element *p*, which is a grounded predicate, then *not p* is true if *p* is false (absent). In

this case, ¬ *p* may or may not be true. The difference between strong and weak negation for a predicate *p* is that the former (¬ *p)* represents the existence of negative (contradictory) information, while the latter (*not p*) represents the absence of positive information about the predicate. The two definitions are not equivalent in an environment where *p* and ¬ *p* may coexist.

- **Conjunction:** DEAL supports logical conjunction of literals with the use of comma (",") symbol.
- **Strict entailment:** DEAL supports strict entailment with the use of the single line arrow, "←". Strict entailment can be used to express rules with the classical sense of logical implication (deductive reasoning). Given a conjunction of literals *X* at the right side of the operator and a literal *Y* at the left, whenever *X* is true, *Y* can be derived as a logical consequence. The only restriction is that literal *Y* cannot be a weak negated predicate. Rules using strict entailment are called *strict rules*.
- **Defeasible entailment:** DEAL supports defeasible entailment with the use of the double line arrow, "⇐". Defeasible entailment is used to express authorization rules in the following sense (defeasible reasoning based on rule preference): Given a conjunction of literals *X* at the right side of the operator and a literal *Y* at the left side, whenever *X* is true, *Y* can be derived as a logical consequence, only if ¬ *Y* cannot be derived by a preferred conflicting rule. Rules using defeasible entailment are called *defeasible rules*.

Rule labels is a set of symbols of the form <*rule-x*>, where *rule-x* takes its value from the set of constants. In DEAL, each rule is identified by its unique rule label.

DEAL Rules

In DEAL we distinguish four types of authorization rules: (a) *final rules*; (b) *priority rules*; (c) *hierarchy rules*; and (d) *user-defined rules*.

Direct knowledge (i.e., *facts*) is expressed by rules with empty body, while *derived knowledge* is expressed as conclusions of rules with non-empty body.

Below, we define the first three types of rules. User-defined rules are those that follow the syntax of DEAL rules but do not fall under any of the first three types of rules.

Definition 1. A hierarchy rule is a rule of the following form:

```
<rule-label> belongs(X, Y) ← L₁,
L₂,.., Lₙ.
```

The hierarchy rule supports the representation of hierarchical categories. The body of the rule is a conjunction of literals ($L_1, L_2,.., L_n$) or the empty set. The rule concludes to a transitive relation. For example, consider the following hierarchy rules:

```
<rule-1> belongs(a, b) ←.
<rule-2> belongs(b, c) ←.
```

In this case, we conclude: *belongs(a, c)*.

Definition 2. A final rule is a rule of the following form:

```
<rule-label> G ⇐ L₁, L₂,.., Lₙ.
```

The final rule concludes to literal *G* which represents a predicate from the set {*granted, grant*} or their respective strong negations ¬ *granted*, ¬ *grant*}, while $L_1, L_2,.., L_n$ is a conjunction of any literals that are supported in DEAL or the empty set. In other words, the final rule concludes to an authorization, which is specified by *G*, while its fulfillment requirements are specified by the

conjunction of literals $L_1, L_2,.., L_n$. Moreover, the final rule supports hierarchical category authorization. For example, consider the following rules:

```
<rule-1> belongs(a, b) ←.
<rule-2> granted(b, q) ⇐.
```

In this case, we conclude: *granted(a, q)*.

Note that a final rule is specified with defeasible entailment. This is due to the fact that an authorization policy may include many and possibly contradictory final rules that lead to authorization conflicts. Therefore, a final rule is specified as a defeasible rule, which can be blocked by a superior rule supporting a contradictory conclusion.

Definition 3. A priority rule is a rule of the following form:

```
<rule-label> superior(<r1>, < r2>) ←.
```

The priority rule is used to express a preference on a pair of conflicting rules (rules with contradictory conclusions). Given a pair of conflicting rules with labels *<r1>*, *<r2>*, *superior(<r1>,<r2>)* denotes that rule labeled by *<r1>* is preferred to rule labeled by *<r2>*. This actually means that in case that both rules can be applied, only the conclusion of rule <r1> can be derived. In case there is no priority relation associating the two rules, both their conclusions are blocked. In this way, inconsistency caused by contradictory conclusions is avoided.

The priority rule concludes to an acyclic relation. For example, the knowledge encoded by the following rules is considered invalid:

```
<rule-1> superior(<a>, <b>) ←.
<rule-2> superior(<b>, <c>) ←.
<rule-3> superior(<c>, <a>) ←.
```

DEAL Characteristics

In this subsection, we illustrate the expressive characteristics of DEAL through examples from the hospital scenario.

The authorization policy of the hospital departments is expressed by the following DEAL rules.

```
<deal1> granted(X, right(read, Z)) ⇐
belongs(X, doctors), belongs(Y, pa-
tients), treat(X,Y), examResults(Y,
Z).
<deal2> granted(X, right(read, Z))
⇐ belongs(X, trainees), belongs(Y,
patients), belongs(W, doctors),
treat(W,Y), examResults(Y, Z),
grant(W, X, right(read, Z)).
<deal3> ¬ granted(X, right(read, Z))
⇐ belongs(X, retDoctors),
belongs(Y, patients),
examResults(Y, Z).
<deal4> belongs(retDoctors, doctors)
←.
<deal5> superior(deal3, deal2) ←.
```

Rules *deal1* and *deal2* correspond to authorization statements 1 and 2 of the motivating scenario, respectively. Rules *deal3* and *deal4* correspond to statement 3, while rule *deal5* corresponds to statement 4.

Rules *deal1* and *deal2* express positive authorization (permission) for doctors and trainees to access patients' examinations, while *deal3* expresses negative authorization (denial) for retired doctors. Rule *deal5* expresses a rule priority of *deal3* over *deal2*. Finally, *deal4* specifies the class of retired doctors as a subclass of doctors (hierarchy categorization).

The same policy could by implemented by replacing rules *deal1*, *deal3* and *deal5* with rules *deal6* and *deal7*.

```
<deal6> granted(X, right(read, Z)) ⇐
belongs(X, doctors), belongs(Y, pa-
```
```
tients), treat(X,Y), examResults(Y,
Z),
not belongs(X, retDoctors).
<deal7>
¬granted(retDoctors,right(read, Z))
⇐ belongs(Y, patients),
examResults(Y, Z).
```

Rule *deal6* uses negation as failure in its body, while *deal7* expresses hierarchical category authorization through the derivation of the negative authorization (denial) to all elements of the category *retDoctors*. Note that the two rules cannot lead to authorization conflicts because their premises cannot be simultaneously satisfied for the same grantee.

Finally, rules *deal1*, *deal2*, *deal3*, *deal6* and *deal7* implement distributed authorization in the sense that their evaluation requires collecting information from one or more remote devices. For instance, *deal2* requires the evaluation of (a) *belongs* and *treat* predicates by the secretariat department; (b) *examResults* predicate by the Xray department; and (c) a *grant* predicate by Alice's PDA.

DEAL Semantics

In this subsection we illustrate the semantics of DEAL through transformation into Defeasible Logic (DL) and CDL.

DL supports constants and variables exactly as they are specified in DEAL. It also supports rules identification using unique rule labels. DL also enables the specification of user-defined predicates. Therefore, all DEAL predicates can be implemented in DL. Moreover, DL supports directly the features of strong negation, logical conjunction, and strict and defeasible entailment, as they are defined in DEAL. Weak negation is not directly supported by DL, but can be simulated using a technique based on auxiliary predicates, which was first presented in Antoniou, Maher, and Billington (2001). Specifically, every declaration of *not X*, where *X* is a language literal, can be equivalently replaced with *not(X)* (where *not* is an auxiliary predicate) and the addition of the following two rules.

```
r1: not(X) ⇐.
r2: ¬ not(X) ⇐ X.
```

Furthermore, all DEAL rules can be translated into DL. The priority rules of DEAL are implemented in DL using the acyclic superiority relation on the set of rules. A superiority relation is defined with the use of ">". Given a rule name *r1* at the left side of the operator and a rule name *r2* at the right side, it is denoted that *r1* is preferred to *r2*. If in a defeasible theory *D* both rules may be applied, only the conclusion of *r1* can be derived from *D*.

The hierarchy rule is specified in DL exactly as in DEAL, while the transitivity of the *belongs* relation is supported with the addition of the following two rules.

```
belongs(X, Y) ← belongsTo(X, Y).
belongs(X, Y) ← belongsTo(X,Z),
belongs(Z, Y).
```

The auxiliary *belongsTo* predicate is used to meet the requirement that the relation expressed by *belongs* should be acyclic, so as to avoid loops in DEAL policies.

Final rules are specified in DL exactly as in DEAL, while hierarchical category authorization is implemented using the following four sets of DL rules. The first set implements grantee hierarchies.

```
granted(X, Q) ⇐ belongs(X, Y),
granted(Y, Q).
¬ granted(X, Q) ⇐ belongs(X, Y), ¬
granted(Y, Q).
grant(G, X, Q) ⇐ belongs(X, Y),
grant(G, Y, Q).
¬ grant(G, X, Q) ⇐ belongs(X, Y), ¬
grant(G, Y, Q).
```

The second set service hierarchies.
```
granted(X, Q) ⇐ belongs(Q, Y),
granted(X, Y).
¬ granted(X, Q) ⇐ belongs(Q, Y),
¬ granted(X, Y).
grant(G, X, Q) ⇐ belongs(Q, Y),
grant(G, X, Y).
¬ grant(G, X, Q) ⇐ belongs(Q, Y),
¬ grant(G, X, Y).
```

The third set implements action hierarchies.

```
granted(X, right(A,O)) ⇐
belongs(A,Y),
granted(X, right(Y,O)).
¬ granted(X, right(A,O)) ⇐
belongs(A, Y),
¬ granted(X, right(Y,O)).
grant(G, X, right(A,O)) ⇐ belongs(A,
Y),
grant(G, X, right(Y,O)).
¬ grant(G, X, right(A,O)) ⇐
belongs(A, Y),
¬ grant(G, X, right(Y,O)).
```

The last set implements object hierarchies.

```
granted(X, right(A,O)) ⇐ belongs(O,
Y), granted(X, right(A,Y)).
¬ granted(X, right(A,O)) ⇐
belongs(O, Y), ¬granted(X,
right(A,Y)).
grant(G, X, right(A,O)) ⇐ belongs(O,
Y), grant(G, X, right(A,Y)).
¬ grant(G, X, right(A,O)) ⇐
belongs(O, Y), ¬grant(G, X,
right(A,Y)).
```

Finally, distributed authorization is implemented using the notion of contexts and mapping rules of CDL. Specifically, each different entity (e.g., each computer/device in the hospital scenario) is defined as a context in a Multi-Context System *C*. Each rule that combines both local knowledge of the entity (local context) and foreign knowledge from other contexts in *C* is defined as a mapping rule of the local context. In the hospital scenario, rules *deal1*, *deal2*, *deal3*, *deal6* and *deal7* are implemented as mapping rules of the cardiology, X-rays and gastroenterology departments. For example, *deal1*, which is used by the cardiology department to determine access rights for doctors, is defined as a mapping rule of the form:

```
<deal2> granted(X, right(read, Z))_c ⇐
belongs(X, doctors)_s, belongs(Y, pa-
tients)_s, treat(W,Y)_s, examResults(Y,
Z)_c.
```

The above rule combines knowledge from the local context (*examResults(Y, Z)*$_C$) with foreign knowledge from other system contexts, namely the secretariat (*belongs(X, doctors)*$_S$, *belongs(Y, patients)*$_S$, *treat(W,Y)*$_S$), to conclude about a local context conclusion (*granted(X, right(read, Z))*$_C$). The subscript at the end of each literal name is used to denote the context that the respective literal is defined by.

RELATED WORK

Over the past twenty years, several authorization approaches have been proposed for distributed environments. In this chapter we present the approaches that are related to our work and describe their main limitations.

The trust-management approach, which was initially proposed by Blaze, Feigenbaum, and Lacy (1996), is focused on the credential-based method for distributed authorization and views the authorization decision as a "proof-of-compliance" problem: *Does a set of credentials prove that a request complies with a policy?* The frameworks of PolicyMaker (Blaze, Feigenbaum, & Lacy, 1996; Blaze, Feigenbaum, & Strauss, 1998), REFEREE (Chu, Feigenbaum, LaMacchia, Resnick, & Strauss, 1997), Keynote (Blaze, Feigenbaum,

Ioannidis, & Keromytis, 1999a, 1999b) and SPKI/SDSI (Clarke, Elien, Ellison, Fredette, Morcos, & Rivest, 1999, 2001; Elien, 1998; Ellison, Frantz, Lampson, Rivest, Thomas, & Ylonen, 1999) are more recent attempts towards a trust management framework. As they are not based on formal logics, most of them do not provide declarative semantics and lack important expressive characteristics. The first three approaches do not support negative authorization, whereas the last one does not support conjunction of attributes and attributes with fields.

On the other hand, logic-based authorization methodology is a very flexible and declarative approach that achieves separation of authorization policies from implementation mechanisms and provides policies with precise semantics. The logic-based authorization approaches that are proposed by Jajodia, Samarati, and Subrahmanian (1997, 2001), Jajodia, Samarati, Subrahmanian, and Bertino (1997), Bertino, Buccafurri, Ferrari, and Rullo (1999), and Bertino, Catania, Ferrari, and Perlasca (2003) are quite expressive. Jajodia et al. proposed the Flexible Authorization Framework (FAF) that incorporates an authorization specification logic language (ASL). ASL can be used to encode the system security needs. ASL supports negative authorizations, hierarchical category authorizations, and nonmonotonic reasoning through the use of negation as failure. Bertino et al. proposed a logic formalism for expressing authorization policies, enabling features such as hierarchical category authorization, negative authorizations (through the use of stong negation) and nonmonotonic reasoning (through the use of negation as failure). The main limitation of both approaches is that they do not support distributed authorization; they are more focused on centralized applications.

Decentralized logic-based approaches have also been proposed in the recent literaure (Li, Grosof, & Feigenbuam, 2000, 2003; Liu, Hu, & Chen, 2005; Wang & Zhang, 2005, 2007). Compared to DEAL their main limitations are: (a) do not support negative authorization, nonmonotonic reasoning and rule priorities (Li et al., 2003; Li, Mitchell, & Winsborough, 2002); (b) The D2LP language proposed in Li et al. (2000), which implements the nonmonotonic version of Li et al. (2003), and the nonmonotonic framework FACL4DE proposed in Liu et al. (2005), do not support hierarchical category authorization; (c) the AL language proposed in Wang and Zhang (2005, 2007) does not integrate any type of priority/preference information.

In conclusion, logic-based approaches have been proven very successful in specifying authorizations. However, none of the existing authorization logic-based approaches combines all desirable characteristics dictated by the real needs of Ambient Intelligence environments.

CONCLUSION AND FUTURE WORK

To conclude this paper, we summarize and discuss its main contributions, and propose possible directions for future research.

This paper studies the problem of authorization in Ambient intelligence environments. First, it describes in detail the basic concepts of the authorization problem and the desirable characteristics of an authorization language for AmI environments. Then, it proposes an approach that meets the predefined criteria. It introduces the formal high level logic-based language, DEAL for addressing authorization issues in Ambient Intelligence environments. The syntax and semantics of DEAL language are described thoroughly. Moreover, it provides an authorization scenario from the Ambient Intelligence domain that is used to demonstrate the expressive power of the language.

This work is just one step in an ambitious research plan, and there are concrete ideas on further work. Our approach addresses the authorization problem by making identification and authentication assumptions. However, the overall access control process requires strong identification and authentication techniques. It is among our priorities to combine our framework with appropriate methods and techniques from this field. Another interesting future direction would be to study a hybrid solution of the connection-based and credential-based approach for supporting distributed authorization. Finally, DEAL can be enriched with additional language characteristics that would empower its expressiveness such as defeaters and conflicting literals, which are supported by alternative versions of Defeasible Logic.

Overall, we believe that Ambient Antelligence environments provide a rich testbed for authorization approaches. Ambient Intelligence is a rich area with special requirements in terms of openness, distribution, heterogeneity and efficiency. Therefore, it can serve as a source of inspiration for future work on the authorization problem.

REFERENCES

Aarts, E. (2004). Ambient intelligence: a multimedia perspective. *IEEE MultiMedia*, *11*(1), 12–19. doi:10.1109/MMUL.2004.1261101

Abowd, G. D., Dey, A. K., Brown, P. J., Davies, N., Smith, M., & Steggles, P. (1999). Towards a Better Understanding of Context and Context-Awareness. In *Proceedings of the 1st International Symposium on Handheld and Ubiquitous Computing* (LNCS 1707, pp. 304-307).

Antoniou, G., Billington, D., Governatori, G., & Maher, M. J. (2001). Representation results for Defeasible Logic. *ACM Transactions on Computational Logic*, *2*(2), 255–287. doi:10.1145/371316.371517

Antoniou, G., Maher, M. J., & Billington, D. (2001). Defeasible Logic versus Logic Programming without Negation as Failure. *The Journal of Logic Programming*, *41*(1), 45–57.

Bertino, E., Buccafurri, F., Ferrari, E., & Rullo, P. (1999). A Logical Framework for Reasoning on Data Access Control Policies. In *Proceedings of the 12th IEEE Computer Security Foundations Workshop (CSFW-12)*, Mordano, Italy (pp. 175-189).

Bertino, E., Catania, B., Ferrari, E., & Perlasca, P. (2003). A Logical Framework for Reasoning about Access Control Models. *ACM Transactions on Information and System Security*, 6(1), 71–127. doi:10.1145/605434.605437

Bikakis, A., & Antoniou, G. (2010). Defeasible Contextual Reasoning with Arguments in Ambient Intelligence. *IEEE Transactions on Knowledge and Data Engineering*, 22(11), 1492–1506. doi:10.1109/TKDE.2010.37

Bikakis, A., & Antoniou, G. (2011). Partial Preferences and Ambiguity Resolution in Contextual Defeasible Logic. In *Logic Programming and Nonmonotonic Reasoning*, (LNCS 6645, pp. 193-198).

Bikakis, A., Antoniou, G., & Hassapis, P. (2011). Strategies for contextual reasoning with conflicts in ambient intelligence. *Knowledge and Information Systems*, 27(1), 45–84. doi:10.1007/s10115-010-0293-0

Blaze, M., Feigenbaum, J., Ioannidis, J., & Keromytis, A. D. (1999a). *The KeyNote Trust-Management System, Version 2* (RFC 2704). Retrieved from http://www.ietf.org/rfc/rfc2704.txt

Blaze, M., Feigenbaum, J., Ioannidis, J., & Keromytis, A. D. (1999b). The role of trust management in distributed systems. In *Secure Internet Programming* (LNCS 1603, pp. 185-210).

Blaze, M., Feigenbaum, J., & Lacy, J. (1996). Decentralized trust management. In *Proceedings of the 1996 IEEE Symposium on Security and Privacy* (pp. 164-173). Washington, DC: IEEE Computer Society.

Blaze, M., Feigenbaum, J., & Strauss, M. (1998). Compliance-checking in the PolicyMaker trust management system. In *Proceedings of the 2nd International Conference on Financial Cryptography* (LNCS 1465, pp. 254-274).

Chu, Y., Feigenbaum, J., LaMacchia, B., Resnick, P., & Strauss, M. (1997). REFEREE: Trust management for web applications. *World Wide Web Journal*, 2, 706–734.

Clarke, D., Elien, J., Ellison, C., Fredette, M., Morcos, A., & Rivest, R. L. (1999). *Certificate Chain Discovery in SPKI/SDSI*. Retrieved from http://people.csail.mit.edu/rivest/ClarkeElElFrMoRi-CertificateChainDiscoveryInSPKISDSI.ps

Clarke, D., Elien, J., Ellison, C., Fredette, M., Morcos, A., & Rivest, R. L. (2001). Certificate chain discovery in SPKI/SDSI. *Journal of Computer Security*, 9(4), 285–322.

Elien, J. (1998). *Certificate Discovery Using SPKI/SDSI 2.0 Certificates*. Unpublished master's thesis, Massachusetts Institute of Technology, Cambridge, MA. Retrieved from http://groups.csail.mit.edu/cis/theses/elien-masters.pdf

Ellison, C., Frantz, B., Lampson, B., Rivest, R., Thomas, B., & Ylonen, T. (1999). *Simple Public Key Certificate*. Retrieved from http://world.std.com/~cme/spki.txt

Giunchiglia, F., & Serafini, L. (1994). Multi-language hierarchical logics, or: how we can do without modal logics. *Artificial Intelligence*, 65(1). doi:10.1016/0004-3702(94)90037-X

Governatori, G., Maher, M. J., Billington, D., & Antoniou, G. (2004). Argumentation Semantics for Defeasible Logics. *Journal of Logic and Computation*, 14(5), 675–702. doi:10.1093/logcom/14.5.675

Henricksen, K., & Indulska, J. (2004). Modelling and Using Imperfect Context Information. In *Proceedings of the PERCOMW 2004 Conference* (pp. 33-37). Washington, DC: IEEE Computer Society.

Jajodia, S., Samarati, P., & Subrahmanian, V. S. (1997). A logical language for expressing authorizations. In *Proceedings of the 1997 IEEE Symposium on Security and Privacy* (pp. 31-42). Washington, DC: IEEE Computer Society.

Jajodia, S., Samarati, P., & Subrahmanian, V. S. (2001). Flexible Support for Multiple Access Control Policies. *ACM Transactions on Database Systems, 26*(2), 214–260. doi:10.1145/383891.383894

Jajodia, S., Samarati, P., Subrahmanian, V. S., & Bertino, E. (1997). A unified framework for enforcing multiple access control policies. In *Proceedings of the ACM SIGMOD International Conference on Management of Data* (pp. 474-485).

Li, N., Grosof, B. N., & Feigenbaum, J. (2000). *A nonmonotonic delegation logic with prioritized conflict handling.* Unpublished manuscript.

Li, N., Grosof, B. N., & Feigenbaum, J. (2003). Delegation Logic: A logic-based approach to distributed authorization. *ACM Transactions on Information and System Security, 6*(1), 128–171. doi:10.1145/605434.605438

Li, N., Mitchell, J. C., & Winsborough, W. H. (2002). Design of a role-based trust management framework. In *Proceedings of the 2002 IEEE Symposium on Security and Privacy* (pp. 114-130). Washington, DC: IEEE Computer Society.

Liu, P., Hu, J., & Chen, Z. (2005). A Formal Language for Access Control Policies in Distributed Environment. In *Proceedings of the 2005 IEEE WIC ACM International Conference on Web Intelligence (WI05)* (pp. 766-769).

Maher, M. J. (2002). A Model-Theoretic Semantics for Defeasible Logic. In *Proceedings of the Workshop on Paraconsistent Computational Logic* (pp. 67-80).

Nute, D. (1994). Defeasible logic. In *Handbook of Logic in Artificial Intelligence and Logic Programming* (*Vol. 3*, pp. 355–395). Oxford, UK: Oxford University Press.

Remagnino, P., & Foresti, G. L. (2005). Ambient Intelligence: A New Multidisciplinary Paradigm. *IEEE Transactions on Systems, Man, and Cybernetics, 35*(1), 1–6. doi:10.1109/TSMCA.2004.838456

Wang, S., & Zhang, Y. (2005). A formalization of distributed authorization with delegation. In *Proceedings of the 10th Australasian Conference on Information Security and Privacy* (LNCS 3574, pp. 303-315).

Wang, S., & Zhang, Y. (2007). Handling distributed authorization with delegation through answer set programming. *International Journal of Information Security, 6*, 27–46. doi:10.1007/s10207-006-0008-4

This work was previously published in the International Journal of Ambient Computing and Intelligence, Volume 3, Issue 4, edited by Kevin Curran, pp. 9-24, copyright 2011 by IGI Publishing (an imprint of IGI Global).

Chapter 20

Ambient Assisted Living and Care in The Netherlands:
The Voice of the User

J. van Hoof
Fontys University of Applied Sciences, The Netherlands

E. J. M. Wouters
Fontys University of Applied Sciences, The Netherlands

H. R. Marston
University of Waterloo, Canada

B. Vanrumste
MOBILAB and Katholieke Universiteit Leuven, Belgium

R. A. Overdiep
Fontys University of Applied Sciences, The Netherlands

ABSTRACT

Technology can assist older adults to remain living in the community. Within the realm of information and communication technologies, smart homes are drifting toward the concept of ambient assisted living (AAL). AAL-systems are more responsive to user needs and patterns of living, fostering physical activity for a healthier lifestyle, and capturing behaviours for prevention and future assistance. This study provides an overview of the design-requirements and expectations towards AAL-technologies that are formulated by the end-users, their relatives and health care workers, with a primary focus on health care in The Netherlands. The results concern the motivation for use of technology, requirements to the design, implementation, privacy and ethics. More research is required in terms of the actual needs of older users without dementia and their carers, and on AAL in general as some of the work included concerns less sophisticated smart home technology.

DOI: 10.4018/978-1-4666-2041-4.ch020

1. INTRODUCTION

With an ageing population, an ever growing group of older adults wish to remain living in the community; the so-called ageing-in-place. Apart from receiving family and professional care at home, there are architectural and technological solutions to facilitate this desire. Within the domain of technological solutions, home automation, telehealth services, and 'ambient intelligence' are increasingly becoming tools to support and monitor older adults, both with or without cognitive impairments (Schuurman et al., 2007). In addition, such technologies form a welcome support for family carers, clinicians and care professionals.

Information and communication technology (ICT) forms a substantial part of everyday technology, and thus, becomes an omnipresent part of the living environment. At the same time, such ICT collects and disperses a high volume of personal data, and gets increasingly intelligent and autonomous (van Hoof et al., 2007). Poland et al. (2009) outlined that smart homes are environments facilitated with technology that act in a protective and proactive function to assist in managing one's daily life. A typical smart home implementation would include sensors and actuators to detect changes in status and to initiate beneficial interventions. According to Virone (2009), smart homes are drifting toward the concept of ambient assisted living (AAL) and are more responsive to users' needs and patterns of living, fostering physical activity for a healthier lifestyle, and capturing behaviours for prevention and future assistance. The philosophy guiding smart home technology or AAL, which offer a wide variety of options (Table 1), is that the monitored environment should be transparent and minimally intrusive to the person being monitored (Kang et al., 2010).

The wide range of (networked) technological possibilities in the home environment of older people is shown by the model of a health smart home by Stefanov et al. (2004) and van Hoof et al. (2007) (Figure 1). For the purposes of this investigation, we distinguish between two kinds of technologies: (i) assistive technologies and devices that are not connected to a network, and (ii) state-of-the-art ICT-solutions, connected to a (single) home network. In Figure 1, the home network is connected to a call centre that includes clinicians, carers, security, and maintenance services. In practice, governments, family and unidentified parties could be connected via the network enabling data access.

Recently, there has been a growing interest in the automatic recognition of human actions and activities, for instance, in the care for older persons with dementia (for instance, van Hoof et al., 2011; Tapia & Corchado, 2009). The general idea of using computers to automatically recognise (patterns in) human activities has been applied to several different research domains and applica-

Table 1. Examples of in situ monitoring technologies for older people (Kang et al., 2010)

Technology	Risk Monitoring Systems	Interventional, Alert System
Portable	Heart rate and blood pressure monitors Activity monitor Oximetry Glucose monitor Sociometer Portable telephone	Mobility monitoring in people with Parkinson's disease Warning systems for unsafe behaviours in people with dementia Cueing of gait for rehabilitation
Environmental	Motion sensor Instrumented carpet Refrigerator door sensor Toilet flush sensor	Video Acute fall detection Electronic pillbox

Figure 1. Various forms of technology transmitting data in an intelligent home environment

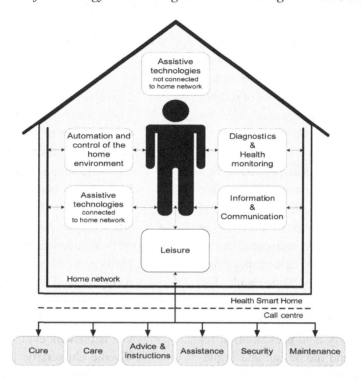

tions. One important subfield of action and activity recognition is the automatic recognition of activities in the home setting and more specifically to monitor the activities of daily living (ADL) of older persons living at home. In relation to smart homes, Frisardia and Imbimbob (2011) state that ADL abilities are the main predictors of informal care hours, and both ADL and neuropsychiatric symptoms are important predictors of perceived burden on carers. ADL monitoring by human observers may be viewed as being inefficient in terms of both time and cost, it is stressful to both parties, and in some instances is deemed to be too invasive, whereas an automatic activity monitoring systems may be more acceptable (Hong & Nugent, 2011). Atallah et al. (2009, p. 1031) stipulated ideally, *"physiological parameters would be observed continuously rather than providing a snap-shot recording of a person's health that is available only when patients are seen in the clinic or visited at home"*. Hong and Nugent (2011) state that automated recognition

of ADL may be considered as one of the most desirable computational functions within a smart home for older people, as there is a direct relationship between physical activity performance and health status. Through monitoring ADL and offering assistance when needed, there is now the potential of technology enriched environments to help older people age-in-place with an acceptable level of independence. To date, researchers have mostly relied on data from video cameras on the one hand and wearable wireless sensors on the other.

Understudied but important aspects of AAL are the views of actual and potential users of such technologies to monitor aspects of daily living. These perceptions may greatly influence the way AAL-technologies are designed and implemented into practice. Dewsbury et al. (2003, p. 191) state, in relation to the design of smart homes that *"[t]here is a need to determine the needs of the occupant(s) and reflect these needs within the overall design"*.

Furthermore, Steele et al. (2009, p. 789) state;

"While there is a plethora of studies addressing the technical improvement of wireless sensor network [...] health technologies, there is a lack of literature that explores the perceptions of [older] persons towards such technology and their potential acceptance or otherwise of it".

This study presents design-requirements and expectations towards AAL-technologies that are formulated by the end-users, their relatives and the health care workers in relation to the provision of care and ageing-in-place. As such expectations and needs may differ from one region to the other; focus is on the situation in The Netherlands. The findings from The Netherlands are discussed in relation to results from international studies. One of the goals of this study is to present input for future AAL-projects and the design and implementation of such technologies.

2. METHODOLOGY

A literature review focusing upon The Netherlands was conducted to assess the attitudes of expected end-users, their relatives and carers towards AAL technologies. The studies had to deal with user research, in particular the investigation of attitudes and thoughts towards AAL-systems, and effects on end-users. Given the rapid developments in the field, studies older than 5 years old were not included. Peer reviewed journal papers, dissertations and scientific reports were considered for the study. Publications merely providing a description of an AAL-system were rejected for inclusion.

The study has identified a number of studies published by research groups in The Netherlands, namely; the University of (Applied Sciences) Amsterdam, Fontys University of Applied Sciences, Rathenau Instituut, the University of Applied Sciences Rotterdam, the University of Applied Sciences Utrecht, Eindhoven University

of Technology, Twente University, the SOPRANO Consortium, and the Free University of Amsterdam. The following numbers of documents were identified per institute:

- University of Applied Sciences Amsterdam / University of Amsterdam: n=1 (rejected: van Kasteren et al., 2010)
- Fontys University of Applied Sciences: n=1 (rejected: Sponselee et al., 2008)
- Rathenau Instituut: n=1 (rejected: Schuurman et al., 2007)
- University of Applied Sciences Rotterdam: n=1 (included: Schikhof et al., 2010)
- University of Applied Sciences Utrecht: n=1 (included: van Hoof et al., 2011)
- Eindhoven University of Technology: n=2 (included: Mohammadi, 2010; rejected: van Bronswijk et al., 2005)
- Twente University: n=2 (included: Nijhof et al., 2009; Neven, 2011)
- SOPRANO Consortium: n=1 (included: Sixsmith et al., 2009)
- Free University of Amsterdam: n=2 (included: Lauriks et al., 2008; rejected Niemeijer et al., 2010)

The results described in the various studies are different in character and detail. Therefore, the description of the projects and their results differ in quality and quantity.

3. RESULTS

This section presents results from the qualitative interviews and data collection, each study is treated on an individual basis, as the designs and goals of the studies are different. The following studies are described:

- Schikhof et al. (2010): Remote monitoring system for dementia

- van Hoof et al. (2011): Unattended autonomous surveillance
- Nijhof et al. (2009): ICT interventions for dementia
- Neven (2011): Design of ambient intelligence technologies
- Mohammadi (2010): Home automation for older adults
- Sixsmith et al. (2009): The SOPRANO Project
- Lauriks et al. (2008): Home automation in institutional dementia care

Three of the studies focus on dementia (Schikhof et al., 2010; Nijhof et al., 2009; Lauriks et al., 2008), mainly in institutional settings, whereas the study by van Hoof et al. (2011) also included a number of respondents with dementia living at home. The study by Mohammadi (2010) deals with older adults in general. The SOPRANO Project aims to support frail and disabled older people.

3.1. Remote Monitoring System for Dementia

The project by Schikhof et al. (2010) involved the development of a remote monitoring system for use at night in institutional dementia care. Nursing-assistants, nurse team leaders and residents were identified as potential (end) users. Dementia makes independent persons dependent on decision-making by others. Therefore, involving persons with dementia in the design was considered to be a difficult issue. Representatives, usually family members, provided information, and were implemented into the design.

Schikhof et al. (2010, pp. 413-414) stated:

"[t]he premise was that privacy and other values could be respected through a conscientious design of the system and guidelines. [... Cameras should start recording only when activated by a sensor. In addition the staff member on duty should be able to see life images (and hear sounds) to make a

proper decision whether to respond to the alarm and go to the bedroom. [...] However, privacy and other important values had to be guaranteed. These values [...] had to be incorporated in the designing process. [...] Also we found that we had different kind of stakeholders / users to work with: management, staff, residents, family".

Acceptance by relatives of residents and staff was crucial for the implementation of the proposed remote monitoring system. Participants were asked what was important to them in caring for and monitoring of people with dementia. All stakeholders named privacy and consent (Table 2). The management had requested that consent was sought prior to testing of the system. Privacy was incorporated into the final design phase of the system, having discovered the importance of such a facet.

A total of 18 persons participated in the survey. Staff members (n=8) and family members (n=13) attended the informational meetings. Six staff and family members found limited camera surveillance in the bedroom of a resident with dementia to be unacceptable. After a round of informational meetings, all staff members and family members found such cameras acceptable or highly acceptable. In addition, concerns were highlighted by some relatives relating to the redundancy of night-shift staff in preference to a remote system, add-

Table 2. Identified values by the different stakeholders (Schikhof et al., 2010)

Residents and Relatives	Staff	Management
Privacy	Privacy	Privacy
Consent	Consent	Consent
Respect	Respect	Quality of care
Individuality	Autonomy	feasibility
Dignity		
Warmth		
Safety		
Well-being		

ing further concerns from staff, who thought the system would be used to control their activities.

Several requirements should be fulfilled for the new system, leading onto a number of design decisions, implementing images and sound in case of emergencies, including a personalisation of the alarm (linking a situation to a certain individual). Qualified carers should retain access to data, and cameras should only be operational when activated by a sensor. The camera itself should freely rotate 360 degrees but without a zooming functionality. Alarm calls should be received by a nursing station or care centre. Door switches may be used to detect if a resident leaves or enters a room. Infrared bed sensors can be placed within the environment, enabling additional monitoring of people exiting their beds. Signal reception should be optimal throughout the building. The system should be designed as such that it cannot be switched on or off (by staff).

3.2. Unattended Autonomous Surveillance

Van Hoof et al. (2011) studied the needs and motives of 18 community-dwelling older adults, receiving ambient intelligence technologies (Unattended Autonomous Surveillance (UAS) system). They investigated how their experience of these technologies contributed to aspects of ageing-in-place. The UAS-system aims to support ageing-in-place and delay the demand for expensive institutional care by increasing the clients' and family carers' sense of safety and security through unobtrusive monitoring at home. The UAS-system offers a large range of functionalities, which include mobility monitoring, voice response, fire detection, as well as wandering detection and prevention.

Technology was perceived to support the wish to age-in-place and, therefore, embraced, accepted or tolerated as a support tool. Matters of great concern included; fear of burglars, falling, the risk of power outages (in the case of electrical assis-

tive devices), and the risk of fires. The majority of respondents in this study possess emergency response systems: neck-worn pendants, wrist bands, and audio/voice alarm systems. The UAS-system was seen as a welcome addition to safety and security because the majority of respondents do not continuously wear the emergency response systems, or because of the fear of not being able to use the emergency response system if necessary. Overall, there seemed to be a supplementary value of the new technologies in terms of improving the sense of safety and security among the respondents. Finally, a major perceived benefit of the ambient intelligence technologies the apparent 24-hour care it provides.

False alarms were frequently mentioned, many related to the infrared movement detectors. Not all respondents regarded false alarms as something negative: it was also a positive sign that the UAS-system responded to the home environment. Moreover, there were unwanted sound effects produced by the new technologies. People may also pull out plugs when a system is producing unwanted effects: this in turn may harm the system.

New technologies should not interfere with the old technologies, such as telephones or (digital) television. In addition, some pieces of technology require equipment to be on stand-by day and night, therefore, people with dementia may turn off this equipment. Moreover, the stand-by mode consumes additional energy. Prior to the interview, one respondent placed a large flower pot right in front of one of the cameras, which, as a result, could not transmit images. There are some issues concerning the operation of the technology, which may impact the safety and security of the respondents. In homes with balconies, respondents remarked that the systems do not work on their balcony. The system also included an algorithm that excludes the presence of pets.

Problems may occur with persons who experience low vision with electrical appliances at home. "Talking" equipment which communicates in English is not an option for older users without the appropriate second-language skills. It is important that technology goes unnoticed or blends in with the interior design. Complaints and comments pertain to the amount of cables used and the placement of the black box in the living room. Some may compare the appearance of the sensors to an anti-burglary system one used to have in a former home.

Respondents would appreciate if care professionals could answer basic questions about the technology. Prior to the introduction of the technologies, professional carers received extensive information about how the system works. The majority of respondents were satisfied with the way the technicians carried out their work. Home visits from these professionals are considered as unavoidable and necessary. Some consider the presence of installers as pleasant occasions.

Privacy does not seem to be a major concern in relation to the new ambient intelligence technologies. The respondents with psychogeriatric health problems, in particular, express no privacy-related issues. Respondents do not feel watched or monitored, and some are even not fully aware of the presence of the UAS-system at home.

3.3. ICT Interventions for Dementia

Nijhof et al. (2009) explored the possibilities for ICT interventions in care of older persons with dementia through a literature review. Eighteen international and eight national (Dutch) studies were included in the review. Three categories of technology were considered: (i) help with symptoms of dementia (ii) social contact and company for the patient, and (iii) health monitoring and safety. The foci of technological applications are in lowering the demands for care; by enhancing the independence, of persons' diagnosed with dementia, and in turn, by supporting informal carers. Some of the studies reviewed dealt with the needs of users. The studies on health monitoring and safety show that there are a number of such technologies available on the market place, in

particular, sensor systems. Some technological systems focus on registration of (in) activity.

One conclusion of the review was that informal carers and care professionals are satisfied with sensor technology, as it is a convenient way to substitute continuous vigilance (the sensor technology can generate an alarm call when needed). Moreover, sensor technology enables informal carers to control their time/agenda. Residents have more freedom of movement due to the system.

In case of sensor technology, informal carers remarked that it may be seen as a burden to need a computer with internet access for the transmission of data. Some of the informal carers are concerned about the fit between technological solutions and individual needs of a person with dementia. In some of the studies, views of persons with dementia were explored (with the help of informal carers). GPS telephony and wearing electric bracelets is not seen as helpful, mainly due to the design of the systems. Automated lighting may be seen as confusing, as if someone else in the room turned on the lighting. Persons with dementia are more prone to accept technology at home when installers mention that the technology is part of a scientific study, compared to when persons are told they need the technology as a support tool to counteract problems. People with dementia may find this stigmatising, as they often do not acknowledge they have a health problem.

3.4. Design of Ambient Intelligence Technologies

Neven (2011) studied the user representation of older users that are created in design processes and scripted into technologies. Moreover, Neven addressed how the diversity is taken into account in such processes and scripts. The work was related to the emergence of ambient intelligence technologies. Neven (2011) has come up with a set of seven design guidelines for designing technologies for older users. The suggestions start from the premise that the views, images and ideas about older people that designers and engineers may have, have a significant effects on the design, acceptance and the use of a technological solutions. The seven recommendations are:

1. Reflect on cultural representations of older people, without making simplifications. Older people often reject this kind of positioning as well as ageism.
2. Reflect on the effects of the ageing-and-innovation discourse. Take a focus on the third age (i.e., still active and healthy older adults), which may offer opportunities for design.
3. Older people are not technologically illiterate. Try to analyse and tap into the technological literacy that they do have.
4. Some older people can participate in design processes
5. Reflexive scripting and scenario-writing
6. Older people also change: adaptability as a pre-requisite
7. Selective use, modification and resistance as input for design. Older people may choose to use a technology in different ways than intended by a designer in order to satisfy their particular needs and preferences. Instead of designing "closed" technologies, applications should have multiple usages in order to be acceptable.

According to Neven (2011), more than any other category of people, older adults are likely to be the object of others' preconceptions about their capabilities, needs and preferences. These are often simplified homogeneous images, while older people are of course diverse. It is thus not easy to predict or speculate about what older people are like, what they want, need or prefer. That is why it is so important to design and implement technologies together with older people.

3.5. Home Automation for Older Adults

Mohammadi (2010) considered the use of home automation systems in the homes of older adults in relation to ageing-in-place. In response to focus group sessions (n=9), in-depth interviews (n=9) and a large questionnaire survey (n=497), Mohammadi (2010) concluded that the attitudes of older adults regarding home automation are in principle positive, as long as they have had the chance to be informed and get acquainted to the technology. Older adults have a positive attitude towards a possible acquisition of such future technologies, although this group is not convinced of the added value of the offered functionalities for the present life. Solutions that support safety and security are valued highly by the participants, including smoke detectors and fall detection, technology to identify visitors (intercoms) and burglar alarms. As far as smart environmental control is concerned, automatic registration of data such as energy use, phone use, status of the alarm system, and the signalling of technical problems, the valuations and opinions on usefulness and necessity are diverse. Technical problems, power failures and sensitivity to failure of the devices are considered risk factors. Privacy concerns were not mentioned by participants. It is possible that this is a problem experienced more by the experts rather than by the end-users.

Mohammadi (2010) concludes that home automation can be characterised as a mismatch between demand and supply. As long as home automation systems are associated with impairment and disease, whereas older adults are increasingly living a healthy and independent life, a breakthrough of home automation technology is likely to be postponed. This leads to what Mohammadi calls an anti-diffusion and non-adoption of home automation systems by the majority of older adults. Functionalities that are not related to care, such as comfort and safety and security, may break the deadlock. Residents value the entirety of living, not the functionalities as such: one does not purchase home automation as such, but merely for the sake of ease and comfort.

In Mohammadi's study of professional stakeholders (n=362), three quarters of the respondents mentioned that unfamiliarity with end-users was seen as the major problem. This is not in line with the findings from the older users, who simply do not have interest in home automation systems. It is concluded that professionals on the supply side are not familiar themselves with needs in the field, whereas 60% of them claim to be well-informed about the demand side.

3.6. The SOPRANO Project

Sixsmith et al. (2009) described the SOPRANO (Service-oriented programmable smart environments for Older Europeans) project, which aims to develop an AAL system to enhance the lives of frail and disabled older people. SOPRANO is a consortium of commercial companies, service providers and research institutes with over 20 partners from in Greece, Germany, UK, The Netherlands, Spain, Slovenia, Ireland and Canada. SOPRANO uses pervasive technologies to create a more supportive home environment. SOPRANO provides additional safety and security, supporting independent living and social participation and improving quality of life (QoL). The SOPRANO system and its technical components are designed as part of a *socio-technical* system that models both the human and machine domains within a single conceptual framework.

Potential frail and disabled older users were involved in order to gather their feedback on the key challenges related to independence and QoL from their perspective without specific reference on how technology could be used to cope with these challenges. This qualitative approach involved 14 focus groups (with more than 90 participants) as well as individual interviews. A number of themes emerged from the user research:

- *Social isolation* (loneliness, depression, boredom, social exclusion and disruption of patterns of daily living);
- *Safety and Security*: (falls, disorientation, control of household equipment);
- *Forgetfulness* (appears to be a challenge to independence for many and concerns, for example, taking medication or finding objects in the house);
- *Keeping healthy and active* (included physical and mental activity, exercise, good nutrition, daily routines and adherence to medications);
- *Community participation and contribution to local community; Accessing information/keeping up to date* (was a crucial issue as well as finding help and tradesmen to do jobs around the home);
- *Getting access to shops and services* (problematic for some people);
- *Quality management of care provision* (is an important issue to ensure that the right amount and right quality of care is delivered in people's homes);
- *Mobility inside and outside the home* (challenges to personal mobility in terms of walking in the neighbourhood and use of public transport).

These themes reflect the needs of potential users, and can thus be used as input for future AAL-projects.

3.7. Home Automation in Institutional Dementia Care

Lauriks et al. (2008) studied the effects of home automation technologies in small-scale group accommodation for people with dementia in terms of QoL of the residents, and the labour satisfaction and workload of care professionals. The randomised controlled trial consisted of a 4 month intervention of home automation systems, with a pre- and post-test set-up using questionnaires (including the Dementia Quality of Life Instrument (DQoL) and QUALIDEM scales, labour satisfaction (MAS-GZ) and workload (UBOS)). There were 54 persons with dementia participating (n=30 intervention group, n=24 control group) as well as 25 care professionals. Significant improvements were found in terms of self-reported QoL (DQoL), and the QUALIDEM domains of social isolation, having something to do, and aesthetics. A significantly higher grade was given when judging their QoL. In addition, the number of fall incidents in the bathroom/toilet was significantly lower through the intervention. An explanation may be sought in an enhanced freedom of movement, independence and exposure to daylight. Although the participants were not asked for their view and requirements, nevertheless, the results of this study are among the few randomised controlled trials in this domain.

Care professionals experienced no significant effects on labour satisfaction and workload. Explicitly mentioned key factors in the successful implementation of the technology were adequate preparation and proper motivation of staff. Home automation systems in dementia care ask for a different way of working. Training, reflection and supervision are important for a successful implementation and integration in work practice.

4. DISCUSSION

A limited number of studies report the concern and needs of older adults and other users of AAL-technologies in the home environment. Therefore, this study is based on views of end-users on the implementation and use of other home technologies. It includes smart home technologies, ambient assisted living, and in-home monitoring. Due to the position of The Netherlands in this field, there are a relatively large number of Dutch studies, which have been included in this report. There is though a need for more studies, conducted with real users; not just potential users and focus group

sessions. In the following section, the results from the Netherlands are compared to international findings. This is followed by a discussion on how to move forward to a needs-based design and implementation of ambient assisted living systems.

Apart from studies conducted in The Netherlands, there are some international studies that have focused on user needs in relation to AAL-technologies.

Lorenz and Oppermann (2009) discuss that in the field of mobile health monitoring the current most important user groups are those aged 50 and over. The group is said to show less perception and control capability and has less experience in the use of information technology. When compared to young people, older people are said to suffer from a wide range of restrictions. The group of 50+ users shows more diversity in their cognitive, sensory and motor skills than younger people. User interfaces for older people should therefore be designed for different capabilities and needs. These conclusions are in line with the human factors requirements identified by the studies from The Netherlands.

In a review on smart home technology, Chan et al. (2008) reviewed the user needs, acceptability and satisfaction. They recall an expert group document of France's National Center for Scientific Research—Science for Engineering. This group recommended the:

(i) Consideration of participants. People with special needs have a clear use for this technology, which will help them express their needs and guide their choices. One must avoid using technologies that are not suitable to their needs; these have to be identified and excluded as early as possible.

(ii) Consideration of the participant's immediate surroundings: family, informal and formal carers. All these persons have their own needs, and will play a major role in determining the conditions of an efficient health care system.

(iii) The manufacturers and commercial parties must build, disseminate, and maintain products that satisfy all these needs. If a given need is not perfectly conceived early in the process, it will not be incorporated into the design.

Steele et al. (2009) conducted an exploratory study (focus groups) into the perceptions, attitudes and concerns of community-dwelling older adults towards wireless sensor network (WSN) technologies for healthcare purposes. The attitudes were generally positive. Independence is highly valued by older people and hence any supportive technology is highly regarded. Moreover, the privacy of WSN health data might not be as important as typically considered. These findings are similar to the results from The Netherlands.

There are indications that cost may be the most prominent determinant influencing the acceptance of WSNs. The majority of the participants have had at least one negative experience with technology. There is a desire to have a system that is simple to understand. The capability to (successfully) interact with the system is a significant concern to the participants. There is a desire for a demonstration or training to be given, as well as a jargon-free manual.

There are three main approaches to implementing sensor networks; wearable sensors, ambient monitoring and embedded sensors. The participants were asked to comment on which implementation approach they prefer and outlined the perceived flaws.

- *Wearable sensors.* Most enthusiasm towards embedding sensors into clothing accessories (comparison to hearing aid). Concerns about forgetting to wear sensor or when nude. Most people do not want to be seen wearing a "health monitoring device".
- *Ambient monitoring.* Concerns: expensive, occurrence of accidents beyond the vicini-

ty of the sensors. Combination of both ambient and embedded sensors may be better equipped in solving a number of perceived problems.

- *Embedded sensors.* Strong interest in, and acceptance of, embedding sensors (under the skin). Advantages: 'invisible to others', one would always wear them. Comparison to dog chipping. Potential disadvantage: change of batteries, pain.

Each one of the participants expressed different desires towards the three approaches, had different perceptions on what functionalities were needed, and how they should be implemented within a health monitoring system. Some participants suggested that they would like to access the system's status on a screen; others said that they preferred to have a beeping sound that alerts them of errors. Some level of control or interaction with the system is preferred. The ability to detect falls and monitor basic bodily functionalities should be among the functionalities implemented into a WSN health monitoring system. A system monitoring 24/7 is considered acceptable, but the incorporation of a camera into such system would be "too intrusive". Moreover, users should be allowed to turn the system off when desired. There are also suggestions to put a time limit on how long it can be turned off before it turns itself back on again. If the system is to be turned off, then it should notify relatives. As the system's purpose is to ensure that medical assistance will arrive promptly when emergencies happen, it should not allow users to turn it off.

Most of these findings relate the results from The Netherlands, for instance, in terms of the use of cameras and the inclusion of potential functionalities. The results are similar to the outcomes of the evaluation of the UAS-system, particularly in terms of acceptance of sensors. The UAS-system was not supposed to be switched off by the participants during operation.

Kang et al. (2010) conducted focus group sessions of dementia monitoring. They state that in the case of dementia monitoring, adoption of the technology by family carers can vary. It is important that technology serves a clear purpose, that is meaningful and that it offers easily perceived benefits. The features must be practical, compelling, economical, and user-friendly. There are family carers willing to pay out of pocket for technologies that meet their needs for safety oversight. Older users have a willingness to trade privacy for technology oversight if it enables them to remain independent. A focus group of older adults on the acceptability of monitoring technology indicated that they are concerned primarily about user-friendliness, the lack of human contact, and the need for specialised training. Some may feel embarrassed and view technology as an admission of dependence. Others may feel pressured to adopt technology just to remain independent. In addition, there are concerns to clinicians, including the overload of information. The use of monitoring technology can create large amounts of information that may have limited clinical value. Moreover, there are a number of technical issues concerning technology (Table 3). The results by Kang et al. (2010) are similar to those found by the dementia-related studies in The Netherlands. Although family carers are identified as major stakeholders in adaption of the technologies, their needs and concerns are not studied in great detail.

Mahoney et al. (2009) conducted qualitative research involving eight sets of focus groups comprised of either older residents from independent living residences (ILR), relatives of residents, building managers and superintendents, or affili-

ated nurse practitioners providing residential services. Residents, family members, and staff members were enrolled in the focus group sessions, which focused on whether remote residential monitoring, using off-the-shelf wireless sensors, might help in daily care. The second part of the study consisted of an intervention.

Across the end-user subgroups similar concerns were mentioned. These included, worries about the safety and well-being of the residents. Specific memory-related issues included medications, meals, and shutting off the toilet/bath water. The Automated Technology for Elder Assessment, Safety and Environment (AT EASE) remote home monitoring system was developed to uniquely tailor the type of sensor and activities monitored to the individual's particular concern(s). The monitoring system consisted of motion sensors in each room, an additional water sensor in the bathroom, a system remote to enable/disable the system, a processing unit, a Zigbee computer interface and custom automation software application to operate the processing unit. Additional sensors available but not desired by participants in this setting included contact sensors for doors, pressure sensors for beds and chairs, and appliance on/off sensors. Each sensor was mounted via a special non-damaging strip of removable adhesive, activated by movement and wirelessly transmitted its signal to a base unit connected to a personal computer.

Multiple safety and well-being concerns arose that could be addressed through sensor based residential monitoring but most residents under-

Table 3. Technical issues identified by Kang et al. (2010)

Communication Infrastructure	Technology Performance, Safety, and Glitches
A proper computer system architecture and data infrastructure is important to reliably handle growing communication and storage needs. Various ways to transmit data need to be considered. Using standardised technology is important for future upgrades and compatibility. Internet-based communications may be subject to requirements for information security.	Hardware incompatibility, the lack of cellular telephone coverage, power outages, and unexpected automated operating system software updates requiring computer reboots can easily hamper implementation of monitoring technologies. Robust systems, validated in community settings, are required before widespread use can be considered. Providers need to proactively address safety concerns by informing end-users not to depend exclusively on technology surveillance because it can experience technical glitches.

estimated their personal vulnerability. Key to acceptance was the residents' perceived need and usefulness of the system to maintain independence and prevent being relocated to a more restrictive environment. Families found the system easy to use and were very satisfied. Building staff highly valued the water overflow alerts and having an additional means to oversee residents' safety that did not increase their workload. Care professionals were non-adopters (feared information overload) favouring personal interaction with residents to medication compliance monitoring. End users favoured passive alert notices (over proactively monitoring the website for residents' status), that were few in number, and valid. They did not want to monitor the monitoring data and believed that accurate alerting was critical and achieved.

The study by Mahoney et al. (2009) shows, in agreement to Dutch studies, that many of the carers involved were non-adopters or at least not most willing to use the new technologies. Even though carers work with a large range of technologies, their primary focus is on the well-being of the care recipient and not as much on the actual tools and methods.

Courtney et al. (2008) investigated the factors that influence the willingness of older adults living in independent and assisted living to adopt smart home technology using a qualitative, descriptive approach. Fourteen participants were recruited from community-dwelling older adults, aged 65 or older (independent living and assisted living type facilities). There were four focus groups with 11 unique respondents. Findings were confirmed through additional individual interviews (n = 3). Courtney et al. (2008) found that, though privacy can be a barrier for older adults', the own perception of their need for the technology can override privacy concerns. These results are similar to those by, for instance, van Hoof et al. (2011) from The Netherlands.

5. THE ROAD TO A NEEDS-BASED AMBIENT ASSISTED LIVING

The Netherlands Institute for Telemedicine (van Nispen, 2004) concluded that in the early days home automation systems were introduced as care technology, in particularly for persons with a demand for care. This was one of the most important reasons why home automation technologies did not emerge as successful consumer goods. According to the report, such technologies were labelled as 'grey, old elderly technology". Moreover, older persons in general often were not very willing to use these technologies because they did not feel they needed such technologies, had a so-called fear of technology, or did not yet feel old enough. These negative feelings and attitudes were often ignored in many Dutch pilot projects. In order to make home automation systems more successful in practice, van Nispen (2004) suggests moving the focus of such systems from older persons to younger persons with functional limitations.

In addition, van Bronswijk et al. (2005) concluded that home automation projects, as part of ambient assisted living, were often unsuccessful because there were many malfunctioning functionalities, and because the majority of functionalities were not used at all. There is also a large diversity in individual lifestyles, for which service providers offer standardised solutions. Moreover, the demand for care differs, the reimbursement systems are not transparent, interfaces often too complicated and installers do not have the proper skills to install the technologies. Oppenauer (2009) states that technology use in old age is influenced by a variety of factors such as technology generation, education, socioeconomic status, cognitive abilities, and attitudes. Furthermore, motivation to use technology in later life is an important issue for a better understanding of technology acceptance.

Niemeijer et al. (2010) concluded that more research is recommended to determine ethical and practical viability of surveillance technologies whereby research should be specifically focused on the resident perspective. These conclusions were drawn based on an overview of ethical and practical aspects of surveillance technologies in the residential care of people with dementia and intellectual disabilities. According to Niemeijer et al. (2010) the ethical debate centres not so much around the effects of this technology (although these effects have scarcely been studied), but rather around the moral acceptability of those effects, especially when a conflict arises between the interests of the institution and the interests of the resident. Safety appears to be a key issue when deciding whether or not to use surveillance technologies.

In order to make ambient assisted living projects more fruitful, we need a multifactorial approach, including more focused technological solutions, better integration in health care, installing technologies matching expectations and needs. The actual needs have not been investigated in their full width. There are numerous studies on technology requirements by older people, although only a few studies focus on sensor-based networks. There is a tendency to focus on older persons with dementia, whereas there should be a balanced between studies focusing on people with or without dementia. Moreover, persons with other diseases and disabilities should be considered as potential users as well, for instance, persons with COPD or mental health problems, or persons recovering from a stroke. Differences are expected between the design of user interfaces and the understanding of the functionalities (cognition), acceptance of technology, and behavioural patterns. There are even fewer studies including the needs of family carers and care professionals. These carers seem to value items as privacy and dignity of the care recipients. Also, studies investigating the implementation of AAL-technologies into the work processes of carers and the skills, and competencies carers need to possess, are required. Future AAL-technologies should attempt to balance between the needs of the various stakeholders: safety and security needs of the care recipient, monitoring of

one's functional and cognitive decline, the need for care support, and the need for secure transfer and processing of data without breeching the standards for ethical practice and privacy.

Sponselee et al. (2008) described several methods that have been used in order to analyse and evaluate users' needs in the context of telecare. Selected methods to capture users' needs, including workshops, role play, demonstration facilities and in-home experience, are all helpful to come to a list of requirements attuned to the needs of the various users. Their usefulness differs depending on the stage of the project, and goes together with divergent pros and cons. Depending on the goals and stage of the project, a method can be selected, taking into account other methodological issues regarding the selection of participants, the use of questionnaires and the test phase situation. When designing an AAL-system, additional focus group sessions with all potential end-users are recommended, not merely as a tool go gain additional insight in the needs of the stakeholders, but also to increase support for the project (increase acceptance) and in order to make people familiar with the new technology (even though the technology is 'ambient', contactless and cloaked) and to provide a preliminary type of training.

6. CONCLUSION

Few studies have been conducted on the needs of older people and carers in relation to ambient assisted living. The Dutch literature shows that user involvement, during the design phase, is crucial for proper implementation of the AAL-technologies. Most of all, technologies should be considered a necessity by the end-users and perceived to be useful. Moreover, technologies need to be user-friendly and require and minimum of training, even though AAL-technologies are said to be minimally intrusive. Much of the research focuses on (institutional) dementia care, whereas technologies to support ageing-in-place (of both persons with and without dementia) seems to be understudied. None of the projects identified dealt with the actual needs of younger age-groups. The research from The Netherlands seems to be supported by findings from international studies, which indicates that the acceptance of technologies may be similar for Western contexts. Persons with dementia and their family carers require systems with simple and robust designs that are easy to understand. More research is required for carers, also in relation to their competencies and integration in work practice, and on AAL in general as some of the work included concerns less sophisticated smart home technology. The few results reported in the literature can be used for the design and implementation of current and future AAL-technologies, and provide guidance for policy makers and health care managers having to decide on such systems.

ACKNOWLEDGMENT

The AMACS consortium is thanked. This work is (partly) financed by the EU EraSME (FP7) project AMACS (IWT 100404): Automatic Monitoring of Activities using Contactless Sensors.

REFERENCES

Atallah, L., Lo, B., Ali, R., King, R., & Yang, G.-Z. (2009). Real-time activity classification using ambient and wearable sensors. *IEEE Transactions on Information Technology in Biomedicine, 13*(6), 1031–1039. doi:10.1109/TITB.2009.2028575

Chan, M., Estève, D., Escriba, C., & Campo, E. (2008). A review of smart homes - Present state and future challenges. *Computer Methods and Programs in Biomedicine, 9*(1), 55–81. doi:10.1016/j.cmpb.2008.02.001

Courtney, K. L., Demiris, G., Rantz, M., & Skubic, M. (2008). Needing smart home technologies: the perspectives of older adults in continuing care retirement communities. *Informatics in Primary Care, 16*(3), 195–201.

Dewsbury, G., Clarke, K., Rouncefield, M., Sommerville, I., Taylor, B., & Edge, M. (2003). Designing acceptable 'smart' home technology to support people in the home. *Technology and Disability, 15*(3), 191–199.

Frisardia, V., & Imbimbob, B. P. (2011). Gerontechnology for demented patients: Smart homes for smart aging. *Journal of Alzheimer's Disease, 23*(1), 143–146.

Hong, X., & Nugent, C. (2011). Implementing evidential activity recognition in sensorised homes. *Technology and Health Care, 19*(1), 37–52.

Kang, H. G., Mahoney, D. F., Hoenig, H., Hirth, V. A., Bonato, P., Hajjar, I., & Lipsitz, L. A. (2010). In situ monitoring of health in older adults: Technologies and issues. *Journal of the American Geriatrics Society, 58*(8), 1579–1586. doi:10.1111/j.1532-5415.2010.02959.x

Lorenz, A., & Oppermann, R. (2009). Mobile health monitoring for the elderly: Designing for diversity. *Pervasive and Mobile Computing, 5*(5), 478–495. doi:10.1016/j.pmcj.2008.09.010

Mahoney, D. F., Mahoney, E. L., & Liss, E. (2009). AT EASE: Automated technology for elder assessment, safety, and environmental monitoring. *Gerontechnology (Valkenswaard), 8*(1), 11–25. doi:10.4017/gt.2009.08.01.003.00

Mohammadi, M. (2010). *Empowering seniors through domotic homes. Integrating intelligent technology in senior citizens homes by merging the perspectives of demand and supply.* Unpublished doctoral dissertation, Eindhoven University of Technology, Eindhoven, The Netherlands.

Neven, L. B. M. (2011). *Representations of the old and ageing in the design of the new and emerging. Assessing the design of ambient intelligence technologies for older people.* Unpublished doctoral dissertation, Twente University, Enschede, Eindhoven, The Netherlands.

Niemeyer, A. L., Frederiks, B. J. M., Riphagen, I. I., Legemaate, J., Eefsting, J. A., & Hertogh, C. M. P. M. (2010). Ethical and practical concerns of surveillance technologies in residential care for people with dementia or intellectual disabilities: an overview of the literature. *International Psychogeriatrics*, *22*(7), 1129–1142. doi:10.1017/S1041610210000037

Nijhof, N., van Gemert-Pijnen, J. E. W. C., Dohmen, D. A. J., & Seydel, E. R. (2009). Dementie en technologie. Een studie naar de toepassingen van techniek in de zorg voor mensen met dementie en hun mantelzorgers. [in Dutch]. *Tijdschrift voor Gerontologie en Geriatrie*, *40*(3), 113–132. doi:10.1007/BF03079573

Oppenauer, C. (2009). Motivation and needs for technology use in old age. *Gerontechnology (Valkenswaard)*, *8*(2), 82–87. doi:10.4017/gt.2009.08.02.006.00

Poland, M. P., Nugent, C. D., Wang, H., & Chen, L. (2009). Smart home research: Projects and issues. *International Journal of Ambient Computing and Intelligence*, *1*(4), 32–45. doi:10.4018/jaci.2009062203

Schikhof, Y., Mulder, I., & Choenni, S. (2010). Who will watch (over) me? Humane monitoring in dementia care. *International Journal of Human-Computer Studies*, *68*(6), 410–422. doi:10.1016/j.ijhcs.2010.02.002

Schuurman, G. J., Moelaert-El-Hadidy, F., Krom, A., & Walhout, B. (2007). *Ambient intelligence. Toekomst van de zorg of zorg van de toekomst?* The Hague, The Netherlands: Rathenau Instituut. [in Dutch]

Sixsmith, A., Meuller, S., Lull, F., Klein, M., Bierhoff, I., Delaney, S., & Savage, R. (2009). SOPRANO – An ambient assisted living system for supporting older people at home. In M. Mokhtari, I. Khalil, J. Bauchet, D. Zhang, & C. Nugent (Eds.), *Proceedings of the 7th International Conference on Smart Homes and Health Telematics* (LNCS 5597, pp. 233-236).

Sponselee, A., Schouten, B. A. M., & Bouwhuis, D. G. (2008). Analyzing users' needs for telecare: Several case studies. In *Proceedings of the Ami Workshop on Capturing Ambient Assisted Living Needs*, Nürnberg, Germany.

Steele, R., Lo, A., Secombe, C., & Wong, Y. K. (2009). Elderly persons' perception and acceptance of using wireless sensor networks to assist healthcare. *International Journal of Medical Informatics*, *78*(12), 788–801. doi:10.1016/j.ijmedinf.2009.08.001

Stefanov, D. H., Bien, Z., & Bang, W.-C. (2004). The smart house for older persons and persons with physical disabilities: Structure, technology arrangements, and perspectives. *IEEE Transactions on Neural Systems and Rehabilitation Engineering*, *12*(2), 228–250. doi:10.1109/TNSRE.2004.828423

Tang, Y., Jin, S., Yang, Z., & You, S. (2006). Detection elder abnormal activities by using omni-directional vision sensor: Activity data collection and modeling. In *Proceedings of the SICE-ICASE International Joint Conference*, Busan, South-Korea.

Tapia, D. I., & Corchado, J. M. (2009). An ambient intelligence based multi-agent system for Alzheimer health care. *International Journal of Ambient Computing and Intelligence*, *1*(1), 15–26. doi:10.4018/jaci.2009010102 van Bronswijk, J. E. M. H., van Hoof, J., Franchi-mon, F., Koren, L. G. H., Pernot, C. E. E., & van Dijken, F. (2005). De intelligente thuisomgeving. Een betaalbare zorg voor de lange duur. In *Handboek zorg thuis* (pp. C 5.3-1-C 5.3-28). Maarssen, The Netherlands: Elsevier gezondheidzorg.

van Hoof, J., Kort, H. S. M., Markopoulos, P., & Soede, M. (2007). Ambient intelligence, ethics and privacy. *Gerontechnology (Valkenswaard)*, 6(3), 155–163. doi:10.4017/gt.2007.06.03.005.00

van Hoof, J., Kort, H. S. M., Rutten, P. G. S., & Duijnstee, M. S. H. (2011). Ageing-in-place with the use of ambient intelligence technology: perspectives of older users. *International Journal of Medical Informatics*, 80(5), 310–331. doi:10.1016/j.ijmedinf.2011.02.010

van Kasteren, T. L. M., Englebienne, G., & Kröse, B. J. A. (2010). An activity monitoring system for elderly care using generative and discriminative models. *Personal and Ubiquitous Computing*, 14(6), 489–498. doi:10.1007/s00779-009-0277-9

van Nispen, B. (2004). *Zorgdomotica. Een inventarisatie van knelpunten en struikelblokken met aanbevelingen om de grootschalige implementatie van zorgdomotica voor ouderen en mensen met functiebeperkingen in Nederland te versnellen en te verbeteren.* The Hague, The Netherlands: Nederlands Instituut voor Telemedicine. [in Dutch]

Virone, G. (2009). Assessing everyday life behavioral rhythms for the older generation. *Pervasive and Mobile Computing*, 5(5), 606–622. doi:10.1016/j.pmcj.2009.06.008

This work was previously published in the International Journal of Ambient Computing and Intelligence, Volume 3, Issue 4, edited by Kevin Curran, pp. 25-40, copyright 2011 by IGI Publishing (an imprint of IGI Global).

Chapter 21
Towards a Mission-Critical Ambient Intelligent Fire Victims Assistance System

Ling Feng
Tsinghua University, China

Yuanping Li
China National Software and Service Co. Ltd., China

Lin Qiao
Shanghai Mobile Company, China

ABSTRACT

While various ambient computing and intelligence techniques have been used to assist human beings in different aspects of their daily lives and work, this paper investigates potential ambient intelligence support in mission-critical scenarios such as firefighting. The paper reviews state-of-the-art ubiquitous techniques and tools assisting firefighting. Based upon these great research results, the authors then report the design and implementation of an ambient intelligent fire victims assistance application. By sensing the physical environment and occupants in a fire building, the system suggests the safest and fastest route along which the building occupants could evacuate; and when escaping from the building is not possible, the system tries to calm down and inform the trapped ones an action list. The channels to convey the guide assistance include traditional lights, speakers, and occupants' mobile phones (if existing). The empirical experiments show that ambient intelligence in such a fire response guide can help improve the egress time performance of building occupants. The presented ambient smart fire victims' assistance system is supposed to work at an early stage of fire in a building. As a complement of existing firefighting techniques, it still faces a number of open questions to be resolved in the future.

DOI: 10.4018/978-1-4666-2041-4.ch021

INTRODUCTION

In the past, fire hazards have caused many injuries and casualties. According to the statistics done by Brushlinsky et al. (2006), each year there are around 7-8 million fire disasters all over the world, which killed 70-80 thousand people and injured 500-800 thousand more. In 2008 in China, the number of fire disasters was 133 thousand (excluding forest, grassland, army, and underground mine fire). In total, 1385 people were killed and 684 people were injured. The direct loss estimate was about 1.5 billion RMB Yuans (CMPS, 2009).

In fire disasters, many people lost lives due to bad judgment. Poor decisions are likely made in life-critical urgent situations. Let us take a close look at two recent fire disasters. One happened in a college dormitory, and the other in a club.

Case 1: On September 20, 2008, a fire occurred at Wuwang Club at Long Gang Street, Shenzhen, China. According to the police, the fire originated from the fireworks being set off on the stage. The disaster killed 44 people with 88 people being injured (Wang et al., 2008). At the beginning of the fire, people in the club mistook it for a show. The fire quickly led to lots of smoke, and many people were smothered. As the customers were not familiar with the back door where the emergency exit is located, hundreds of people rushed to the front door through which they entered, causing many people being stumbled to the ground. In contrast, as the employees of the club knew the emergency exit, the majority of them succeeded in escaping from the fire via this exit gate. The death rate for the total 150 employees is far less than that for the club customers.

Case 2: On November 14, 2008, at the Shanghai Business College in China, a dormitory room at the sixth floor caught fire at 6:10am in the morning. The fire expanded very quickly and gave off a lot of smoke. The door was incidentally closed. The four trapped girls fell back to try to keep away from the fire. Eventually, the fire flame spread to the balcony. The girls jumped from the balcony before the firefighters arrived. They may have thought it was safer to do so, yet none of them could survive. The police received the fire report at 6:12am. The firefighters soon arrived, and the fire was put out at 6:30am (Liu, 2009).

A critical lesson we learn from these tragedies is that on-site occupants' assistance in an unexpected and urgent fire situation is very much desirable. While lots of great efforts have been made to deliver tour guide or museum guide, we ask ourselves: *"can we design a mission critical fire response guide to calm and assist on-site victims in a fire building to survive?"*

If there had been such an assistance system, which could point nervous and chaotic people to the right emergency exits along with the proper escape path (in case 1); or which could adaptively advise the four trapped girls to use the sheets in the dormitory and tie them to their bodies and climb down to the lower floors, e.g., the fifth floor, rather than directly jump down to the ground (in case 2), their lives might have been saved.

According to the physiological, psychological, and social behavioral studies (Song, 2002), at times of urgency, people tend to make unsound situational judgments and take wrong actions and, at times, even lose consciousness. Shouting loudly, losing confidence, disregarding exhortations, running in all directions, etc. are typical behaviors of people confronted with emergency situations. Even worse, poisonous smoke from the fire, e.g., CO, HCL, HCN, etc., can easily cause physiological disorders, such as impairment in the sense of smell, breathing difficulty, blurred vision, damage to the visceral and cranial nerve system, etc., which soon lead to mental confusion, behavior disorders, dizziness, coma, and suffocation (Song, 2002). There is no doubt that prompting ambient intelligent ubiquitous computing support to occupants is in demand.

However, common human behavior makes the problem particularly challenging.

The aim of this study is to investigate ambient smart context-aware techniques for assisting fire victims to react properly when confronted with an emergent fire disaster from a technical perspective. Such an assisting system is not meant to substitute existing firefighting facilities and systems, but as a complementary user-centric technology to calm and help some people in a fire building. The system is mainly used before firefighters come. We have the following assumptions in this study.

- The layout of the fire building is available beforehand.
- Fire locations can be detected by smoke and temperature sensors.
- IDs of frequent occupants and number of occupants in each cell unit (room or corridor) of the fire building can be sensed by techniques such as RFID.
- Occupants may or may not carry mobile phones. Mobile phone numbers of occupants are available from a database. For those carrying mobile phones, their mobile phone numbers can either be available from a database (for frequent occupants) or be detected, e.g., by blue-tooth beacons.

Upon the rise of a fire in a building, by sensing the context of the building on fire and the occupants in the building, our fire response assistance system quickly figures out the fastest safe evacuation route or works out an action-list for trapped "no-way-out" people.

In the study, the fire building is modeled as a graph, containing a number of vertices corresponding to doors, rooms, certain points at corridors, and exits. The system generates the escaping route guide based on referential location (vertex in the graph). To achieve real-time response, the system pre-computes all possible evacuation routes, and stores them in a database beforehand. In case of a fire, the fastest and safest routes will be picked up

immediately for differently localized occupants, taking into account the current distribution of building occupants so as to avoid potential escaping bottleneck due to human's inherent collective crow behaviors in the chaotic situation (Mataric, 1993; Helbing et al., 2001; Helbing, 2007; Wang & Luh, 2008; Wirz et al., 2009, 2010). In the study, the system tries to evenly disperse people to valid exits.

Based on the locations of installed speakers in the building, occupants per room, and "referential location", the fire assistance system will announce directional guide by means of lights and speakers without detecting the initial orientation of the people. For occupants with mobile phones, a brief guide will also be delivered to their mobile phone screens.

We evaluate the empirical experiences, effectiveness, and efficiency of the system by user studies and experiments, which show that context-aware technology in such a fire response guide enables the improvement of fire egress time. We also pinpoint some limitations of the system and some lessons we learned in building such a mission-critical ambient intelligence application.

The remainder of the paper is organized as follows. We review state-of-the-art ubiquitous techniques and tools assisting firefighting. Solution requirements for the context-aware fire response assistance for building occupants are further analyzed. We describe the design of the system architecture, and detail the techniques used. We report our performance study in. We summarize the paper and discuss future work.

STATE-OF-ART UBIQUITOUS TECHNIQUES IN FIREFIGHTING

Emergency response to fire is a topic that has been investigated for a long history. People have built a variety of excellent modern fire fighting systems, which can detect a fire, sound an alarm, and start corresponding activities to extinguish the fire. Such systematic facilities react quite well as a whole against a fire disaster. However, its assistance may not always reach each individual on site. Taking the above Wuwang club fire as an example (case 1), when the fire started, the fire fighting equipments, e.g., water showers, inside the club did begin to work. However, the turmoil still led to serious fire casualties. In fact, insufficient direction to individual occupants is a shortcoming of many modern fire fighting systems.

With the development of pervasive computing technology, technical supports to both firefighters and on-site victims are becoming important.

SUPPORT TO FIREFIGHTERS

Fischer and Gellersen (2010) have made a good survey on indoor location and navigation support products and projects for emergency responders, and concluded that techniques of wireless sensor networks, inertial sensing, and preinstalled location systems all have benefits and drawbacks when considering emergency response requirements (Renaudin et al., 2007; Miller, 2006; Wilson et al., 2007). Klann (2009) presented a concept and implementation for supporting tactical navigation of firefighters in structural fires called LifeNet. It is based on a sensor network that firefighters deploy on-the-fly during an intervention and a wearable system that provides them with navigational support. Wada et al. (2009) proposed a device that can indicate the direction through the tactile sensation of the head in an invisible fire environment full of smoke. Chen et al. (2007) described an application in helping emergency first responders in a fire exercise by the local police department and fire department at Lebanon airport (NH) in the spring of 2004. Blood oxygen saturation, as well as cardiac and respiratory states, is monitored for the first responders, and the surrounding environment is deployed with sensors. In the system, the fire state of propagation and location of each first responder are monitored. Besides, the system can also report

injured responders and their physiological status. Responders wear PDAs as the user interface, and the commanders can probe the history of sensor data and issue one-shot queries for situation assessment. Landgren and Nulden (2007) analyzed the patterns of mobile interaction in the emergency response work. Salam et al. (2008) evaluated a class of strategies to support efficient sensor energy workforce management used in mission-critical wireless sensor networks. Chen et al. (2007) presented a map synchronization table strategy to support firefighters to cooperatively make decisions in ad-hoc situations. Jiang et al. (2004) presented a context-aware system called "Siren" to help professional firefighters. The system can support tacit communication between firefighters and support multi-channel communication. Firefighters take PDAs both as a communication tool and a wireless sensing device. One firefighter can place the wireless-enabled sensors on the fly when he sizes up the situation. A new design of head-mounted displays for increased indoor firefighting safety and efficiency was also proposed in Steingart et al. (2005), Wilson et al. (2005), and Wilson and Wright (2009). Luyten et al. (2006) designed a system to support fire brigades with a role-based focus+context user interface on PDAs and Tablet computers. Klann (2007) described an approach of using game-like techniques to engage firemen from the Paris Fire Brigade into a participatory design process of wearable computing for emergency response. Denef et al. (2007, 2009) did field study for design of new interactive technologies for firefighting. Toups and Kerne (2007) also discussed developing education systems for teaching fire emergency responders.

SUPPORT TO ON-SITE FIRE VICTIMS

While the previous research greatly extends the mission critical disaster applications of context-awareness techniques, they mainly focused on saving professionals' lives, such as firefighters or people involved in dangerous work. While we recognize that protecting professionals is very important, civilian occupants rather than professionals are the main casualties of disasters today. Occupants are different from professionals in some respects. For instance, we can have every professional wear certain electronic devices, but it is more difficult to have all the ordinary people wear electronic devices, although in some places this is possible if a certain regulation is set up for wearing such devices. Instead of posing requirements for ordinary people, we may turn to the ubiquitous computing support and let the environment wear electronic "eyes" and "mouths". Capote et al. (2008) presented an evacuation model of fire scenarios in passenger trains. Wang and Luh (2008) further gave a probabilistic model to comprehensively characterize how fire propagation affects crowds in stressful conditions and in turn egress time performance. Ferscha and Zia (2009) proposed a belt like wearable device for vibro tactile directional guidance, called LifeBelt, to notify individuals in panic about exits. Blohberger and Grundler (2009) had a patent which can dynamically activate the escape identification lights according to the situation.

This study builds upon the above great research results, and research into the possible use of mobile phones of building occupants in a fire situation.

SOLUTION REQUIREMENTS

To deliver a context-aware ubiquitous computing support for occupants to survive in a fire, we conducted a field study by analyzing real fire disaster cases like the ones in Shanghai and Shenzhen described previously, reading firefighting literatures on how to behave and save lives on a fire occasion, interviewing firefighting administrators and a professional firefighting system manufacturer. As a result, we have the following criteria which will serve as design guidelines for our context-aware fire response guide.

- *Building Structures.* As fire situations are complex, the type of building greatly influences the design of the fire victims assistance system greatly. As a first step, we consider two typical building models, taking the former Shanghai College Dormitory Building and Shenzhen Club Building for reference. The first building represents a large public room, such as a restaurant, a supermarket, a club, etc., where customers are relatively unfamiliar with the building, while the second has a regular-sized small room construction and residents are relatively familiar with the building construction. Their lego models are illustrated in Figure 1. We can later extend the developed technologies to more types of buildings.
- *Timeliness.* Fire usually expands in minutes to the whole building. At public gathering places, it takes about 7 minutes for fire to spread. Only 6 minutes after the starting of a fire, the actual site temperature reaches 300-400°C. At a fire scene, people tend to be extremely sensitive to environmental and thermal radical temperature and can tolerate 65°C for a very limited time. At 120°C, people can endure for 15 minutes, and less than 1 minute at 175°C. When thermal radical temperature is $12000W/m2$, people can only stand for a few seconds. After that, people will go into a state of coma and shock (Song, 2002). Thus, the fire victims assistance system should have very high performance in decision making.
- *Simple Interaction.* We discussed with the engineers in a firefighting manufacture company whether to use more user-machine interaction, like voice interaction to solve some ambiguities. The engineers said using complex interactions might not be a good idea, but repeating the same instruction words several times might be helpful

so that occupants can grasp the meaning of the words.

- *Reliability.* As a mission-critical application, the fire victims assistance system must be reliable in terms of both hardware and software in fire emergencies. The underlying strategies should be as much reliable as possible. For instance, correct decisions depend on highly reliable context information. This is similar to the patient safety system developed by Bardram and Nørskov (2008), who used short-range RFID tags rather than long-range ones in order to get more precise context information. We once tried to incorporate several sophisticated fire expansion prediction models into the design of the fire response assistance system. One of the leading fire simulation systems called Fire Dynamics Simulator (FDS) was specifically tested in our experiment. However, as such a system needs a comprehensive model of the building (including furniture, window status, wall materials, etc.), it takes hours to compute a simulated fire expansion result. More important, solid validation is still lacking for the precision of prediction in the real world, since in reality there are too many details to be modeled. In other words, we cannot predict exactly where the fire will expand in the next minute. Therefore, we mainly use the real-time sensor data in our fire victims assistance system.

SYSTEM ARCHITECTURE

The fire victims assistance system works in a building, where each room has a smoke sensor at the middle of the ceiling, and another sensor, which can be either smoke or temperature sensor, at the entrance of the room. In addition, smoke sensors are attached on the corridors and exits of the whole building. Both kinds of sensors are

Figure 1. The Shanghai and Shenzhen fire building models

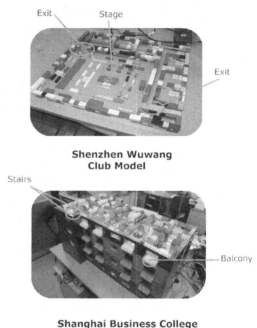

Shenzhen Wuwang Club Model

Shanghai Business College Dormitory Model

connected to the fire victims assistance system's backend server via sensory data acquisition cards. Multiple sensor data acquisition methods can be supported here. For output channels, each room, corridor, and exit has a speaker. Emergency red lights are also installed at each exit and along each corridor. For frequent occupants whose mobile phone numbers are known and stored in a database beforehand, corresponding fire response guides will also be sent to their mobile phones via a GPRS modem. Hardware deployment of the fire victims assistance system is given in Figure 2.

Figure 3 plots the software architecture of the fire victims assistance system. It contains four major components, namely, *context acquisition, fire status judgment, guidance generating*, and *guidance delivery*. In response to a fire, the *context acquisition* module quickly gathers low-leveled raw sensor values, and performs context aggregation and interpretation according to the

Figure 2. Hardware setting of the fire victims assistance system

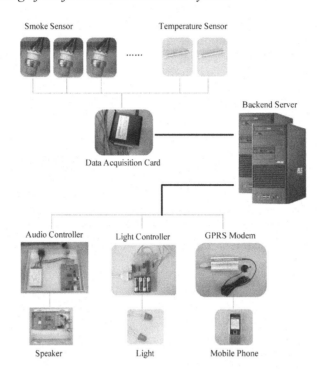

building and fire-related ontologies, which is manipulated using the protégé API. These ontologies are used to model the devices, building structure, and their relationships, as illustrated in Figure 4. Based on derived high-level context information and domain knowledge, the *fire status judgment* decides the pattern of expansion and extinguishing of the fire in the fire building. The change of the fire status triggers the update of the occupants' situations and influences the most

appropriate fire response manner for them. There are basically two choices for occupants: 1) finding the shortest safe way out, meanwhile ensuring occupants are evenly guided to different safe exits to avoid clogging and exit bottlenecks; or 2) taking proper self-protection actions if trapped.

The *guidance generation* then works out the evacuation route under choice 1), or the ToDo list for those who are trapped under choice 2). Implementation of the guidance generation module will

Figure 3. Software structure of the fire victims assistance system

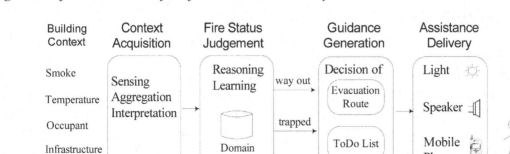

Figure 4. Ontology used in the fire victims assistance system

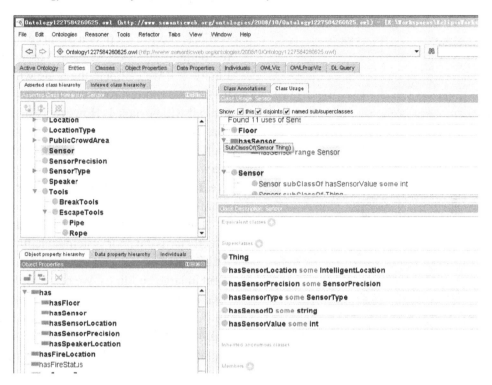

be detailed in the next section. In order to provide different guides to people at different locations, the *guidance delivery* module can support multiple audio cards and different output communication protocols. Fire victims are notified via nearby speakers and wearable mobile phones, whose aims are to deliver the escape route if it exists and safe response guide. Red lights along the escape route and exits will be set on as well.

GUIDANCE GENERATION

The fire victims assistance system delivers two types of guidance for two types of fire victims, i.e., ones who can escape and ones who are trapped.

EVACUATION ROUTE GENERATION

The emergency evacuation route algorithms have been already studied in Muir et al. (1996), Tseng et al. (2006), Shastri (2006), Barnes et al. (2007), Wang and Luh (2008), Tabirca et al. (2009), and Zeng et al. (2009). Based on these great research results, we further designed the method to generate the guide output. Experiences tell us the right way to escape from a fire is via emergency exits, which could be the inner or outer stairs for a building. The guidance using the command *"Go west!"* may be hard for the occupants to accurately follow, particularly in an unfamiliar building. Also, if the system guides the occupants to *"Go to the stairs!"* directly, the stairs might be too far away to see. Hence, we adopt a nearby referential vertex approach to give the route guide. *"Go left of the elevator!"* is one such guidance example.

The administrator of the fire victims assistance system off-line annotates the floor plan of the building, as shown in Figure 5, and this annotated floor plan is then converted into a graph model by the program.

Figure 5. Conversion from an annotated floor plan to a graph

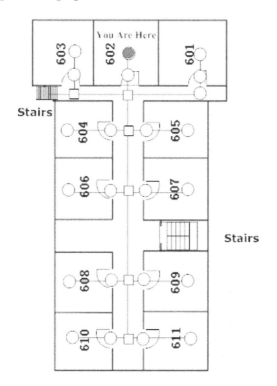

Here, circles stand for ordinary vertices and the boxes stand for referential vertices. Two heuristics are employed to identify referential vertices.

- Crossings in the path are taken as referential vertices. This is judged by whether the out-degree of a vertex is greater than two. For example, in Figure 6, *A* is a room, *E* is its door, and *B* is a crossing out of the room. Taking *B* as referential vertex for *E*, we can go "*left*" or "*right*" at this vertex.
- The referential vertices can be obtained by user-defined rules, e.g., all the big screens on the wall are treated as referential vertices.

To point out the correct way at run-time, the fire victims assistance system computes the shortest safe path between every two vertices in the graph and stores them in advance. In case of a

fire, dangerous vertices will be detected. If the fire does block the shortest path between the two vertices, the fire victims assistance system will re-compute the shortest path. For example, in Figure 7, if we compute the route when there is no fire, the shortest route from "*You are here*" to the exit will be path 1. However, when a fire occurs nearby, the stair vertex is blocked, so the shortest safe route becomes path 2. We increase the weight of edges connected to the unsafe vertices to make the computed path pass around unsafe vertices.

However, using the shortest safe path algorithm directly turns out poor system scalability, making it difficult to meet the real-time response requirement in large buildings. We made further special optimizations in the algorithm, greatly decreasing the time complexity and making the final performance of the fire victims assistance system acceptable, as evidenced by our experiments.

1. We initialize all the shortest paths for each vertex offline. In the run-time period, only a subset of the paths will be recomputed online according to the context.

2. If a fire occurs at or expands to stairs, we leverage the structural characteristics of the building. That is, in a vertical staircase, if one location of the staircase is blocked by the fire, the fire victims assistance system

Figure 6. Referential vertex selection example

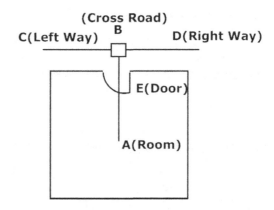

Figure 7. A dynamic route selection example

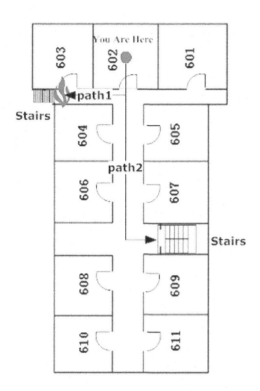

will not guide people to pass down through the firing stairs in the upper floors. This optimization reduces the complexity from the 3-dimension graph model to an approximate 2-dimension graph model.

Another issue that needs to be tackled is to explain directions in a natural language. Let $A(x_A, y_A, z_A)$ and $C(x_C, y_C, z_C)$ denote two different locations, and $B(x_B, y_B, z_B)$ denote the referential vertex from A to C. Let vector $\vec{a} = B-A = (a_x, a_y, a_z)$ and $\vec{b} = C-B = (b_x, b_y, b_z)$. Let $P_c = a_x b_y - a_y b_x$, $P_i = a_x b_x + a_y b_y$, and $r = \sqrt{a_x a_x + a_y a_y} \cdot \sqrt{b_x b_x + b_y b_y}$. Then the direction D is composed into three elements (d_1, d_2, d_3):

$$d_1 = \begin{cases} left & (P_c > 0)^\wedge(|\,P_c\,/\,r\,| > \varepsilon_1) \\ right & (P_c < 0)^\wedge(|\,P_c\,/\,r\,| > \varepsilon_1) \\ center & (|\,P_c\,/\,r\,| \le \varepsilon_1) \end{cases} \quad (1)$$

$$d_2 = \begin{cases} forward & (P_i > 0)^\wedge(|\,P_i\,/\,r\,| > \varepsilon_2) \\ backward & (P_i < 0)^\wedge(|\,P_i\,/\,r\,| > \varepsilon_2) \\ center & (|\,P_i\,/\,r\,| \le \varepsilon_2) \end{cases} \quad (2)$$

where ε_1 and ε_2 are the thresholds in the range of $[0,1]$.

$$d_3 = \begin{cases} up & (z_C > z_B) \\ down & (z_C < z_B) \\ center & (z_C = z_B) \end{cases} \quad (3)$$

With all the methods stated above, the fire victims assistance system generates guide information in the natural language such as "*In the corridor, turn right!*" An algorithm description of a typical transformation from an evacuation path to guide speech is shown in Figure 8.

In addition, in a big room like a dance hall illustrated in Figure 9, there may be more than one exit, and occupants might not see all the exits. To attract the occupants to the safe exits, we add speakers at the exits, repeating "*Here is the exit!*"

TODO-LIST GENERATION FOR TRAPPED OCCUPANTS

Our current study is based on the following two rules to determine whether one is trapped by the fire or not.

[Rule 1] The door of the room where one is situated has been blocked by the fire.
[Rule 2] All the paths from which one can escape out of the floor have been blocked by the fire.

Situations complying with Rule 1 could be detected by either a temperature sensor or a smoke sensor close to the door, while those complying with Rule 2 could be detected via smoke sensors.

Figure 8. A typical transformation from an evacuation path to guide speech

```
----------------------------------------------------------------------------------------
Input: Path P that starts from o₁ to o₂; and the layout graph G (V, E)
Output: Guide speech for path P

1    foreach vertex v in P from o₁ to o₂ do
2      if v has more than 2 adjacent vertices in G then
3        v₁ = v;
4        break;
5      endif

6    v₂ = v₁'s next vertex in the path P;
7    v₃ = v₁'s previous vertex in the path P;
8    direction = get the direction from v₁ to v₃ by referential v₂;

9    if v₂ is a door then
10     if direction is "forward" then
11       speech = "go through" + v₂'s name + ", go forward";
12     else
13       speech = "go through" + v₂'s name + ", turn " + direction;
14     endif
15   else if v₂ is a corridor then
16     if direction is "forward" then
17       speech = "In " + v₂'s name + ", go forward";
18     else
19       speech = "In " + v₂'s name + ", turn " + direction;
20     endif
21   endif
----------------------------------------------------------------------------------------
```

There exist the possibility that even if one is blocked, with wet covers s/he could dash out of the burning place. This challenges the fire victims assistance system to be smart enough to have a great insight into the surrounding and give the most appropriate instruction. We leave this issue to our further research. A To Do list advised by the fire victims assistance system for trapped ones includes the following:

Action 1: Tie knotted sheets to the window/ balcony and your body, climb downward!
Action 2: Close the door and keep smoke out!
Action 3: Ask for help!
Action 4: Stick to the wall foot!

Figure 10 illustrates the fire response guides sent to a victim's mobile phone. This is done by using a GPRS modem.

EVALUATION

We implemented the prototype of our fire victims assistance system using Java and C++ programming languages. C++ code is used for sensors and speakers, which are called by the Java Native Interface (JNI). The speech is generated by the Microsoft Text to Speech (TTS) SDK. Currently, our smoke sensors are connected to the fire victims assistance system server directly by a data acquisition card. Regarding the output channels,

Figure 9. A big room example

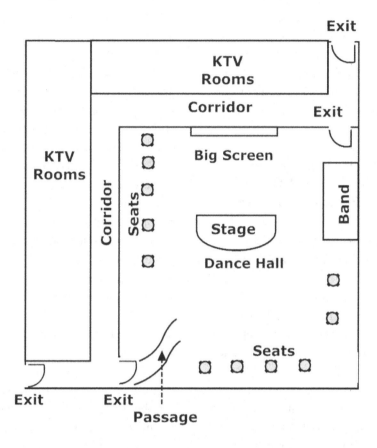

Figure 10. Guide sent to the mobile phone of a building occupant

 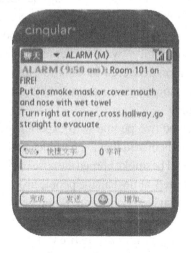

Route picture sent to the mobile phone   **Text guide sent to the mobile phone**

a control component has been implemented for multiple audio cards connected to the fire victims assistance system server, which is a desktop computer of 3GHz CPU and 2GB RAM. Experiments were conducted to evaluate efficiency and effectiveness of the fire victims assistance system through user studies and experiments.

INTERVIEWS WITH DOMAIN EXPERTS, FIRE-EXPERIENCING PEOPLE, AND ORDINARY USERS

We interviewed the firefighting administration department in the university. It is a subordinate division of the Public Safety Ministry. They gave us a brochure of fire response principles which were summarized by experienced firefighters and researchers. These principles were implemented in the fire victims assistance application, especially in the ToDo list.

We interviewed three senior experts in a professional firefighting system manufacturer. They acknowledged the usefulness of the system, and suggested that the system is suited for the places like hotels and dormitories. One of the experts is the member of the firefighting product standardization committee of the country. He emphasized the hazard of smoke inhalation, and suggested, if possible, guiding people to put on smoke-proof masks. This suggestion was implemented as general information delivered in our fire victims assistance application, besides the adaptive route or ToDo list guide.

We interviewed two people who experienced real fires. One of them said that the particles in the smoke were large. The smoke burned the nose badly. When the fire started, almost all the people around the fire were in a sudden confusion. Some people even used a cotton quilt to put out the fire, but the fire grew even faster. A system like fire victims assistance application is in demand to help the people protect themselves. The other person said, in the real fire which he experienced, all people were in

a panic, running and colliding in the passageway chaotically. Both of them argue that people do need a guide to reduce the collision so as to reduce the number of the injuries.

We further presented two questions to 52 undergraduate and graduate students in different majors at the university in order to understand ordinary users' attitude towards an ambient intelligent fire victims assistance application. The answers are illustrated in Figure 11. 51 out of 52 people believed that the guide could increase the possibility of survival in the Shanghai dormitory fire disaster. 42 of 52 people thought that alarm together with voice route guide is the best in guiding occupants in unfamiliar places. 5 people argued that voice route guide is the best in the second question, and over 90% people selected voice route guide.

Discussion

The interviews above indirectly identified the requirement for fire victims assistance application. To obtain an on-site experience, two of the lab members participated in a fire drill in a 14-floor dormitory building organized by the firefighting department. Hundreds of people took part in the drill. The experiences told us that when we were at the very stage of deciding where to go at the door, the flashlights which show the arrows and diagrams marking exit routes, were not always directly in front of us. Whichever way we selected, we were not confident. The fire victims assistance application does not mean to substitute the flashlights, but it will be useful if it could calm and help people encounter the right flashlights more quickly.

EMPIRICAL EXPERIENCE WITH THE FIRE VICTIMS ASSISTANCE APPLICATION

We conducted an empirical experience study with the fire victims assistance application. 20 subjects,

Figure 11. People's attitudes towards the ambient intelligent fire victims assistance application

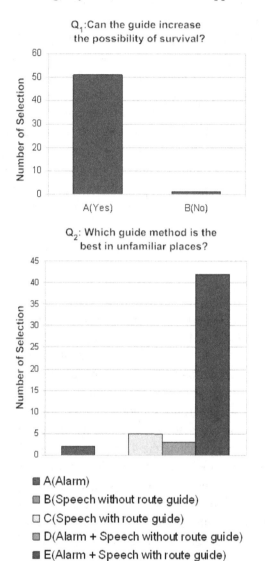

A(Alarm)
B(Speech without route guide)
C(Speech with route guide)
D(Alarm + Speech without route guide)
E(Alarm + Speech with route guide)

including 3 university staff, 3 administrative staff, and 14 graduate students, participated in the experiment.

Method

Before the study, the subjects were told that one kind of emergency might happen, and we were to see whether they could behave correctly. But we did not tell them what would actually happen. We designed two scenarios. The first scenario was to guide them to a safe exit. But this safe exit was not the one through which people entered the building. The second scenario was to simulate a situation that they are trapped by the fire outside near the door. The system guided them to close the door and wait for rescue. After the test, the subjects were asked to fill in a questionnaire.

Result

Except for one invalid questionnaire which selected more than one item for one question, we collected 19 completed valid questionnaires. The results are tabulated in Table 1 (Likert scale, 1-5 point, 5 for best and 1 for worst). Overall, the system was perceived as useful (4.33) and had almost no adverse interference with people's normal life (4.64). People scored high on usefulness of voice guiding (4.14) and the clarity of short message guide on mobile phones (4.41). The reaction time of voice guiding was fine (4.11). However, the message receiving time was complained by some subjects (3.81). The mobile phones are provided by us, and the delay of short messages sent to the mobile phones was compared to the voice guide delivery.

Table 1. Questionnaire result

Empirical Experience	Mean	Standard Deviation
System Usefulness	4.33	0.60
Usefulness of Voice Guiding	4.41	0.78
Reaction Time of Voice Guiding	4.11	0.93
Usefulness of Short Message Guiding	3.92	0.84
Clarity Effect of Short Message Guiding	4.41	0.79
Reaction Time of the System	3.81	0.69
Unobtrusiveness in People's Normal Life	4.64	0.61

Discussion

Benefits and constraints of using mobile phones. Using mobile phones are better than nothing. We want the victims to leave or take other self-protection actions before firemen come. People can adjust the position of mobile phones by themselves to see the guide more clearly. The mobile phone can use the public wireless communication channels which are not destroyed by the fire. However, there are some constraints with mobile phones. Firstly, not all occupants have access to mobile phones. Secondly, a slow message receiving time was incurred when we adopted the public mobile network to connect the system to users' mobile phones. A more efficient method might be using the combination of both public and local networks. Thirdly, it is still an open question that whether the mobile phone is useful in a very crowded building, where watching mobile phone might become difficult for users. Displaying very simple guide, such as only a directional arrow on the screen with the aid of the compass in the mobile phone, might be a good choice. Crowd, noise and people's communications. In this user study, we observed that people communicated with each other when they were in a small crowd. Even if some people did not catch the guide, they could follow those who catch the guide. The people who had mobile phones could also help those who did not have. But the crowd also impeded the speed of evacuation. These phenomena deserve further researches (Steingart et al., 2005).

EFFECTIVENESS OF THE FIRE VICTIMS ASSISTANCE APPLICATION

To investigate more rigorously whether context-awareness in the guide takes effect in an emergent state, we performed this user study. One challenge in designing such an experiment lies in designing an emergency state, because we cannot put people into real danger. Previous researches on disaster rescue and evacuation were often carried out in simulation environments (Li et al., 2003; Blohberger & Grundler, 2009). Hence, our user study was also conducted as a drill. We referred to the famous bonus method successfully used by Helen Muir's group at Cranfield in the domain of aircraft evacuations (Li et al., 2003). In their pioneering aircraft egress experiments, bonus was used to simulate an emergent state among the subjects. Another challenge is that, as in reality, people's attention is not always on the emergency. To make the subjects' attentions not fully on fire alarms, we let the subjects focus on some work in the experiment, i.e., doing some mathematical exercises.

Method

Twenty-four subjects, 8 female, and 16 male of age 19-48, participated in the experiment. They were recruited through an open internet advertisement in the city and were arranged into 6 groups randomly, with 4 subjects per group. Each group was allocated to 2 rooms, with 2 subjects per room. Each group attended 8 tests. Figure 12 plots the test setting. To eliminate the effect of position difference, the 4 subjects changed their positions clock-wise in every test in turn. As soon as a voice alarm arose, the subjects at different rooms needed to evacuate to a safe place, i.e., one of the two stairs at the two ends of the corridor.

To investigate the effectiveness of the fire route guide, we considered two types of voice alarms, one with route guide "The building is on fire, please cover your mouth with wet cloth, in the corridor turn right/left, go to the safe exit quickly!", and the other without route guide "The building is on fire, please cover your mouth with wet cloth!". The same voice alarm was repeated in one test until the test finished. In each test, one of the two stairs was blocked by a "fire" randomly. When a subject reached the "fire" stairs, a staff would notify her/him about being blocked by fire, and the subject then needed to turn around, and run to the opposite side, i.e., the safe stairs.

Figure 12. Experiment setting

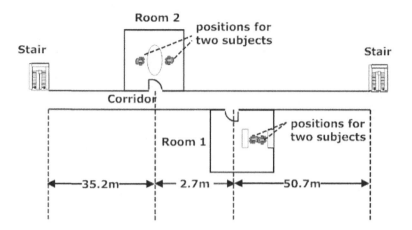

Which type of voice alarm would arise in one test was a random choice. The experiment took place in a real building, and the distances from the two rooms to the two stairs were not equal. This might have influenced the egress time. Therefore, for each kind of voice alarms, we let the number of "fire" on the left stairs be equal to the number of "fire" on the right stairs. We recorded both the egress time and the mathematical exercise score for each subject. The bonus was divided into 3 categories for a competitive atmosphere. (1) If a subject obtains top 50% exercise score and also is among top 50% to arrive at a safe place, s/he will get 40 RMB (Yuan) bonus; (2) If a subject does not obtain top 50% exercise score but is among top 50% to arrive at a safe place, s/he will get 30 RMB (Yuan) bonus; (3) The rest will get 20 RMB (Yuan) bonus.

Result

In total, 96 measurements of egress time for voice route guide and 96 measurements for voice without route guide were noted down. The ranked measurements are shown in Figure 13. The Wilcoxon-Mann-Whitney statistic (Landgren & Nulden, 2007) was used to do the inference test. Let f be the continuous cumulative distribution function for egress time e_1 without route guide, and g be

the continuous cumulative distribution function for egress time e_2 with route guide. We examined the hypothesis H_0: $f = g$ against the alternative H_1: $f(x) > g(x)$ for every x (i.e., e_1 is statistically larger than e_2). The statistic U is 2516.5 and z is 5.43. The statistics reject H_0 in favor of H_1 with the significance level $a < 0.001$. The sample medians and means are shown in Table 2. The result supports a first but valuable finding, that is, the voice alarm with context-aware route guide leads to less egress time than the voice alarm without route guide in a similar building layout statistically, although we observed not all the subjects followed the guide exactly in this experiment.

Discussion

Building type. It is noteworthy that this user study was conducted in an office building. The result is for the situation when the fire is just beginning and the crowd is relatively small. This might not be suitable for a very crowded club. Equipment failure. In this study, the result was obtained in a situation where the equipments, e.g., the sensors, or at least some of them work. Equipment failure should be considered for the system deployment. For example, reserve battery and fire proof materials should be used to protect the equipments. Actually, the influence of equipment failure and

Figure 13. Egress time measurements for voice alarms with/without route guide

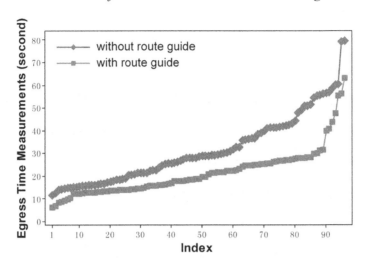

Table 2. Sample medians and means of egress time

Voice Alarm Type	Sample Size	Median	Mean
without route guide	96	28.35	31.53
with route guide	96	18.83	21.39

how to reduce such a negative influence deserve further research.

EFFICIENCY OF THE FIRE VICTIMS ASSISTANCE APPLICATION

Context judgment, path finding, and ToDo-list generation constitutes the inner kernels of the system. while context sensing and delivery time are beyond the control of the system, we evaluate the system reaction time, which is the time interval when a smoke sensor value is read till the assistance guidance is issued to the user in a building. We simulated on the two real building models, i.e., Shanghai Business College Dormitory and Shenzhen Wuwang Club, where the former has 11 rooms per floor and the later has 7 small rooms and 1 big room (dance hall) per floor. Then we varied the floor number, exit number, and fire spot number of the buildings to examine the system

performance. The experimental result presented in Figure 14 showed that all the response times are less than 1 second.

CONCLUSION AND FUTURE WORK

In this paper, we report our technical design of an ambient intelligent context-aware fire response guide, aiming to calm and guide panicked occupants to properly react to an emergent fire. The presented ambient smart fire victims assistance system is supposed to work at an early stage of fire in a building, and serve as a complement to the existing optical and acoustic guidance techniques. We evaluate the performance of the system through user studies and experiments. The experimental results show the feasibility, effectiveness, and some limitations of the system. To have the system truly work in the real world, we still need to resolve a number of open questions.

Figure 14. System scale-up performance

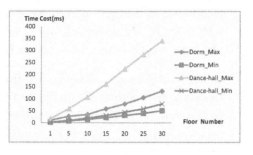

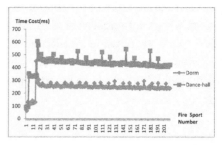

(a) Time cost versus total number of floors   (b) time cost versus number of fire spots

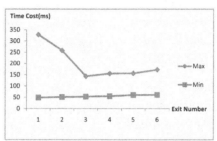

(c) Time cost versus total number of exits

- The success of an evacuation process relies on precise behavioral, psychological, physical, and social studies related with both individuals and groups. Users' collective effects must be seriously considered when designing an evacuation assistance system (Fersche & Zia, 2009). To evaluate and improve the work, the guidance obtained by our approach must be incorporated in crowd simulation.

- For a mission-critical application like the one presented in the paper, it is very important to address the liability issue introduced by potential faulty sensors, burning hardware, and software bugs of the system in a life-threatening situations.

- Although the shortest safe path solution is presented to direct fire victims to different exits, finding the optimal guiding strategy still remains challenging, for example, when some exits are blocked by the crowd or collapsed by secondary effects from the

fire. In addition to sensor data, some other factors, like dynamic crowd density detection and phased evacuation, can be incorporated in computing appropriate escape routes.

- Besides displaying evacuation routes and action list, users' mobile phones could be employed to communicate with outside for help. Some public available displays in buildings can also be explored as an assistance interface.

ACKNOWLEDGMENT

The authors would like to thank Yiping Li, Shoubin Kong, and Yu Yi for their great implementation work. Comments from Daqing Zhang, Weijun Qin, and Shanghai Huyi firefighting electronic equipment company are very inspiring and helpful. We also like to thank National Natural Science Foundation of China (60773156, 61073004) and

Chinese Major State Basic Research Development 973 Program (2011CB302203-2) for supporting this work. A preliminary conference version of this article entitled "A Context-Aware Fire Response Guide for Victims" appeared in the Proceedings of the 5th International Conference on Smart Sense and Context.

REFERENCES

Bardram, J., & Nørskov, N. (2008). A context-aware patient safety system for the operating room. In *Proceedings of the 10th International Conference on Ubiquitous Computing* (pp. 272-281).

Barnes, M., Leather, H., & Arvind, D. (2007). Emergency evacuation using wireless sensor networks. In *Proceedings of the 32nd International Conference on Local Computer Networks* (pp. 851-857).

Blohberger, F., & Grundler, G. (2009). *U. S. Patent No. 20090102619: Evacuation system having escape identification lights*. Washington, DC: United States Patent & Trademark Office.

Brushlinsky, N., Sokolov, S., Wagner, I. P., & Hall, J. (2006). *World fire statistics*. Retrieved from http://ec.europa.eu/consumers/cons safe/presentations/21-02/ctif.pdf

Capote, J., Alvear, D., Abreu, O., Lázaro, M., & Cuesta, A. (2008). Evacuation modeling of fire scenarios in passenger trains. In *Proceedings of the International Conference on Pedestrian and Evacuation* (pp. 705-711).

Chen, G., Li, M., & Kotz, D. (2007). Data-centric middleware for context-aware pervasive computing. *International Journal of Pervasive and Mobile Computing*, 216-253.

Chinese Ministry of Public Security (CMPS). (2009). *2008 fire statistics in China*. Retrieved from http://www.mps.gov.cn/n16/n1282/n3553/1778249.html

Denef, S. (2009). Human-computer interaction techniques in firefighting. In *Proceedings of the 12th IFIP TC 13 International Conference on Human-Computer Interaction: Part II* (p. 867).

Denef, S., Ramirez, L., & Dyrks, T. (2009). Letting tools talk: Interactive technology for firefighting. In *Proceedings of the 27th International Conference on Human Factors in Computing Systems* (pp. 4447-4452).

Ferscha, A., & Zia, K. (2009). LifeBelt: Silent directional guidance for crowd evacuation. In *Proceedings of the 13th International Symposium on Wearable Computers* (pp. 19-26).

Fischer, C., & Gellersen, H. (2010). Location and navigation support for emergency responders: A survey. *International Journal of IEEE Pervasive Computing*, 38-47.

Helbing, D., Farkas, I., & Vicsek, T. (2000). Simulating dynamical features of escape panic. *International Journal of Letters to Nature*, *407*(6803), 487–490. doi:10.1038/35035023

Helbing, D., & Johansson, A., & AI-Abideen, H. (2007). Dynamics of crowd disasters: An empirical study. *International Journal of Physical Review*, *75*, 1–7.

Jiang, X., Chen, N., Hong, J., Wang, K., Takayama, L., & Landay, J. (2004). Siren: Context-aware computing for firefighting. In *Proceedings of the 2nd International Conference on Pervasive Computing* (pp. 87-105).

Klann, M. (2007). Playing with fire: User-centered design of wearable computing for emergency response. In *Proceedings of the International Conference on Mobile Response* (pp. 116-125).

Klann, M. (2009). Tactical navigation support for firefighters: The LifeNet ad-hoc sensor-network and wearable system. In *Proceedings of the International Conference on Mobile Response* (pp. 41-56).

Landgren, J., & Nulden, U. (2007). A study of emergency response work: Patterns of mobile phone interaction. In *Proceedings of the International Conference on Human Factors in Computing Systems* (pp. 1323-1332).

Li, Q., De Rosa, M., & Rus, D. (2003). Distributed algorithms for guiding navigation across a sensor network. In *Proceedings of the 9th International Conference on Mobile Computing and Networking* (pp. 313-325).

Liu, D. (2009). *Shanghai business college dormitory fire: Four students dead.* Retrieved from http://news.xinhuanet.com/newscenter/2008-11/14/content 10357255 1.htm

Luyten, K., Winters, F., Coninx, K., Naudts, D., & Moerman, I. (2006). A situation-aware mobile system to support fire brigades in emergency situations. In R. Meersman, Z. Tari, & P. Herrero (Eds.), *Proceedings of the On the Move Workshops* (LNCS 4278, pp. 1966-1975).

Mataric, M. (1993). Designing emergent behaviors: From local interactions to collective intelligence. In *Proceedings of the 2nd International Conference on Simulation of Adaptive Behavior* (pp. 1-10).

Miller, L. (2006). *Indoor navigation for first responders: A feasibility study.* Washington, DC: US National Institute Standards and Technology.

Muir, H., Bottomley, D., & Marrison, C. (1996). Effects of motivation and cabin configuration on emergency aircraft evacuation behavior and rates of egress. *The International Journal of Aviation Psychology, 6*(1), 57–77. doi:10.1207/s15327108ijap0601_4

Renaudin, V., Yalak, O., Tomé, P., & Merminod, B. (2007). Indoor navigation of emergency agents. *European Journal of Navigation, 5,* 36–45.

Salam, H., Rizvi, S., Ainsworth, S., & Olariu, S. (2008). A durable sensor enabled lifeline support for firefighters. In *Proceedings of the Computer Communications Workshop* (pp. 1-6).

Shastri, J. (2006). *Safe navigation during fire hazards using Specknets.* Unpublished master's thesis, The University of Edinburgh, Edinburgh, UK.

Song, G. (2002). *Firefighting in public places.* Beijing, China: Chinese People's Public Security University Press.

Steingart, D., Wilson, J., Redfern, A., Wright, P., Romero, R., & Lim, L. (2005). Augmented cognition for fire emergency response: An iterative user study. In *Proceedings of the 1st International Conference on Augmented Cognition.*

Tabirca, T., Brown, K., & Sreenan, C. (2009). A dynamic model for fire emergency evacuation based on wireless sensor networks. In *Proceedings of the 8th International Symposium on Parallel and Distributed Computing* (pp. 29-36).

Toups, Z., & Kerne, A. (2007). Implicit coordination in firefighting practice: Design implications for teaching fire emergency responders. In *Proceedings of the SIGCHI Conference on Human Factors in Computing Systems* (pp. 707-716).

Tseng, Y., Pan, M., & Tsai, Y. (2006). A distributed emergency navigation algorithm for wireless sensor networks. *IEEE Computers, 39*(7), 55–62.

Wada, C., Yoneda, Y., & Sugimura, Y. (2009). Proposal of a direction guidance system for evacuation. In *Proceedings of the International Conference on Human-Computer Interaction* (pp. 221-227).

Wang, P., & Luh, P. (2008). Modeling and optimization of crowd guidance for building emergency evacuation. In *Proceedings of the 4th IEEE International Conference on Automation Science and Engineering* (pp. 328-334).

Wang, P., Ying, A., & Jiang, B. (2008). *Analysis of the fire caused heavy casualties in Shenzhen: the fire was mistaken as a show.* Retrieved from http://news.sina.com.cn/c/2008-09-22/121716333822.shtml

Wilson, J. (2007). A wireless sensor network and incident command interface for urban firefighting. In *Proceedings of the 4th IEEE International Conference on Mobile and Ubiquitous Systems: Network & Services* (pp.1-7).

Wilson, J., Steingart, D., Romero, R., Reynolds, J., Mellers, E., Redfern, A., et al. (2005). Design of monocular head-mounted displays for increased indoor firefighting safety and efficiency. In *Proceedings of SPIE on Helmet-and Head-mounted Displays X: Technologies and Applications* (pp. 103-114).

Wilson, J., & Wright, P. (2009). Head-mounted display efficacy study to aid first responder indoor navigation. *Proceedings of the Institution of Mechanical Engineers. Part C, Journal of Mechanical Engineering Science, 223*(3), 675–688. doi:10.1243/09544062JMES1213

Wirz, M., Roggen, D., & Tröster, G. (2009). Decentralized detection of group formations from wearable acceleration sensors. In *Proceedings of the International Conference on Computational Science and Engineering* (pp. 952-959).

Wirz, M., Roggen, D., & Tröster, G. (2010). A methodology towards the detection of collective behavior patterns by means of body-worn sensors. In *Proceedings of the 8th Pervasive Computing Conference.*

Zeng, Y., Murphy, S., Sitanayah, L., Tabirca, T., Truong, T., Brown, K., & Sreenan, C. (2009). Building fire emergency detection and response using wireless sensor networks. In *Proceedings of the 9th IT & T Conference.*

This work was previously published in the International Journal of Ambient Computing and Intelligence, Volume 3, Issue 4, edited by Kevin Curran, pp. 41-61, copyright 2011 by IGI Publishing (an imprint of IGI Global).

Chapter 22
The Core Aspects of Search Engine Optimisation Necessary to Move up the Ranking

Stephen O'Neill
University of Ulster, UK

Kevin Curran
University of Ulster, UK

ABSTRACT

Search engine optimization (SEO) is the process of improving the visibility, volume and quality of traffic to website or a web page in search engines via the natural search results. SEO can also target other areas of a search, including image search and local search. SEO is one of many different strategies used for marketing a website but SEO has been proven the most effective. An Internet marketing campaign may drive organic search results to websites or web pages but can be involved with paid advertising on search engines. All search engines have a unique way of ranking the importance of a website. Some search engines focus on the content while others review Meta tags to identify who and what a web site's business is. Most engines use a combination of Meta tags, content, link popularity, click popularity and longevity to determine a sites ranking. To make it even more complicated, they change their ranking policies frequently. This paper provides an overview of search engine optimisation strategies and pitfalls.

1. INTRODUCTION

Search Engine Optimisation (SEO) is the technique by which we can optimize a website in accordance with search engine requirements (Agarwal, 2009). It has transformed into a highly controlled science, crucial to every website marketing plan as it targets website traffic. When SEO started in late 1990's it was easily manipulated and abused but search engines developed algorithms that would remove any factors that help influence a websites ranking, this solution was links, but with this development came problems and so Search Engines had to develop Link Building. This even-

DOI: 10.4018/978-1-4666-2041-4.ch022

tually stopped people manipulating their website rankings. The evolution of SEO happened with the introduction of Authority, this process was measuring the Authority of a website instead of the popularity of incoming links a website received. The search engine industry is always changing, and as industry standards and trends change so does the methods of SEO. Statistics (Porter, 2011) show how crucial SEO is to a website and how important it is to get ranked as high as possible.

- 42% of search users click the top-ranking link.
- 8% click the second-ranking link
- 62% of search users click a link on the first page of search results
- 23% of searches progress to the second page
- 80% of unsuccessful searches are followed with keyword refinement.
- 41% of searches unsuccessful *after the first page* choose to refine their keyword
- 77% of search users choose organic over paid listing when searching
- 67% choose organic search when purchasing
- 40% of SEO campaigns aware of their ROI achieve returns in excess of 500%

It is important to understand that search engines read and like pure HTML. Major keywords should therefore be placed in the <HEAD> area by using Meta tags and repeated again in the <BODY> area of the page. It is also recommended to emphasize targeted key phrases by putting them in <h1> or <h2> tags plus the early paragraphs on the page. Another useful approach is to place information into all the <ALT> tags associated with each photo/picture. This will then tell search engine robots what the graphic is depicting. Time should be spent deliberating over the actual text surrounding a link (or links from other sites to your site). This is given special precedence by the engines and

care should be taken to avoid 'wasting' keyword 'points' on senseless text such as 'Click here to..'.

Search engines do not like Flash, JavaScript, Frames, words in graphics and (in many cases) dynamically produced pages (like.asp) which include symbols such as ? in the URL. These types of pages make it difficult to achieve good rankings. Static HTML pages are much more preferable for search engine listings. Spamming the engines is attempting to 'fool' the ranking system into presenting a 'spammed' site higher than it deserves to be in the results. All engines however are aware of spamming methods and there is a risk of becoming banned should a site be discovered to be using covert methods. Tricks that can get a site banned include repeating words over and over in tiny or invisible text, filling Meta tags with irrelevant terms, using competitor's names or trademarks and any other method of keyword 'stuffing'. Although meta tags are often ignored, search engines are aware that so-called 'experts' fill them with words to attract surfers so many now check to see if the words listed are actually on the web page, if they are not then a site could be downgraded or banned for spamming (Evans, 2007).

Improved results can be obtained by having the title of each page state clearly in 8-12 words what the page is about, ensuring also that the first 20-30 words of text on the page explain what service or product is being promoted, and making sure that there is also clearly written information about the subject and other sites linking back. Each site that links to a page is an extra vote of confidence in that site, but care has to be taken to ensure that the links are from a reputable third party or related web-site/portal. FFA (Free for All link page) sites and 'link-farms' (which contain links that no-one is likely to ever click on) can have the opposite effect and is now a day deemed as another method of trying to fool the search engines. Attempts should be made to copy the potential keywords that each surfer will attempt in their web session. It may be easy to get a top ranking for a company name or an obscure product but how many people will actually come to the site as a result of the obscure products or typing in a company name? Yes, selection of the proper phrases for each market is crucial. Targeting the wrong keywords will be a wasted effort and possibly an expensive mistake if Google AdWords (https://adwords.google.com) mechanism was been used. However, selection of the correct keywords could see traffic growth and sales increases beyond a marketing manager's wildest dream.

A good practice is to check out what people are searching for. To help with this, there are a number of free and inexpensive tools available to help such as wordtracker.com or Google Analytics service. Some keywords are always going to be much more competitive than others. For example, ranking well on the single word "Digital" will be much more difficult than ranking in the top 10 for "Digital Prints." In general, single keywords usually return the least targeted leads. Targeting multi-word keyword phrases can result in achieving the highest quality leads. A recent study showed that only 34% of Web site owners knew to include the appropriate words on their Web page. Adding words in the keywords tag is not enough. Many search engines ignore the keyword tag therefore the correct words have to be on the page. It makes simply makes sense (Weitzner, 2008).

There are a number of commonly used techniques to influence a page's position within search results. These include indexing (registering a site and its pages with a search engine and creating an XML site map), on-site optimization techniques (changes made to the HTML code on the site itself) and off-site optimization (which are activities that occur on other sites to draw traffic to a particular site) (Jones, 2008; Frydenberg & Miko, 2011; Curran, 2004; Malaga, 2010).

2. ON PAGE SEO

On Page SEO is involved with the areas of optimising the title, the keywords, the description and the content. The title is the most important aspect of On – Page SEO, the idea is to have a unique title for each page on the site, and if the titles on pages are similar they are treated as 'duplicates' by the search engines. To avoid using titles like 'untitled' or a title that isn't relate to the pages' content, the best way is to choose a title that communicates the content of the page and allows the person to know exactly what's on each that particular page. Also make sure that the title is short and isn't too long as the search engine usually shows snippets in the search if this is the fact. The description Meta tag is another important element when it is getting indexed by the search engines (Figure 1). Sometimes search engines use this as a snipped of the page for the results on the search engine; this usually happens if it relates more to what the user query. Another way is if your site is listed within the Open Directory project, the Search Engine might use the description provided there. One can prevent them displaying ODP data by adding the following *"<Meta name="robots" content="NOODP">"*.

Figure 1. Code snippet of where meta tag is inserted

```
<html>
<head>
<title>Brandon's Baseball Cards - Buy Cards, Baseball News, Car
<meta name="description" content="Brandon's Baseball Cards prov
</head>
<body>
...
```

Meta Tags should summarise the whole pages content, this should also avoid writing descriptions that are unrelated to the pages content. The description should only contain 160 characters this will increase the SEO. Meta tags should also be unique, the same as for each page of the site, using the same Meta Tag could make the search engine only show one instead of all of them and sending the rest to the supplement results index. Another factor is URLs structuring, this helps search engine crawl you website better and makes it look more appealing for people to link your content. User also use anchor text (Figure 2), the link show relevant words this helps the search engines and other users find the relevant content.

URLs are more likely to be better if words are used instead f numbers, Ids, and etc, but the words need to be kept to a minimum to allow full exposure to the search engines. Also only provide a single version of a URL to reach a document, this helps to prevent users link to one URL and other linking to a different version.

3. OFF PAGE SEO

Off-page SEO is performed outside the web page itself – primarily on other people's web sites. Off – page SEO is the creation of inbound links that are optimised for the web pages' keywords or keyword phrase. When search engines acknowledge that there is a lot of inbound links to your page that have similar topics to your pages' theme, usually keywords, they will assume that your page is viewed by other web pages specialising in your chosen Keyword and to accomplish this there is many factors to take into account.

The objective is not to make your links appear natural; the objective is that your links are natural (Matt Cutts – mattcutts.com). Linking is one of the primary elements in links to your website and improving the ranking and optimisation of the website, the relationship between other websites is helped using back links and the overall goal is to get traffic to the site. The Quality of the back link is a key factor for the ranking of the site, the more back links there is the better for the site and the better the quality and location of the back links will help to dramatically make a difference with SEO. No matter how much you spend on SEO, a web site is invisible until somebody links to it (Eric Ward). Using other methods like blogs, forums and social networking are other ways in building significant and diverse amount of high quality back links to the site. The increase of popularity of people using social networks can help build a higher presence among the users and results for your website. Some of the best methods in implementing back links are:

- Register the site with online directories
- Build a relationship and gain links to your site with other quality and on-topic websites
- Publishing press releases and articles online
- Develop a viral on the Web from a worthy link resource or tool

The age of the Domain is a factor that affects Optimisation. The older the domain is results in higher ranking points with regards optimisation. The thinking behind this is that if a domain has been in existence for years, then it can be assumed

Figure 2. Example of link to website on a blog

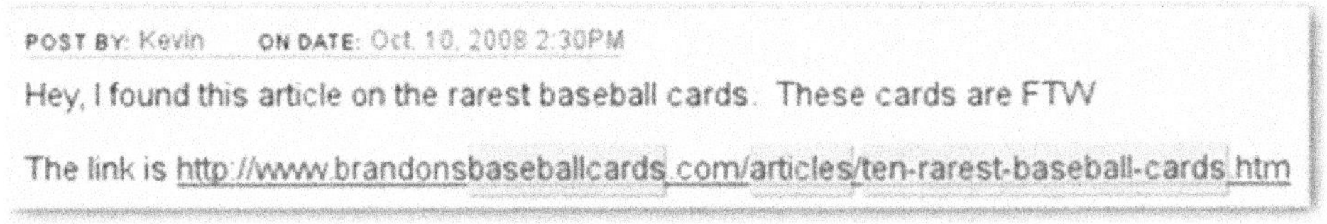

POST BY: Kevin   ON DATE: Oct. 10, 2008 2:30PM

Hey, I found this article on the rarest baseball cards. These cards are FTW

The link is http://www.brandonsbaseballcards.com/articles/ten-rarest-baseball-cards.htm

that it is an established site and less likely to be a spam site or host of malicious software. Not only is the Domain Name important but also the hosting, there is many factors that is important to help with SEO, you need to know where the hosting comes from if you are a U.K business get a UK host. Websites like 'http://www.123-reg.co.uk/' usually have hundreds of websites on one server. Make sure that your neighbour's that are on the same server as you are not classified as spam; this will affect your SEO. The structure of your URL is also important make sure strings are not random and is clear to follow, this helps keep the optimisation process well. Visitor behaviour is the aspect of how a visitor behaves when they visit a site. This can have an impact on ranking, Bounce rate measures the people viewing your site. It can measure if a visitor does not stay on long. This could be easily avoidable if useful content is added with an intuitive and engaging style. This will help lower the bounce rate and overall help the rank of the Website. Finding where the sources of the traffic come from is necessary, because it can affect ranking. We should aim for good sources and eliminate the bad sources. The building of a site is a gradual procedure and generally involves continually adding more pages and content with more links.

There are a number of basic Search Engine Optimisation key factors that if implemented on a website will immediately improve the search engine ranking. These are as follows.

Meta Tags

Meta tags are snippets of code that are placed at the start of the HTML code that contains the information about the sites name and purpose. Other than title tags, these tags aren't visible to visitors on the site, but provide valuable information to the search engines. In the past they were the main criteria for search engines rankings, but after many arguments and discussion between the top webmaster, majority of people now believe

that it is less important in optimising a website. The first Meta tag is Meta Description tag, this is the tag that is important because search engines use it for the sites SERP listing, and this is the perfect place to help entice traffic to your site, if the search engines cannot generate an abstract of the visible content within the site. This does not affect the ranking of the site but helps with the marketing. Another aspect of Meta Tags or Meta Keywords tags they are use for providing a list of keyword suggestions to search engines, this can help them then rank your page, although it is getting less important in ranking the site, it still get used by various search engines.

Title Tag

This process involves creating a keyword rich 'Title Tag' which is embed at the head section of your HTML document or title section of your blog configuration. It is the single most influential piece of information on your site. Usually the Title Tag is shown in the search results. When selecting a Title Tag it has to be highly relevant to the page, the title needs to be under the 70 characters limit and try to feature the keywords in the title tag as soon as possible. Naming your site with your chosen keywords is the best possible outcome for SEO. Title tags are currently considered the most important Meta tag from a search engine; it is a MUST to be successful in SEO. Title Tags are similar to Meta Tags because you place the most important keywords at the start and the less important at the end of the tag. Also when you are naming the pages and articles refer to you keywords and helps rank faster. When potential traffic looks at your link you want to make sure that when optimising the Title Tag you make it enticing for the visitors and not to make look like a spam site.

Two features that are part of HTML specification are ALT and TITLE attributes, ALT is focused on images and TITLE is for links. ALT attributes provides a description of an image for the blind or those with images turned off their web browsers. The Title attribute provides a description of the linked to the page to give the browser more information before clicking the link. Both are prime places for the placement of keywords, this does not mean you want to stuff them with Keywords as this will affect you optimisation. A bad example of title attribute would be "Click for more information." This approach does not let the potential traffic know what the topic of the site is. The method you would use instead would be to use an image that is relevant to your site and including your keywords within the code.

An ALT attribute is used for a site logo a bad example of using ALT is to say "my logo." A Title Tag helps with your sites optimisation and it doesn't affect the ranking of the site but helps the site look more professional to potential traffic.

Keyword Research

This process is very critical to get right for getting good rankings for your website. When researching for keywords the main objective is to find a keyword that best describes your subject on your website. There are many ways in researching keywords, a popular choice is people use simple popularity metric, this is that you perform a search and look at the size of results returned, the problem with this process is that if you do include keywords on your doesn't mean that they are actively optimising keywords, words can just be common and may have no influence for SEO. There are many different approaches to this but once you have found your keyword you then need to test it on available sites online to find tail keywords which have high searches and low competing websites. This process is very time consuming but powerful in SEO. Minor Keywords are also important but can be very difficult to get ranked for them; it could make the difference of where you are positioned on the Website. These can be place at the footer of the site along with the copyright statement; this helps place minor

keywords on every page of the site and overall helps the ranking.

Keyword Anchor Text

Ensuring the keyword Anchor text is when the words that are used in your linking structure should be Keywords. They are called 'Anchor' text when they are used as the phrases that they are linked to and tell the search engine what the user is searching for based on the 'click' action. This is the key factor used for in search engine optimisation consulting.

Linking

URL linking, this helps the webpage crawling programs to find all your webpage's in your website. Search engine crawling programs, sometimes called spiders, crawls your website's pages, indexing its content. If the content is hard to find behind badly formatted HTML, chances are that the search engines will not be able to access all of it or correctly index it. When creating a linking structure you have to ensure that all links are referenced using their full URL. The rule of the thumb is to build a website for users, not for spiders (Dave Naylor).

Creating Search Engine Accessible HTML

The mark up on a site has to be clean, limited and as clear as possible, to test this you can pull open the source code of a page and check how it looks, if it is badly done, you can trim it down or switch to another mark up CSS. They could affect the density of the code and could potentially hut the keyword density. One main rule to remember is that search engines are not search for grammar mistakes but having a clean, accessible, quick loading, validated mark up is a bonus as this will provide the user with a good experience and they may recommend the site. The less and cleaner the mark up, the faster the server is to upload.

Crawling Spiders

The main goal of a Crawling Spider is to read all the source code and content, usually the top end gets more attention than the bottom half. They have limits to how much they read so it is important to prioritise the content on a site. Always ensure that the site structure code is at the top. This tends to be at various places within the code.

Content

Content is critical to helping SEO. It needs to be SEO friendly as search engines are constantly being updated so when managing a website, one has to ensure that the content is also updated and based on more relevant keywords. When embedding keywords into the text at a high level, one

has to make sure that the search engines knows what keywords are the important ones and that it is not 'over done' to avoid making the website look like spam. This could lead to a low ranking or even removal on a search engine. Gaining trust is the important factor of SEO. One should keep a long term focus as tricks and shortcuts are not the way to earn trust (Matt McGee). Figure 3 demonstrates what HTML code should look like.

Unpopular Methods of SEO

HTML frames are no longer as powerful but are still used. They were used when the connection speed was at 9600 baud, and this overcame the problem with reloading the header and menu every time the user went to another page. Although the increase in bandwidth is positive this has also lead to the decrease of Frames being used. The unpopularity of frames is also caused by the search engines problem of crawling them; this

Figure 3. Example of the layout of HTML code

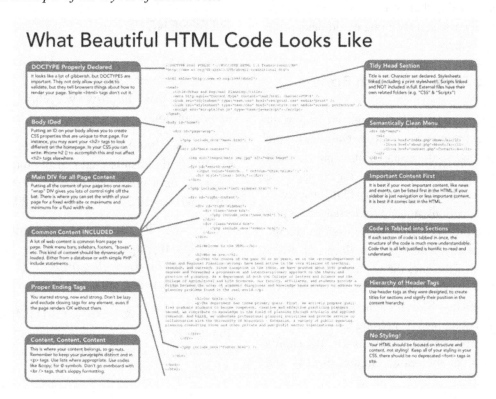

makes them undesirable and useless now. Another decrease has been seen in JavaScript and DHTML with the highly popular use of HTML and CSS. The problems associated with Java Script and DHTML is that with the change in Search engines algorithms, crawling programs can't crawl through Java Script and DHTML coding which then affects SEO.

Flash is unpopular but is now being redesigned so crawling programs can crawl the necessary information to help rank the site. This is because flash sites tend to be graphic based. If the homepage is flash, this will dramatically decrease the chances of a high ranking website. To avoid this, offer people the option of viewing the flash, but make the default site CSS and HTML. You can then detect Flash with JavaScript and open a new window to play it. Search engines do not support Forms but these are necessary to allow browsers to interact with web pages. A search engine will not submit a form on a site. If this is the only way to reach a website then the search engine will not reach the content. This can be an advantage as if there is a link that you do not want a search engine to access, and then one could design the page as a form.

Heading Tags, Fonts and Sizes

Heading tags, specifically h1 tags, are important to denote content on your site, but similar to title tags you need to do research and find the best possible tags. H1 tags are used for on page tile (e.g., article title at top of page), H2 is for secondary content sections, and H3 for tertiary ones and so on done the line. CSS can be used to change the appearance of the tags but does not affect the ranking of the site; the content doesn't have to be big font but as long as is used with good keyword density. Search engines also weigh up the content contained b or strong tags or tags that indicate emphasis but is now as the algorithms change so does the search engines priority and

it is now steering away from these areas but it is still important to use these appropriately.

4. CONCLUSION

Search Engine Optimisation (SEO) has many factors that affect the performance of a website ranking within the Search Engines. It is important to tailor a strategy for each search engine you wish to get high rankings in. Researching keywords is important in declaring to the search engines what type of website you own. There are a number of approaches that can be taken to optimise a website. The factors that help rank a site are important to understand when building a site. Strong factors to SEO are Relationships and communication with other websites. To increase traffic to a site, build more links online. SEM is also a powerful way in promoting a website but SEO is free and a 'natural' method in achieving high rankings within search engines.

REFERENCES

Agarwal, N. (2009, September 11). SEO – An effective online marketing tool. *Digital Marketing*. Retrieved from http://www.eyebridge.in/blog/seo-definition/

Curran, K. (2004). Tips for achieving high positioning in the results pages of the major search engines. *Information Technology Journal*, *3*(2), 202–205. doi:10.3923/itj.2004.202.205

Evans, M. P. (2007). Analyzing Google rankings through search engine optimization data. *Internet Research*, *17*(1), 21–37. doi:10.1108/10662240710730470

Frydenberg, M., & Miko, J. (2011). Taking it to the top: A lesson in search engine optimization. *Information Systems Education Journal*, *9*(1), 24–40.

Jones, K. B. (2008). *Search engine optimization.* Indianapolis, IN: Wiley.

Malaga, R. A. (2007). The value of search engine optimization: An action research project at a new e-commerce site. *Journal of Electronic Commerce in Organizations*, *5*(3), 68–82. doi:10.4018/jeco.2007070105

Malaga, R. A. (2010). Search engine optimization - black and white hat approaches. *Advances in Computers*, *78*, 2–41. doi:10.1016/S0065-2458(10)78001-3

Porter, I. (2011). *10 statistics that demonstrate the value of SEO.* Retrieved from http://www.intraspin.com/news/10-statistics-that-demonstrate-the-value-of-seo/

Weitzner, D. (2008). Web science: an interdisciplinary approach to understanding the web. *Communications of the ACM*, *51*(7), 60–69.

This work was previously published in the International Journal of Ambient Computing and Intelligence, Volume 3, Issue 4, edited by Kevin Curran, pp. 62-70, copyright 2011 by IGI Publishing (an imprint of IGI Global).

Compilation of References

Aarts, E., & Marzano, S. (2003). *The new everyday: Visions of ambient intelligence.* Rotterdam, Netherlands: 010 Publishing.

Aarts, E. (2004). Ambient intelligence: a multimedia perspective. *IEEE MultiMedia, 11*(1), 12–19. doi:10.1109/MMUL.2004.1261101

Aarts, E. H., & Encarnação, J. L. (2006). *True visions: The emergence of ambient intelligence* (1st ed.). New York, NY: Springer.

Abowd, G. D., Dey, A. K., Brown, P. J., Davies, N., Smith, M., & Steggles, P. (1999). Towards a Better Understanding of Context and Context-Awareness. In *Proceedings of the 1ˢᵗ International Symposium on Handheld and Ubiquitous Computing* (LNCS 1707, pp. 304-307).

Abraham, T., & de Vel, O. (2002). Investigative profiling with computer forensic log data and association rules. In *Proceedings of the IEEE International Conference on Data Mining* (pp.11-18).

Agarwal, N. (2009, September 11). SEO – An effective online marketing tool. *Digital Marketing.* Retrieved from http://www.eyebridge.in/blog/seo-definition/

Alavi, S. M. M., Walsh, M. J., & Hayes, M. J. (2009). Robust distributed active power control technique for IEEE 802.15.4 wireless sensor networks - a quantitative feedback theory approach. *Control Engineering Practice, 17*(7), 805–814. doi:10.1016/j.conengprac.2009.02.001

Alavi, S. M. M., Walsh, M. J., & Hayes, M. J. (2010). Robust power control for IEEE 802.15.4 wireless sensor networks with round-trip time-delay uncertainty. *Wireless Communications and Mobile Computing, 10*(6), 811–825.

Alemdar, H., & Ersoy, C. (2010). Wireless sensor networks for healthcare: A survey. *Computer Networks, 54*(15), 2688–2710. doi:10.1016/j.comnet.2010.05.003

Alexa. (2010). *ThePirateBay.org site info.* Retrieved from http://alexa.com/siteinfo/thepiratebay.org

Andreasen, F. (2010, March 24). *SDP Capability Negotiation.*

Andreasen, F. (2002). *Session Description Protocol (SDP).* Simple Capability Declaration.

Antoniou, G., Billington, D., Governatori, G., & Maher, M. J. (2001). Representation results for Defeasible Logic. *ACM Transactions on Computational Logic, 2*(2), 255–287. doi:10.1145/371316.371517

Antoniou, G., Maher, M. J., & Billington, D. (2001). Defeasible Logic versus Logic Programming without Negation as Failure. *The Journal of Logic Programming, 41*(1), 45–57.

Ares, B. Z., Fischione, C., Speranzon, A., & Johansson, K. H. (2007). On power control for wireless sensor networks: System model, middleware component and experimental evaluation. In *Proceedings of the* European Control Conference, Kos, Greece.

Arthur, C. (2010, February). *Opposition to digital economy bill grows.* Retrieved from http://www.guardian.co.uk/technology/2010/feb/05/digital-economy-bill

Arthur, W. B., Durlauf, S. N., & Lane, D. A. (1997). *The economy as an evolving complex system II. SFI studies in the sciences of complexity.* Reading, MA: Addison-Wesley.

Asgaut Eng. (1996). *Passive and active attacks.* Retrieved from http://www.pvv.org/~asgaut/crypto/thesis/node10.html

Atallah, L., Lo, B., Ali, R., King, R., & Yang, G.-Z. (2009). Real-time activity classification using ambient and wearable sensors. *IEEE Transactions on Information Technology in Biomedicine*, *13*(6), 1031–1039. doi:10.1109/TITB.2009.2028575

Avilés-López, E., & García-Macías, J. (2009). TinySOA: A service-oriented architecture for wireless sensor networks. *Service Oriented Computing and Applications*, *3*(2), 99–108. doi:10.1007/s11761-009-0043-x

Avizienis, A., Laprie, J., Randell, B., & Landwehr, C. (2004). Basic concepts and taxonomy of dependable and secure computing. *IEEE Transactions on Dependable and Secure Computing*, *1*(1), 11–33. doi:10.1109/TDSC.2004.2

Bailey, T., & Durrant-Whyte, H. (2006). Simultaneous localization and mapping (SLAM). *IEEE Robotics & Automation Magazine*, *13*(3), 108–117. doi:10.1109/MRA.2006.1678144

Banala, S. K., Kulpe, A., & Agrawa, S. K. (2007, April 10-14). A powered leg orthosisfor gait rehabilitation of motor-impaired patients. In *Proceedings of the IEEE International Conference on Robotics and Automation*, Rome, Italy (pp. 401-407).

Bardram, J., & Nørskov, N. (2008). A context-aware patient safety system for the operating room. In *Proceedings of the 10th International Conference on Ubiquitous Computing* (pp. 272-281).

Barnes, M., Leather, H., & Arvind, D. (2007). Emergency evacuation using wireless sensor networks. In *Proceedings of the 32nd International Conference on Local Computer Networks* (pp. 851-857).

Baronti, P., Pillai, P., Chook, V. W. C., Chessa, S., Gotta, A., & Hu, Y. F. (2007). Wireless sensor networks: A survey on the state of the art and the 802.15.4 and ZigBee standards. *Computer Communications*, *30*(7), 1655–1695. doi:10.1016/j.comcom.2006.12.020

Barringer, H., Goldberg, A., Havelund, K., & Sen, K. (2004). Rule-based runtime verification. In *Proceedings of the 5th International Conference on Verification* (pp. 44-57).

BBC. (2008, February). *Games firms 'catching' non-gamers.* Retrieved from http://news.bbc.co.uk/1/hi/technology/7697898.stm

Bellavista, P., Cinque, M., Controneo, D., & Foschini, L. (2009). Self-Adaptive Handoff Management for Mobile Streaming Continuity. *IEEE Transactions on Networks and Service Management, 6*(2).

Bernstein, D. S., & Michel, A. N. (1995). A chronological bibliography on saturating actuators. *International Journal of Robust and Nonlinear Control*, *5*, 375–380. doi:10.1002/rnc.4590050502

Berry, M. (2005). *A virtual learning environment in primary education.* Retrieved from http://www.world-citizens.net/ftp/Primary%20VLE.pdf

Bertino, E., Buccafurri, F., Ferrari, E., & Rullo, P. (1999). A Logical Framework for Reasoning on Data Access Control Policies. In *Proceedings of the 12th IEEE Computer Security Foundations Workshop (CSFW-12)*, Mordano, Italy (pp. 175-189).

Bertino, E., Catania, B., Ferrari, E., & Perlasca, P. (2003). A Logical Framework for Reasoning about Access Control Models. *ACM Transactions on Information and System Security*, *6*(1), 71–127. doi:10.1145/605434.605437

BigScreenLive. (2010). Retrieved April 8, 2010, from http://bigscreenlive.com/

Bikakis, A., & Antoniou, G. (2011). Partial Preferences and Ambiguity Resolution in Contextual Defeasible Logic. In *Logic Programming and Nonmonotonic Reasoning,* (LNCS 6645, pp. 193-198).

Bikakis, A., & Antoniou, G. (2010). Defeasible Contextual Reasoning with Arguments in Ambient Intelligence. *IEEE Transactions on Knowledge and Data Engineering*, *22*(11), 1492–1506. doi:10.1109/TKDE.2010.37

Bikakis, A., Antoniou, G., & Hassapis, P. (2011). Strategies for contextual reasoning with conflicts in ambient intelligence. *Knowledge and Information Systems*, *27*(1), 45–84. doi:10.1007/s10115-010-0293-0

BitTorrent. (2008). *The BitTorrent Protocol specification.* Retrieved from http://bittorrent.org/beps/bep_0003.html

Blaze, M., Feigenbaum, J., & Lacy, J. (1996). Decentralized trust management. In *Proceedings of the 1996 IEEE Symposium on Security and Privacy* (pp. 164-173). Washington, DC: IEEE Computer Society.

Blaze, M., Feigenbaum, J., & Strauss, M. (1998). Compliance-checking in the PolicyMaker trust management system. In *Proceedings of the 2nd International Conference on Financial Cryptography* (LNCS 1465, pp. 254-274).

Blaze, M., Feigenbaum, J., Ioannidis, J., & Keromytis, A. D. (1999a). *The KeyNote Trust-Management System, Version 2* (RFC 2704). Retrieved from http://www.ietf.org/rfc/rfc2704.txt

Blaze, M., Feigenbaum, J., Ioannidis, J., & Keromytis, A. D. (1999b). The role of trust management in distributed systems. In *Secure Internet Programming* (LNCS 1603, pp. 185-210).

Blohberger, F., & Grundler, G. (2009). *U. S. Patent No. 20090102619: Evacuation system having escape identification lights.* Washington, DC: United States Patent & Trademark Office.

Bohn, J., Gärtner, F. C., & Vogt, H. (2003). Dependability issues of pervasive computing in a healthcare environment. In *Proceedings of the Statistical Process Control Conference* (pp. 53-70).

Bohn, J., Coroama, V., Langheinrich, M., Mattern, F., & Rohs, M. (2005). Social, economic, and ethical implications of ambient intelligence and ubiquitous computing. In Weber, W., Rabaey, J., & Aarts, E. (Eds.), *Ambient intelligence*. New York, NY: Springer. doi:10.1007/3-540-27139-2_2

Booth, R. (2009, February 12). Video games are good for children – EU report. *The Guardian*, 2.

Borghesani, C., Chait, Y., & Yaniv, O. (2003). *The QFT frequency domain control design toolbox for use with MATLAB*. Arlington Heights, IL: Terasoft.

Boulos, M. K., Rocha, A., Martins, A., Vicente, M. E., Bolz, A., & Feld, R. (2007). CAALYX: A new generation of location-based services in healthcare. *International Journal of Health Geographics, 6*(1), 9. doi:10.1186/1476-072X-6-9

Bouzit, M., Popescu, G., Burdea, G., & Boian, R. (2002). The Rutgers Master II-ND force feedback glove. In *Proceedings of the 10th Symposium on Haptic Interfaces for Virtual Environment and Teleoperator Systems*, Orlando, FL (p. 145).

Brenton, C., Bird, T., & Ranum, M. J. (2006). *Top 5 essential log reports.* Retrieved from http://www.sans.org/security-resources/top5_logreports.pdf

Brownell, B. (2008). *Transmaterial 2: A catalog of materials that redefine our physical environment*. Princeton, NJ: Princeton Architectural Press.

Brushlinsky, N., Sokolov, S., Wagner, I. P., & Hall, J. (2006). *World fire statistics*. Retrieved from http://ec.europa.eu/consumers/cons safe/presentations/21-02/ctif.pdf

Bubb, H. (1993). *Carl-Hanser Verlag*. München-Wien, Germany: Systemergonomische Gestaltung. In Ergonomie.

Buiza, C., Gonzalez, M. F., Etxaniz, E., Urdaneta, E., Yanguas, J., Geven, A., et al. (2008). *Technology support for cognitive decline and independent living – Presenting the HERMES project.* Paper presented at the Gerontological Society of America Conference, Washington, DC.

Buiza, C., Gonzalez, M. F., Facal, D., Martinez, V., Diaz, U., Etxaniz, A., et al. (2009). Efficacy of cognitive training experiences in the elderly: Can technology help? In *Proceedings of the 5th International Conference on Universal Access in Human Computer Interaction*.

Buiza, C., Etxeberria, I., Galdona, N., González, M. F., Arriola, E., & López de Munain, A. (2008). A randomized, two-year study of the efficacy of cognitive intervention on elderly people: the Donostia Longitudinal Study. *International Journal of Geriatric Psychiatry, 23*, 85–94. doi:10.1002/gps.1846

Bulling, A., Roggen, D., & Tröster, G. (2008). It's in your eyes: Towards context-awareness and mobile hci using wearable eog goggles. In *Proceedings of the 10th International Conference on Ubiquitous Computing* (pp. 84-93). New York, NY: ACM Press.

Bulling, A., Ward, J. A., Gellersen, H., & Tröster, G. (2011). Eye movement analysis for activity recognition using electrooculography. *IEEE Transactions on Pattern Analysis and Machine Intelligence, 33*(4), 741–753. doi:10.1109/TPAMI.2010.86

Burdick, D., & Kwon, S. (2004). *Gerotechnology: Research and practice in technology and aging.* New York: Springer.

C2K. (2010). Retrieved from http://www.c2kni.org.uk

Cacioppo, J., & Patrick, W. (2008). *Loneliness: Human Nature and the Need for Social Connection.* New York: W. W. Norton & Co.

Cai, L. L., Fong, A. J., Liang, Y., Burdick, J., Otoshi, C. K., & Edgerton, V. R. (2006). Effects of assist-as-needed robotic training paradigms on the locomotor recovery of adult spinal mice. In *Proceedings of the IEEE/RAS-EMBS International Conference on Biomedical Robotics and Biomechatronics* (pp. 62-67).

Cai, Y., & Abascal, J. (2006). *Ambient intelligence in everyday life.* Berlin, Germany: Springer-Verlag.

Cameron, C. (2010). *Military-grade augmented reality could redefine modern warfare.* Retrieved from http://www.readwriteweb.com/archives/military_grade_augmented_reality_could_redefine_modern_warfare.php

Cañete, E., Chen, J., Díaz, M., Llopis, L., & Rubio, B. (2011). A service-oriented approach to facilitate WSAN application development. *Ad Hoc Networks, 9*(3), 430–452. doi:10.1016/j.adhoc.2010.08.022

Capote, J., Alvear, D., Abreu, O., Lázaro, M., & Cuesta, A. (2008). Evacuation modeling of fire scenarios in passenger trains. In *Proceedings of the International Conference on Pedestrian and Evacuation* (pp. 705-711).

Carmen, J. (2005). Using augmented reality to treat phobias. *IEEE Computer Graphics and Applications, 25*(6), 31–37. doi:10.1109/MCG.2005.143

Carroll, J. (1995). *Scenario-based design: Envisioning work and technology in systems development.* New York: John Wiley & Sons.

Caudell, T., & Mizell, D. (1992). Augmented reality: An application of heads-up display technology to manual manufacturing processes. In *Proceedings of the IEEE Hawaii International Conference on Systems* (pp. 26-32).

Cawood, S., & Fiala, M. (1998). *Augmented reality – a practical guide.* Raleigh, NC: The Pragmatic Bookshelf.

Cerami, E. (2002). *Web services essentials: Distributed applications with XML-RPC, SOAP, UDDI & WSDL* (1st ed.). Sebastopol, CA: O'Reilly Media.

Chakraborty, S., Poolsappasit, N., & Ray, I. (2007, July 8-11). Reliable delivery of event data from sensors to actuators in pervasive computing environments. In S. Barker & G. JoonAhn (Eds.), *Proceedings of the 21st Annual IFIP WG 11.3 Working Conference on Data and Applications Security*, Redondo Beach, CA (LNCS 4602, pp. 77-92).

Chang, Z., & Hao, Y. (2009).The research of disaster recovery about the network storage system base on "safety zone". In *Proceedings of the Conference on Apperceiving Computing and Intelligence Analysis* (pp. 290-293).

Chan, M., Estève, D., Escriba, C., & Campo, E. (2008). A review of smart homes - Present state and future challenges. *Computer Methods and Programs in Biomedicine, 9*(1), 55–81. doi:10.1016/j.cmpb.2008.02.001

Chen, G., Li, M., & Kotz, D. (2007). Data-centric middleware for context-aware pervasive computing. *International Journal of Pervasive and Mobile Computing,* 216-253.

Chen, M., Gonzalez, S., & Leung, V. C. (2007). Applications and design issues for mobile agents in wireless sensor networks. *IEEE Wireless Communications, 14*(6), 20–26. doi:10.1109/MWC.2007.4407223

Chen, Y.-H., Lee, B.-K., & Chen, B.-S. (2006). Robust Hinf power control for CDMA cellular communication systems. *IEEE Transactions on Signal Processing, 54*(10), 3947–3956. doi:10.1109/TSP.2006.880237

Chiba, K., & Hiraishi, K. (1998). Iterated continuous prisoner's dilemma game and its usefulness in analyzing multi-agent systems. In *Proceedings of the IEEE International Conference on System, Man and Cybernetics* (pp. 644-649).

Chin, C., & Barreto, A. (2006a). Electromyograms as physiological inputs that provide efficient computer cursor control. In *Proceedings of the WSEAS International Conference on Mathematical Biology and Ecology*, Miami, FL.

Chin, C., & Barreto, A. (2006b). Performance comparison of electromyogram-based computer cursor control systems. *WSEAS Transactions on Biology and Biomedicine*, *3*, 118.

Chinese Ministry of Public Security (CMPS). (2009). *2008 fire statistics in China.* Retrieved from http://www.mps.gov.cn/n16/n1282/n3553/1778249.html

Choi, S. H., & Lee, M. (2006). Brain computer interface using EEG sensors based on an fMRI experiment. In *Proceedings of the International Joint Conference on Neural Networks* (pp. 4656-4663).

Cho, J., Shim, Y., Kwon, T., & Choi, Y. (2007). SARIF: A novel framework for integrating wireless sensor and RFID networks. *IEEE Wireless Communications*, *14*(6), 50–56. doi:10.1109/MWC.2007.4407227

Chu, Y., Feigenbaum, J., LaMacchia, B., Resnick, P., & Strauss, M. (1997). REFEREE: Trust management for web applications. *World Wide Web Journal*, *2*, 706–734.

Clarke, D., Elien, J., Ellison, C., Fredette, M., Morcos, A., & Rivest, R. L. (2001). Certificate chain discovery in SPKI/SDSI. *Journal of Computer Security*, *9*(4), 285–322.

Clarke, E. M., Grumberg, O., & Peled, D. A. (1999). *Model checking*. Cambridge, MA: MIT Press.

Cohen, P. (1992). The role of Natural Language in a Multimodal Interface. In *Proceedings of the 5th Annual Symposium on user interface software and technology*, Montreau, CA (pp. 143-149). New York: ACM.

Cook, D., Augusto, J., & Jakkula, V. (2009). Ambient intelligence: Technologies, applications, and opportunities. *Pervasive and Mobile Computing*, *5*(4), 277–298. doi:10.1016/j.pmcj.2009.04.001

Corchado, J. M., Bajo, J., Paz, Y. D., & Tapia, D. I. (2008). Intelligent environment for monitoring Alzheimer patients, agent technology for health care. *Decision Support Systems*, *44*(2), 382–396. doi:10.1016/j.dss.2007.04.008

Coronato, A., & Esposito, M. (2008). Towards an implementation of smart hospital: A localization system for mobile users and devices. In *Proceedings of the Sixth Annual International Conference on Pervasive Computing and Communications* (pp. 715-719).

Coronato, A., & De Pietro, G. (2010). Formal design of ambient intelligence applications. *IEEE Computer*, *43*, 60–68.

Courtney, K. L., Demiris, G., Rantz, M., & Skubic, M. (2008). Needing smart home technologies: the perspectives of older adults in continuing care retirement communities. *Informatics in Primary Care*, *16*(3), 195–201.

Cowper, T., & Buerger, M. (2003). Improving our view of the world: Police and augmented reality technology. *FBI Law Enforcement Bulletin*, *77*(5).

Craik, F. I. M. (2000). Age-related changes in human memory. In Park, D. C., & Schwartz, N. (Eds.), *Cognitive aging* (pp. 75–92). Philadelphia: Psychology Press.

Crutzen, C. K. M. (2006). Invisibility and the meaning of ambient intelligence. *International Review of Information Ethics*, *6*(12), 52–62.

Cuomo, F., Luna, S. D., Monaco, U., & Melodia, T. (2007). Routing in ZigBee: Benefits from exploiting the IEEE 802.15.4 association tree. In *Proceedings of the IEEE International Conference on Communications* (pp. 3271-3276).

Curran, K. (2004). Tips for achieving high positioning in the results pages of the major search engines. *Information Technology Journal*, *3*(2), 202–205. doi:10.3923/itj.2004.202.205

Curran, K. (2009). Ambient intelligence - the link between the sciences - paving the way where no recommender system has gone before. *International Journal of Ambient Computing and Intelligence*, *1*(4), 1–2.

Dean, K. (2004, November). *A kinder, gentler copyright bill?* Retrieved from http://www.wired.com/politics/law/news/2004/11/65796

Denef, S. (2009). Human-computer interaction techniques in firefighting. In *Proceedings of the 12th IFIP TC 13 International Conference on Human-Computer Interaction: Part II* (p. 867).

Denef, S., Ramirez, L., & Dyrks, T. (2009). Letting tools talk: Interactive technology for firefighting. In *Proceedings of the 27ᵗʰ International Conference on Human Factors in Computing Systems* (pp. 4447-4452).

Dewsbury, G., Clarke, K., Rouncefield, M., Sommerville, I., Taylor, B., & Edge, M. (2003). Designing acceptable 'smart' home technology to support people in the home. *Technology and Disability, 15*(3), 191–199.

Dey, A. K., Abowd, G. D., & Salber, D. (2001). A conceptual framework and a toolkit for supporting the rapid prototyping of context-aware applications. *Human-Computer Interaction, 16*(2), 97–166. doi:10.1207/S15327051HCI16234_02

Di Giacomo, V., Felici, M., Meduri, V., Presenza, D., Riccucci, C., & Tedeschi, A. (2008). Using security and dependability patterns for reaction processes. In *Proceedings of the 19th International Conference on Database and Expert Systems Application* (pp. 315-319).

Drewes, H., & Schmidt, A. (2007). Interacting with the computer using gaze gestures. In C. Baranauskas, P. Palanque, J. Abascal, & S. DinizJunqueira Barbosa (Eds.), *Proceedings of the 11th IFIP TC13 International Conference on Human-Computer Interaction*, Rio de Janeiro, Brazil (LNCS 4663, pp. 475-488).

Drewes, H., Atterer, R., & Schmidt, A. (2007). Detailed monitoring of user's gaze and interaction to improve future e-learning. In *Proceedings of the 4th International Conference on Universal Access in Human-Computer Interaction: Ambient Interaction* (pp. 802-811).

Duman, H., Hagras, H., & Callaghan, V. (2010). A multi-society-based intelligent association discovery and selection for ambient intelligence environment. *ACM Transactions on Autonomous and Adaptive Systems, 5*(2).

Dunkels, A., Gr̈onvall, B., & Voigt, T. (2004). *Contiki - a Lightweight and Flexible Operating System for Tiny Networked Sensors.*

Eclipse Foundation. (2011). *Explore the Eclipse universe.* Retrieved from http://www.eclipse.org/

Elien, J. (1998). *Certificate Discovery Using SPKI/SDSI 2.0 Certificates.* Unpublished master's thesis, Massachusetts Institute of Technology, Cambridge, MA. Retrieved from http://groups.csail.mit.edu/cis/theses/elien-masters.pdf

Ellison, C., Frantz, B., Lampson, B., Rivest, R., Thomas, B., & Ylonen, T. (1999). *Simple Public Key Certificate.* Retrieved from http://world.std.com/~cme/spki.txt

Ember Corporation. (n.d.). *Designing with an inverted-F PCB antenna.* Retrieved from http://www.ember.com/pdf/120-5052-000_Designing_with_a_PCB_Antenna.pdf

Engelbart, D. C. (1968). *The demo.* Retrieved from http://sloan.stanford.edu/MouseSite/1968Demo.html

Engelbart, D. C. (1970). *U. S. Patent 3541541: X-Y position indicator for a display system.* Washington, DC: U. S. Patent and Trademark Office.

Erman, D. (2005). *BitTorrent traffic measurements and models.* Unpublished licentiate thesis, Blekinge Institute of Technology, Hogskola, Sweden.

Evans, M. P. (2007). Analyzing Google rankings through search engine optimization data. *Internet Research, 17*(1), 21–37. doi:10.1108/10662240710730470

Extensible Messaging and Presence Protocol (XMPP). (n.d.). Retrieved from http://xmpp.org/

Facal, D., González, M. F., Martínez, V., Buiza, C., Talantzis, F., Petsatodis, T., et al. (2009). *Cognitive games for healthy elderly people in a multitouch screen.* Paper presented at DRT4ALL2009 Conference, Barcelona, Spain.

Facal, D., González, M. F., Buiza, C., Laskibar, I., Urdaneta, E., & Yanguas, J. J. (2009). Envejecimiento, deterioro cognitivo y lenguaje: Resultados del Estudio Longitudinal Donostia [Aging, cognitive impairment and language. Results from the Donostia Longitudinal Study]. *Revista de Logopedia, Foniatría y Audiología, 29*(1), 4–12.

Felzer, T., & Nordmann, R. (2008). Evaluating the hands-free mouse control system: An initial case study. In K. Miesenberger, J. Klaus, W. Zagler, & A. Karshmer (Eds.), *Proceedings of 11th International Conference of Computers Helping People with Special Needs*, Linz, Austria (LNCS 5105 pp. 1188-1195).

Ferencz, D. C., Zhenxing, J., & Chizeck, H. J. (1993). Estimation of center-of-pressure during gait using an instrumented ankle-foot orthosis. In *Proceedings of the 15ᵗʰ Annual International Conference on Engineering in Medicine and Biology Society* (pp. 981-982).

Fernández, C., Lázaro, J. P., & Benedí, J. M. (2009). Workflow Mining Application to Ambient Intelligence Behavior Modeling. In *Proceedings of Universal Access in HCI, Part II (HCII 2009)* (LNCS 5615, pp. 160-167).

Fernández, C., Mocholí, J. B., Moyano, A., & Meneu, T. (2010). *Semantic Process Choreography for Distributed Sensor Management.* Paper presented at the International Workshop on Semantic Sensor Web (SSW 2010).

Fernández-Ballesteros, R. (2003). Una perspectiva psico-social: Promoción del envejecimiento activo. [A psycho-social perspective: Promotion of active aging] In Salvador, L. A., Cabo, J. R., & Alonso, F. (Eds.), *Longevidad y vida saludable* [Longevity and healthy life]. Madrid, Spain: AECES.

Fernández-Ballesteros, R., Zamarrón, M. D., & Tárraga, L. (2005). Learning potential: a new method for assessing cognitive impairment. *International Psychogeriatrics, 17,* 119–128. doi:10.1017/S1041610205000992

Ferscha, A., & Zia, K. (2009). LifeBelt: Silent directional guidance for crowd evacuation. In *Proceedings of the 13ᵗʰ International Symposium on Wearable Computers* (pp. 19-26).

Fischer, C., & Gellersen, H. (2010). Location and navigation support for emergency responders: A survey. *International Journal of IEEE Pervasive Computing,* 38-47.

Fitts, P. M. (1992). The information capacity of the human motor system in controlling the amplitude of movement. *Journal of Experimental Psychology. General, 121*(3), 262–269. doi:10.1037/0096-3445.121.3.262

Fitts, P. M., & Peterson, J. R. (1964). Information capacity of discrete motor responses. *Journal of Experimental Psychology, 67*(2), 102–113. doi:10.1037/h0045689

Franco, F. D., Tachtatzis, C., Graham, B., Bykowski, M., Tracey, D. C., Timmons, N. F., & Morrision, J. (2010). Current Characterisation for Ultra Low Power Wireless Body Area Networks. In *Proceedings of the 8th IEEE Workshop on Intelligent Solutions in Embedded Systems (WISES 2010),* Heraklion, Crete, Greece.

Franke, A. (2008). *Arbeitsmarktkompetenzen im sozialen Wandel. In Kompetenz-Bildung: Soziale, emotionale und kommunikative Kompetenzen von Kindern und Jugendlichen* (pp. 169-190). Wiesbaden, Germany: VS Verlag für Sozialwissenschaften / GWV Fachverlage GmbH.

Frisardia, V., & Imbimbob, B. P. (2011). Gerontechnology for demented patients: Smart homes for smart aging. *Journal of Alzheimer's Disease, 23*(1), 143–146.

Frund, J., Gausemeier, J., Matysczok, C., & Radkowski, R. (2004, May 26-28). Cooperative design support within automobile advance development using augmented reality technology. In *Proceedings of the 8th International Conference on Computer Supported Cooperative Work in Design* (Vol. 2, pp. 492–497).

Frydenberg, M., & Miko, J. (2011). Taking it to the top: A lesson in search engine optimization. *Information Systems Education Journal, 9*(1), 24–40.

Gajos, K. Z., & Weld, D. S. (2004). Supple: Automatically generating user interfaces. In *Proceedings of the 9th International Conference on Intelligent User Interfaces* (pp. 93-100). New York, NY: ACM Press.

Gajos, K. Z., Weld, D. S., & Wobbrock, J. O. (2010). Automatically generating personalized user interfaces with supple. *Artificial Intelligence, 174*(12-13), 910–950. doi:10.1016/j.artint.2010.05.005

Gamma, E., Helm, R., Johnson, R., & Vlissides, J. M. (1994). *Design patterns: Elements of reusable object-oriented software.* Reading, MA: Addison-Wesley.

Gao, T., Pesto, C., Selavo, L., Chen, Y., Ko, J.-G., Lim, J.-H., et al. (2008). Wireless medical sensor networks in emergency response: Implementation and pilot results. In Proceedings of the IEEE International Conference on Technologies for Homeland Security, Waltham, MA (pp. 187-192).

Georgalis, Y., Grammenos, D., & Stephanidis, C. (2009). Middleware for ambient intelligence environments: Reviewing requirements and communication technologies. In C. Stephanidis (Ed.), *Proceedings of the 5th International on Conference on Universal Access in Human-Computer Interaction. Part II: Intelligent and Ubiquitous Interaction Environments* (LNCS 5615, pp. 168-177).

Giunchiglia, F., & Serafini, L. (1994). Multilanguage hierarchical logics, or: how we can do without modal logics. *Artificial Intelligence, 65*(1). doi:10.1016/0004-3702(94)90037-X

Goldsmith, A. (2006). *Wireless communications.* Cambridge, UK: Cambridge University Press.

Gomez, D. (1997). *A dexterous hand master with force feedback for virtual reality.* Unpublished doctoral dissertation, Rutgers University, Rutgers, NJ.

Governatori, G., Maher, M. J., Billington, D., & Antoniou, G. (2004). Argumentation Semantics for Defeasible Logics. *Journal of Logic and Computation, 14*(5), 675–702. doi:10.1093/logcom/14.5.675

Grau, J. W., Barstow, D. G., & Joynes, R. L. (1998). Instrumental learning within the spinal cord: I. Behavioral properties. *Behavioral Neuroscience, 112*, 1366–1386. doi:10.1037/0735-7044.112.6.1366

Greenfield, A. (2006). *Everyware – the dawning age of ubiquitous computing.* Indianapolis, IN: New Riders.

Grenier, C. (2004). *HoneyNet scan of the month 31: Solution.* Retrieved from http://old.honeynet.org/scans/scan31/sub/grenier/attacks.html

Gronlund, S. D., Carlson, C. A., & Tower, D. (2007). Episodic memory. In Durso, F. (Ed.), *Handbook of applied cognition* (2nd ed.). New York: John Wiley & Sons. doi:10.1002/9780470713181.ch5

Guttman, E., Perkins, C., Veizades, J., & Day, M. (1999). *Service Location Protocol RFC 2608.*

H.323 v7. (2009). *ITU-T Recommendation Packet Based multimedia Communication systems.*

Hall, R., & Cervantes, H. (2004). An osgi implementation and experience report. In *Proceedings of the Consumer Communications and Networking Conference* (pp.394-399).

Handley, M., & Jacobson, V. (1998). *SDP: Session Description Protocol RFC 2327.*

Handley, M., Schulzrinne, H., & Schooler, E. (2002). *SIP: Session Initiation Protocol RFC3261.*

Hannaway, A., & Kechadi, M.-T. (2009). An analysis of the scale and distribution of copyrighted material on the Gnutella network. In *Proceedings of the International Conference on Information Security and Privacy*, Orlando, FL.

Hanus, R., Kinnaert, M., & Henrotte, J. (1987). Conditioning technique a general anti-windup and bumpless transfer method. *Automatica, 23*, 729–739. doi:10.1016/0005-1098(87)90029-X

Harrison, C., & Dey, A. K. (2008). Lean and zoom: proximity-aware user interface and content magnification. In *Proceeding of the Twenty-Sixth Annual SIGCHI Conference on Human Factors in Computing Systems* (pp. 507-510). New York, NY: ACM Press.

Haung, C.-M., Lin, C.-W., & Yang, C.-C. (2010). *Mobility Management for Video Streaming on Heterogeneous Networks.* Washington, DC: IEEE Computer Society. ITU-T Study Group 16. (n.d.a). *AMS Third generation of ITU-T Multimedia Systems and Terminals.* Retrieved from http://www.itu.int/ITU-T/studygroups/com16/ams/index.html

Helbing, D., Farkas, I., & Vicsek, T. (2000). Simulating dynamical features of escape panic. *International Journal of Letters to Nature, 407*(6803), 487–490. doi:10.1038/35035023

Helbing, D., & Johansson, A., & AI-Abideen, H. (2007). Dynamics of crowd disasters: An empirical study. *International Journal of Physical Review, 75*, 1–7.

Henn, H. (2008). Web4me – User Centric Infrastructure for Ambient Assisted Living. In *Proceedings AAL Kongress* (pp. 27-31). Berlin: VDE Verlag. ISBN 978-3-8007-3076-6

Henricksen, K., & Indulska, J. (2004). Modelling and Using Imperfect Context Information. In *Proceedings of the PERCOMW 2004 Conference* (pp. 33-37). Washington, DC: IEEE Computer Society.

Herold, R., Vogel, U., Richter, B., Kreye, D., Reckziegel, S., Scholles, M., et al. (2009, June 20-22). OLED-on-CMOS integration for augmented-reality systems. In *Proceedings of the International Students and Young Scientists Workshop on Photonics and Microsystems* (pp. 19-22).

Herrmann, G., Turner, M., & Postlethwaite, I. (2006). Discrete-time and sampled-data anti-windup synthesis: stability and performance. *International Journal of Systems Science, 37*(2), 91–114. doi:10.1080/00207720500444074

Herrmann, G., Turner, M., Postlethwaite, I., & Guo, G. (2004). Practical implementation of a novel anti-windup scheme in a HDD-dual-stage servo-system. *IEEE/ASME Transactions on Mechatronics, 9*(3). doi:10.1109/TMECH.2004.835333

Hickey, M. (2010). *Virtual mirror – tells you how to look better.* Retrieved from http://news.cnet.com/8301-17938_105-20015260-1.html

Hirschheim, R., & Klein, H. (1989). Four paradigms of information systems development. *Communications of the ACM, 32*(10), 1199–1216. doi:10.1145/67933.67937

Holden, W. (2011). *Mobile augmented reality: Forecasts, applications & opportunity appraisal.* Retrieved from http://www.juniperresearch.com/shop/viewreport.php?id=197

Holleis, P., Kranz, M., Winter, A., & Schmidt, A. (2006). Playing with the real world. *Journal of Virtual Reality and Broadcasting, 3*(1).

Höllerer, T., & Feiner, S. (2004). Mobile augmented reality. In Karimi, H. A., & Hammad, A. (Eds.), *Telegeoinformatics: Location-based computing and services*. Boca Raton, FL: Taylor & Francis.

HoneyNet. (2004). *Scan 31.* Retrieved from http://old.honeynet.org/scans/scan31/

Hong, X., & Nugent, C. (2011). Implementing evidential activity recognition in sensorised homes. *Technology and Health Care, 19*(1), 37–52.

Horowitz, I. (2001). Survey of quantitative feedback theory (QFT). *International Journal of Robust Nonlinear Control, 11*, 887–921. doi:10.1002/rnc.637

Houle, K. J., & Weaver, G. M. (2001). *Trends in denial of service attack technology.* Pittsburgh, PA: CERT® Coordination Centre.

Huang, Y., & Pang, A. (2007). A comprehensive study of low-power operation in IEEE 802.15.4. In *Proceedings of the 10th ACM Symposium on Modeling, analysis, and Simulation of Wireless and Mobile Systems*, Chania, Crete Island, Greece (pp. 405-408).

Humphries, M. (2010). *GM experimenting with augmented reality in cars.* Retrieved from http://www.geek.com/articles/news/gm-experimenting-with-augmented-reality-in-cars-20100318/

IEEE. Computer Society. (2006). *IEEE Std 802.15.4: Wireless lan medium access control (mac) and physical layer (phy) specifications for low-rate wireless personal area networks (lr-wpans).* Washington, DC: IEEE Computer Society.

Ilyas, M., & Dorf, R. C. (Eds.). (2003). *The handbook of ad hoc wireless networks*. Boca Raton, FL: CRC Press.

International Federation of the Phonographic Industry. (2011). *Digital music report 2011.* Retrieved from http://www.ifpi.org/content/section_resources/dmr2011.html

International Telecommunication Union (ITU). (2005). *ITU Internet Reports 2005: The Internet of Things.* Geneva, Switzerland: Author.

International Telecommunication Union. (2010). *Report on Internet.* Retrieved from http://www.itu.int

ISB. (2000). *Copyright and related rights act.* Retrieved from http://www.irishstatutebook.ie/2000/en/act/pub/0028/index.html

ITU-T Study Group 16. (2008). *Advanced Multimedia System (AMS) – AMS Project Description.* Retrieved from http://www.packetizer.com/ipmc/h325/doc_status.html

ITU-T Study Group 16. (n.d.b). *AMS Architecture.* Retrieved from http://wftp3.itu.int/av-arch/avc-site/2009-2012/AMS_emeetings/AMS-0020.zip

ITU-T Study Group 16. (n.d.c). *Advanced Multimedia System (AMS) – AMS Applications, Application Capabilities, and Capability Advertisement.* Retrieved from http://wftp3.itu.int/av-arch/avc-site/2009-2012/AMS_emeetings/AMS-0015a.zip

ITU-T Study Group 16. (n.d.d). *Advanced Multimedia System (AMS) – System Architecture.* Retrieved from http://www.packetizer.com/ipmc/h325/doc_status.html

ITU-T Study Group 16. (n.d.e). *Advanced Multimedia System (AMS) – Service Node Architecture.* Retrieved from http://www.packetizer.com/ipmc/h325/doc_status.html

ITU-T Study Group 16. (n.d.f). *Advanced Multimedia System (AMS)* (2009) - *H.325 Overview.* Retrieved from http://www.packetizer.com/ipmc/h325/papers

Jacob, R. (1990). What you look at is what you get: Eye movement-based interaction techniques. In *Proceedings of the SIGCHI Conference on Human Factors in Computing Systems* (pp. 11-18). New York, NY: ACM Press.

Jajodia, S., Samarati, P., & Subrahmanian, V. S. (1997). A logical language for expressing authorizations. In *Proceedings of the 1997 IEEE Symposium on Security and Privacy* (pp. 31-42). Washington, DC: IEEE Computer Society.

Jajodia, S., Samarati, P., Subrahmanian, V. S., & Bertino, E. (1997). A unified framework for enforcing multiple access control policies. In *Proceedings of the ACM SIGMOD International Conference on Management of Data* (pp. 474-485).

Jajodia, S., Samarati, P., & Subrahmanian, V. S. (2001). Flexible Support for Multiple Access Control Policies. *ACM Transactions on Database Systems, 26*(2), 214–260. doi:10.1145/383891.383894

Jang, W. S., & Healy, W. M. (2009). Wireless sensor network performance metrics for building applications. *Energy and Buildings Journal*, 862-868.

Jayaputera, G. T., Zaslavsky, A., & Loke, S. W. (2007). Enabling run-time composition and support for heterogeneous pervasive multi-agent systems. *Journal of Systems and Software, 80*(12), 2039–2062. doi:10.1016/j.jss.2007.03.013

Jezernik, S., Scharer, R., Colombo, G., & Morari, M. (2003). Adaptive robotic rehabilitation of locomotion: A clinical study in spinally injured individuals. *Spinal Cord, 41*, 657–666. doi:10.1038/sj.sc.3101518

Jiang, X., Chen, N., Hong, J., Wang, K., Takayama, L., & Landay, J. (2004). Siren: Context-aware computing for firefighting. In *Proceedings of the 2nd International Conference on Pervasive Computing* (pp. 87-105).

JISC. (2009). *Tangible benefits of e-learning*. Retrieved from http://www.jiscinfonet.ac.uk/case-studies/tangible

Johannsen, G. (1993). *Mensch-Maschine-Systeme*. Berlin: Springer Verlag.

Johnson, W. L., & Rickel, J. (1997). Steve: an animated pedagogical agent for procedural training in virtual environments. *SIGART Bulletin, December, 8*(1-4), 16-21.

Jones, E. P. (2007). Rapporteur ITU-T Q12/16. *A Concept for the Advanced Multimedia System*. Retrieved from http://www.packetizer.com/ipmc/h325/papers/

Jones, K. B. (2008). *Search engine optimization*. Indianapolis, IN: Wiley.

Jones, Q., Grandhi, S., Terveen, L., & Whittaker, S. (2005). People-to-people-to-geographical places: The P3 framework for location-based community systems. *Computer Supported Cooperative Work, 13*, 249–282. doi:10.1007/s10606-004-2803-7

Juncos-Rabadán, O., Facal, D., Rodríguez, M. S., & Pereiro, A. X. (in press). Lexical knowledge and lexical retrieval in ageing: Insights from a tip-of-the-tongue (TOT) study. *Language and Cognitive Processes*.

Kang, H. G., Mahoney, D. F., Hoenig, H., Hirth, V. A., Bonato, P., Hajjar, I., & Lipsitz, L. A. (2010). In situ monitoring of health in older adults: Technologies and issues. *Journal of the American Geriatrics Society, 58*(8), 1579–1586. doi:10.1111/j.1532-5415.2010.02959.x

Katsarakis, N., & Pnevmatikakis, A. (2009). *Face Validation Using 3D Information from Single Calibrated Camera*. Paper presented at DSP 2009, Santorini, Greece.

Kempermann, G., Gast, D., & Gage, F. H. (2002). Neuroplasticity in Old Age: Sustained Fivefold Induction of Hippocampal Neurogenesis by Long-term Environmental Enrichment. *Annals of Neurology, 52*(2), 135–143. doi:10.1002/ana.10262

Killijian, M., Powell, D., Banâtre, M., Couderc, P., & Roudier, Y. (2004). Collaborative backup for dependable mobile applications. In *Proceedings of the 2nd Workshop on Middleware for Pervasive and Ad-Hoc Computing*.

Kim, H., & Lee, H. (2009). *Accelerated Three Dimensional Ray Tracing Techniques using Ray Frustums for Wireless Propagation Models*. Seoul, South Korea: Sogang Unversity.

King, R. (2009). *Augmented reality goes mobile*. Retrieved from http://www.businessweek.com/technology/content/nov2009/tc2009112_434755.htm

Klann, M. (2007). Playing with fire: User-centered design of wearable computing for emergency response. In *Proceedings of the International Conference on Mobile Response* (pp. 116-125).

Klann, M. (2009). Tactical navigation support for firefighters: The LifeNet ad-hoc sensor-network and wearable system. In *Proceedings of the International Conference on Mobile Response* (pp. 41-56).

Klein, G., & Murray, D. (2009). Parallel tracking and mapping on a camera phone. In *Proceedings of the 8th IEEE International Symposium on Mixed and Augmented Reality* (pp. 830-86).

Knezik, J., & Drahansky, M. (2007). Simple EEG driven mouse cursor movement. *Advances in Soft Computing, 45*, 526–531. doi:10.1007/978-3-540-75175-5_66

Korba, J. (2000). *Windows NT attacks for the evaluation of intrusion detection systems.* Unpublished master's thesis, Massachusetts Institute of Technology, Cambridge, MA.

Küsters, I. (2009). *Narrative Interviews. Grundlagen und Anwendungen. Wiesbaden 2009 Lehrbuch Studientexte zur Soziologie.* Germany: VS Verlag.

Kutcher, O. B. (2005). *Session Description and Capability Negotiation.*

KZero Services. (2010). *Consulting and analytics, augmented reality brand tracking.* Retrieved from http://www.kzero.co.uk/

Landgren, J., & Nulden, U. (2007). A study of emergency response work: Patterns of mobile phone interaction. In *Proceedings of the International Conference on Human Factors in Computing Systems* (pp. 1323-1332).

Lee, T. (2006). *Circumventing competition: The perverse consequences of the digital millennium copyright act: Policy analysis, no. 564.* Washington, DC: Cato Institute.

Leguay, J., Lopez-Ramos, M., Jean-Marie, K., & Conan, V. (2008). An efficient service oriented architecture for heterogeneous and dynamic wireless sensor networks. In *Proceedings of the 33rd IEEE Conference on Local Computer Networks* (pp. 740-747).

Leonardi, P. M., & Barley, S. R. (2008). Materiality and change: Challenges to building better theory about technology and organizing. *Information and Organization, 18*, 159–176. doi:10.1016/j.infoandorg.2008.03.001

Lester, J. C., Converse, S. A., Kahler, S. E., Todd Barlow, S., Stone, B. A., & Bhogal, R. S. (1997). The Persona Effect: Affective Impact of Animated Pedagogical Agents. In *Proceedings of the SIGCHI conference on Human factors in computing systems,* Atlanta (pp. 359-366). New York: ACM.

Letts, Q. (2011, May 24). *Good man John Hemming brought an end to the farce.* Retrieved from http://www.dailymail.co.uk/debate/article-1390215/Ryan-Giggs-super-injunction-John-Hemming-brought-end-farce.html#ixzz1O24eCqmw

Leucker, M., & Schallhart, C. (2009). A brief account of runtime verification. *Journal of Logic and Algebraic Programming, 78*(5), 293–303. doi:10.1016/j.jlap.2008.08.004

Levis, P., Madden, S., Polastre, J., Szewczyk, R., Whitehouse, K., & Woo, A. (2005). In Weber, W., Rabaey, J. M., & Aarts, E. (Eds.), *TinyOS: An Operating System for Sensor Networks in Ambient Intelligence* (pp. 115–148). Berlin: Springer Verlag.

Li, N., Grosof, B. N., & Feigenbaum, J. (2000). *A nonmonotonic delegation logic with prioritized conflict handling.* Unpublished manuscript.

Li, N., Mitchell, J. C., & Winsborough, W. H. (2002). Design of a role-based trust management framework. In *Proceedings of the 2002 IEEE Symposium on Security and Privacy* (pp. 114-130). Washington, DC: IEEE Computer Society.

Li, Q., De Rosa, M., & Rus, D. (2003). Distributed algorithms for guiding navigation across a sensor network. In *Proceedings of the 9th International Conference on Mobile Computing and Networking* (pp. 313-325).

Li, N., Grosof, B. N., & Feigenbaum, J. (2003). Delegation Logic: A logic-based approach to distributed authorization. *ACM Transactions on Information and System Security, 6*(1), 128–171. doi:10.1145/605434.605438

Lindwer, M., Marculescu, D., Basten, T., Zimmennann, R., Marculescu, R., Jung, S., & Cantatore, E. (2003). Ambient intelligence visions and achievements: Linking abstract ideas to real-world concepts. In *Proceedings of the Design, Automation and Test in Europe Conference and Exhibition* (pp. 10-15).

Liu, D. (2009). *Shanghai business college dormitory fire: Four students dead.* Retrieved from http://news.xinhuanet.com/newscenter/2008-11/14/content 10357255 1.htm

Liu, P., Hu, J., & Chen, Z. (2005). A Formal Language for Access Control Policies in Distributed Environment. In *Proceedings of the 2005 IEEE WIC ACM International Conference on Web Intelligence (WI05)* (pp. 766-769).

Lorenz, A., & Oppermann, R. (2009). Mobile health monitoring for the elderly: Designing for diversity. *Pervasive and Mobile Computing, 5*(5), 478–495. doi:10.1016/j.pmcj.2008.09.010

Luca, A. D., Weiss, R., & Drewes, H. (2007). Evaluation of eye-gaze interaction methods for security enhanced PIN-entry. In *Proceedings of the Australian Computer-Human Interaction Conference*, Adelaide, Australia (pp. 199-202). New York, NY: ACM Press.

Luyten, K., Winters, F., Coninx, K., Naudts, D., & Moerman, I. (2006). A situation-aware mobile system to support fire brigades in emergency situations. In R. Meersman, Z. Tari, & P. Herrero (Eds.), *Proceedings of the On the Move Workshops* (LNCS 4278, pp. 1966-1975).

Lyytinen, K., & Yoo, Y. (2002). Introduction. *Communications of the ACM*, *45*(12), 62–65. doi:10.1145/585597.585616

Macal, C. M., & North, M. J. (2010). Tutorial on agent-based modelling and simulation. *Journal of Simulation*, *4*, 151–162. doi:10.1057/jos.2010.3

MacKenzie, S., Kauppinen, T., & Silfverberg, M. (2001). Accuracy measures for evaluating computer pointing devices. In *Proceedings of the CHI Conference on Human Factors in Computing Systems* (pp. 9-16). New York, NY: ACM Press.

Macy, M. W., & Willer, R. (2002). From factors to actors: Computational sociology and agent-based modeling. *Annual Review of Sociology*, *28*, 143–166. doi:10.1146/annurev.soc.28.110601.141117

Maher, M. J. (2002). A Model-Theoretic Semantics for Defeasible Logic. In *Proceedings of the Workshop on Paraconsistent Computational Logic* (pp. 67-80).

Mahoney, D. F., Mahoney, E. L., & Liss, E. (2009). AT EASE: Automated technology for elder assessment, safety, and environmental monitoring. *Gerontechnology (Valkenswaard)*, *8*(1), 11–25. doi:10.4017/gt.2009.08.01.003.00

Malaga, R. A. (2007). The value of search engine optimization: An action research project at a new e-commerce site. *Journal of Electronic Commerce in Organizations*, *5*(3), 68–82. doi:10.4018/jeco.2007070105

Malaga, R. A. (2010). Search engine optimization - black and white hat approaches. *Advances in Computers*, *78*, 2–41. doi:10.1016/S0065-2458(10)78001-3

Malatras, A., Asgari, A., Baugé, T., & Irons, M. (2008). A service-oriented architecture for building services integration. *Journal of Facilities Management*, *6*(2), 132–151. doi:10.1108/14725960810872659

Mana, A., Rudolph, C., Spanoudakis, G., Lotz, V., Massacci, F., Malideo, M., & Lopez-Cobo, J. S. (2007). Security engineering for ambient intelligence: A manifesto. In Mouratidis, H., & Giorgini, P. (Eds.), *Integrating security and software engineering: Advances and future visions* (pp. 244–270). Hershey, PA: IGI Global.

Margolis, L., & Robinson, A. (2007). *Living systems – Innovative materials for architecture and design*. Boston, MA: Birkhäuser.

Marin-Perianu, M., Meratnia, N., Havinga, P., de Souza, L., Muller, J., & Spiess, P. (2007). Decentralized enterprise systems: A multiplatform wireless sensor network approach. *IEEE Wireless Communications*, *14*(6), 57–66. doi:10.1109/MWC.2007.4407228

Martin, M., & Schumann-Hengsteler, R. (2001). How task demands influence time-based prospective memory performance in young and older adults. *International Journal of Behavioral Development*, *25*(4), 386–391. doi:10.1080/01650250042000302

Masri, T., Chew, S. P., Wong, C. P., & Lias, K. (2005). *A Study of Signal Penetration into Building Materials*. Sarawak, Malaysia: University Malaysia Sarawak.

Mataric, M. (1993). Designing emergent behaviors: From local interactions to collective intelligence. In *Proceedings of the 2nd International Conference on Simulation of Adaptive Behavior* (pp. 1-10).

Mather, T., Kumaraswamy, S., & Latif, S. (2009). *Cloud Security and Privacy*. New York: O'Reilly.

Matthias, K., Jäger, T., & Philips, L. H. (2008). Adult age differences in event-based prospective memory: A meta-analysis on the role of focal versus nonfocal cues. *Psychology and Aging*, *23*(1), 203–208. doi:10.1037/0882-7974.23.1.203

MaxMind. (2010). *GeoLite country database*. Retrieved from http://www.maxmind.com

Mayhorn, C. B., Rogers, W. A., & Fisk, A. D. (2004). Designing technology based on cognitive aging principles. In Burdick, D. C., & Kwon, S. (Eds.), *Gerotechnology: Research and practice in technology and aging* (pp. 42–53). New York: Springer Publising Company.

McCullough, M. (2004). *Digital ground: Architecture, pervasive computing, and environmental knowing, cloth.* Cambridge, MA: MIT Press.

McFarlane, A., Sparrowhawk, A., & Heald, Y. (2002). *Report on the educational use of games: An exploration by TEEM of the contribution which games can make to the education process.* Retrieved from http://www.teem. org.uk/publications/teem_gamesined_full.pdf

McFedries, P. (2008, August). The Cloud Is The Computer. *IEEE Spectrum.*

Meyer, R. (2008). *Detecting attacks on web applications from log files.* Bethesda, MD: SANS Institute.

Mikkilineni, R., & Sarathy, V. (2009). Cloud Computing and the Lessons from the Past. In *Proceedings of the 18th IEEE International Workshops on Enabling Technologies: Infrastructures for Collaborative Enterprises*, Groningen, The Netherlands.

Milgram, P., & Kishino, K. (1994). A taxonomy of mixed reality visual displays. *Transactions on Information and Systems, 77*(12).

Miller, L. (2006). *Indoor navigation for first responders: A feasibility study.* Washington, DC: US National Institute Standards and Technology.

Mistry, P., & Maes, P. (2009). *SixthSense: A wearable gestural interface.* Cambridge, MA: MIT Media Lab.

Mitchell, W. (2000). *City of bits – Space, place and the Infobahn.* Cambridge, MA: MIT Press.

Mohammadi, M. (2010). *Empowering seniors through domotic homes. Integrating intelligent technology in senior citizens homes by merging the perspectives of demand and supply.* Unpublished doctoral dissertation, Eindhoven University of Technology, Eindhoven, The Netherlands.

Moreno, R., & Mayer, R. (2007). Interactive Multimodal Learning Environments. *Educational Psychology Review, 19*, 309–326. doi:10.1007/s10648-007-9047-2

Moteiv Corporation. (n.d.). *Ultra low power IEEE 802.15.4 complaint wireless sensor module.* Retrieved from http://sentilla.com/files/pdf/eol/tmote-sky-datasheet.pdf

Muir, H., Bottomley, D., & Marrison, C. (1996). Effects of motivation and cabin configuration on emergency aircraft evacuation behavior and rates of egress. *The International Journal of Aviation Psychology, 6*(1), 57–77. doi:10.1207/s15327108ijap0601_4

Mukherjee, S., Aarts, E., Roovers, R., Widdershoven, F., & Ouwerkerk, M. (2006). *Amiware: Hardware technology drivers of ambient intelligence.* New York, NY: Springer. doi:10.1007/1-4020-4198-5

Müller, D., Bruns, W., Erbe, H., Robben, B., & Yoo, Y. (2007). Mixed reality learning spaces for collaborative experimentation: A challenge for engineering education and training. *International Journal of Online Engineering, 3*(1), 36–42.

Murphy, D. (2009, April 17). *The Pirate Bay founders sentenced to prison, website soldiers on.* Retrieved from http://www.engadget.com/2009/04/17/the-pirate-bay-founders-head-to-prison-website-soldiers-on/

Muto, T., Herzberger, B., Hermsdörfer, J., Miyake, Y., & Pöppel, E. (2007, October 29-November 2). Interactive gait training device 'walk-mate' for hemiparetic stroke rehabilitation. In *Proceedings of the IEEE/RSJ International Conference on Intelligent Robots and Systems*, San Diego, CA (pp. 2268-2274).

Nebusens. (2011). *n-Core: A faster and easier way to create wireless sensor networks.* Retrieved from http://www.n-core.info

Nehmer, J., Karshmer, A., Lamm, R., & Becker, M. (2006). Living assistance systems: An ambient intelligence approach. In *Proceedings of the 28th International Conference on Software Engineering* (pp. 43-50).

Neven, L. B. M. (2011). *Representations of the old and ageing in the design of the new and emerging. Assessing the design of ambient intelligence technologies for older people.* Unpublished doctoral dissertation, Twente University, Enschede, Eindhoven, The Netherlands.

NGSON Working Group of IEEE Standards Committee. (2008). *Draft White Paper for Next Generation Service Overlay Network.*

Nichols, J., Myers, B. A., Litwack, K., Higgins, M., Hughes, J., & Harris, T. K. (2004). Describing appliance user interfaces abstractly with xml. In *Proceedings of the Workshop on Developing User Interfaces with XML: Advances on User Interface Description Languages.*

Nichols, J., Rothrock, B., Chau, D. H., & Myers, B. A. (2006). Huddle: Automatically generating interfaces for systems of multiple connected appliances. In *Proceedings of the 19th Annual ACM Symposium on User Interface Software and Technology* (pp. 279-288). New York, NY: ACM Press.

Nichols, J., & Myers, B. A. (2009). Creating a lightweight user interface description language: An overview and analysis of the personal universal controller project. *ACM Transactions on Computer-Human Interaction, 16*(4), 1–37. doi:10.1145/1614390.1614392

Niemeyer, A. L., Frederiks, B. J. M., Riphagen, I. I., Legemaate, J., Eefsting, J. A., & Hertogh, C. M. P. M. (2010). Ethical and practical concerns of surveillance technologies in residential care for people with dementia or intellectual disabilities: an overview of the literature. *International Psychogeriatrics, 22*(7), 1129–1142. doi:10.1017/S1041610210000037

Nijhof, N., van Gemert-Pijnen, J. E. W. C., Dohmen, D. A. J., & Seydel, E. R. (2009). Dementie en technologie. Een studie naar de toepassingen van techniek in de zorg voor mensen met dementie en hun mantelzorgers. [in Dutch]. *Tijdschrift voor Gerontologie en Geriatrie, 40*(3), 113–132. doi:10.1007/BF03079573

Nilsson, H. (2009, October). *Sweden implements IP rights enforcement directive for copyright.* Retrieved from http://www.twobirds.com/English/News/Articles/Pages/Sweden_implements_IP_Rights_Enforcement_Directive_for_Copyright.Aspx

Nute, D. (1994). Defeasible logic. In *Handbook of Logic in Artificial Intelligence and Logic Programming* (*Vol. 3*, pp. 355–395). Oxford, UK: Oxford University Press.

O'Malley, C., Vavoula, G., Glew, J., Taylor, J., Sharples, M., & Lefrere, P. (2003). *MOBILearn WP4 – guidelines for Learning/Teaching/Tutoring in a Mobile Environment.* Retrieved from http://www.mobilearn.org/download/results/guidelines.pdf

Ofsted, (2009). *Virtual learning environments: an evaluation of their development in a sample of educational settings.* Retrieved from http://www.ofsted.gov.uk/Ofsted-home/Publications-and-research

Ohlman, B., Eriksson, A., & Rembarz, R. (2009). What Networking of Information Can Do for Cloud Computing. In *Proceedings of the 18th IEEE International Workshops on Enabling Technologies: Infrastructures for Collaborative Enterprises*, Groningen, The Netherlands.

Old, S. R., & Naveh-Benjamin, M. (2008). Differential effects of age on item and associative measures of memory: a meta-analysis. *Psychology and Aging, 23*(1), 104–118. doi:10.1037/0882-7974.23.1.104

Oppenauer, C. (2009). Motivation and needs for technology use in old age. *Gerontechnology (Valkenswaard), 8*(2), 82–87. doi:10.4017/gt.2009.08.02.006.00

Orlikowski, W. J. (2007). Sociomaterial practices: Exploring technology at work. *Organization Studies, 28*(9), 1435–1448. doi:10.1177/0170840607081138

Orlikowski, W. J., & Scott, S. V. (2008). Sociomateriality: Challenging the separation of technology, work and organization. *Academy of Management Annals, 2*(1), 433–474. doi:10.1080/19416520802211644

Ortiz, A., Carretero, M., Oyarzun, D., Yanguas, J., Buiza, C., Gonzalesm, M., & Etxeberria, I. (2007). Elderly Users in Ambient Intelligence: Does an avatar improve the interaction? In *Universal Access in Ambient Intelligence Environments* (LNCS 4397, pp. 99-114). Berlin: Springer.

O'Shaughnessy, S., & Gray, G. (2010). Development of a dataset generator for testing and evaluating knowledge discovery techniques and forensics or network security analysis tools. In *Proceedings of the 10th International Conference on Information Technology and Telecommunication.*

Park, K.-L., Yoon, U., & Kim, S.-D. (2009). Personalized service discovery in ubiquitous computing environments. *IEEE Pervasive Computing / IEEE Computer Society [and] IEEE Communications Society, 8*(1), 58–65. doi:10.1109/MPRV.2009.12

Payatagool, C. (2008). *War is Halo.* Retrieved from http://www.telepresenceoptions.com/2008/07/war_is_halo/

Peng, C.-J., Chen, M.-X., & Hwang, R.-H. (2008). SSIP: Split a SIP Session over Multiple Devices. *Computer Standards & Interfaces*, 29(5).

Peng, L., Wu, L., & Zeng, J. Z. (2008). Research on the service-oriented solution for integrating WSN with grid. *Journal of Computer Applications*, 28, 1861–1865. doi:10.3724/SP.J.1087.2008.01861

Peréz, J., Álvarez, J., Fernández-Montes, A., & Ortega, J. (2009). Service-oriented device integration for ubiquitous ambient assisted living environments. In J. A. Pérez, J. A. Álvarez, A. Fernández-Montes, & J. A.Ortega (Eds.), *Proceedings of the 10th International Work-Conference on Artificial Neural Networks: Part II: Distributed Computing, Artificial Intelligence, Bioinformatics, Soft Computing, and Ambient Assisted Living* (LNCS 5518, pp. 843-850).

Petsatodis, Th., & Boukis, C. (2009). *Efficient Voice Activity Detection in Reverberant Enclosures using Far Field Microphones.* Paper presented at IEEE DSP2009 Conference, Santorini, Greece.

Piekarska, P. (2006). *Tinmith AR system, research into mobile outdoor augmented reality.* Retrieved from http://www.tinmith.net/

Poland, M. P., Nugent, C. D., Wang, H., & Chen, L. (2009). Smart home research: Projects and issues. *International Journal of Ambient Computing and Intelligence*, 1(4), 32–45. doi:10.4018/jaci.2009062203

Porter, I. (2011). *10 statistics that demonstrate the value of SEO.* Retrieved from http://www.intraspin.com/news/10-statistics-that-demonstrate-the-value-of-seo/

Prinsloo, J. M., Schulz, C. L., Kourie, D. G., Theunissen, W. H. M., Strauss, T., Heever, R. V. D., et al. (2006). A service oriented architecture for wireless sensor and actor network applications. In *Proceedings of the Annual Research Conference of the South African Institute of Computer Scientists and Information Technologists on IT research in Developing Countries*, Somerset West, South Africa (pp. 145-154).

RapidMiner. (2010). *RapidMiner homepage.* Retrieved from http://rapid-i.com/content/view/181/190/

Read, J., & McFarlane, S. (2006). Using the Fun Toolkit and Other Survey Methods to Gather Opinions in Child Computer Interaction. In *Proceedings of the 2006 conference on interaction design and children*, Tampere, Finland (pp. 81-88). New York: ACM.

ReadWriteWeb. (2009). *Augmented reality: A human interface for ambient intelligence.* Retrieved from http://www.readwriteweb.com/archives/augmented_reality_human_interface_for_ambient_intelligence.php

Regenbrecht, H., Baratoff, G., & Wilke, W. (2005). Augmented reality projects in the automotive and aerospace industries. *IEEE Computer Graphics and Applications*, 25(6), 48–56. doi:10.1109/MCG.2005.124

Remagnino, P., & Foresti, G. L. (2005). Ambient Intelligence: A New Multidisciplinary Paradigm. *IEEE Transactions on Systems, Man, and Cybernetics*, 35(1), 1–6. doi:10.1109/TSMCA.2004.838456

Renaudin, V., Yalak, O., Tomé, P., & Merminod, B. (2007). Indoor navigation of emergency agents. *European Journal of Navigation*, 5, 36–45.

Rianovosti. (2006, June 16). *Moscow court gives lengthy jail terms to credit card fraud gang.* Retrieved from http://rianovosti.com/russia/20060616/49635773.html

Ritterfeld, U., Cody, M. J., & Vorderer, P. (2009). *Serious Games. Mechanisms and effects.* London, UK: Routledge.

Riva, G., Vatalaro, F., Davide, F., & Alcañiz, M. (2005). *Ambient Intelligence*. Amsterdam, The Netherlands: IOS Press.

Robles, E., & Wiberg, M. (2011). From materials to materiality. *Interactions (New York, N.Y.)*, 18(1). doi:10.1145/1897239.1897248

Rodden, T., & Benford, S. (2003, April 5-10). The evolution of buildings and implications for the design of ubiquitous domestic environments. In *Proceedings of the CHI Conference on Human Factors in Computing.*

Rosas, R., Nussbaum, M., Cumsille, P., Marianov, V., Correa, M., & Flores, P. (2003). Beyond Nintendo: design and assessment of educational video games for first and second grade students. *Computers & Education*, 40(1), 71–94. doi:10.1016/S0360-1315(02)00099-4

Rosenberg, J., & Schulzrinne, H. (2002). *An offer/Answer Model with the Session Description Protocol.*

Rosenberg, J., Peterson, J. L., Schulzrinne, H., & Camarillo, G. (2004). *Best Current Practices for Third Party Call Control (3pcc) in the Session Initiation Protocol.*

Rosu, G., & Havelund, K. (2005). Rewriting-based techniques for runtime verification. *Automated Software Engineering, 12,* 151–197. doi:10.1007/s10515-005-6205-y

RTE. (2008, April 21). *Eircom rejects record firms' claims.* Retrieved from http://www.rte.ie/business/2008/0421/eircom.html

Saffer, D. (2007). *Designing for interaction: Creating smart applications and clever devices.* Berkeley, CA: New Riders.

Salam, H., Rizvi, S., Ainsworth, S., & Olariu, S. (2008). A durable sensor enabled lifeline support for firefighters. In *Proceedings of the Computer Communications Workshop* (pp. 1-6).

Sánchez, M. (2007, September 19-21). *Buenas Prácticas en la Creación de Serious Games (Objetos de Aprendizaje Reutilizables).* Paper presented at the IV Simposio Pluridisciplinar sobre Diseño, Evaluación y Desarrollo de Contenidos Educativos Reutilizables (SPDECE 2007).

Sanders, J. (1999). The regulation of indecent material accessible to children on the Internet. *Catholic Law,* 125-129.

Sarangapani, J. (2007). *Wireless ad hoc and sensor networks: Protocols, performance, and control* (1st ed.). Boca Raton, FL: CRC Press.

Sauer, K. L., Yfantis, E. A., Teruel, M. B., & Elkhater, R. W. (2006). A novel approach to camera calibration as part of an hci system. *Journal of Systemics. Cybernetics and Informatics, 4*(1), 8–13.

Scanlon, M., Hannaway, A., & Kechadi, M.-T. (2010). A week in the life of the most popular BitTorrent swarms. In *Proceedings of the 5th Annual Symposium on Information Assurance and the Academic Track of the 13th Annual New York State Cyber Security Conference,* Albany, NY (pp. 32-36).

Schikhof, Y., Mulder, I., & Choenni, S. (2010). Who will watch (over) me? Humane monitoring in dementia care. *International Journal of Human-Computer Studies, 68*(6), 410–422. doi:10.1016/j.ijhcs.2010.02.002

Schmidt, A., Holleis, P., & Kranz, M. (2004). Sensor Virrig – A balance cushion as controller. In *Proceedings of the Workshop on Playing with Sensors in Conjunction UbiComp.*

Schramm, P., Naroska, E., Resch, P., Platte, J., Linde, H., Stromberg, G., & Sturm, T. (2004). A service gateway for networked sensor systems. *IEEE Pervasive Computing / IEEE Computer Society [and] IEEE Communications Society, 3*(1), 66–74. doi:10.1109/MPRV.2004.1269133

Schuurman, G. J., Moelaert-El-Hadidy, F., Krom, A., & Walhout, B. (2007). *Ambient intelligence. Toekomst van de zorg of zorg van de toekomst?* The Hague, The Netherlands: Rathenau Instituut. [in Dutch]

Scott, S. D., Mandryk, R. L., & Inkpen, K. M. (2003). Understanding children's collaborative interactions in shared environments. *Journal of Computer Assisted Learning, 19*(2), 220–228. doi:10.1046/j.0266-4909.2003.00022.x

Sengers, P., Kaye, J., Boehner, K., Fairbank, J., Gay, G., Medynskiy, Y., & Wyche, S. (2004). Culturally embedded computing. *Pervasive Computing, 3*(1).

Serpanos, D., & Henkel, J. (2008). Dependability and security will change embedded computing. *IEEE Computer, 41*(1), 103–105.

Shacham, R., Schulzrinne, H., Thakolsri, S., & Kellerer, W. (2007). Ubiquitous Device Personalization and Use: The Next Generation of IP Multimedia Communications. *ACM Transactions on Multimedia Computing, Communications and Applications, 3*(2).

Shacham, R., Schulzrinne, H., Thakolsri, S., & Kellerer, W. (2009). *Session Initiation Protocol (SIP). Session Mobility.*

Shastri, J. (2006). *Safe navigation during fire hazards using Specknets.* Unpublished master's thesis, The University of Edinburgh, Edinburgh, UK.

Siebenthal, T. (1998). Online-erfassung von handschrift mit einer videokamera (Doctoral dissertation, Universität Bern). *Neubrückstrasse, 10,* 3012.

Sielhorst, T., Obst, T., Burgkart, R., Riener, R., & Navab, N. (2004). An augmented reality delivery simulator for medical training. In *Proceedings of the AMI-ARCS/ MICCAI Joint International Workshop on Augmented Environments for Medical Imaging* (pp. 11-20).

Simoncini, L. (2003). Architectural challenges for "ambient dependability". In *Proceedings of the 9th IEEE International Workshop on Object-Oriented Real-Time Dependable Systems* (p. 245).

Singer, J. (2010). *Augmented reality e-books: Mmm, smell the Jumanji.* Retrieved from http://www.fastcompany.com/1597320/augmented-reality-e-books-bringing-jumanji-to-the-freaky-next-level

Singh, C. K., Kumar, A., & Ameer, P. M. (2008). Performance evaluation of an IEEE 802.15.4 sensor network with a star topology. *Wireless Networks*, *14*(4), 543–568. doi:10.1007/s11276-007-0043-8

Sinnreich, H., & Johnston, A. (2010). *SIP APIs for Communication on the Web*. Internet Engineering Task Force.

Sippl, A., Holzmann, C., Zachhuber, D., & Ferscha, A. (2010). Real-time gaze tracking for public displays. In B. de Ruyter, R. Wichert, D. V. Keyson, P. Markopoulos, N. Streitz et al. (Eds.), *Proceedings of the First International Joint Conference on Ambient Intelligence* (LNCS 6439, pp. 167-176).

Sixsmith, A., Meuller, S., Lull, F., Klein, M., Bierhoff, I., Delaney, S., & Savage, R. (2009). SOPRANO – An ambient assisted living system for supporting older people at home. In M. Mokhtari, I. Khalil, J. Bauchet, D. Zhang, & C. Nugent (Eds.), *Proceedings of the 7th International Conference on Smart Homes and Health Telematics* (LNCS 5597, pp. 233-236).

Slocum, J. (2005). A breakdown of the psychomotor components of input device usage. Usability News, 71.

Song, E. Y., & Lee, K. B. (2008). STWS: A unified web service for IEEE 1451 smart transducers. *IEEE Transactions on Instrumentation and Measurement*, *57*(8), 1749–1756. doi:10.1109/TIM.2008.925732

Song, G. (2002). *Firefighting in public places*. Beijing, China: Chinese People's Public Security University Press.

Sponselee, A., Schouten, B. A. M., & Bouwhuis, D. G. (2008). Analyzing users' needs for telecare: Several case studies. In *Proceedings of the Ami Workshop on Capturing Ambient Assisted Living Needs*, Nürnberg, Germany.

Srinivasan, K., & Levis, P. (2006). RSSI is under appreciated. In Proceedings of the Third Workshop on Embedded Networked Sensors EmNets.

Staten, J. (2009, March 7). Is Cloud Computing Ready for the Enterprise? *Forrester Report*.

Steele, R., Lo, A., Secombe, C., & Wong, Y. K. (2009). Elderly persons' perception and acceptance of using wireless sensor networks to assist healthcare. *International Journal of Medical Informatics*, *78*(12), 788–801. doi:10.1016/j.ijmedinf.2009.08.001

Stefan, F. (2008). Herausforderungen bei der Marktimplementierung von AAL-Systemen bei Anbieters von sozialen Dienstaleistungen. In *Proceedings AAL Kongress* (pp. 291-292). Berlin: VDE Verlag. ISBN 978-3-8007-3076-6

Stefanov, D. H., Bien, Z., & Bang, W.-C. (2004). The smart house for older persons and persons with physical disabilities: Structure, technology arrangements, and perspectives. *IEEE Transactions on Neural Systems and Rehabilitation Engineering*, *12*(2), 228–250. doi:10.1109/TNSRE.2004.828423

Steingart, D., Wilson, J., Redfern, A., Wright, P., Romero, R., & Lim, L. (2005). Augmented cognition for fire emergency response: An iterative user study. In *Proceedings of the 1st International Conference on Augmented Cognition*.

Stelmack, T. (2004). *HoneyNet scan of the month 31: Solution.* Retrieved from http://old.honeynet.org/scans/scan31/sub/tina_stelmack/tina_stelmack.pdf

Stingley, M. (2009). *Check point firewall log analysis in-depth*. Bethesda, MD: SANS Institute.

Streitz, N. A., Tandler, P., & Müller-Tomfelde, C. (2002). Roomware: Toward the next generation of human-computer interaction based on an integrated design of real and virtual worlds. In Carroll, J. (Ed.), *Human computer interaction in the next millennium*. Reading, MA: Addison-Wesley.

Su, W., & Alzagal, M. (2008). Channel propagation characteristics of wireless MICAz sensor nodes. *Ad Hoc Networks Journal*, 1183-1193.

Subasi, Ö., Leitner, M., Geven, A., Dittenberger, S., Tscheligi, M., & Buiza, C. (2009). User requirement analysis for ambient assistive living (AAL): Affective improvement of methods for technologyh acceptance evaluation. In *Evaluating new interactions in healthcare in conjunction with CHI'09*, Boston.

Subramanian, A., & Sayed, A. H. (2005). Joint rate and power control algorithms for wireless networks. *IEEE Transactions on Signal Processing, 53*(11), 4204–4214. doi:10.1109/TSP.2005.857044

Sunderland, A., Watts, K., Baddeley, A. D., & Harris, J. E. (1986). Subjective memory assessment and test performance in the elderly. *Journal of Gerontology, 41*, 376–384.

Sundmaeker, H., Guillemin, P., Friess, P., & Woelfflé, S. (2010). *Vision and challenges for realising the Internet of Things*. Brussels, Belgium: European Commission.

Tabirca, T., Brown, K., & Sreenan, C. (2009). A dynamic model for fire emergency evacuation based on wireless sensor networks. In *Proceedings of the 8th International Symposium on Parallel and Distributed Computing* (pp. 29-36).

Tang, Y., Jin, S., Yang, Z., & You, S. (2006). Detection elder abnormal activities by using omni-directional vision sensor: Activity data collection and modeling. In *Proceedings of the SICE-ICASE International Joint Conference*, Busan, South-Korea.

Tapia, D. I., & Corchado, J. M. (2009). An ambient intelligence based multi-agent system for Alzheimer health care. *International Journal of Ambient Computing and Intelligence, 1*(1), 15–26. doi:10.4018/jaci.2009010102

Tech Target. (2007). *Honeypot definition*. Retrieved from http://searchsecurity.techtarget.com/sDefinition/0,sid14_gci551721,00.html

Tenable Network Security. (2010). *Tenable nesssus*. Retrieved from http://www.nessus.org/nessus/

Texas Instruments. (n.d.). *2.4GHz IEEE 802.15.4/Zigbee-ready RF Transceiver*. Retrieved from http://focus.ti.com/lit/ds/symlink/cc2420.pdf

The Pirate Bay. (n. d.). *Total top 100*. Retrieved from http://www.thepiratebay.org/top/all

Thórisson, K. (1996). *Communicative Humanoids: A Computational Model of Psychosocial Dialogue Skills*. Unpublished doctoral dissertation, Massachusetts Institute of Technology, Cambridge, MA.

Toups, Z., & Kerne, A. (2007). Implicit coordination in firefighting practice: Design implications for teaching fire emergency responders. In *Proceedings of the SIGCHI Conference on Human Factors in Computing Systems* (pp. 707-716).

Tseng, Y., Pan, M., & Tsai, Y. (2006). A distributed emergency navigation algorithm for wireless sensor networks. *IEEE Computers, 39*(7), 55–62.

Turner, M., Herrmann, G., & Postlethwaite, I. (2007). Incorporating robustness requirements into anti-windup design. *IEEE Transactions on Automatic Control, 52*(10), 1842–1855. doi:10.1109/TAC.2007.906185

Turner, M., & Postlethwaite, I. (2004). A new perspective on static and low-order anti-windup synthesis. *International Journal of Control, 77*, 27–44. doi:10.1080/0020717031000164011 6

Urdaneta, E., Buiza, C., Gonzalez, M. F., Facal, D., Geven, A., & Höller, N. (2009). Addressing cognition needs in three European countries with the help of technology. *The Journal of Nutrition, Health & Aging, 13*(1), 620.

Uttl, B. (2008). Transparent Meta-Analysis of Prospective Memory and Aging. *PloS One, 3*(2), e1568. doi:10.1371/journal.pone.0001568

Vaarandi, R. (2004). A breadth-first algorithm for mining frequent patterns from event logs. In *Proceedings of the IFIP International Conference on Intelligence in Communication Systems* (pp. 293-308).

van Bronswijk, J. E. M. H., van Hoof, J., Franchimon, F., Koren, L. G. H., Pernot, C. E. E., & van Dijken, F. (2005). De intelligente thuisomgeving. Een betaalbare zorg voor de lange duur. In *Handboek zorg thuis* (pp. C 5.3-1-C 5.3-28). Maarssen, The Netherlands: Elsevier gezondheidzorg.

van der Hoog, W., Keller, I., & Stappers, P. J. (2004) Gustbowl: Technology Supporting Affective Communication through Routine Ritual Interactions. In *Proceedings of CHI 2004*, Vienna, Austria. New York: ACM.

van der Hoog, W., Keller, I., & Stappers, P. J. (2004 b, September/October). Connecting Mother and Sons: A Design Using Routine Affective Rituals. *Interaction*, 68–69. doi:10.1145/1015530.1015564

van Hoof, J., Kort, H. S. M., Markopoulos, P., & Soede, M. (2007). Ambient intelligence, ethics and privacy. *Gerontechnology (Valkenswaard)*, *6*(3), 155–163. doi:10.4017/gt.2007.06.03.005.00

van Hoof, J., Kort, H. S. M., Rutten, P. G. S., & Duijnstee, M. S. H. (2011). Ageing-in-place with the use of ambient intelligence technology: perspectives of older users. *International Journal of Medical Informatics*, *80*(5), 310–331. doi:10.1016/j.ijmedinf.2011.02.010

van Kasteren, T. L. M., Englebienne, G., & Kröse, B. J. A. (2010). An activity monitoring system for elderly care using generative and discriminative models. *Personal and Ubiquitous Computing*, *14*(6), 489–498. doi:10.1007/s00779-009-0277-9

Van Krevelen, D., & Poelman, R. (2010). A survey of augmented reality technologies, applications and limitations. *International Journal of Virtual Reality*, *9*(2), 1–20.

van Nispen, B. (2004). *Zorgdomotica. Een inventarisatie van knelpunten en struikelblokken met aanbevelingen om de grootschalige implementatie van zorgdomotica voor ouderen en mensen met functiebeperkingen in Nederland te versnellen en te verbeteren*. The Hague, The Netherlands: Nederlands Instituut voor Telemedicine. [in Dutch]

Virone, G. (2009). Assessing everyday life behavioral rhythms for the older generation. *Pervasive and Mobile Computing*, *5*(5), 606–622. doi:10.1016/j.pmcj.2009.06.008

von Hippel, W. (2007). Aging, executive functioning, and social control. *Current Directions in Psychological Science*, *16*(5), 240–244. doi:10.1111/j.1467-8721.2007.00512.x

Wada, C., Yoneda, Y., & Sugimura, Y. (2009). Proposal of a direction guidance system for evacuation. In *Proceedings of the International Conference on Human-Computer Interaction* (pp. 221-227).

Walsh, M. J., Alavi, S. M. M., & Hayes, M. J. (2008, December 9-11). On the effect of communication constraints on robust performance for a practical 802.15.4 wireless sensor network benchmark problem. In *Proceedings of the 47th IEEE Conference on Decision and Control*, Cancun, Mexico (pp. 447-452).

Walsh, M. J., Alavi, S. M. M., & Hayes, M. J. (2010). Practical assessment of hardware limitations on power aware wireless sensor networks- an anti-wind up approach. *International Journal of Robust and Nonlinear Control*, *20*(2), 194–208. doi:10.1002/rnc.1475

Walsh, M. J., Hayes, M. J., & Nelson, J. (2009). Robust performance for an energy sensitive wireless body area network - an anti-windup approach. *International Journal of Control*, *82*(1), 59–73. doi:10.1080/00207170801983109

Walters, K., Iliffe, S., See Tai, S., & Orrell, M. (2000). Assessing needs from patient, carer and professional perspectives: The Camberwell Assessment of Need for Elderly people in primary care. *Age and Ageing*, *29*, 505–510. doi:10.1093/ageing/29.6.505

Wang, P., & Luh, P. (2008). Modeling and optimization of crowd guidance for building emergency evacuation. In *Proceedings of the 4th IEEE International Conference on Automation Science and Engineering* (pp. 328-334).

Wang, P., Ying, A., & Jiang, B. (2008). *Analysis of the fire caused heavy casualties in Shenzhen: the fire was mistaken as a show*. Retrieved from http://news.sina.com.cn/c/2008-09-22/121716333822.shtml

Wang, S., & Zhang, Y. (2005). A formalization of distributed authorization with delegation. In *Proceedings of the 10th Australasian Conference on Information Security and Privacy* (LNCS 3574, pp. 303-315).

Wang, S., & Zhang, Y. (2007). Handling distributed authorization with delegation through answer set programming. *International Journal of Information Security*, *6*, 27–46. doi:10.1007/s10207-006-0008-4

Wayner, P. (2008, July 21). Cloud versus cloud - A guided tour of Amazon, Google, AppNexus and GoGrid. *InfoWorld*.

Weiss, A. (2007). Computing in the Clouds. *Networker*, *11*(4), 16–25. doi:10.1145/1327512.1327513

Weitzner, D. (2008). Web science: an interdisciplinary approach to understanding the web. *Communications of the ACM, 51*(7), 60–69.

Wenke, L., & Stolfo, S. J. (1998). Data mining approaches for intrusion detection. In *Proceedings of the 7th Conference on USENIX Security* (Vol. 7).

Weston, P. F., & Postlewaite, I. (1998). Analysis and design of linear conditioning schemes for systems containing saturating actuators. In Proceedings of the IFAC Nonlinear Control System Design *Symposium*.

Whitehead, R., & Spikes, P. (2003, July). *Determining Internet jurisdiction*. Retrieved from http://www.nysscpa.org/cpajournal/2003/0703/features/f072403.htm

Wiberg, M. (2005). *An architecturally situated approach to place-based mobile interaction design*. Paper presented at the Location Awareness & Community Workshop at the 9th European Conference on Computer-Supported Cooperative Work.

Wiberg, M. (2011). *Interactive textures for architecture and landscaping – digital elements and technologies*. Hershey, PA: IGI Global.

Wiberg, M., & Robles, E. (2010). Computational compositions: Aesthetics, materials, and interaction design. *International Journal of Design, 4*(2), 65–76.

Wilkins, A. (2010). *Meta cookie – can taste like any cookie you want*. Retrieved from.

Wilson, J. (2007). A wireless sensor network and incident command interface for urban firefighting. In *Proceedings of the 4th IEEE International Conference on Mobile and Ubiquitous Systems: Network & Services* (pp.1-7).

Wilson, J., Steingart, D., Romero, R., Reynolds, J., Mellers, E., Redfern, A., et al. (2005). Design of monocular head-mounted displays for increased indoor firefighting safety and efficiency. In *Proceedings of SPIE on Helmet-and Head-mounted Displays X: Technologies and Applications* (pp. 103-114).

Wilson, R. (2002). *Propagation Losses Through Common Building Materials 2.4GHz vs 5 GHz*. Los Angeles: University of Southern California. WiSAR Lab. (n.d.a). *WiSAR Lab Development Mote*. Retrieved from http://www.wisar.org/

Wilson, J., & Wright, P. (2009). Head-mounted display efficacy study to aid first responder indoor navigation. *Proceedings of the Institution of Mechanical Engineers. Part C, Journal of Mechanical Engineering Science, 223*(3), 675–688. doi:10.1243/09544062JMES1213

Wirz, M., Roggen, D., & Tröster, G. (2009). Decentralized detection of group formations from wearable acceleration sensors. In *Proceedings of the International Conference on Computational Science and Engineering* (pp. 952-959).

Wirz, M., Roggen, D., & Tröster, G. (2010). A methodology towards the detection of collective behavior patterns by means of body-worn sensors. In *Proceedings of the 8th Pervasive Computing Conference*.

WiSAR Lab. (n.d.b). *WiSAR Lab Office Testbed*. Retrieved from http://monitor.wisar.ie/

Witt, H. (2005). A toolkit for context-aware user interface development for wearable computers. In *Proceedings of the Doctoral Colloquium at the 9th International Symposium on Wearable Computers*.

Witt, H., Nicolai, T., & Kenn, H. (2007). The WUI-toolkit: A model-driven UI development framework for wearable user interfaces. In *Proceedings of the 27th International Conference on Distributed Computing Systems Workshop* (pp. 43). New York, NY: ACM Press.

Wool, R. N., Siegel, D., & Fine, P. R. (1980). Task performance in spinal cord injury: Effect of helplessness training. *Archives of Physical Medicine and Rehabilitation, 61*, 321–325.

Wu, X., Berger, S., Sidiroglou, S., & Schulzrinne, H. (2003). *Ubiquitous Computing using SIP*. Paper presented at the International Workshop on Network and Operating System support for Digital Audio & Video.

Xiaotao, W., & Schulzrinne, H. (2004). SIPc, a Multifunction SIP User Agent. In *Proceedings of the 7th IFIP/IEEE International Conference, Management of Multimedia Networks and Services*.

XML VM. (2011). *Overview*. Retrieved from http://xmlvm.org/

Yanguas, J. J., Buiza, C., Echeverria, I., Galdona, N., González, M. F., & Arriola, E. (2006). *Estudio longitudinal Donostia de enfermedad de Alzheimer*. Salamanca, Spain: Tempora.

Zamora-Izquierdo, M., A., Santa, J., & Gomez-Skarmeta, A., F. (2010). An integral and networked home automation solution for indoor ambient intelligence. *IEEE Pervasive Computing / IEEE Computer Society [and] IEEE Communications Society, 9*(4), 66–77. doi:10.1109/MPRV.2010.20

Zeng, Y., Murphy, S., Sitanayah, L., Tabirca, T., Truong, T., Brown, K., & Sreenan, C. (2009). Building fire emergency detection and response using wireless sensor networks. In *Proceedings of the 9th IT & T Conference.*

Zhang, J. (2007). An evolutionary game model of resources-sharing mechanism in P2P networks. In *Proceedings of the Workshop on Intelligent Information Technology Application* (pp. 282-285).

Zhang, W. (2009). A Uniform Negotiation and Delivery Mechanism for SIP-based Conferencing System. In *Proceedings of the International Conference on Communication Software and Networks.*

Zhou, F., Duh, H., & Billinghurst, M. (2008). Trends in augmented reality tracking, interaction and display: A review of ten years of ISMAR. In *Proceedings of the IEEE/ACM International Symposium on Mixed and Augmented Reality* (pp. 193-202).

Zhu, P., & Zhang, C. (2001). Data mining for network intrusion detection: A comparison of alternative methods. *Decision Series, 32*(4), 635–660. doi:10.1111/j.1540-5915.2001.tb00975.x

About the Contributors

Kevin Curran, BSc (Hons), PhD, SMIEEE, FBCS CITP, SMACM, FHEA, is a Reader in Computer Science at the University of Ulster and group leader for the Ambient Intelligence Research Group. His achievements include winning and managing UK & European Framework projects and Technology Transfer Schemes. Dr. Curran has made significant contributions to advancing the knowledge and understanding of computer networking and systems, evidenced by over 700 published works. He is perhaps most well-known for his work on location positioning within indoor environments, pervasive computing, and internet security. His expertise has been acknowledged by invitations to present his work at international conferences, overseas universities, and research laboratories. He is a regular contributor to BBC Radio & TV news in the UK and is currently the recipient of an Engineering and Technology Board Visiting Lectureship for Exceptional Engineers and is an IEEE Technical Expert for Internet/Security matters. He is listed in the *Dictionary of International Biography*, Marquis *Who's Who in Science and Engineering*, and in *Who's Who in the World*. Dr. Curran was awarded the Certificate of Excellence for Research in 2004 by Science Publications and was named Irish Digital Media Newcomer of the Year Award in 2006. Dr. Curran has performed external panel duties for various Irish Higher Education Institutions. He is a fellow of the British Computer Society (FBCS), a senior member of the Association for Computing Machinery (SMACM), a senior member of the Institute of Electrical and Electronics Engineers (SMIEEE), and a fellow of the higher education academy (FHEA). Dr. Curran's stature and authority in the international community is demonstrated by his influence, particularly in relation to the direction of research in computer science. He has chaired sessions and participated in the organising committees for many highly-respected international conferences and workshops. He is the Editor in Chief of the *International Journal of Ambient Computing and Intelligence* and is also a member of 15 journal editorial committees and numerous international conference organising committees. He has authored a number of books and is the recipient of various patents. He has served as an advisor to the British Computer Society in regard to the computer industry standards and is a member of BCS and IEEE Technology Specialist Groups and various other professional bodies.

* * *

Claas Ahlrichs is a student at the University Bremen. He enrolled in 2007, and started to study computer science and is currently preparing for graduation. Claas Ahlrichs is working as a student assistant at the Centre for Computing Technology (TZI) in the field of wearable computing.

Seyed Mohammad Mahdi Alavi received his Bachelor and Master degrees in Control Engineering from K.N. Toosi University of Technology in 2001 and 2003, respectively and Ph.D. from University of Limerick, Ireland in 2009. He is currently a post doctorate researcher at Simon Fraser University, BC, Canada. His research interests include robust control theory (in particular Quantitative Feedback Theory) and fault detection and isolation technique with applications to wired/wireless networks as well as power systems. He received the best student award from K.N. Toosi University of Technology (2001); Ph.D. scholarship from Science Foundation Ireland (May 2006–October 2008). He has held visiting positions at Centre for Embedded Software System, Aalborg University, Denmark (February–April 2007), and at Automatic Control Laboratory, EPFL, Switzerland (May–October 2007).

Ricardo S. Alonso (PhD. Student). He is a PhD. student at the University of Salamanca (Spain). He obtained an Engineering in Telecommunications degree in 2008 at the University of Valladolid (Spain) and an MSc in Intelligent Systems at the University of Salamanca (Spain) in 2009. He has also been a co-author of several papers published in recognized workshops and symposiums.

María Amparo Navarro Salvador is Telecommunications Engineer from the Polytechnic University of Valencia since 2009. She made her Final Project at ITACA-TSB UPV Department and she received the Orange Foundation Award for best Final Project in new technologies applied to digital inclusion and independent living promotion in 2010. She currently works as a researcher at ITACA-TSB UPV Department, working on eHealth area projects. She has participated in the European project PREVE, aimed at the implementation of ICT in health promotion and disease prevention. Currently works as technical and development head of the Enjoy.IT! project, whose main objective is the design and planning of an entertainment applications and multimedia and multimodal contents platform.

Grigoris Antoniou is Professor of Computer Science at the University of Crete, and Head of the Information Systems Laboratory at FORTH-ICS, the top-rated research institute in Greece. His research interests lie in semantic technologies, particularly knowledge representation and reasoning, and its application to ambient intelligence, e-commerce, and cultural informatics. He has published over 200 technical papers in scientific journals and conferences. He is author of three books with international publishers (MIT Press, Addison-Wesley); his book "A Semantic Web Primer" is internationally the standard textbook in the area, and has been or is about to be translated to Japanese, Chinese, Korean, Spanish and Greek. In recognition of his work, he was elected an ECCAI Fellow in 2006.

Elena Urdaneta Artola: Ph.D. in Pharmacy. Professor of Physiology at Public University of Navarra (Spain), Deputy Head of the R&D Department at Ingema. Main areas of research: Successful Aging and Health. She has a long-lasting experience in Physiology, human and animal longitudinal studies, and ageing-related research. She has been Principal Investigator in numerous European and Spanish research projects. Strong skills and knowledge of ethical issues related to biomedical and clinical research. She also peer-reviews scientific articles for international journals and is author or co-author of more than 25 publications (articles, books and book chapters).

John Barton received his M.S degree from University College Cork in 2006. He joined the Interconnection and Packaging Group of the National Microelectronics Research Centre (now Tyndall National Institute) as a research engineer in 1993. Currently in the Wireless Sensor Networks team where his recent research interests include ambient systems research, wearable computing and deployment of wireless sensor networks for personalized health applications. As PI on the Enterprise Ireland funded D-Systems project John has been the leader of the development of the Tyndall Wireless Sensor Mote platform. He has authored or co-authored over 90 peer reviewed papers.

Antonis Bikakis is a lecturer in the Department of Information Studies at University College London (UCL). He holds a PhD and a M.Sc. in Computer Science from the University of Crete and a degree in Electrical and Computer Engineering from the Aristotle University of Thessaloniki. His main research interests are in the areas of Knowledge Representation, Nonmonotonic Reasoning and Ambient Intelligence. He has published a number of journal and conference papers on defeasible reasoning and its application to reasoning on Semantic Web and Ambient Computing systems. Since 2006, he is a member of the Hellenic Association for Artificial Intelligence (EETN).

Marek Bykowski holds a Ph.D (2006) from the Institute of Telecommunication, Teleinformatics and Acoustics, Wroclaw University of Technology and an M.A.(2001) in Electronics from the Wroclaw University. He also has a postgraduate certificate in Project Management from the Dublin Business School. He joined the WiSAR Lab in November 2009 having been a Postdoctoral Research Fellow in the Communication Network Research Institute in the Dublin Institute of Technology for 3 years. Previous roles included those of Senior Specialist in the Radiocommunication Department of the Polish Military Communication Institute and in the design and maintenance of Terrestial and Satellite TV for Ostrowski Ltd. His current research interests are in the areas of Wireless Sensor Networks, WLAN/Mesh Networks, Link Adaptation, Routing, Indoor and Outdoor Radio Propagation, Interference Mitigation, Signal Processing.

Sean Carlin is an Computer Science student at the University of Ulster. He has worked for a number of years in the software industry and his research interests include web design, network protocols and security.

Marcello Cinque graduated with honours from University of Naples, Italy, in 2003, where he received the PhD degree in computer engineering in 2006. Currently, he is Assistant Professor at the Department of Computer and Systems Engineering (DIS) of the University of Naples Federico II. Dr. Cinque is chair and/or TPC member of several tecnica conferences and workshops on dependable, mobile, and pervasive systems, including IEEE PIMRC, DEPEND, and ACM ICPS. His research interests include dependability analysis of mobile and sensor systems, and middleware solutions for mobile ubiquitous systems.

Aodhan L. Coffey received his B.E. (Electronic) degree from the National University of Ireland (NUI), Maynooth in 2010. He is currently undertaking his Ph.D (Biomedical Engineering) at the National University of Ireland, Maynooth. His current primary research area is the application of robotics interfaces for neurorehabilitation, particularly in stroke rehabilitation.

Juan M. Corchado (PhD.). Received a PhD. in Computer Science from the University of Salamanca in 1998 and a PhD. in Artificial Intelligence (AI) from the University of Paisley, Glasgow (UK) in 2000. At present he is the Dean of the Faculty of Computer Science and Director of the BISITE Research Group (http://bisite.usal.es). He has leaded several Artificial Intelligence research projects sponsored by Spanish and European public and private institutions. He has been president of the organising and scientific committee of several international symposiums and co-author of more than 250 books, book chapters, journal papers, technical reports, etc. published in recognized journal, workshops and symposiums.

Antonio Coronato is a researcher at the Institute of High-Performance Computing and Networking (ICAR) of the National Research Council (CNR) of Italy. His research focuses on pervasive computing and component-based architectures. Coronato received an MSc in computer engineering from "Federico II" University in Naples. He is a member of the ACM.

Fabio Di Franco received a Masters degree in Microwave Communications from the Universita' di Messina (Italy) in 2004 and a Bachelor's Degree from the University of Palermo in 2001. He also holds a Project Management certificate from the Open University. Since May 2009, Fabio has held the position of senior RF researcher in the WiSAR Lab team. Prior to that, he gained extensive experience in mobile phone design from working in Motorola and Cambridge Silicon Radio (CSR) where he provided support for Radio Frequency and Hardware design to the top five mobile phone manufacturers. His current research interests are the modelling and testing of the RF environment around the Human Body, techniques to improve the radio performance in BAN's and also approaches to measuring and analysing power consumption in sensor networks in order to optimise lifetime.

David Facal. PhD in Developmental Psychology (University of Santiago de Compostela) in 2008 and Master Degree in Clinical Gerontology by the University of A Coruña. He has published papers in international journals and book chapters about language and communication changes in the aging process. He was awarded the Humanitas Award 2007 (from the Social Council of the University of Santiago de Compostela) to their social labour as psychologist in AGADEA (Alzheimer's Association of Santiago). Currently he is working in Ingema as researcher in different projects related to life span development and assistive technologies.

Enda Fallon joined Athlone Institute of Technology (AIT)<http://www.ait.ie/> from Ericsson in 2002. In 2003 he founded the Software Research Institute (SRI) <http://www.ait.ie/sri/> at AIT. Since 2003, Enda has been a principal investigator on over 20 collaborative industry/academic research projects. His research interest focuses on service mediation and adaptation for heterogeneous networking environments. Enda holds a BSc in Computer Science and Mathematics from University College Galway and an MSc in Software Engineering from Athlone Institute of Technology. He is currently undertaking a PhD at the Performance Engineering Laboratory <http://pel.ucd.ie/> at University College Dublin.

Ling Feng is a professor of computer science and technology at Tsinghua University in China. Her research interests include context-aware data management towards Ambient Intelligence, knowledge-based information systems, data mining and warehousing, and distributed object-oriented database management systems, etc. She has published over 140 scientific articles in high-quality international conferences or journals, and received the 2004 innovational VIDI Award by the Netherlands Organization for Scientific Research, 2006 Chinese ChangJiang professorship Award by the Ministry of Education, and 2006 Tsinghua Hundred-Talents Award.

Carlos Fernández-Llatas is foresight and research coordinator in Health & Wellbeing Technologies Group in ITACA institute at Universidad Politecnica de Valencia. He received the PhD degree in Computer Science in the Pattern Recognition and artificial Intelligence Program of that university. He participated in more than 20 projects through IV, V VI and VII european Framework program and Spanish Goverment funded projects He has published more than 30 scientific papers. His research is mainly focused in process management learning, representation and execution techniques and its automatic learning for their application in health and human behavior modeling. He also has a wide experience on software platforms and Business Process Management technology.

Irini Genitsaridi graduated in Computer Science from the University of Crete in 2009. She completed her MSc at the Computer Science Department at University of Crete in 2011. She worked as a research Assistant at the Information Systems Laboratory at the Institute of Computer Science of FORTH in Greece since 2009. Her research interests include Knowledge Representation, Ambient Intelligence, and mobile computing.

Arjan Geven holds an MSc in Technology and Society from the Eindhoven University of Technology with a specialization in Human Technology Interaction. He participated in various national and European research projects, specifically working on motivational aspects of technology, translation of user attitudes into corresponding behaviour, and HCI methodology.

Mari Feli Gonzalez degree in Psychology (Public University of Salamanca) in 2004 and Masters Degree in Clinical Psychology and Neuropsychology by the University of Barcelona. PhD Student. Currently she is working in Ingema as a research assistant in different projects related to elderly and people with physical or mental disability.

Ben Graham has a B.Eng(Hons) in Embedded System Design from the Letterkenny Institute of Technology (LYIT). Ben joined the WiSAR Lab in May 2009 as a Research Technician. Prior to that, he had worked for 4 years in the EPICentre at LYIT on collaborative projects with industry involving PCB Design and Layout, Electronics System Design. His current research interests are in the areas of Wireless sensor networks (WSNs), Low Power Measurement techniques, Wireless Testbed Infrastructure, Embedded System Design and the use of Energy Harvesting in WSN's.

Geraldine Gray is a lecturer with the Informatics Department at the Institute of Technology Blanchardstown(ITB) Dublin, Ireland, specialising in the design and delivery of modules in the areas of data mining, text mining and enterprise application development, including ITB's online masters in Business Intelligence and Data Mining. Prior to joining ITB, Geraldine lectured in IT Tallaght, and also has a number of years of industrial experience developing software for distribution and inventory management. Research interests and publications include educational data mining, data mining techniques for computer forensics, mining unstructured data, semantic web technologies and web services. She is currently completing her PhD in the field of Educational Data Mining, based on ongoing research in partnership with the National Learning Network to assess the impact of inclusive teaching practices on student performance.

Alan Hannaway graduated from the UCD Centre for Cybercrime Investigation, School of Computer Science & Informatics at University College Dublin, Ireland with a M.Sc. for his research into building tools to investigate problems in environments where the use of P2P technology is predominant. He received a B.Sc. (Hons.) in Computer Science from UCD in 2006. Alan's research interests lie in the areas of Distributed Computing, Cloud Computing, P2P Networking, Computer Forensics and Cybercrime Investigation on large online networks.

Martin J. Hayes has lectured at the University of Limerick since 1997, is currently course leader for the B.S. in Electronics programme, and is a researcher in the Wireless Access Research Centre. He teaches undergraduate and postgraduate courses in electrical science, automatic control, computer controlled systems and the control of nonlinear systems. His research interests lie in the area of systems theory in general and in particular on the intelligent use of system resources within biomedical or safety critical wireless systems that are subjected to channel and/or performance uncertainties. He is also interested in how the dynamic delivery of information to handheld devices at tourist attractions can add value to the visitor experience.

Jennifer Hyndman BSc (Hons) is a PhD student researching in the area of ambient intelligence within creative technologies in the School of Computing and Intelligent Systems, Faculty of Computing and Engineering at the University of Ulster. Her research interests include multimodal interfaces, learning environments and serious games.

Hendrik Iben is with TZI (Center for Computing and Communication Technologies) of University Bremen since 2007. He is a PhD candidate involved in wearable computing projects and lectures. He is a 2007 graduate of University Bremen.

Gerrit Kalkbrenner is working in the field of mobile media, multimedia, broadband network communication, and mobile communication now for 15 years. 1996 he finished his Dr.-Ing. thesis in the field of Teleservices and E-Learning. With several projects (Multimedia Home Platform. E-Learning modules / virtual laboratories, Campus Mobil, Ubiquitous Media, Self Organizing Traffic System) he is concerned with mobile media. He played for instance a central role in the development of an open source Multimedia Home Platform.

Mohand-Tahar Kechadi was awarded Ph.D. in Computer Science from the University of Lille 1, France. After working as a post-doctoral researcher under TMR program at UCD, he joined the UCD School of Computer Science and Informatics in 1999. He is the director of the PCRG laboratory and head of teaching and learning at the School of Computer Science and Informatics. His research interests span the areas of Optimisation Techniques, Distributed Data Mining, Forensic Computing and Grid computing. He is a member of the Communication of the ACM and IEEE Computer Society.

Paul Mc Kevitt is Chair in Intelligent MultiMedia at the School of Computing & Intelligent Systems, Faculty of Computing & Engineering, University of Ulster, Magee, Derry/Londonderry, Northern Ireland. Previously, he was Associate Professor (Senior Lecturer) in the School of Electronics, Electrical Engineering and Computer Science, The Queen's University of Belfast, Northern Ireland. He has been Visiting Professor of Intelligent MultiMedia Computing in the Institute of Electronic Systems, Aalborg

University, Denmark and a British EPSRC (Engineering and Physical Sciences Research Council) Advanced Fellow in the Department of Computer Science, University of Sheffield, England. The Fellowship, commenced in 1994, and released him from his Assistant Professorship (tenured Lectureship) for 5 years to conduct full-time research on the integration of natural language, speech and vision processing. He has been Visiting Professor at LIMSI-CNRS, Orsay, Univ. Paris Sud, France, Visiting Fellow at the School of Electronic Engineering, Dublin City University, Dublin, Ireland, and Research Scientist and Research Fellow in The Department of Computer Science, New Mexico State University, New Mexico, USA. He completed a Master's degree in Education (M.Ed.), at the University of Sheffield, England in 1999, his Ph.D. in Computer Science, at the University of Exeter, England in 1991, his Master's degree in Computer Science (M.S.), at New Mexico State University, New Mexico, USA in 1988 and his Bachelor's degree in Computer Science (B.Sc., Hons.), at University College Dublin (UCD), Ireland in 1985. He has published numerous research papers in international conferences, research books and journals and has been awarded 4 UK/international patents. He has obtained research and education funding from the European Union (Esprit [Open-LTR], TEMPUS, Erasmus, Socrates), British Engineering and Physical Sciences Research Council (EPSRC), The Royal Society, The British Council, Invest Northern Ireland (Proof-of-Concept, RTD Networking), InterTradeIreland (Fusion), Enterprise Ireland (Innovation Vouchers), UK Teaching Company Scheme (TCS) and industry (US WEST Advanced Technologies, USA).

Daniel Kohlsdorf is a student at the University Bremen. He enrolled in 2007 and started to study computer science and is currently preparing for graduation. Daniel Kohlsdorf is working as a student assistant at the Centre for Computing Technology (TZI) in the field of wearable computing.

Karunakar A Kotegar received the Master of Computer Applications degree from Karnataka University, Dharwad in 1998 and PhD from Manipal University for his work on Wavelet Based Scalable Video Coding in 2009. He is having 12 years of research and teaching experience at Manipal Institute of Technology, Manipal India. Currently, he is a Postdoctoral Research Fellow in Software Research Institute at Athlone Institute of Technology, Athlone Ireland. His areas of interest are Image Processing and Scalable Video Coding. He published 18 research papers in National and International Conferences and Journals.

Roisin Lautman is currently working in the Irish computing industry. Her research interests include internet law and network security.

Michael Lawo is with TZI (Center for Computing and Communication Technologies) of Universitaet Bremen since 2004. He is professor for applied computer science involved in numerous projects of wearable computing and artificial intelligence. He is a 1975 graduate of Ruhr- Universitaet- Bochum, got his PhD in 1981 from Essen University and became professor there in 1992. He has more than 15 years of experience in the IT industry in different management positions, and is author, co-author and co-publisher of eight books and more than 120 scientific papers on numerical methods and computer applications also in healthcare, optimization, IT-security and wearable computing.

Brian Lee is Research Manager of the SRI and joined the Institute in August 2009. Previously he had been Research Manager in LM Ericsson in Ireland where he supervised a team of 20 researchers investigating solutions in network management for Ericsson's Operations Support System (OSS) for mobile and fixed networks. He has over twenty years experience in research and system design of network management solutions for large scale telecommunication networks. He has participated in many national and international research projects. He holds a PhD from Trinity College Dublin in the area of policy management applied to charging. His research interest focuses self-adaptive software systems for network management.

Yuanping Li received his Bachelor degree from University of Science and Technology in Beijing, China in 2004, and Master degree in software engineering from Tsinghua University in Beijing, China in 2007, and PhD degree in computer science and technology from Tsinghua University in Beijing, China in 2011. His research interest is context-aware data management. He is now working at China National Software and Service Co. Ltd.

Tom Lunney BSc (Hons), MSc, P.G.C.E, PhD, MIEEE, MBCS received his degrees from Queen's University Belfast, and is now a Senior Lecturer in Computer Science in the University of Ulster. His research areas include concurrent and distributed systems, artificial intelligence and multi-modal computing. He has presented papers at a range of International Conferences and participated in the organising committees for a number of international conferences and workshops. He has taught at other educational institutions including Queens University, Belfast and The University of Pau, France. He is currently Course Director for postgraduate masters programmes in the University of Ulster.

Hannah R. Marston, PhD, MSc, BSc, PGCE (1980) has a background in multimedia and computing. Her research interests lie within technology use and gerontology. She has recently completed a post-doctoral fellowship at the University of Waterloo, which involved the study of audience usage and access of content through digital devices.

Teresa Meneu, Degree in Telecommunications Engineering (2001-Polytechnic University of Valencia), Master's Degree in Business Administration – MBA (2004-Instituto Universitario de Posgrado), and is currently in the research phase of her PhD studies in Business Organizations at UPV, focused in the impact of ICT in the reengineering of the healthcare delivery chain and the empowerment of the effective adoption of ICT solutions by citizens & professionals including technological, social, organizational and economical considerations. She is responsible of the eHealth Strategic Programme of the 'Health & Wellbeing Group (TSB)' at ITACA and Member of the Board of the Telecommunications Engineer Professional Association of the region of Valencia. Since 2001, she has actively participated in more than 10 national and international projects, working in all the project phases, being specialist in the definition of the project proposal, the acquisition of the user requirements, the definition of business models, the evaluation and assessment of the impact of the solution and the project management. She has been involved in several technical audits, under the e-TEN programme, as an expert for the project evaluation for health related business models and evaluation outcomes and as peer reviewer in several European Projects and in the Scientific Committee of several international congresses and conferences.

Richard H. Middleton received his B.Sc. (1983), B.Eng. (Hons-I)(1984) and Ph.D. (1987) from the University of Newcastle, Australia. He is currently a Research Professor at the Hamilton Institute, The National University of Ireland, Maynooth; a Senior Research Associate of the University of Newcastle;

President Elect (2010) of the IEEE Control Systems Society and Senior Editor of the IEEE Transactions on Automatic Control. His research interests include a broad range of Control Systems Theory and Applications.

Jim Morrison holds a PhD (2006) in Digital Security from the University of Limerick, an MSc (1992) in Industrial Applications of Computing from the Open University and a BEng (1981) in Electronics and Electrical Engineering from Queens University of Belfast. He has been a member of the IEEE and its Communications Society and Computer Society for over 20 years. He joined LYIT in 1985 as a Lecturer and became Head of Department of Electronics and Mechanical engineering in 2004. He was a co-founder of the WISAR Lab in 2009 and was a co-founder of the associated EpiCentre in 2004. His current research interests are in the areas of Wireless Sensor Networks (WSNs), Medical Body Area Networks (MBAN), Sensors, Ultra Low Power Communication Protocols and associated security issues.

Niall Murray received his BE in Electronic and Computer Engineering from the National University of Ireland, Galway in 2003. He obtained a MEng in Computer and Communication Systems from the University of Limerick in 2004. After spending a number of years in telecommunication and software development industries, he started his PhD in the Software Research Institute, Athlone Institute of Technology (AIT) in 2010. His interests include Inter-Device and Inter-Service Collaboration, SOA, Multimedia Service Composition techniques and Multimedia Communication Systems.

Ana Belén Navarro PhD in Psychology of Aging (University of Salamanca) in 2007 and Masters Degree in Gerontology by the University of Salamanca. She was granted Extraordinary Award to the Ph.D. thesis defended on 2007. She has participated in various national and international projects within the research group in Aging at the University of Salamanca. She has been awarded the best Oral Communication Award in different Congresses of Gerontology. Currently she is working in Ingema as a research in different projects related to elderly and people with physical or mental disability.

Brendan O'Flynn received his B.E. degree from University College Cork in 1993, and his M.S. degree from University College Cork, National Microelectronics Research Centre in 1995. Brendan is a senior staff researcher at the Tyndall national Institute and is Research Activity Leader for the Wireless Sensor Network (WSN) Group. As such he has been responsible for directing the research activities of the group in a variety of industry funded, nationally funded and European projects. He has been involved in the development of the AES Intern Program, and conducting research into miniaturized wireless sensor systems as well as the supervision activities associated with postgraduate students PhD and Masters Level. His research interests include low power microelectronic design, RF system design system integration of miniaturized sensing systems and embedded system design on resource constrained platforms. Brendan was one of the founders of Inpact Microelectronics Ireland Ltd. and has significant expertise in the commercialization of technology. Inpact (a spin off from the National Microelectronics Research Centre (NMRC)) miniaturized in the development of system in a package (SiP) solutions for customers. Inpact offered a complete solution to customers enabling the development of a product concept through to volume product supply; miniaturizing in radio frequency (RF) system development and product miniaturization.

Cian O'Mathuna is head of Tyndall National Institutes Microsystems Centre. His research interests include microelectronics integration for ambient electronic systems, biomedical microsystems, and energy processing for information and communications technologies. He received his Ph.D. in Microelectronics from University College Cork. He is a member of the IEEE.

Stephen O'Shaughnessy is currently studying for a MSc. in Computing by research in the Institute of Technology Blanchardstown (ITB), Dublin. The MSc. combines the disciplines of Computer Forensics and Data Mining to propose a solution to consolidate forensic data in order to effectively track the activity of users on a Windows system. Stephen is also a part-time lecturer in the College of Computer Training (CCT) in Dublin. Areas of interest include programming and algorithm design, Data Mining and Computer Forensics, particulary the combination of both disciplines as an efective means of gathering and processing forensics data.

Rienk A. Overdiep MSc, PT (1962) has a background in physical therapy and public health, and works with the Institute of Allied Health professions of Fontys University of Applied Sciences in Eindhoven as a research and business manager.

Lin Qiao received her Bachelor and Master degrees in computer science and technology from Tsinghua University in Beijing, China in 2003 and 2011, respectively. She is now working at Shanghai Mobile Company in China.

Yuansong Qiao is the Principal Investigator at the Software Research Institute (SRI), Athlone Institute of Technology (AIT), Ireland. He received his Ph.D. in Computer Applied Technology from the Institute of Software, Chinese Academy of Sciences (ISCAS), Beijing, China, in 2007. As part of his Ph.D. research programme he joined the SRI at AIT in 2005. He continued his research in the SRI as a postdoctoral researcher in 2007. He completed a B.Sc. and an M.Sc. in Solid Mechanics from Beihang University, Beijing, China in 1996 and 1999 respectively. After graduation Yuansong Qiao joined the ISCAS immediately where he held roles as a network administrator and as a research engineer & team leader in research & development, working on protocols and products in the areas of computer networking, multimedia communication and network security. His research interests include network protocol design and multimedia communications for the Future Internet.

Andreas Riener carried out his PhD at the Institute for Pervasive Computing, Johannes Kepler University Linz, Austria from which he received his PhD degree in 2009. In his PhD thesis he has confirmed driver-vehicle interfaces as complex configurations of technological system components and services, and implicit interaction therein as a major research challenge. In a substantial part of his thesis he dealt with implicit interaction modalities based on vibrotactile sensations and notifications affecting the driver-vehicle feedback loop. From March 2006 to July 2009 he was also an employee at the Research Institute for Pervasive Computing (RIPE) in Hagenberg. In June 1999 he received an "Excellence Scholarship" from the technical and natural scientific faculty, JKU Linz, in autumn 2008 he was awarded the "Talent Funding Award for Science" from the Upper Austrian Federal State Government as honor for his performance in research. Since 2009 he is a Postdoctoral research fellow at the same institute. Andreas Riener is and was engaged in several EU-and-industrial-funded research projects, for instance in cooperation projects with Siemens AG or in the FP7 project "SOCIONICAL". His research interests include multimodal sensor and actuator systems with a focus on implicit human-computer interaction. Furthermore, he is interested in driver vital state recognition from embedded sensors and context-sensitive data processing. His core competence and research focus is context-aware computing and implicit interaction influencing the driver-vehicle interaction loop.

Ana Belén Sánchez, Bachelor in Sociology (2000) at the Universidad Complutense de Madrid. PhD on Social Psychology (2009) at the Universidad Complutense de Madrid. She has participated in several different EU-funded projects within the VII Framework Program such as HEARTCYCLE, PREVE or VERITAS and Spanish funded projects as FASyS, enjoy.IT!, EMOTIVA or CMA, most of them associated with health care and social services making use of Information Communication Technologies. Her research is focused on the study of human behavior, analysis of values, attitudes, beliefs and behaviors related to health and wellbeing. In particular she has experience in applied research focused on motivation and attitude modification, using qualitative methodology, and also Analysis of Discourse techniques. Her wide experience in social and psychological research covers epistemological and ontological approaches. She also has teaching experience (2007-2009) at the Department of Social Psychology at the Political Science and Sociology Faculty (Universidad Complutense de Madrid). She has worked in the private sector in CENGRASS, National Data Center for Social Security (2004-2005) as a researcher on a population study based on comparison of demographic patterns: population structure, educational and activity variables and population projections.

Mark Scanlon is currently a Ph.D. candidate at the UCD Centre for Cybercrime Investigation, School of Computer Science & Informatics at University College Dublin, Ireland, under the supervision of Prof. Mohand-Tahar Kechadi. He received his B.A. (Hons.) degree in Computer Science and Linguistics in 2006 and his research M.Sc. in Computer Forensics focused on designing and implementing a remote digital evidence capturing system in 2009. The Irish Research Council for Science, Engineering and Technology (IRCSET) and Intel Ireland Ltd. co-fund his current research through the Enterprise Partnership Scheme. Mark's research interests include Computer Forensics and Cybercrime Investigation, Networking and Internet protocols, Peer-to-Peer Technologies.

Christos Tachtatzis has a PhD (2008) in Electronic and Electrical Engineering and an MSc (2002) in Communications, Control and DSP both from the University of Strathclyde and a BEng (2001) in Communications Systems from the University of Portsmouth. He joined the WiSAR Lab in May 2009 having been a Postdoctoral Research Fellow in the University of Strathclyde for 2 years, working on a variety of Wireless Sensor Network projects in collaboration with industry. Previously he had worked as a Research Assistant in the University of Strathclyde performing research in the area of Ultra Wideband (UWB) wireless communications. Christos has 3 patents granted in Channel Switching, improving Network Capacity and a Beacon Co-ordinated MAC Protocol for UWB. His current research interests are in Wireless sensor networks (WSNs), low power MAC Protocols, Co-existence and Interference mitigation techniques, Embedded System hardware and software design.

Dante I. Tapia (PhD.). Received a PhD. in Computer Science from the University of Salamanca (Spain) in 2009. He obtained an Engineering in Computer Sciences degree in 2001 and an MSc in Telecommunications at the University of Colima (Mexico) in 2004. At present he is a full-time researcher at the BISITE Research Group (http://bisite.usal.es) of the University of Salamanca (Spain). He has been member of the organising and scientific committee of several international symposiums and co-author of more than 50 papers published in recognized journal, workshops and symposiums.

Alessandro Testa received in 2008 his MS degree in computer engineering from the University of Naples "Federico II", Italy. He is a Ph. D. Student in the MobiLab Group at the Computer and Systems Engineering Department of the University of Naples "Federico II". He is a research fellow at the Italian National Research Council (CNR) - Institute for High-Performance Computing and Networking (ICAR), where he is involved in the design of RunTime Verification Techniques in the Ambient Intelligence Systems used in the Healthcare Field. Alessandro Testa's research interests focus on analysis and implementation of platforms for monitoring of Wireless Sensor Networks. He is an IEEE Member since 2009.

Nick Timmons holds an M.Sc (2004) in Satellite Engineering Design from the University of Surrey and a B.Eng (Hons)(1989) from the University of Ulster, Jordanstown. He is also a member of the ECIT Radio Communications research group at Queen's University Belfast. He joined LYIT in 1997 as a Lecturer and was a co-founder of the WISAR Lab in 2009. Prior to that he had 10 years industrial experience in the area of RF design including roles as a Product Manager for Connaught Electronics leading the development of low power RF transceivers for the automobile industry and as a Senior Principal RF Engineer in Siemens working on Satellite Communications RF/microwave design. His current research interests are in the areas of Wireless Sensor Networks (WSNs), Medical Body Area Networks (MBAN), Sensors, Ultra Low Power Communication Protocols: MAC and Network/Routing protocols and Energy harvesting.

David Tracey holds an M.Sc in Computer Science from Trinity College Dublin and a B.E. (Electronic) from University College Dublin. He joined the WiSAR Lab in June 2009 and has over 20 years industrial experience in a range of product and research areas in software architecture and design, particularly related to Real-time Systems, System Management, Network Protocols and Thin Clients. His previous positions include those of founding architect and VP of Engineering at SIMtone, Senior Staff Engineer at Sun Microsystems, Head of Product Strategy at Datalex and Senior Researcher at Broadcom Eireann Research. He has had 5 US patents granted with 5 more pending. His current research interests are in the areas of Network and Routing Protocols (particularly the use of P2P in Sensor networks), Smart Spaces and Embedded System Software Design.

Manfred Tscheligi is founder and director of CURE and since March 2004 he is also Full Professor for Human-Computer Interaction & Usability at the University of Salzburg and has been active in the area of Interactive Systems, Human Computer Interaction, Usability Engineering, User Interface Design for around 20 years. He has been successfully managing numerous research and industrial projects as well as established national and international initiatives. He is a distinguished speaker at conferences and seminars and has taught at several universities and technical colleges.

Joost van Hoof, PhD, MSc, Eur Ing (1980) has a background in building physics and systems, with a specialisation in dementia, housing and technology. He works with the Institute of Allied Health professions of Fontys University of Applied Sciences in Eindhoven. Van Hoof is involved in the development of an interfacultary centre for education and research in the field of health care and technology.

Bart Vanrumste PhD, MSc (1971) has a background in electrical engineering, communication engineering, and biomedical sciences. He works as a lecturer with the Department of Industrial and Biosciences of K.H.Kempen in Geel. His research interests lie within biomedical technology. He is head of the biomedical technology subgroup at MOBILAB.

Michael J. Walsh received a first class honors B.E. degree in Electronic Engineering from the University of Limerick in 2005. He subsequently applied for and was awarded a Ph.D. scholarship sponsored by the Embark Initiative's Postgraduate Research Scheme under the Irish Council for Science, Engineering and Technology (IRCSET). He completed his PhD, entitled "An AntiWindup Approach to Reliable Communication and Resource Management in Wireless Sensor Networks", as a member of the Wireless Access Research Centre in the Electronic and Computer Engineering Department at the University of Limerick in 2009. Following completion of his Ph.D., Michael joined the Tyndall National Institute in Cork, where he is currently a post-doctoral researcher funded by the Clarity Centre for Sensor Web Technologies. His research interests are presently centred on the development of wearable body area networks and more specifically the design and practical evaluation of new miniaturized heterogeneous wearable technologies. He is also concerned with protocol development for wireless body area networks, where his goal is to apply systems science and optimization techniques in the wireless ambient healthcare environment.

Tomas E. Ward received the B.E. (Electronic), M.Eng.Sc. (Biomedical Engineering) and Ph.D (Biomedical Engineering) degrees from University College, Dublin, Ireland in 1994, 1996 and 1999 respectively. In 1999 he was appointed Lecturer in the Department of Computer Science at the National University of Ireland (NUI), Maynooth. In 2000 he was appointed Lecturer in the Department of Electronic Engineering at NUI Maynooth where he is now Senior Lecturer. His current primary research areas include the application of brain computer interfaces for neurorehabilitation particularly in stroke, closed loop communication protocols for distributed interactive applications and virtual environments for cognitive and physical rehabilitation.

Mikael Wiberg, PhD is a chaired professor in Human-Computer Interaction at the department of Informatics and Media at Uppsala university, Sweden. In his research, mostly focused on mobile interaction, the emerging interaction society, interaction design and interactive architecture, he has published his work in a number of international journals, including e.g. IJDesign, IJACI, ToCHI, HCI, BIT, IEEE Network, IEEE Pervasive Computing, etc. and he has also published his work in books, encyclopedias, and in international conference proceedings including e.g. CHI, HCI, GROUP, etc.

Eveline J. M. Wouters, PhD, MD, MSc (1958) has a background in medicine and epidemiology. She works with the Institute of Allied Health professions of Fontys University of Applied Sciences in Eindhoven. She is the head of the research group Bridging Innovations to Sustainable Care, which investigates themes in the field of health care and technology, with an explicit focus on user perspectives.

Javier Yanguas, Ph.D. in Psychology, holds a Master's Degree in Neuro-psychology. His work in the field of care-giving, attention for the elderly and ageing-related research started twenty years ago. His innovative and challenging proposals led Matia Foundation to set up Ingema Foundation, where he works as Head of the R&D Department since 2002. His main research interests are the prevention of dependency and promotion of healthy ageing, as well as the binomial quality of life-quality of attention. Not only is he Principal Investigator in several European, national and local research projects, but he also takes part in Spain's main Professional Associations such as the Spanish Society of Gerontology and Geriatrics and the Basque Association of Professional in Gerontology and Geriatrics since 2001.

Index